F 11

shelf.

Richard

6 Oct. 2013

MAKING LEGAL HISTORY

Making Legal History

Essays in Honor of William E. Nelson

EDITED BY
Daniel J. Hulsebosch and R. B. Bernstein

NEW YORK UNIVERSITY PRESS
New York and London

NEW YORK UNIVERSITY PRESS
New York and London
www.nyupress.org

© 2013 by New York University

References to Internet websites (URLs) were accurate at the time of writing. Neither the author nor New York University Press is responsible for URLs that may have expired or changed since the manuscript was prepared.

Library of Congress Cataloging-in-Publication Data
Making legal history : essays in honor of William E. Nelson / edited by Daniel J. Hulsebosch and R. B. Bernstein.
pages cm   Includes bibliographical references and index.
ISBN 978-0-8147-2526-9 (cl : alk. paper)
1. Law—United States—History. I. Nelson, William Edward, 1940– honouree.
II. Hulsebosch, Daniel Joseph, editor of compilation. III. Bernstein, Richard B., 1956– editor of compilation.
KF352.M35   2013
349.73—dc23   2013014007

New York University Press books are printed on acid-free paper, and their binding materials are chosen for strength and durability. We strive to use environmentally responsible suppliers and materials to the greatest extent possible in publishing our books.

Manufactured in the United States of America

10 9 8 7 6 5 4 3 2 1

Also available as an ebook

CONTENTS

Making Legal History

MORTON J. HORWITZ

It is a pleasure to offer a foreword to this volume of essays in honor of Bill Nelson—one of the most generous scholars working in the field of legal history. I've known Bill from the beginning, when we were both Charles Warren Fellows at Harvard Law School some forty years ago. At that time we were researching our first books. Every day Bill would travel to one or another archive. "I was in the Dedham courthouse today," he would say, and the next day he was in another courthouse. Each day I would wait for him to come back and debrief him on his research—for self-interested reasons.

Now, here's the point: Bill Nelson shared *all* of his research with me. We were not working on identical topics, but they were similar. I have not seen that happen in the subsequent forty years of my academic life. Bill showed a sense of generosity and of investment in a common purpose. If we were going to make legal history a *field*, we needed to try to help each other as best we could, and Bill really did make a big difference in my understanding of my own work.

What Bill did for *Americanization of the Common Law* was, I think, something that had not been done before: He literally covered the court records. If you think about the state of the published work at that time on the Massachusetts colonial period, you have to say, in terms of primary sources, there was little. You had Nathan Dane's *General Abridgment and Digest of American Law*, published in the 1820s, and you had William Cushing's legal notes in the Massachusetts Historical Society. There were also Josiah Quincy's reports from the Superior Court of Judicature just before the Revolution. But 98 percent of the materials of colonial Massachusetts law had never been read.

I was doing work through the published sources and the easily accessible manuscripts, but they represented only a small, not necessarily representative, sample. They were basically great cases. Bill, on the other hand, was looking at everyday cases. Let me give you a typical example of the many ways that Bill's work helped me understand what I was writing about. I was writing about the emergence of negligence, and it became clear to me that the intellectual key to the emergence of negligence was the collision case—mostly carriage collisions, occasionally ship collisions. It was interesting because plaintiffs usually sued in trespass, in which, according to the doctrine at the time, the plaintiff won a *prima facie* case on the basis of a direct injury. There were many cases in which, although the plaintiff sued in trespass and proved a direct injury, the defendant nevertheless won. There was not an articulate doctrinal explanation for *why* the defendant won. It became clear that the way in which the juries broke the tie was by asking who caused the collision, or, in effect, who was at fault. Here was negligence emerging under the radar in jury determinations, well before it was recognized in the distinctions between trespass and case, or in the overt emergence of the doctrine of negligence. Now, on the basis of the materials I had accessible to me, it was possible to look at only a handful of collision cases, and I didn't know whether these collision cases were quirky or representative. By the time Bill returned from all of his courthouse visits, it was clear that there were many collision cases in which the plaintiffs had pleaded and proved that a collision involving the defendant had occurred, and yet the defendant still won. Something was going on beyond the formalistic pleading. That something was jury decision making: The jury was choosing who was at fault. One needed Bill's rampage through the archives to be able to establish that that was a pattern based on the relatively recent emergence of collision cases in a prospering society with a growing, urbanized, more concentrated population that had enough carriages to have collisions. So here was a way that I could discover the development of the negligence principle below the doctrinal radar. Bill's work in the archives allowed me to claim that there was a much wider pattern than I could have found from my sources alone.

I could give you equally detailed accounts of how Bill's research helped me in other areas and illuminated things that I would not

otherwise have seen. I thank him for it, and I think it was an extraordinary act of generosity on his part in, if there is such a thing, the true
spirit of scholarship. But it also illustrates what was so pathbreaking about Bill's first book: He was the first person to follow Frederic
William Maitland's example and go into the *American* archives, read
comprehensively, and write legal history on the basis of those archival
sources. Today this practice is much more common, and many people
do it. But Bill was the first, and for that we should thank him as well.
He has been enjoying a great career. I am glad that I was present at the
beginning.

Introduction

Making Legal Historians

The subjects of the essays included in *Making Legal History* range from local government in seventeenth-century New England to executive power in the Reagan administration and illustrate the variety of subjects and methods now being pursued by historians of American law. Some cast new light on perennial questions; others move in entirely new directions. About half focus on private law, the other half on public law. All rest on original research, and each could stand alone as an original contribution to the field. Taken together, they offer a unique and illuminating cross-section of the questions, sources, and narratives used by historians working in the field of American legal history today.

It is therefore fitting that these essays were first presented at a conference at New York University School of Law honoring William E. Nelson. Few fields of history as are vital and diverse today as American legal and constitutional history. That was not so in 1965, when Bill Nelson graduated from New York University School of Law and began doctoral studies in history at Harvard University. At that time, legal history often fell between law schools and history departments, with no home in either. Half a century later, the situation is quite different. Legal historians teach in law schools, history departments, and elsewhere, and the field has an array of journals, book series, and professional organizations. Annual conventions feature dozens of scholarly papers, and the literature of the field is growing exponentially. Indeed, the pace of publication outstrips the ability of even the most assiduous readers to keep up.

Probably no legal historian in the past generation has undertaken more original research, exploring a wider range of sources to pursue a broader array of questions, than Bill Nelson. Nor would it be easy to identify a legal historian who has composed more pages of compelling narrative answers to those questions. Bill Nelson has produced a remarkable body of scholarship—to date, fourteen books and more than seventy articles and essays—spanning the full course of American legal and constitutional history, from its colonial origins to twentieth-century New York. (A bibliography of Nelson's work is appended to this volume.) Several of his books are methodologically innovative as well as essential for understanding their subjects. He also served for ten years as assistant editor of the *American Journal of Legal History* and many terms on the Board of Directors of the American Society for Legal History, an institution that supports the publication of books and a journal. Nelson's record of scholarship alone would mark him as a central figure in the modern efflorescence of American legal history, and his writings have shaped the contributions of dozens of younger scholars.

Yet Bill Nelson has not been just an excavator, digging into legal records on a heroic scale. Nor has he been only a prolific author. He has also been one of the field's great institution-builders. Through the Samuel I. Golieb Fellowship Program and the Legal History Colloquium, which he created and has administered at NYU since 1981, Nelson has shaped the careers of a generation of legal historians. Not only has he made much legal history—he also has helped to make a generation of legal historians.

The "Goliebs," as they are often known, owe Nelson an enduring debt of gratitude, both for the year of training in legal history at NYU and for years of mentoring thereafter. The contributors to this volume (as well as its editors) are all former Golieb Fellows. The authors were students when they were Goliebs, typically completing their dissertations in history. Now they are tenured professors who have produced substantial publications, on average more than one book per contributor. For most of us, the year at NYU was our initiation into the field of legal and constitutional history. The Legal History Colloquium has long been one of the premier workshops for legal historians, who present work-in-progress to a revolving membership, including each year's Golieb Fellows, for a demanding two hours of commentary and critique. In almost every session of the Colloquium comes a moment when Nelson leans forward and says, "There are at least two things going on in this paper. Let's set aside the things that are not all that original and have been done before. What's new and interesting and hasn't been done before is this. . . ." As Nelson talks, outlining a sometimes radically reconceptualized version of the paper before the group, the presenter will seize a pen and begin to scribble notes destined to become a roadmap for recasting the project into a new, more interesting and useful form. Many of the leading studies in the field of legal history have first taken shape as papers presented to the Colloquium, and the distance between the original papers and the final articles and books is a measure of the value of the Colloquium and the assistance it has brought to generations of young and established scholars alike. These features make the Golieb Fellowship and the Colloquium unique in the field.

Yet Bill gave and continues to give the Goliebs even more. For all of his impressive achievements as a scholar and critic, perhaps his greatest contribution to the field has been the creation of a tight yet expanding network of scholars. Each Golieb is connected to Bill, and through Bill they connect to one another. It is an impressive web. More than one hundred Golieb alumni teach at dozens of law schools and history departments throughout the United States and around the world. Not only is Bill Nelson an indefatigable investigator of past communities; along the way, he has created a vibrant one that did not exist thirty years ago. Now, it's difficult to imagine the field without it. We offer these essays to Bill in a tribute to his generous spirit and in appreciation of his tireless efforts on behalf of the Golieb Fellows and the field of legal and constitutional history.

*   *   *

Our goal is to honor Bill Nelson's convictions about the historical enterprise, above all the central importance of identifying a genuine problem, undertaking original research, and telling a compelling story. Bill's "foundational assumption," as he lays it out in *The Legalist Reformation*, his pathbreaking analysis of liberal jurisprudence in the courts of twentieth-century New York, is that "historians should rediscover forgotten data rather than rehash what is already familiar."[1] Time and again he has told the Colloquium that deep, comprehensive research in the records of legal institutions and the legal profession distinguishes legal history from many academic pursuits in the legal academy, where theory and abstraction are often the starting and concluding points. The commitment to concrete historical facts of the law—facts revealing the fate of real people who staffed and used the legal institutions that created, regulated, and disciplined liberty and power—also distinguishes his historical vision from some of the more abstract concerns current in history departments. We have also heard him say that good data, though necessary, is not sufficient. The historian must also weave those sources into a story that illuminates important developments in the legal culture as well as in the larger society framing it. This enterprise enables the historian as well as the reader to "delight in the discovery of new knowledge and insight."[2]

A preference for original sources, arguments, and narratives is compatible with a wide variety of historical methods. In his approach to historical method as to the past itself, Nelson is reflexively pluralist.[3] He is catholic about the types of history that count as contributions to the field, and his evaluative standards for judging scholarship are consciously nondoctrinaire. He has celebrated the boisterous diversity of "traditional history," by which he means scholarship that does not hew to one methodology, and he has argued that it is "precisely this variety of theme, objective, and method that gives [historical] scholarship . . . its power."[4] The goal of legal history is first to identify real problems and then to offer evidence that enlightens or solves them. *How* precisely they are solved is not the main issue. The nature of the problem usually suggests the sorts of evidence and methods that might best produce answers. As long as the research is "competent," meaning simply factually accurate, then the work cannot be criticized as bad—or as good.[5] To be good, or powerful, a work must be both "unconventional" in some way and ultimately "influential."[6] By "unconventional," he means the use of new sources and interpretations. His concern with influence speaks to a work's ability to shape research agendas throughout the field. Methods are means to those ends, not the main event, and especially not the main measure of scholarly value.

Nelson often says that history is an intrinsically comparative enterprise, an exercise in comparative law.[7] Unlike comparative law scholars, though, American legal historians do not regularly compare different legal cultures in different places at the same time.[8] Instead, they often examine legal ideas, institutions, and practices in the past and, with differing degrees of consciousness, compare and contrast them with formal or functional equivalents in the present. The point is not usually to trace legal genealogies but rather to understand the function and meaning of the law as rooted in particular times and places. Formal training in the law is not necessary to gain this insight—three of our contributors are not lawyers—though it has not hurt Nelson that he is an accomplished lawyer.[9] (Indeed, listening to Bill's descriptions of colonial legal practice—his first field of inquiry, to which he has returned in the past decade—is like being in the presence of the last surviving member of the eighteenth-century bar.)

Accordingly, the contributors to this volume set out to identify, interpret, and explain original sources in ways illuminating contemporary methods of writing legal history. They do not subscribe to a single programmatic theme or method. Instead, they ask different questions, use an array of sources, and tell their stories in individual ways. Together, they provide a kaleidoscopic image of the men, women, institutions, ideas, and practices that have made American legal history in the past and how historians make it into scholarship today. So the essays exemplify less a "school" of legal or constitutional history than a shared sense of scholarly purpose, one not limited to Bill Nelson or the Legal History Colloquium but one that he epitomizes in his own work and that he has inculcated into the Golieb Fellows for three decades. Call it a sort of ethical unity: an ethos of making history faithful to the past and yet alive for readers in the present.[10]

*   *   *

Two civil wars punctuate American legal history: the American Revolution and the Civil War of 1861–65. Contrary to Cicero's dictum that in times of war the laws are silent, law pervaded both wars: before as a cause, during as a means, and after as a mechanism for changing the resultant political and social world. In "The Landscape of Faith: Religious Property and Confiscation in the Early Republic," Sarah Barringer

Gordon explores the fascinating story of the legal battles over colonial church property ownership in the new republic. Much is known about the law and politics of disestablishment in the early Republic. But what happened to all the land, such as glebe lands, that established churches had received from colonial governments before the Revolution? Forgotten today, this question burned brightly in a few of the postrevolutionary states. Fights over how best to disestablish—how to think about church property in a newly disestablished jurisdiction—consumed state legislatures and courts for decades. Gordon traces the litigious fate of Church of England lands in Virginia and Vermont.

In "'It cant be cald stealin': Customary Law Among Civil War Soldiers," Thomas C. Mackey explores the cognitive dissonance that Civil War soldiers, Union and Confederate, experienced as they left their ordinary lives, suffused with customary common-law understandings of property, and entered the military, where according to the laws of war they could appropriate personal property in a variety of circumstances. Back home, that appropriation might be called "stealing." During wartime, however, such foraging was often legitimate and necessary. That it was "legal" did not, for many soldiers, lessen their unease. Instead, they felt compelled to explain their behavior to civilian correspondents back home—and to themselves. Examining rarely used personal correspondence by these soldiers, Mackey wonderfully captures the lived experience of legal pluralism among ordinary Americans who found themselves pulled between two legal orders, civilian and military, in the extraordinary circumstance of a civil war fought at home.

Daniel W. Hamilton turns in his essay, "Debating the Fourteenth Amendment: The Promise and Perils of Using Congressional Sources," to the historically and constitutionally crucial question of the congressional understanding of the Fourteenth Amendment. Building on Bill Nelson's insight that the congressional debates offer a view into deeply contested principles of legal and constitutional ideology, Hamilton argues that historians can analyze congressional debates (and others like them) as examples of legal ideology-in-action. Highly charged political debates over constitutional principles offer wonderful case studies for testing the relative autonomy of those principles.

The function of law as a mechanism of social regulation has long been a central concern to legal historians. The next four essays explore this old question in exciting new ways. In "Was the Warning of Strangers Unique to Colonial New England?," Cornelia H. Dayton and Sharon V. Salinger examine the previously unused logbook of a colonial official charged with "warning out" strangers and discover that the warning-out usually did not result in banishment, as we might think, but served rather to mark that stranger as ineligible for *local* poor relief. Instead, those newcomers could stay (and many did stay, for many years), engaging fully in the town's economic and civic life, and even remaining eligible for welfare from the *provincial* rather than the town government. Warning-out, it appears, functioned to sort those who could apply for local welfare from those who would have to seek aid from the colony.

Barry Cushman reads lawyers' briefs and judicial opinions closely to explore free-labor ideology in "Ambiguities of Free Labor Revisited: The Convict Labor Question in Progressive-Era New York." In the context of the debate over whether states could prohibit the sale of goods made with convict labor, the sellers invoked free-labor ideology as a defense of their right to trade in those goods. It's an irony that recalls Nelson's early work on the connection between antebellum antislavery ideology and late-nineteenth-century judicial formalism.[11] Here, the sword of free labor also could be used as a shield, to protect manufacturers from legislation designed to promote goods made with "free" labor.

In "The Long, Broad, and Deep Civil Rights Movement: The Lessons of a Master Scholar and Teacher," Tomiko Brown-Nagin asks how the legal history of the Civil Rights Movement would look if historians turned the focus away from such leading litigators as Thurgood Marshall and concentrated instead on "local people and ordinary Americans." Approaching that history "from the bottom up" and focusing in particular on the complicated dynamics within local Southern communities, she finds an extraordinary diversity of views among local African American activists, including many who held more radical and hopeful views of the possibilities of constitutional change than did the leading NAACP lawyers, but also including those who preferred a "pragmatic" approach by emphasizing the economic and political empowerment of black communities rather than integration and colorblindness. Local community studies offer one way to recover the history made by ordinary people in American legal culture. The aggregation of data offers quite a different method toward the same goal.

John Wertheimer focuses on the promise and limits of quantitative method for legal historians in his essay, "Counting as a Tool of Legal History." He rightly argues that some legal institutions, such as the jury, agency prosecutors, and the state census, cry out for more quantitative work, which, as he demonstrates with three examples, can illuminate the social and racial politics of law enforcement and statutory regulation in American history.

Courts, judges, and lawyers are traditional subjects for legal history. The essays in the final section demonstrate that when historians approach these institutions from new angles, ask new questions, and unearth new material, studies of courts, judges, and lawyers remain the richest topics in the field. In "A Mania for Accumulation: The Plea of Moral Insanity in Gilded Age Will Contests," Susanna L. Blumenthal explores one of the most fascinating civil trials of the late nineteenth century—that focusing on the attempt to probate the will of "Commodore" Cornelius Vanderbilt, the controversial railroad magnate who died as the nation's wealthiest man. The family fight over his fortune also was a source of almost obsessive popular interest owing to the murky circumstances of his last days. As Blumenthal shows, the legal and journalistic controversies swirling around the clashing attempts to challenge and to defend Vanderbilt's ability to make a will shed new and unsettling light on evolving ideas of testamentary capacity, the effects of enormous wealth on the values and psychology of testators, and the roles of courts and psychological experts in resolving disputes over the dispositions of vast estates.

John Fabian Witt's essay, "The Political Economy of Pain," explores one of the great puzzles in twentieth-century tort law: How did pain and suffering damages move from the backwater of American law to become one of its main currents? Witt finds that plaintiff's lawyers used pain and suffering damages as a vehicle for staving off legislative revision of tort law, a defensive collective action that, ironically, helped produce even more of the common-law litigation that reformers had wished to prevent. In so doing, Witt reminds us that courts include more actors than judges and juries: Trial lawyers sometimes coordinate to act as independent agents and thereby make more than just litigation; they make law and change the course of legal history. The last essay brings the collection up to the end of the twentieth century.

Reuel Schiller, in "An Unexpected Antagonist: Courts, Deregulation, and Conservative Judicial Ideology, 1980–94," argues that the Reagan administration's policy of "executive deregulation" largely failed because the federal courts rejected the administration's attempts to do this—even during Reagan's second term, when his appointees had come to dominate the federal judiciary. Judicial rejection of executive deregulation illustrates some of the contradictions in late-twentieth-century conservative ideology. Reagan-era conservatives were committed to anti-statist beliefs, out of which deregulation naturally flowed, but many also were committed to controlling "judicial activism." The means deployed by these conservatives included textualism and a commitment to originalism in both constitutional and statutory interpretation. These approaches undermined executive deregulation. In this instance, conservative judicial method trumped conservative executive policy.

*   *   *

The power of Bill Nelson's scholarship comes from his hard-earned understanding of the craft-wisdom of past legal communities, his analysis of the social meaning of those ideas and practices, and his ability to put it all together in imaginative narratives written in lucid prose. He has exemplified this method for the Goliebs across three decades. The contributors to this volume wrote their essays with Nelson's example and precepts in mind, and each reveals something strikingly new about the functions of lawyers and of law in past communities. They offer their essays in gratitude for Bill's many years of support.

NOTES
1. William E. Nelson, *The Legalist Reformation: Law, Politics, and Ideology in New York, 1920–1980* (Chapel Hill: University of North Carolina Press, 2001), 1.
2. *Ibid.*
3. William E. Nelson, "Standards of Criticism," *The Literature of American History* (Dobbs Ferry, N.Y.: Oceana Publications, 1985), 322 (originally *Texas Law Review*, 1982).
4. William E. Nelson, "1981–1984," in *The Literature of American History* (Dobbs Ferry, N.Y.: Oceana Publications, 1985), 281.
5. "A critic must distinguish between plain errors of fact and factual interpretations derived from differing perspectives." Nelson, "Standards of Criticism," 323.

6. Nelson, "Standards of Criticism," 327.

7. "[N]o one hypothesis can generate as much insight into the past as can the historian's basic conceptual tool, the examination of changes over time," a belief that Nelson may have learned from his own dissertation advisor, Bernard Bailyn. Nelson, "1981–1984," at 281. For Bailyn's belief that good history analyzes change over time, see James A. Henretta, Michael G. Kammen, and Stanley N. Katz, eds., *The Transformation of Early American History: Society, Authority, and Ideology* (New York: Alfred A. Knopf, 1991).

8. Though of course they do, for example in the new journal *Comparative Legal History*.

9. Nelson was graduated first in his class at New York University School of Law; clerked for Judge Edward Weinfeld of the U.S. District Court for the Southern District of New York, known as a "judge's judge"; and then clerked for U.S. Supreme Court Justice Byron R. White. He has since written illuminatingly about both Weinfeld and White. For example: William E. Nelson, *Edward Weinfeld: In Pursuit of Law and Justice* (New York: New York University Press, 2004); William E. Nelson, "Judge Weinfeld and the Adjudicatory Process: A Law Finder in an Age of Judicial Lawmakers," *New York University Law Review* 50:5 (November 1975): 980–1007; William E. Nelson, "Justice Byron R. White: His Legacy for the Twenty-First Century," *University of Colorado Law Review* 74:4 (2003): 1291–1304; William E. Nelson, "Byron R. White: The Justice Who Never Thought About Himself," *Harvard Law Review* 116 (November 2002): 9–12; William E. Nelson, "Justice Byron R. White: A Modern Federalist and a New Deal Liberal," *Brigham Young University Law Review* 1994:2 (1994): 313–48; William E. Nelson, "Byron White: A Liberal of 1960," in Mark Tushnet, ed., *The Warren Court in Historical and Political Perspective* (Charlottesville: University Press of Virginia, 1993), 139–54; and William E. Nelson, "Deference and the Limits to Deference in the Constitutional Jurisprudence of Justice Byron R. White," *University of Colorado Law Review* 58:3 (Summer 1987): 347–64.

10. William E. Nelson, *Americanization of the Common Law* (Cambridge, Mass.: Harvard University Press, 1975; reprint ed., with new introduction, Athens: University of Georgia Press, 1994).

11. William E. Nelson, "The Impact of the Antislavery Movement upon Styles of Judicial Reasoning in the Nineteenth Century," *Harvard Law Review* 87 (1974): 513–66.

I

Civil Wars and Legal Rights

1

The Landscape of Faith

Religious Property and Confiscation in the Early Republic

SARAH BARRINGER GORDON

In 1805, Hungars Church was looted by local residents. The small structure, situated on the eastern shore of Virginia, was a holdover from
pre-Revolutionary days. The parish included the church and valuable
holdings, including a 1,600-acre farm in one of the most fertile areas
of Northampton County, complete with houses and farm buildings,
and a dozen "servants" (undoubtedly, slaves) who were attached to the
church as part of the glebe dedicated to the maintenance of the minister, the church building, and any associated graveyards and parsonages.[1] The looting was representative of a new era in religious life in the
post-Revolutionary United States.[2] Hungars was an Episcopal Church,
the denomination known until just a few years earlier as the Church of
England. By the early nineteenth century, the remnants of the English
church had been re-christened, born anew as the Protestant Episcopal
Church. But the taint of an English past endured.

Before the Revolution, the threat of an Anglican bishop sent by the
mother church to the colonies had been a constant trouble spot. The
much-discussed threat never materialized, but alarmist predictions by
John and Samuel Adams in Massachusetts and instigator John Wilkes in
London kept it constantly on the political front burner. Together, they
exploited longstanding tensions over doctrine (including priestly vest-
ments, the Book of Common Prayer, and the gulf between clergy and
laity) and stoked them with political flames. The Church of England,
they argued, was allied with Parliament and the Crown in scheming to

undermine the liberties of colonists.[3] One British scholar has titled his recent book on the Revolution "a war of religion."[4] At the time, Loyalist British clergy agreed with him. At the least, the war revealed the fragility of the Protestant empire that missionaries and some colonists embraced before the rupture.[5] Others have noted the religious ferment that accompanied charismatic prophets and their followers in the Revolutionary era, arguing that religious diversity can be traced to independence.[6] Certainly, anti-Catholic invective, long a staple of the defense of British liberties, was turned against British King George III to great popular effect—the monarch had been seduced by popish conspiracies, so the argument went, and now sought to enslave his freedom-loving people in North America.[7]

During the war for independence, many Anglican clerics fled to Canada or back to England.[8] Of those who remained, several dozen were prosecuted for treason, and many others were driven by mobs from their parishes or quietly retired to avoid persecution. One missionary, John Stuart, who worked with Mohawk Indians in New York in the 1770s, was placed under house arrest for three years after he refused to drop the prayer for the English king from his worship services. Eventually, Stuart was fined, his land was "confiscated," and the church he founded was turned into a bar.[9] In Philadelphia, the minister Jacob Duché originally supported the Revolution and was named chaplain to the First Continental Congress. When the British occupied the city in 1777, however, Duché switched sides and eventually left with the British.[10] A third clergyman, the Reverend Ephraim Avery, who had welcomed British troops when they arrived in Rye, New York, was found with his throat cut. Neighbors suspected local rebels of Avery's murder.[11]

Clerics also produced Loyalist literature, arguing for preservation of the hierarchies that Patriots claimed were the equivalent of enslavement. Some argued that the Revolution was really just the product of troublemaking Congregationalist and Presbyterian "factions" who trumped up opposition to Britain to serve their own sectarian interests.[12] Anglican clerics suffered substantial erosion of privilege in their standing and power in every new state during the Revolution. Stories of beatings, dunkings, and worse meant that many were so intimidated that they stayed quiet rather than risk the mobs.[13] Reflecting on the insolence of the Patriot mobs, one outraged Anglican divine preached his final sermon in 1775 with a loaded pistol in his hand and then left Maryland with a hostile crowd in close pursuit. He later denied that "in point of principle, there is a shade of difference between the American revolution and the French rebellion."[14]

Even after the war's end, everyone remembered that legacy of political controversy and Tory sympathies. Sunday services were mocked as "Tories at prayer" for the next century and more. The Episcopal Church limped along in the early Republic; its leaders protested that they were actually patriots, not closet Loyalists plotting for re-colonization by the British.[15] In Virginia, such protestations were met with skepticism, although most Episcopalians had been Patriots. The percentage of Loyalists among clergy was much lower in Virginia and across the South than it was in New England or New York, or even Maryland, where in 1780 only fifteen remained of the fifty-three Anglican ministers who had served the colony in 1775.[16] The strong tradition of local, lay control over the colonial establishment in Virginia meant that Anglican ministers were beholden to the planters who dominated politics and the rebellion against Britain. James Madison even exulted in a 1775 letter to his college friend William Bradford over the expulsion of the Reverend James Herdman, the Anglican rector of Bromfield Parish in Culpeper County, as a suspected Tory. If he did not conform, Madison recommended, the parson should "get ducked in a coat of Tar and a surplice of feathers," which would be a lesson in preparing the reverend for his "new Canonicals" in revolutionary Virginia.[17] Eventually, Madison supported the fight against the glebes to increase his standing among religious dissenters.[18]

Both Virginia's more radical elite landowners and religious dissenters had little sympathy for Episcopal clergy, however. The visceral anticlericalism of Thomas Jefferson was an important source of his disdain for Episcopal divines, of course, but others shared his desire to prune back the authority of clerics. Anglican ministers, after all, had been eager to punish dissenting preachers in the years leading up to the Revolution.[19] Now those dissenters—in particular Baptists and Presbyterians—maintained that the Episcopal Church should not profit from an establishmentarian past that linked the new denomination with old tyranny and religious oppression.[20] Some critics charged that the excesses of the

French Revolution encouraged anti-religious radicalism, particularly among the members of the Virginia Assembly.[21] Many less politically engaged country folk were perfectly happy to melt down the organ of Hungars Church to make sinkers for their fishing lines, or to use its churchyard's tombstones to grind wheat or corn in their mills.[22]

The plundering of Hungars Church is very much a tale of Virginia, which in the early national period occupied a notable place in America's new way of separating church and state.[23] In other states, Anglican churches had been burned decades earlier. Indeed, in Virginia the post-war climate was more hostile to Anglican clerics in many cases than the Revolution had been. The looting and torching of churches is not generally included in the story of American religious liberty as told by historians and legal scholars. This essay argues, by contrast, that the wealth of religious establishments and their ownership of land posed stickier problem for the new states than the revocation of positive tax support that we traditionally associate with disestablishment in Virginia and elsewhere. To explore this obscure yet important corner of American history, this essay focuses on legal, religious, and political developments that presaged and accompanied disestablishment in the Revolutionary and early national periods.

Instead of telling a shopworn story of the "discovery" of religious freedom, therefore, this essay focuses on property and the effects of disestablishment on land ownership by religious organizations.[24] Many related subjects are backlit by the history detailed here, including mortmain statutes and related limits on property rights for religious organizations enacted by states and territories in the nineteenth century, and investigations of confiscation of the property of religious organizations across the original thirteen states during the Revolution. I analyze the former in a forthcoming book; the latter project, the work of a lifetime, is beyond the scope of this foray into the land law as applied to religious property owners as a direct consequence of Revolution and disestablishment. Also of importance, but also beyond the scope of this essay, are the longstanding debates in other state legislatures whether to enact confiscatory legislation that did not result in the widespread forfeiture provisions studied here.[25]

Yet we can confidently say a few things about the changes wrought by the Revolution. After 1776, Committees of Sequestration or Safety routinely charged Anglican ministers with treason, and their property disappeared either through legal process or often through informal looting and occupation.[26] Stories of British soldiers protecting churches and glebes were common during the war; when they left, the forebears of the Hungars Church looters had their way.[27] Trinity Church of Wall Street, one of the largest landowners in Manhattan to this day, was burned early in the war.[28] Much of this history of arson and pillage is lost in the confusion of war and the inadequacy of surviving records, yet the loss of valuable property and the erosion of security in ownership were significant. Redistribution through confiscation or just plain theft meant that an aura of instability hung over newly vulnerable Anglican clerics and their glebes and churches.

In a country where the religion of the (former) oppressor occupied a liminal space yet remained a landowner of considerable wealth in many jurisdictions, the question of how to handle a new and unprecedented regime of disestablishment became urgent. Two early U.S. Supreme Court cases laid the groundwork for the law of property in such situations.[29] The cases were decided within weeks of each other in 1815; both opinions were written by Associate Justice Joseph Story of Massachusetts. Together, these decisions generated a land law of disestablishment of importance for the next century and more. The cases are undeservedly obscure, not even mentioned in leading casebooks on the law of religion, for example.[30] The failure to appreciate the importance of property has in turn obscured the ways that disestablishment actually worked in these formative early decades.

This essay aims to recover a more complete story of disestablishment by looking at the conflicts that produced these two cases. These key but long-overlooked issues of property formed the second generation of debates over how to disentangle church and state. The investigation here is not just focused on Virginia, which has been extensively studied by historians of church and state. Vermont also plays a key role, taking the trajectory out of the South and away from Massachusetts, the only northern state where disestablishment previously has been the subject of sustained scholarly research. In that sense, this essay pushes beyond existing scholarship in its geographic scope as well as its central topic. There is more to be done, but for the first time we can study the far longer and previously obscure stages of disestablishment in the early national period.[31]

As an initial foray into a larger project on government restrictions on land ownership and development by religious organizations across American national history, this essay focuses on the early national period because that era framed the questions that arose later in the nineteenth century and beyond. To frame this study, it is important to note that the relationship between religious vitality and property ownership seems to have grown increasingly close over the past two centuries. Concerns about the amount of property owned by religious institutions have waxed and waned, but as far as we can tell, the relative percentages of total real property in the United States belonging to religious organizations have increased dramatically and steadily since the early nineteenth century.[32] That is, the former religious establishments' property holdings were the focus in the early national period, but today wealth in land is spread far more widely, well beyond mainstream faiths, and far exceeding the rates of ownership and wealth of churches or religious denominations in the colonial and early national periods.

In various ways, including statutory limits on total property, zoning restrictions, and limitations on donations known as mortmain statutes, local and national laws have tried to rein in the capacity of religious institutions to acquire property even after the threat of establishment was long past.[33] Some of these attempts clearly were driven by concern that hierarchical organizations (such as the Catholic Church and the Church of Jesus Christ of Latter-day Saints), if left unfettered, would undermine American liberty by engrossing vast tracts of land. It is also clear, however, that reasons for opposition to unlimited land ownership for religious groups extended well beyond sheer bigotry.

For one thing, the Catholic Church had only minuscule holdings in Virginia or Vermont at the dawn of the nineteenth century. And although it might be fair to call the Anglican Church of the late eighteenth century hierarchical, the colonial church in North America was never equipped with the central instrument of hierarchical polity—a bishop. It was often dominated by lay members, most notably but not only in Virginia. Furthermore, the new Episcopal Church that succeeded the British denomination in the 1780s instituted a broadly democratic religious polity.[34] Instead of an actual or immediate threat, the Catholic Church and eventually the Mormon Church often functioned in political life as cautions; to their opponents even in states or territories where Mormons or Catholics were a small minority, these churches exemplified priestly arrogance and material excess as well as the dangers of religious oppression.[35] Limiting the right of all religious organizations to own property was a handy way to reduce the buying power of such hierarchical and broadly resented institutions.

These conflicts over religious ownership of property run like a seam through American religious and legal history: The centrality of land to debates about religion and government simply cannot be denied, even if just asking how much land is currently owned by religious organizations is a sure-fire way to enter a political thicket of epic proportions and an empirical challenge of commensurate density.[36] The *mise-en-scène* in Virginia and Vermont is as good a place as any to start, for it concentrates our gaze on a basic question: Would the full liberty of property so vital to the Revolution be extended to religious interests? The answer to the question was "no"—eventually. But the issue was hard-fought.

*   *   *

Most religious establishments survived the Revolution, but in substantially weakened form.[37] During the War for Independence, confiscation proceeded apace against Anglican land holdings. In many cases, prosecution of a minister was accompanied by forfeiture not only of land dedicated to the support of the relevant clergyman; frequently, the church itself and any associated glebes were part and parcel of both formal and extralegal processes. John Stuart's sorry experience in New York's Mohawk Valley (discussed earlier) was replicated up and down the eastern seaboard. Many of these formal and informal processes (with looting often an accompaniment even to formal legal proceedings) left no trace in the surviving records. Others, however, lie hidden in the records of the war in the states, where valuable information has long lain unexplored. The research challenge is massive, yet much could be learned from the careful study of even a single jurisdiction.[38] And although the total property wrested from Anglican clutches during the war is unknown, the forfeitures significantly reduced the wealth and power of Anglican establishments even before disestablishment became a recognized policy in many jurisdictions.[39] Massachusetts, Connecticut, New York, and other states were awash with popular and formal actions against Loyalist clerics.[40]

Only Virginia and Vermont enacted confiscatory statutes in the early national period, yet it is worth noting that both jurisdictions had been remarkably free of chances to relieve the Church of England of its property during the War for Independence. Virginia's clergy were less inclined to Loyalist commitments, and only six prosecutions against clerics in the Old Dominion were brought before the official cessation of hostilities, even though the Anglican parishes and clergy in Virginia far outnumbered those of any other state.[41] Vermont was not one of the original thirteen states, of course, but rather a separate and highly unstable (even disreputable) entity. It also was remarkably rebellious and generally dedicated to extracting a pound of flesh from any vulnerable Englishman. British enemies were elusive, however, but enemies from the other states, New York in particular, were thick on the ground. In that sense, both Virginia and Vermont had been denied the redistributive windfall that other jurisdictions enjoyed when doubts about clerics' patriotism opened the window to confiscation or just plain looting.[42]

The received wisdom tends to end the story of disestablishment when positive taxation in favor of the established church was either discontinued or substantially eliminated by allowing taxpayers to direct their monies to the church of their choosing. Scholars have called such individual control over the destination of their tax funds "multiple establishments";[43] in reality, they were short-lived periods of misery for clerics who saw themselves reduced to penury.[44] We know from the work of William E. Nelson (to whom this volume is dedicated) that the religious establishment in Massachusetts was weakened substantially a full generation before disestablishment. In 1811, the legislature allowed taxpayers to direct their funds to almost any religious organization, even fly-by-night evangelists and Baptists.[45] Other scholars have supplemented Nelson's research, demonstrating, for example, that the British government had long had its suspicions that the Massachusetts establishment was a weak link. The town fathers and members of the General Court maintained with a straight face before the Revolution that the Church of England was firmly established in every town in the form of Congregationalist churches. In the early national period, they argued just as strenuously that there was no establishment, even though the same churches survived intact and still enjoyed the support of the townsfolk through their taxes, however meager.[46]

And indeed the Standing Order in Massachusetts was neither as land-rich nor as hidebound as the more robust Anglican establishments had been in other colonies. This weakness helps to explain the technical survival of Massachusetts's anemic establishment until 1833. More likely, it was all but dead by 1815, valuable primarily to long-settled towns in the east of the state where the Standing Order still held sway, but ever more unreliable as one traveled westward.[47] And even then, by 1820 eastern towns were horrified by the example of Dedham, which called a member of the radical Unitarian branch to the pulpit of the once-venerable First Church.[48] Other towns followed suit, and at least eighty Unitarian betrayals of this kind revealed the fundamental weakness of the remaining establishment.[49] There was litigation as a result, but the relative poverty of Massachusetts's churches made them a less attractive target than the rich glebes of the mid-Atlantic states, especially Virginia.[50]

Among the nine states that entered the Revolution with religious establishments, Massachusetts was not typical. In New Hampshire, parts of New York, Maryland, the Carolinas, and more, the Anglican establishment had more bite and far less democratic origins and support.[51] Even if America is not exceptional, as the historians would tell us, Massachusetts was an exception within America. The Bay State's contradictory posture (what was an establishment before the Revolution was no longer an establishment after independence, even though the same system survived pretty much unchanged) understandably exposed state leaders to charges of hypocrisy. Yet Massachusetts's way of doing religion was pliable enough to satisfy ostensibly irreconcilable standards and political regimes.[52] The discomfort produced by the Unitarian heresy raised the temperature, to be sure, but in Massachusetts the collapse came from within the system, as orthodox church members eventually decided that positive tax support just wasn't worth the risk of losing at the polls to ne'er-do-well liberals. And outside Massachusetts, the consequences of disestablishment were proportionately more dire. By the early decades of the nineteenth century, the decision that voluntary rather than public tax support for religion would be the American way of faith had traveled up and down the coast. This is a familiar story, well known to historians, judges, and even some politicians and activists.[53] But this is only half the story of disestablishment.

Religious establishments in many jurisdictions were supported by dedicated land, not just taxes. Scholars' focus on finance misses the other, equally vital source of income: real property—or, as they were commonly called at the time, glebe lands.[54] Such dedicated property was an essential and ubiquitous element of initial church formation and ongoing administration. As Justice Story described the relationship between a community and its church, the glebe was the dowry for the marriage between congregation and Christian faith.[55] The blessing of spiritual guidance and solace required tangible support. The earthly church—the bride of Christ, as it was often called—was endowed with the most recognizable form of wealth: land. Without a glebe, said Story, one did not have a church.[56] Several hundred acres was the usual, and that the former World Trade Center towers were surrounded by land that belonged to the Episcopal Church (the same Trinity Church of Wall Street that was burned in the Revolution and in the second decade of the twenty-first century has become a focus of Occupy Wall Street protestors) should give us a sense of the tangible quality and persistence of such glebes.[57] In Delaware, a glebe farm dating from the pre-Revolutionary period was actively farmed at least until the mid-1960s.[58]

When religious institutions were separated from their traditional grounding in political sovereignty—that is, when they were disestablished—the question of the land that endowed the formerly established church (tax-free in perpetuity, of course) arose immediately and with urgency. What would happen to the dowry, now that the marriage between church and state had devolved into—well, maybe not a divorce—a separation?[59] In many new states, the landscape had long been marked by property dedicated to the support of religion.[60] In grants to form new towns, for example, it was common to set aside a portion of all land both for the support of the contemplated church itself and often for education and mission work as well. One example shows how ingrained this habit had become in the new United States. Debates between the members of the Confederation Congress in 1785 on how to provide for the settlement of western lands pitted most New

England delegates against James Madison. Responding to their proposal that a portion of each new township be set aside "for the support of religion," Madison argued that the plan "smell[ed] strongly of
antiquated bigotry" and vehemently opposed the dedication. He won
that battle, but even so in July 1787—while Madison was at the Federal
Convention in Philadelphia—the Confederation Congress approved a
large sale of land in the new Ohio Territory to the Reverend Manasseh
Cutler, rector of the Congregational Church of Ipswich, Massachusetts
(who doubled as a speculator in land and was well known for his liberality with bribes). The sale quietly included the proviso on lot twenty-
nine in each proposed township, setting it aside from the sale for support of religion, the precise provision that New Englanders had lately
proposed and that Madison had stridently opposed.[61]

*   *   *

Inevitably, disestablishment raised the question of how to treat such
dedicated land—the relic of a prior regime that had been imposed by
imperial Britain and engrossed land in an institution once part of government, but that now in theory existed only in a private space yet still
lived off and profited from the legacy of oppression. At least, that was
how proponents of forfeiture put it, especially Baptists and Presbyterians in the Old Dominion. Each jurisdiction that had disestablished
confronted the issue, although few were as divided and raucous as Virginia.[62] Two decisions by the U.S. Supreme Court in 1815 illustrate how
such questions were debated.

The first case reached the Court from the District of Columbia,
which was called into being in 1801, well after the age of establishment,
at least in theory, and yet the new district included land and buildings
that were part of an earlier era. Because the states of Maryland and Virginia had ceded territory to form the federal district, their legacy was
inherited through the mechanism of the transfer. What had been land
within a state became federal property and was transformed invisibly
but crucially by the new legal environment. When land from Virginia
was transferred to the District of Columbia, the Supreme Court became
another voice in the ways and means of disestablishment. By the time
the Court heard argument in a case involving lands that formerly had

been part of Virginia (and were returned to the state about thirty years after the Court's decision), the first phase of disestablishment was substantially complete in most of the new states.

Taxes came first, to be sure, and consumed attention in the late eighteenth century, but simple revocation of tax support hardly completed the process. The transition from conflict over taxation to the question of property took less than a generation. After the outbreak of the Revolutionary War, many former colonies moved to ensure that Anglican clerics would receive no tax support. New York (1776), Virginia (1776), North Carolina (1777), New Hampshire (1777), Georgia (1778), and other new states quickly terminated support for ministers of the Church of England. A decade later, when Virginia formally disestablished, moderate and loyalist Anglican clergymen had been forced out. Even Patrick Henry, no pushover for lazy churchmen, had been moved to pity by the penurious and hangdog lot who remained.[63]

Truth be told, however, the church itself tended to be socially elitist and spiritually moribund, especially in tidewater Virginia. Virginia's "Mother Church," as it was called, was dominated by the planter elite, who also controlled the General Assembly, which dictated when and how churches could acquire or sell real property. Both on their own and through the legislature, the planter elite effectively resisted clerical power.[64] The church was already cash-poor but still land-rich—a tempting target. The decision to "establish" religious freedom in 1786 made permanent and official what had existed for a decade: No tax could thereafter be levied to support clergy of any denomination.[65] Disestablishment also occurred just as the new Episcopal Church, clearly conceived as the successor to the colonial establishment, developed its own internal governance and rewrote the Book of Common Prayer. There was even talk of bishops.[66]

Especially in light of a successor church, disestablishment raised the follow-on question. What about the wealth of the church in glebes, accumulated over 150 years through imperial mandates? Virginia was thickly settled with Anglican churches: 107 parishes, many with three or four churches each, were spread across Virginia before the Revolution, far outnumbering those in other colonies. And although some of these parishes must have included land and buildings that were among the least valuable in a given district, Hungars Church and many others illustrate the choice and productive acreage that had been set aside to support the worship of God. Had not the dedication of such land been a kind of theft of valuable real estate from the good people of the Old Dominion?

Resentment lingered, as the value of glebes to both clergy and the new Episcopalian denomination was backlit after the revocation of tax support. The longstanding elitism of the Episcopal clergy and the spiritual torpor of their churches only added to the malaise. More popular and egalitarian Baptist and Presbyterian critics sputtered with outrage at the material advantage that—they claimed—was still held by the new Episcopal Church.[67] They and their supporters advocated leveling the playing field—and after a decade or so of chipping away at lingering Anglican privileges, the Glebe Act of 1802 killed two birds with one stone. The act united charity with confiscation: It provided for the forfeiture of all vacant parishes and glebes, authorizing the Overseers of the Poor in each county to sell the land, and dedication of the proceeds of those sales to the relief of poverty or any other purpose "which a majority of the voters might decide."[68]

The results were predictable. Litigation followed immediately as defenders of the church argued that the confiscation of vested property was a violation of the liberty of property for which the Revolution had been fought, but devastation was around the corner. Plundering churches and glebe houses became a brief but intensive (and profitable) sport. "Vacancy" may have been achieved by scaring away the minister, but once abandoned the land was immediately vulnerable to both forfeiture and less formal and often boisterous pillage by local commonfolk who may well have long resented the elitism of the Anglican clergy. The ascendancy of Baptists in particular was proportional to the humiliation of the Episcopalians by a radical change in the physical landscape. The idea of wresting vested property from an apparently valid successor institution did trouble some consciences in Virginia. The few legal scholars who have mentioned the Glebe Act have criticized its radical nature, either calling the Act's legality "doubtful" or arguing that it would have been "wiser" to avoid caving in to "cupidity and sectarian jealousy."[69] Clearly, the free-for-all that followed the Act released pent-up feelings that do not reflect well on the respect for property often cited as a cardinal feature of American life and law.[70]

The Episcopal Church brought suit in hopes that the Act would be declared unconstitutional. But in October 1803 the venerable but aged Edmund Pendleton, president judge of the Court of Appeals (then Virginia's highest court), died in his rooms at the Swan Tavern in Richmond. Pendleton had been a well-known opponent of seizure of the glebes.[71] The full opinion striking down the Glebe Act was found on the table next to his lifeless body, but Pendleton's death before the decision was handed down meant that the case remained open. Unfortunately for historians of church and state, the draft opinion apparently has not survived. Pendleton's successor, St. George Tucker, famous as the first American editor of Blackstone's *Commentaries on the Laws of England*, voted to sustain the Act, thereby snatching defeat for the Episcopal Church from the jaws of victory. Tucker's reasons for sustaining the forfeiture were never recorded, but history has judged the court's decision as indefensible.[72]

There was a great deal of property at stake, although precise numbers may never be known. Churches in Virginia were mandated by law to be provided with glebe houses and farms of at least 200 acres (often the actual amount was double or triple that acreage); frequently, there were multiple churches in each parish.[73] As one sympathetic observer commented, that Anglican clergy no longer collected salaries at taxpayers' expense had been mitigated by income from the glebes; after the Glebe Act, they had nothing to fall back on.[74] More than sixty parishes were vacant by the time the Glebe Act took effect in 1802, and only thirty-five survived into the mid–nineteenth century. The forfeiture of glebe lands and vacant parishes proceeded with breathtaking speed. Churches stripped of their valuable materials fell into ruin. Denominational histories are full of stories of plunder and desecration.[75] Many such stories are confirmed by outside materials.

Across the state, forfeitures brought about the virtual dissolution of the traditional faith. But the District of Columbia, the one hundred square miles that included what are now the cities of Washington and Alexandria, was organized and placed under federal jurisdiction in 1801, just as the Glebe Act gathered overwhelming political support but before it was enacted.[76] And when the vestry of the Episcopal Church in Alexandria tried to sell their 516-acre glebe several years later, Virginia's Fairfax County overseers claimed the land was theirs by virtue of the Glebe Act. The resulting dispute was finally resolved by the U.S. Supreme Court in February 1815. In his opinion for the Court in *Terrett v. Taylor*, Justice Story noted drily the "remarkable diversity of opinion in the [Virginia] legislature" as to the proper treatment of religion and property.[77] The better path would be to respect "all sects" by giving them management of their property and power to regulate their own affairs, he added complacently.[78] His serenity belied the brewing controversy over religious establishment in his home state of Massachusetts. Story instead used the occasion of writing for the Court in *Terrett v. Taylor* to strike a blow for property rights and against the vagaries of politics.

The Virginia legislature had mistaken its power, Story said, in ways that "would uproot the very foundation of almost all the land titles in Virginia."[79] A republican government, Story stressed, must protect the liberty of property from such overreaching. Property that had vested before the Revolution, he held, was protected by the same limitations that had restrained the Crown before independence. Virginia succeeded only to the powers of the "regal government . . . and, we may add, with many a flower of prerogative struck from its hands."[80] There was no power to declare that entire swaths of religious property now belonged to the state, Story concluded, just as the king would have been powerless to do the same before the Revolution. Virginia's Glebe Act was held unconstitutional by the unanimous U.S. Supreme Court, thus protecting the glebe lands of the Episcopal Church of Alexandria from the grasping claims of the Fairfax County overseers.

But the case was of little practical value outside the District of Columbia, because the Supreme Court's writ did not extend to land law outside the bounds of federal territories, whatever persuasive effect Story thought his holding would have outside the District. In Virginia, many forfeitures had already taken place and, after Pendleton's death and Tucker's vote to sustain, no reconsideration of the constitutionality of the statutory mandate that unleashed the devastation was contemplated. Sporadic litigation arguing that one or another parish or glebe was not in fact "vacant" lasted until the late 1850s, but the handwriting was on the wall. Nothing that the Supreme Court could say made a difference, however much Story lamented the excitability of the Virginia legislature.

* * *

Less than a month after the Alexandria case, Justice Story confronted an equally turbulent history, this one far closer to his New England home. Vermont, infamous in the Revolutionary and early national periods for its thugs and outlaws, was also dotted with what became known by the euphemism "lease lands." As the sole historian of these lands reflected in 1950, the 250 towns then in the state were almost all established with dedicated land set aside for pious and charitable purposes.[81] These towns include grants made during the colonial period as well as after Vermont became a separate jurisdiction and even after it had joined the United States.

Most numerous were the "Wentworth towns," so called after the crafty and grasping colonial governor of New Hampshire, Benning Wentworth. Gazing westward from New Hampshire in the 1740s, Wentworth took advantage of the imprecision of the eastern border separating New Hampshire from the far larger and more powerful but notoriously dysfunctional colony of New York. The Green Mountains were generally ignored by New York. In 1749, Wentworth began to experiment; he established the town of Bennington on the western shore of the Connecticut River. When he encountered no resistance from New York, Wentworth moved quickly. Over the next two decades, he granted anywhere from a low estimate of 126 towns to a high of 148 in what is now Vermont. Each town was six miles square, and all of them included "shares" (a minimum of 250 acres per share) for each of four public purposes: one for a glebe for the Church of England, one for the Society for the Propagation of the Gospel in Foreign Parts (SPG—a British missionary society established in 1701 as an arm of the Anglican Church), one for the first settled minister in the town, and one for a school.[82]

Settlement of these new towns was spotty, and many of the private grantees were veterans of the Seven Years' War and protégés of Wentworth. Others bought into the governor's speculative bubble, including the notorious Ethan Allen and his gang of Green Mountain Boys, who hoped to make quick money.[83] From the 1760s through the 1780s, this speculation fueled rapid growth and migration to many of Wentworth's new towns. This doughty collection of settlers resisted New York's intermittent attempts to regain control of what it had thought of as its "northeastern counties."[84]

In 1777, Vermont took advantage of the distraction provided by the Revolution and became an independent entity, with a separate government and a rollicking approach to religion as well as to government. The Green Mountain State was admitted to the Union in 1791 as the first post-independence American state. One observer has argued that Vermont came closer than any other state to embodying the New England ideal of a truly pluralist establishment, because Baptist and Methodist parishes almost matched Congregationalists in number by the late eighteenth century.[85] The few historians who have paid attention to such issues tend to write off Vermont's establishment, generally concluding that it was less onerous than others in the early Republic, and that egalitarianism dominated.[86]

Yet Vermont established an additional 131 towns in the late eighteenth century and continued the practice of setting aside shares of 250 acres each for a glebe, the SPG, the first settled minister, and education. These gifts in support of religion were themselves tax-free in perpetuity, often a valuable gift. Despite their arguments elsewhere in the new nation that support for religion should be entirely voluntary and private, Baptists in Vermont accepted glebes and minister's portions in some two dozen towns and also split the gift with ministers of other denominations when the township was divided among religious groups.[87] But as with so much in Vermont, the implementation of the mandate for support in land for religion varied from place to place and might be ignored entirely or modified locally. The chaotic government and paucity of records before the nineteenth century mean that many details of this local control are unrecoverable.[88]

It is clear, however, that the Vermont legislature encountered controversy and attempted to mediate disputes over glebe and other gifted lands in several different statutes, with only partial success. True, Vermont formally ended taxation in support of religion in 1807, but its early state constitutions all included the instructions that "every sect or denomination of Christians ought to observe the Sabbath . . . and keep up some sort of religious worship which to them shall seem most agreeable to the revealed word of God." This aspiration was codified in 1783 legislation that detailed how townships could "Erect Proper Houses for Public Worship and Support Ministers of the Gospel" whenever two-thirds of eligible voters chose to select a location for a church and call a minister.[89] Over the next twenty years, the state steadily reduced restrictions on dissenters, until it ended tax support altogether with the repeal of earlier legislation in the interest of "harmony and good order in Civil Society."[90] The revocation of tax support was not especially acrimonious within Vermont, although other New Englanders predicted that the "leveling spirit of democracy [in the Green Mountain State] . . . would eradicat[e] every moral virtuous and religious principle from the human heart."[91] Nonetheless, one Baptist missionary from Connecticut reported several years later that no minister in Vermont had lost his post as a result of the cessation of tax support.[92]

The real battles were over land, not taxes. The eighteenth-century grants set aside at least 750 acres per town for the direct support of religion, with one share for the first settled minister, one to generate income for the church, and—remarkably—one for the Society for the Propagation of the Gospel, even after Vermont had declared itself independent of Britain.[93] In the post-Revolutionary period, the state legislature authorized town selectmen to lease such lands, eject trespassers, and so on, but with the proviso that all proceeds must be used for "the support of religious-worship."[94] Vermont ministers proved a quarrelsome bunch: Not only did Baptists fight with Congregationalists and Presbyterians with some frequency, but some of them proved unreliable once they were granted the minister's portion in a town. Elder Hezekiah Eastman led a small Baptist church in Danby. A few months after being installed as the "first settled minister in the town," he sold his land to the highest bidder and moved on, much to the chagrin of the congregation.[95] One Congregationalist minister reportedly collected rights in seven separate towns for a total of at least 1,750 acres, making a handsome profit on the scheme.[96]

In 1805, the Vermont legislature took a bold new step: It re-granted all lands set aside for religious support to the towns for the "use of the schools of such towns."[97] Again, a significant amount of land was at stake: The best estimate at the time put the amount at more than 150,000 acres.[98] And once again, the predictable result was litigation, which lasted for several decades. It included two U.S. Supreme Court decisions, the first and more important of which was the 1815 case of *Town of Pawlet v. Clark*, with an opinion written by Justice Story close on the heels of his decision in *Terrett v. Taylor*.[99] A young Daniel Webster argued for the township, claiming that the land had reverted to the town (which no doubt contemplated leasing or resale of the 750 acres at stake in the case). Webster's presence was one facet of his fight against the Standing Order in New Hampshire, then raging over the control of Dartmouth College. Indeed, *Terrett* and *Pawlet* were important precedents for the U.S. Supreme Court's decision in the well-known *Dartmouth College* case in 1819.

Webster's interest in the Vermont case was animated by his knowledge that Benning Wentworth not only gave away much of Vermont; Wentworth also promised Eleazer Wheelock 500 acres for the formation of what eventually became Dartmouth College. As the controversy over Vermont's disestablishment simmered to the west, New Hampshire was caught in a battle between religious liberals and the more conservative Congregationalists, whose interests were supported by the dedicated property that Wentworth had made his uniform practice in land grants. The New Hampshire legislature, controlled by the conservatives, sought to restructure the college to protect religious orthodoxy.[100] Webster, himself a dissenter, supported the liberalization of education at Dartmouth and opposed orthodox sectarian preferences.[101] Rededicating public property to liberal educational purposes and away from conservative religious control, therefore, was in his view a worthy project.

His argument found a ready audience at the Supreme Court, especially because *Terrett v. Taylor* already had provided much of the answer to the question of Vermont's legislation. In Virginia, the forfeiture of glebes, like that in Vermont, was of "unoccupied" property. But in Virginia, the glebes supported churches that had been active and that had once had ministers. As the technical language has it, the churches had been "full" (that is, they had all once had ministers in the pulpit), so the gift of the glebe had become irrevocable. The vacancies were the product of the Revolution and of distrust of Anglicans. But the glebes themselves had already "vested," as Story emphasized in *Terrett*, and the change in government did not dissolve title to property. Virginia's attempted divestment of church ownership of glebe lands, therefore, was an unconstitutional interference with property rights—full stop. Virginia, of course, continued on its merry way, undeterred by the Supreme Court, which had power to protect the Fairfax property from the grasp of marauding Virginians only because the state had ceded to the District of Columbia the land on which the church stood.

In the Vermont case, however, the Court had jurisdiction over all disputed lands. The question was whether the original grants from New Hampshire or the subsequent regranting by the state of Vermont would take precedence. The suit, therefore, was by "citizens of the same state claiming lands under grants of different states"[102] and fell squarely within the scope of federal judicial power outlined in Article III of the U.S. Constitution. The crucial difference in Vermont was the vacancy of the lands—unlike Virginia's glebe lands, they had never "vested" in the full-blown sense of the term. So far, so good. But the question of the forfeiture was not answered so readily. Two subsidiary issues occupied Justice Story and the Court. First, Story held that the grant was "in abeyance" for so long as there was no current worthy claimant or occupant. In that legal limbo, the legislature was not free to expropriate the property, any more than the king would have been free to "resume" his control of a donation for the use of a nonexistent church.

This point led to the second question, one involving the law of charities. Because the donation was for an institution—an established church—that did not yet exist, and because it was part of a collection of donations (to schools, to the SPG) for pious and charitable purposes, Story reasoned, its effect "by the common law [was] as a dedication to [general] pious uses."[103] With the consent of the town, therefore, the state could "redirect" the property (before vesting) to a related use. Education had always been part of the dedicated purposes, thus the support of local schools was a respectable and connected interest in the spirit of the initial grants. Had a church or minister capable of laying claim to the glebe lands already been recognized in the jurisdiction, the question would have had a far different answer (see the Fairfax litigation). But given that the Vermont statute had explicitly exempted all such towns from the operation of the statute, the provisions rededicating the shares set aside for the church and the first settled minister were valid exercises of sovereign control, rather than an appropriation of vested property.[104]

End of story—except that the Act and subsequent lawsuits all were based on the assumption that Vermont actually could figure out which lands were granted for religious uses, an exercise that to this day has proved far beyond the state's capacity. There are still pockets claimed by schools, by churches, and by the successor in interest to the Society for the Propagation of the Gospel (the Episcopal Church of Vermont, ironically).[105] Each year, the church reportedly sends a plaintive letter to the State of Vermont, begging for clarification of its holdings. It has now been unclear for more than 200 years what they are all talking about.

*   *   *

It bears noting that both Virginia and Vermont expropriated religious property ostensibly to accomplish two fundamental goals of government that previously had been the responsibilities of an established church: poor relief and education. At least, that's what they said their purpose was. It is doubtful that either worthy object saw much benefit. Yet the redirection of land showed the state's assumption of power over responsibilities that traditionally had been within the purview of religious authorities.

It is vital also to draw attention here to another aspect of this history that has gone unnoticed among historians, including those working in the field of church and state: Even though significant property was involved in each state, the total property owned or dedicated to religious purposes in American establishments was small, certainly less than 3 percent of total land in the state. In several other jurisdictions, deciding to let the current owner of church land keep the property may have been the less onerous choice. Forfeiture of lands inevitably resulted in expensive litigation and was controversial—more controversial than the cessation of tax support. Partly that controversy resulted because significant moral value was attached to land, and partly because taxes always have been a more visible target than ownership of land. But it may well also be worthwhile to investigate the ways in which these places of faith have far deeper meanings than the dollars flowed into them. In political terms, property rights long have been held to be a source of liberty and independence. In religious terms, saving rituals happened in salvific spaces; and forcibly turning spaces having redemptive power to profane even if ostensibly charitable uses rubbed many observers and participants the wrong way.[106]

Many American scholars are just beginning to appreciate the correlation between communities of believers and the physical spaces where they congregate and worship. In some surprising ways, disestablishment has proven far more useful than establishment, from this perspective. In 1837, the minister and activist Lyman Beecher reflected on his deep anxiety at the prospect of disestablishment in Connecticut twenty years earlier: "[W]e shall become slaves," he had said then, "and slaves to the worst of masters."[107] Instead, Beecher and others like him found themselves masters of new dominions after disestablishment. And the wealth of religious organizations grew apace in the new world of church and state. Even the Episcopal Church saw a remarkable recovery in Virginia in the second quarter of the nineteenth century.[108] President Ulysses S. Grant claimed in his 1875 State of the Union Message that the amount of real property owned by religious organizations had doubled in the ten years between 1850 and 1860.[109] It has risen steadily ever since.

Although reliable estimates of the amount of all religiously owned real property are scarce as hen's teeth, the most recent broad surveys— which were conducted a generation ago and were far from precise— place the figure at anywhere from 10 to 20 percent.[110] That is, the federal government owns about 30 percent of all land in the United States,[111] states own about 10 percent,[112] and religious organizations own at least as much as the states, although nobody really knows the total amount in religious hands. This vast wealth in land, of course, is not dedicated only to places of worship: It includes hospitals, schools, seminaries, monasteries, gymnasiums, parsonages, resorts, townships, and more. Yet even to point out the fact of such wide property ownership by religious organizations is controversial. In an era when impoverished governments are searching for new sources of revenue, the argument that such property should be taxed has a more receptive audience than at any time in recent history.[113] Also pervasive are new restrictions on land use that effectively screen out religious acquisition and development of property, particularly in urban redevelopment districts and many suburbs.[114] In urban settings, eminent domain condemnations have become a tool for removing churches and their associated soup kitchens and shelters that cater to poor residents of decaying city centers, all in the interest of "vibrant," taxpaying commercial enterprises that serve a wealthier clientele.

We began with the looting of Hungars Church. It is fitting to close with another phase in the history of Hungars parish. The large and valuable glebe mentioned at the outset survived the first phase of forfeitures. The pulpit was "full" without meaningful gaps for the first several decades of the nineteenth century; Hungars and its glebe escaped forfeiture proceedings, despite rumblings from "antagonists" in the surrounding country.[115] Especially after the Virginia Court of Appeals unequivocally upheld the Glebe Act in 1840, hungry land speculators and aggrieved members of competing Protestant denominations reinvigorated the call for forfeitures. Threatened litigation against Hungars glebe was a constant topic of conversation in the vestry. When the Overseers of the Poor invoked the Glebe Act and sold the land at auction "conditionally," Hungars fought long and hard, claiming that its glebe did not fall within the purview of the forfeiture provisions, and cases in the lower courts went both ways. Finally, in 1859, the Court of Appeals ordered the sale of the glebe.[116] Distraught vestry members raged that the decision flew in the face of the Supreme Court's *Terrett v. Taylor* decision of 1815. They predicted that they would win an appeal to the highest court—but they nonetheless decided that an appeal would be unwise, presumably on legal as well as political grounds. Intervening events apparently delayed the inevitable for more than a decade. Only in 1870 did Virginia appoint a state commission to oversee the sale of Hungars glebe.[117]

Well into the late nineteenth century, in other words, aftershocks of disestablishment redefined local religious life along political and denominational lines. The contours of property law for religious organizations, especially the Episcopal Church, hardly resembled the private space that many historians and lawyers have long assumed nurtured American religious life. Instead, the religious landscape was molded by turbulent and frequently violent eruptions, and then by ongoing legislative and judicial intervention. Forfeiture is not the end of the story— widespread limitations set by states and then federal territories on the amounts and value of real property were imposed on religious organizations in the nineteenth century. Mortmain statutes, in that sense, were the third-generation property consequences of disestablishment.

Insight into patterns of property ownership by American religious institutions, and how much of it they owned at different periods, must now begin with due attention to the earliest days of our national history. Then, greed and treason created an atmosphere that has reverberated through American religious life, even though we have long ignored the ways that disestablishment actually worked in law and on the ground.

NOTES

1. Slaves became part of the glebe itself, authorized by an act of the Virginia General Assembly in 1745, which directed the sale of one portion of the Hungars glebe to finance the purchase of "slaves to be annexed to the land" to build glebe houses and work the land on the main 1,600-acre farm. William W. Hening, *Statutes at Large of Virginia*, 13 vols. (Richmond, Va.: Samuel Pleasants, 1809–23), 5:390–91. Other Virginia glebes also included slaves; Elizabeth City Parish, with 200 acres, owned 24 slaves in 1788. *Virginia Independent Chronicle* (Richmond), 17 September 1788, cited in Thomas E. Buckley, "Evangelicals Triumphant: The Baptists' Assault on the Virginia Glebes, 1786–1801," *William and Mary Quarterly* 3d Ser., 45:1 (January 1988): 33–69, 34. Individual ministers at Hungars and elsewhere also owned slaves. See Susan Stitt, "The Will of Stephen Charlton and Hungars Parish Glebe," *Virginia Magazine of History and Biography* 77:3 (July 1969): 259–76, 265; George MacLaren Brydon, "The Wealth of the Clergy," *Historical Magazine of the Protestant Episcopal Church* 22 (1953): 91–98. Slaveholding was also common in Virginia among both Baptist (68 percent) and Presbyterian (73 percent) ministers in the early national period. Buckley, "Evangelicals Triumphant," 62–63, n.102.
2. Anne Floyed Upshur and Wilson M. Stitt, "The History of Hungars Episcopal Church, Hungars Parish, Northampton County, Bridgetown, Virginia" (n.p., n.d.), reprinted online at http://www.esva.net/ghotes/history/hungars.htm (accessed 15 October 2011); David L. Holmes, *A Brief History of the Episcopal Church* (Harrisburg, Pa.: Trinity Press International, 1993), 26–28.
3. Carl Bridenbaugh, *Mitre and Sceptre: Transatlantic Faiths, Ideas, Personalities, and Politics, 1689–1775* (New York: Oxford University Press, 1962), 207–87.
4. James B. Bell, *A War of Religion: Dissenters, Anglicans, and the American Revolution* (Basingstoke, UK: Palgrave Macmillan, 2008).
5. Katherine Carte Engel, "The SPCK and the American Revolution: The Limits of International Protestantism," *Church History* 81:1 (March 2012): 1–27, 3–4, 26–27; Carla Gardina Pestana, *Protestant Empire: Religion and the Making of the British Atlantic World* (Philadelphia: University of Pennsylvania Press, 2009), 218–50.
6. E.g., Stephen A. Marini, *Radical Sects of Revolutionary New England* (Cambridge, Mass.: Harvard University Press, 1982), 7, 175–76.
7. Brendan McConville, *The King's Three Faces: The Rise and Fall of Royal America, 1688–1776* (Chapel Hill: University of North Carolina Press, 2006), 261–65.
8. Robert W. Shoemaker, *The Origin and Meaning of the Name "Protestant Episcopal"* (New York: American Church Publications, 1959); Nancy Rhoden, *Revolutionary Anglicanism: The Colonial Church of England Clergy during the American Revolution* (New York: New York University Press, 1999); Stephen Taylor, "Whigs, Bishops and America: The Politics of Church Reform in Mid-Eighteenth-Century England," *The Historical Journal* 30 (1993): 338; Arthur L. Cross, *The Anglican Episcopate and the American Colonies* (*Harvard Historical Studies, Vol. IX*) (Cambridge, Mass.: Harvard University Press, 1902; repr., Hamden, Conn.: Archon Books, 1964).

9. *Classified Digest of the Records of the Society for the Propagation of the Gospel in Foreign Parts, 1701–1892*, 4th ed. (London: SPG Office, 1893), 74, 140, 155; Robert Prichard, *A History of the Episcopal Church*, rev. ed. (Harrisburg, Pa.: Morehouse Publishing, 1999), 77–78.
10. S. D. McConnell, *History of the American Episcopal Church from the Planting of the Colonies to the End of the Civil War* (New York: T. Whittaker, 1891); Stephanie Corrigan, "Politics of Faith: The Loyalism of Rev. John Stuart" (presented at Society for the History of the Early Republic, Baltimore, July 2012).
11. Henry Caner to Society for the Propagation of the Gospel in Foreign Parts (SPG), 14 April 1776, SPG, Series B, reel 23, #135.
12. See, e.g., Joseph Galloway, *Historical and Political Reflections on the Rise and Progress of the American Rebellion* (London: G. Wilkie, 1780), 54–55.
13. Rhoden, *Revolutionary Anglicanism*, 88–115.
14. Jonathan Boucher, *A View of the Causes and Consequences of the American Revolution* (London: Printed for G. G. & J. Robinson, 1797), 309; Alan Virta, *Prince George's County, A Pictorial History* (Norfolk, Va.: Donning Co., 1984), 68; http://www.ang-md.org/history.php (accessed 28 December 2011).
15. John F. Woolverton, "Philadelphia's William White: Episcopalian Distinctiveness and Accommodation in the Post-Revolutionary Period," *Historical Magazine of the Protestant Episcopal Church* 43 (December 1974): 279–96.
16. Prichard, *History*, 78.
17. James Madison to William Bradford, 28 July 1775, in William T. Hutchinson and William M.E. Rachal, eds., *The Papers of James Madison*, 17 vols. (Chicago: University of Chicago Press, 1962–77), 1:159–61 (quote at 161; see also 162 n.10); Thomas E. Buckley, *Church and State in Revolutionary Virginia, 1776–1787* (Charlottesville: University Press of Virginia, 1977), 16.
18. Buckley, *Church and State in Revolutionary Virginia*, 171–72.
19. On persecution of dissenters, see John A. Ragosta, *Wellspring of Liberty: How Virginia's Religious Dissenters Helped Win the American Revolution & Secured Religious Liberty* (New York: Oxford University Press, 2010), 15–42 and Appendix A, "Persons Persecuted for Religion, Eighteenth-Century Virginia, Post-1763," 171–81; Rhys Isaac, "'The Rage of Malice of the Old Serpent Devil': The Dissenters and the Making and Remaking of the Virginia Statute for Religious Freedom," in Merrill D. Peterson and Robert C. Vaughan, eds., *The Virginia Statute for Religious Freedom: Its Evolution and Consequences in American History* (New York: Cambridge University Press, 1988), 139–69, 163; Mark D. McGarvie, *One Nation Under Law: America's Early National Struggles to Separate Church and State* (DeKalb: Northern Illinois University Press, 2004), 144–48.
20. Pritchard, *History*, 73–81.
21. Hamilton J. Eckenrode, *Separation of Church and State in Virginia: A Study of the Development of the Revolution* (Richmond, Va.: Davis Bottom, Superintendent of Public Printing, 1910), 144.

22. Holmes claims that in addition to grindstones and sinkers, baptismal fonts were used as planters, pewter communion sets were transformed into utensils and bullets, and the bricks and pews of one church were pirated to build a kitchen and a stable. Holmes, *Brief History*, 26.

23. For a thoughtful exploration of the debate leading up to the Glebe Act, as well as the long debate over whether religious organizations should be allowed to incorporate, a related issue that followed on the property forfeitures discussed here, see Thomas E. Buckley, "After Disestablishment: Thomas Jefferson's Wall of Separation in Antebellum Virginia," *Journal of Southern History* 61:3 (August 1995): 445–80.

24. The exceptions to this rule are Anson Phelps Stokes, *Church and State in the United States*, 3 vols. (New York: Harper, 1950), and Thomas E. Buckley, whose articles have already filled in some gaps, and whose forthcoming book on Virginia's experience of disestablishment from 1789 to 1940 promises a full exploration of such issues.

25. For example, New York state conducted hearings into the extensive property holdings and management practices of Trinity Church of Wall Street on several separate occasions from the 1770s through the early twentieth century. See Morgan Dix, ed., *A History of the Parish of Trinity Church in the City of New York*, 6 vols. (New York: G. P. Putnam's Sons, 1898–1962), *passim*; Elizabeth Mensch, "Religion, Revival, and the Ruling Class: A Critical History of Trinity Church," *Buffalo Law Review* 36:1 (Fall 1987): 427–571 *passim*.

26. See, e.g., *The Black List: A List of those Tories Who Took Part with Great-Britain, in the Revolutionary War, and Were Attainted of High Treason, Commonly Called the Black List!* (Philadelphia: Printed for the Proprietor, 1802).

27. Thomas B. Allen, *Tories: Fighting for the King in America's First Civil War* (New York: HarperCollins, 2010), 15, 166–67, 194; Thomas S. Kidd, *God of Liberty: A Religious History of the American Revolution* (New York: Basic Books, 2010).

28. It is not entirely clear that the fire of 1776 was set with an eye to destroying the church, although the Reverend Charles Inglis, Rector of Trinity, believed that it had been. See Inglis's charge in *Ecclesiastical Records, State of New York*, 7 vols. (Albany: J. B. Lyon, 1901–16), 6: 4298.

29. *Terrett v. Taylor*, 13 U.S. (9 Cranch.) 43 (1815) and *Town of Pawlet v. Clark*, 13 U.S. (9 Cranch) 292 (1815).

30. See, e.g., Leslie C. Griffin, ed., *Law and Religion: Cases and Materials*, 2d ed. (New York: Foundation Press, 2010), 251–331 (chapter on church property dedicated to schisms, employment, sex and race discrimination, tort liability); John T. Noonan Jr. and Edward McGlynn Gaffney Jr., eds., *Religious Freedom: History, Cases, and Other Materials on the Interaction of Religion and Government*, 3d ed. (New York: Foundation Press, 2011), 470–93, 954–86 (same); Steven G. Guy, ed., *Religion and the State*, 2d ed. (Newark, N.J.: LexisNexis, 2006), 1–17, 695–711 (same).

31. Mark McGarvie's fine book *One Nation under Law* is an exception, as it focuses on South Carolina, New York, and New Hampshire, tracing the different

histories of disestablishment in each jurisdiction, although without attention to property issues. See also Buckley, "After Disestablishment," for a helpful longer view in Virginia, but without substantial attention to forfeiture.

32. Supreme Court Justice William O. Douglas dissented in *Walz v. Tax Commission of New York*, 397 U.S. 664 (1970), which upheld state property tax exemptions for religious organizations against an Establishment Clause challenge. Douglas argued that such exemptions were a form of state subsidy, which had allowed religious institutions to acquire vast amounts of property, estimated at a value of $141 billion in the late 1960s with an annual income of at least $22 billion, "and the extent to which they are feeding from the public trough in a variety of forms is alarming." 397 U.S. at 714, citing Martin A. Larson and C. Stanley Lowell, *The Churches: Their Riches, Revenues and Immunities, An Analysis of Tax-Exempt Property* (Washington, D.C.: R. B. Luce, 9), 232.

33. These restrictions have not been widely studied. For brief overviews, see Carl Zollman, *American Civil Church Law* (*Columbia Studies in the Social Sciences*, No. 181) (New York: Columbia University, 1917), 89–102, and Sarah Barringer Gordon, *The Mormon Question: Polygamy and Constitutional Conflict in Nineteenth-Century America* (Chapel Hill: University of North Carolina Press, 2002), 69–71, 187–208.

34. William White, *The Case of the Episcopal Churches in the United States Considered* (Philadelphia: David Claypoole, 1782), available at http://anglicanhistory.org/usa/wwhite/case1782.html (accessed 28 December 2011).

35. On Catholics, see Philip Hamburger, *Separation of Church and State* (Cambridge, Mass.: Harvard University Press, 2002), 201–19; on Mormons, see Gordon, *Mormon Question*, 68–83.

36. On the complexity and controversy of such questions, see Diana B. Henriques, "In God's Name" (eight-part series on religion, taxation, and regulation), *New York Times*, 8 October 2006 to 23 November 2007, http://www.nytimes.com/ref/business/churchstate.html (accessed 26 December 2011).

37. Sarah Barringer Gordon, "Religion and Law, 1790–1820," in *Cambridge History of American Law*, 3 vols. (Cambridge: Cambridge University Press, 2008), 2: 417–48; Martin E. Marty, "Living with Establishment and Disestablishment in Nineteenth-Century Anglo-America," *Journal of Church and State* 18 (Winter 1976): 61–77; Leonard W. Levy, "No Establishment of Religion: The Original Understanding," in *Judgments: Essays on American Constitutional History* (Chicago: Quadrangle Books, 1972), 169–224.

38. In a history dissertation underway at Northwestern University, Howard Pashman claims that the process of confiscation and redistribution of Loyalist property ensured patriotic adherence to the new revolutionary order in New York state. "The People's Property Law: Building a New Legal Order in Revolutionary New York" (presented at the American Society for Legal History Annual Meeting, Atlanta, November 2011), *passim*. The issue of "who should rule at home" is the classic one for such research. See Carl Becker, *History of Political Parties*

in the Province of New York, 1760–1776 (Madison: University of Wisconsin Press, 1909), and Staughton Lynd, "Who Should Rule at Home? Dutchess County, New York in the American Revolution," *William and Mary Quarterly* 3d Ser., 18:3 (July 1961): 330–59.

39. Other jurisdictions cry out for such study, and informal measures clearly were more common than formal ones, making community studies a crucial aspect of any thorough treatment, as well. For extant treatments, see Robert A. East, "Connecticut Loyalists: An Analysis of Loyalist Land Confiscations in Greenwich, Stamford and Norwalk," *Connecticut History* 20 (January 1979): 41–42; Richard D. Brown, "The Confiscation and Disposition of Loyalists' Estates in Suffolk County, Massachusetts," *William & Mary Quarterly* 3d Ser., 21:4 (October 1964): 534–50; Edward Countryman, "'Out of the Bounds of the Law': Northern Land Rioters in the Eighteenth Century," in Alfred F. Young, ed., *The American Revolution: Explorations in the History of American Radicalism* (DeKalb: Northern Illinois University Press, 1976), 56–57; Sarah V. Kalinoski, "Sequestration, Confiscation, and the 'Tory' in the Vermont Revolution," *Vermont History* 45:4 (October 1977): 236–46; Anne M. Outerhout, "Pennsylvania Land Confiscations During the Revolution," *Pennsylvania Magazine of History & Biography* 102:3 (June 1978): 328–43; Robert S. Lambert, "The Confiscation of Loyalist Property in Georgia, 1782–1786," *William & Mary Quarterly* 3d Ser., 20:1 (January 1963): 80–94. On the challenge facing researchers in the field, see Daniel J. Hulsebosch, "A Discrete and Cosmopolitan Minority: The Loyalists, The Atlantic World, and the Origins of Judicial Review," *Chicago-Kent Law Review* 81 (2006): 825–66, 835.

40. Prichard, *History*, 74–81; Bell, *A War of Religion*, 170–86.

41. S. D. Connell, *History of the American Episcopal Church from the Planting of the Colonies to the End of the Civil War* (New York: Thomas Whittaker, 1891), 211. Compare with twelve prosecutions in Massachusetts, ten in New York, and eight in Connecticut, all with only a fraction of Virginia's 130 Anglican clergy. Rhoden, *Revolutionary Anglicanism*, Appendix, 148–52.

42. For the long and at times acrimonious debate over whether the Revolutionary-era confiscations redistributed property more broadly than before Independence, see J. Franklin Jameson, *The American Revolution Considered as a Social Movement* (Princeton, N.J.: Princeton University Press, 1926); Harry Yoshpe, *The Disposition of Loyalist Estates in the Southern District of the State of New York* (New York: Columbia University Press, 1939); Richard B. Morris, "Class Struggle and the American Revolution," *William and Mary Quarterly* 3d Ser., 19:1 (January 1962): 3–29.

43. Daniel R. Ernst, "Church-State Issues and the Law," in John F. Wilson, ed., *Church and State in America: A Bibliographical Guide*, 2 vols. (Westport, Conn.: Greenwood Press, 1986), 1: 335; Levy, "No Establishment of Religion," 201.

44. Elizabeth B. Clark, "Church-State Relations in the Constitution-Making Period," in *Church and State in America*, 1: 157–61.

45. William E. Nelson, *Americanization of the Common Law: The Impact of Legal Change on Massachusetts Society, 1760–1830* (Cambridge, Mass.: Harvard University Press, 1975), 104–9.

46. Thomas J. Curry, *The First Freedoms: Church and State in America to the Passage of the First Amendment* (New York: Oxford University Press, 1986), 163–77; see also McGarvie, *One Nation, Under Law*, 156–65, on New England more generally and the role of education in the move to disestablish outside Vermont.

47. William G. McLoughlin, "The Role of Religion in the Revolution: Liberty of Conscience and Cultural Cohesion in the New Nation," in Stephen G. Kurtz and James H. Hutson, eds., *Essays on the American Revolution* (Chapel Hill: University of North Carolina Press for the Institute of Early American History and Culture, 1973), 197–255.

48. *Baker v. Fales*, 16 Mass. 487 (1820); see also Leonard W. Levy, *The Law of the Commonwealth and Chief Justice Shaw* (Cambridge, Mass.: Harvard University Press, 1957), 29–42.

49. E.g., *Stebbins v. Jennings*, 27 Mass. 171, 10 Pick. 172 (1830).

50. In Massachusetts, New Hampshire, and Connecticut there were undoubtedly glebes (see, for example, "Glebe Roads" in Taunton, Massachusetts; Westmoreland, New Hampshire; and Norwich, Connecticut). The extent of such holdings and their fate in the Revolution and beyond has not been the subject of scholarly inquiry, however.

51. McGarvie, *One Nation Under Law*, 106–17, 131–38; Anglicans in colonial New York, for example, never constituted more than 10 percent of the population. Elizabeth Mensch, "Religion, Revival, and the Ruling Class: A Critical History of Trinity Church," *Buffalo Law Review* 36 (Fall 1987): 467.

52. Curry, *First Freedoms*, 107–17, documents brilliantly how divines in both Massachusetts and Connecticut maintained that their Congregational parishes were established in ways fully consistent with the doctrines and privileges of the Church of England. The Massachusetts branch then studiously avoided the use of the word "establishment" when describing the post-Revolutionary religious settlement that used local taxation to support locally selected ministers. (Connecticut's religious leaders, for the most part, tended toward more openness about their continued establishment but could on occasion descend to the Bay State's level of obfuscation.) *Id.*, 174–85.

53. This is not to say the story's meaning is uncontested. Contrast the treatment of this subject by law professor Philip Hamburger, *Separation of Church and State*, 109–43, with Isaac Kramnick and R. Lawrence Moore, *The Godless Constitution: A Moral Defense of the Secular State* (New York: W. W. Norton & Co., 2005), 88–130 (Kramnick is a political theorist and historian, Moore a historian of American religion).

54. A glebe is defined as "The land which belongs to a church. *Gleba est terra qua consistit dos ecclesiae.*" William Edward Baldwin, ed., *Bouvier's Law Dictionary* (Cleveland: Banks-Baldwin Law Publishing Co., 1946), 468.

55. *Town of Pawlet v. Clark*, 13 U.S. (9 Cranch) 292, 329 (1815).

56. *Id.*, 330: "[N]o parish church . . . could have a legal existence until consecration; and consecration was expressly inhibited unless upon a suitable endowment of land. The canon law, following the civil law, required such endowment to be made or at least ascertained, before the building of the church was begun."

57. Winnifred Fallers Sullivan, "Religion, Land, and Rights: Reflections on the Park51 Controversy," in *Varieties of Religious Establishment*, ed. Winnifred Fallers Sullivan and Lori Beaman (forthcoming, Ashgate, 2013).

58. For current property holdings of Trinity Church see http://www.trinitywall-street.org/about/real-estate (accessed 19 November 2011). Borden W. Painter Jr., former president and emeritus Professor of History at Trinity College, Hartford, Connecticut, stayed with the Rector of Immanuel Church, Newcastle, Delaware, in the early 1960s while doing research as a Ph.D. student and learned that a tenant still worked the Glebe Farm. Email to the author, 2 December 2011. The Glebe House is on the National Historic Register, but there is no mention of the farm on the church's current website. http://www.immanuelonthegreen.org/ (accessed 28 December 2011).

59. For a focus on separation (rather than divorce) as the central focus for collapsing marriages in the nineteenth century, see Hendrik Hartog, *Man and Wife in America: A History* (Cambridge, Mass.: Harvard University Press, 2002), 63–92, *passim*.

60. The doctrine of dedication (reserved for public lands) was extended to church property ownership in the U.S. Zollman, *American Civil Church Law*, 407–13.

61. Ronald A. Smith, "Freedom of Religion and the Land Ordinance of 1785," *Journal of Church and State* 24 (1982): 589–602. Madison also apparently believed that all land owned by religious institutions should be taxed. "Monopolies, Perpetuities, Corporations, Ecclesiastical Endowments," in Elizabeth Fleet, ed., "Madison's Detached Memoranda," *William and Mary Quarterly* 3d Ser., 3:3 (July 1946): 551–62, 555 (pointing to an "attempt in Kentucky for example, where it was proposed to exempt Houses of Worship from taxes" and a violation of separation of church and state).

62. Stokes, *Church and State in the United States*, 1: 366–97; Buckley, "Evangelicals Triumphant," *passim*.

63. On the role of Henry in the Parson's Cause in the 1760s, see Stokes, *Church and State in the United States* 1:367–68; Eckenrode, *Separation of Church and State in Virginia*, 27, 28.

64. On planter dominance of the church, see Ragosta, *Wellspring of Liberty*, 36–38.

65. Thomas Jefferson titled his bill an Act to Establish Religious Freedom; drafted in 1779, it was not enacted until 1786. A useful version, indicating the changes to the original bill in the final statute, appears in John A. Ragosta, "The Virginia Statute for Establishing Religious Freedom," in Francis D. Cogliano, ed., *A Companion to Thomas Jefferson* (Malden, Mass.: Wiley-Blackwell, 2012), 75–90 (esp. 87–88).

66. Prichard, *History*, 82–98. The first bishop, ironically enough, was James Madison, cousin to the author of the "Memorial and Remonstrance" that became the most articulate argument in favor of disestablishment. Bishop Madison, who was consecrated at Canterbury Cathedral in 1790, was an ineffective political actor, especially weak in debates over forfeiture of glebes in the 1790s. Buckley, "Evangelicals Triumphant," 64–68.

67. For a review of petitions submitted by dissenting clergy between 1776 and 1785, see Curry, *First Freedoms*, 135–37, 143–48; and Buckley, *Church and State in Revolutionary Virginia*, 148–50; see also Eckenrode, *Separation of Church and State*, 130–50.

68. Eckenrode, *Separation of Church and State*, 148 (exceptions to the provisions for sale were made when the property had been acquired through private donation and a valid successor to the donor could be found, and for any property acquired since 1777, but both provisions were of little use to Episcopal churches); Buckley, "Evangelicals Triumphant," 54–55.

69. Stokes, *Church and State*, 1:395; Sanford H. Cobb, *The Rise of Religious Liberty in America: A History* (New York: Macmillan, 1902), 511.

70. Eckenrode called the Act "stupid and bad in tendency" especially because "too many people were interested in the sales from personal motives"; predictably, no benefit to the broader public flowed from sales conducted by the overseers, "a usually incompetent class of officials." *Separation of Church and State*, 148. On respect for property rights, see Morris, "Class Struggle," 7–11; Louis Hartz, *The Liberal Tradition in America: An Interpretation of American Political Thought since the Revolution* (New York: Harcourt, Brace, 1955), 5–6.

71. See Pendleton's "Proposed Memorial Concerning the Glebe Lands of the Episcopal Church (1797), in David J. Mays, ed., *The Letters and Papers of Edmund Pendleton, 1734–1803*, 2 vols. (Charlottesville: University Press of Virginia, 1967), 2:638–46; Mays, *The Life and Times of Edmund Pendleton: A Biography*, 2 vols. (Cambridge, Mass.: Harvard University Press, 1952), 2:337–49; Robert Leroy Hilldrup, *The Life and Times of Edmund Pendleton* (Chapel Hill: University of North Carolina Press, 1939), 336–38.

72. The opinion was to have been for a 3–1 majority; after Pendleton's death, the rehearing resulted in a 2–2 tie because of Tucker's vote. The case was then technically affirmed by an equally divided court. *Turpin v. Locket*, 10 Va. (6 Call.) 113 (1804).

73. The Clergy Act of 1748 stipulated that a glebe must be of "good and convenient land," complete with a parsonage and all necessary farm buildings. George MacLaren Brydon, *Virginia's Mother Church: The Story of the Anglican Church and the Development of Religion in Virginia*, 2 vols. (Philadelphia: Church Historical Society, 1952), 2:239.

74. Holmes, *Brief History*, 25–26.

75. See, e.g., William Meade, *Old Churches, Ministers and Families of Virginia*, 2 vols. (Philadelphia: J. B. Lippincott, 1857), 2:196–97; Johann David Schoepf, *Travels in*

the Confederation, 2 vols. Alfred J. Morrison, trans. (Philadelphia: W. J. Campbell, 1911), 2:62–63.

76. Alexandria is no longer part of the District; it was retroceded from the District to Virginia in 1846. Mark David Richards, "The Debates over the Retrocession of the District of Columbia, 1801–2004," *Washington History*, 16:1 (Spring/Summer 2004): 54–82.

77. *Terrett v. Taylor*, 13 U.S. (9 Cranch), 43, 48 (1815).

78. *Id.*, 49.

79. *Id.*, 50.

80. *Id.* Litigation in Virginia continued for many decades, given the lack of decisive precedential value of the 2–2 *Turpin* decision. The constitutionality of the Glebe Act was finally sustained unequivocally in *Selden v. Overseers of the Poor*, 38 Va. 183 (1840).

81. Walter Thompson Bogart, *The Vermont Lease Lands* (Montpelier: Vermont Historical Society, 1950), 1.

82. The good governor always reserved several hundred acres for himself, as well, purely as a private benefit. It is not likely that he profited from them in any significant way before his death in 1767. On the "BW" shares, see Bogart, *Vermont Lease Lands*, 2 n.2. See also Chilton Williamson, *Vermont in Quandary, 1763–1825* (Montpelier: Vermont Historical Society, 1949).

83. Michael A. Bellesiles, *Revolutionary Outlaws: Ethan Allen and the Struggle for Independence on the Early American Frontier* (Charlottesville: University Press of Virginia, 1993), 33–37.

84. On this point, see Daniel J. Hulsebosch, *Constituting Empire: New York and the Transformation of Constitutionalism in the Atlantic World, 1664–1830* (Chapel Hill: University of North Carolina Press, 2005), 114, 156, 221.

85. William G. McLoughlin, *New England Dissent, 1630–1833*, 2 vols. (Cambridge, Mass.: Harvard University Press, 1971), 2:794; Dee E. Andrews, *The Methodists and Revolutionary America, 1760–1800: The Shaping of an Evangelical Culture* (Princeton, N.J.: Princeton University Press, 2000).

86. See, e.g., T. D. Seymour Bassett, *Gods of the Hills: Piety and Society in Nineteenth-Century Vermont* (Montpelier: Vermont Historical Society, 2000), 12.

87. One staunch Baptist recorded his principled decision to forgo such an arrangement, saying that he turned away the township's offer because "I had left all for Christ and thought it wrong and contrary to the new-testament to accept of such an offer [of 250 acres]." Elias Smith, *The Life, Conversion, Preaching, Travelings and Sufferings of Elias Smith, Written by Himself* (Portsmouth, N.H.: Beck & Foster, 1816), 205.

88. The most thorough treatment of this period is Bogart, *Vermont Lease Lands*, 21–97.

89. Dissenters could be exempted upon production of a "certificate" signed by any official representative of an alternative section, an effort to prevent free riding by those who "pretend to differ from the Majority with a Design only to escape

Taxation." An Act to Enable Towns and Parishes to Erect . . . (1783), in John A. Williams, ed., *Laws of Vermont, 1781–84*, in *State Papers of Vermont* (Montpelier, Vt.: H. E. Armstrong, Secretary of State, 1956), 13:195.

90. "An Act to Repeal a Certain Act, and Parts of an Act, Therein Mentioned" (1807), in *Acts and Laws Passed by the Legislature of the State of Vermont* (Randolph, Vt.: Sereno Wright, 1807), 22.

91. David McWilliams Ludlum, *Social Ferment in Vermont, 1791–1850* (Montpelier: Vermont Historical Society, 1948), 47.

92. David Benedict, *A General History of the Baptist Denomination in America, and Other Parts of the World*, 2 vols. (Boston: Lincoln & Edmands, 1813), 1:351–53. This is not to say that harmony prevailed everywhere, just that internal squabbles about division of property pale in comparison to battles over forfeiture.

93. In addition, at least one share was set aside for education in Wentworth towns, and two in post-1777 Vermont towns.

94. In 1787, the state legislature gave town selectmen the power to lease these lands, and to collect rents for the support of religion.

95. Henry Crocker, *History of the Baptists in Vermont* (Bellows Falls, Vt.: P. H. Gobie Press, 1913), 116–17; McLoughlin, *New England Dissent*, 2:823.

96. Bogart, *Vermont's Lease Lands*, 305–7. Bogart reports that the allowed acreage often approached 300 acres per share.

97. *Statutes of the State of Vermont, Revised* (Windsor, Vt.: George Hough and Alden Spooner, 1787), 7–8.

98. This rough calculation is based on Daniel Webster's claim at oral argument in the *Town of Pawlet* case that 200 towns were affected by the 1805 legislation (assuming that all those had three shares of religious lands, at the low end of 250 acres per share). Total acreage of Vermont is just under 6,000,000 acres (meaning that the proportion of land dedicated to religious uses was actually about 2.5 percent of total—much lower than modern, far higher ownership levels). See also Bogart, *Vermont Lease Lands*, 17 (estimating that a total of 280,000 to 300,000 acres were set aside for various forms of public use, including glebes, SPG, and education).

99. 13 U.S. (9 Cranch.) 292 (1815); the second case, *Society for Propagation of the Gospel v. New Haven*, 21 U.S. (8 Wheat.) 464 (1823), simply applied the rule of *Terrett v. Taylor* to Vermont. For a brief discussion of the case and its aftermath, see *infra* note 102.

100. The best treatment of the New Hampshire controversy is McGarvie, *One Nation Under Law*, 152–89.

101. Webster was a Unitarian—a classic supporter of "Christianity in general" rather than by denomination—who believed in religious qualifications for office, for example. George Willis Cooke, *Unitarianism in America: A History of Its Origin and Development* (Boston: American Unitarian Association, 1902), 270–71; Webster's defense of Christianity at the Supreme Court in the case challenging the will of Stephen Girard included this statement: "There can be no charity where

the authority of God is derided and his word rejected." *Vidal v. Girard's Executors*, 42 U.S. (2 How.) 126, 174 (1844). Sarah Barringer Gordon, "Blasphemy and the Law of Religious Liberty in Nineteenth-Century America," *American Quarterly* 52:4 (December 2000): 682–719, 703–4; Robert V. Remini, *Daniel Webster: The Man and His Time* (New York: W. W. Norton & Co., 1997), 588–89.

102. U.S. Constitution, Article III, section 2. The *Pawlet* case is the Supreme Court's first reported application of this constitutional provision; see 9 Cranch. at 322–23: "The first question presented in this case is, whether the Court has jurisdiction. The Plaintiffs claim under a grant from the state of Vermont, and the Defendants claim under a grant from the state of New Hampshire, made at the time when the latter state comprehended the whole territory of the former state. The constitution of the United States, among other things, extends the judicial power of the United States to controversies 'between citizens of the same state claiming lands under grants of different states.' . . . Now it is very clear that although the territory of Vermont was once a part of New Hampshire, yet the state of Vermont, in its sovereign capacity, is not, and never was the same as the state of New Hampshire. The grant of the Plaintiffs emanated purely and exclusively from the sovereignty of Vermont; that of the Defendants purely and exclusively from the sovereignty of New Hampshire." In *Colson v. Lewis*, 15 U.S. 377 (1817), the Court applied *Pawlet's* jurisdictional doctrine to a land dispute as between grants issued by Virginia and Kentucky prior to their separation. See also Rhode Island v. Massachusetts, 37 U.S. 657 (1838), involving a border dispute. A few scattered lower federal court cases have addressed this provision. *Schroeder v. Freeland*, 188 F.2d 517 (8th Cir. 1951) (the provision does not apply when the claim rests from tax sales certificates rather than original conveyances by states); *Port of Portland v. Tri-Club Islands*, 315 F. Supp. 1160 (D. Or. 1970) (ownership of an island in the Columbia River claimed under competing land grants from Oregon and Washington falls under provision, even with presence of additional parties from different states); *Kennedy v. Elliot*, 85 F. 832 (C.C. Wash. 1898) (federal courts have jurisdiction to settle a dispute involving competing grants from Oregon and Washington over another island in the Columbia River). The jurisdiction for lower federal courts to hear such cases is now codified at 28 U.S.C. § 1354. Thanks to Professor Tobias Wolff for his fine research and guidance on this question.

103. 9 Cranch., 333.

104. Story noted his doubt whether the decision in the *Pawlet* case covered the property dedicated to the Society for the Propagation of the Gospel, as that was entirely vested at the time of the initial grant. Sure enough, when that issue was considered by the Supreme Court in 1823, Justice Bushrod Washington (a Virginia Episcopalian who had opposed the state's Glebe Act of 1802) held that *Terrett* and *Dartmouth College* together established that rights respecting vested property survived the Revolution intact. The property interest of the SPG could not be forfeited without justification by the Vermont legislature. Society for Propagation of the *Gospel v. New Haven*, 21 U.S. (8 Wheat.) 464 (1823).

105. After much backing and forthing, SPG transferred its entire interest to the Epis-copal Church, a deal finally consummated in 1927. At that point, the Episcopal Church acquired 131 separate parcels in as many towns (presumably, the total of extant townships from the Wentworth grants). It was discovered then that most of the land acknowledged as belonging to the SPG was "situated in the hilly and less desirable parts of the towns. In theory each holder was assigned his share by lot, but in practice people on the spot drew the best land with astonishing regularity." L. D. Clarke, "Vermont Lands of the Society for the Propagation of the Gospel," *New England Quarterly* 32 (April 1930): 279–96, 283.

106. See, e.g., David Chidester and Edward T. Linenthal, eds., *American Sacred Space* (Bloomington: Indiana University Press, 1995).

107. Lyman Beecher (Barbara H. Cross, ed.), *The Autobiography of Lyman Beecher*, 2 vols. (Cambridge, Mass.: Belknap Press of Harvard University Press, 1961), 1:192.

108. Buckley, "After Disestablishment," 474.

109. James D. Richardson, ed., *A Compilation of the Messages and Papers of the Presi-dents*, 20 vols. (Washington, D.C.: Bureau of National Literature, 1), 9:4288–89.

110. A 1976 study of tax rolls in fourteen cities across the United States found that "more than ten percent of all the real property . . . was owned by churches and exempt from taxes—at a value of at least 155 billion in the fourteen cities alone." Elliott Beard and Elizabeth Lesly, "Pennies from Heaven: It's Time for Uncle Sam to Pass the Collection Plate," *Washington Monthly*, April 1991, at 1ff.

111. http://www.nationalatlas.gov/printable/fedlands.html (accessed 28 December 2011)

112. For older information, see www.nrcm.org/documents/publiclandownership.pdf (accessed 28 December 2011).

113. See, e.g., Jeff Schweitzer, "Separation of Church and Estate," *The Huffington Post*, 24 November 2008, http://www.huffingtonpost.com/jeff-schweiutzer/separa-tion-of-church-and_b_145748.html (accessed 28 December 2011). "Churches have evolved into nothing more than big businesses that strive to influence politics with direct pleas from the pulpit and massive contributions to political campaigns. Let us listen to James Madison, one of the most influential of our Founding Fathers and a great president. As he pleaded, let us impose property taxes on all religious institutions, and let us do so now." In 2008, Schweitzer estimated the investment income of religious organization as between $500 bil-lion and one trillion dollars annually.

114. Although the jurisprudence is divided, most courts have upheld such restric-tions against challenges based on the Religious Land Use and Institutionalized Persons Act of 2000, Pub.L. 106–274, codified as 42 U.S.C. § 2000cc-1 et seq., which was designed to protect such uses against local zoning restrictions. See, e.g., *Lighthouse Institute for Evangelism, Inc. v. City of Long Branch*, 510 F.3d 253 (3rd Cir. 2007); *The Elijah Group, Inc. v. City of Leon Valley*, 643 F.3d 419 (5th Cir. 2011); *Covenant Christian Ministries v. City of Marietta*, 654 F.3d 1231 (11th Cir. 2011).

115. Meade, *Old Churches*, 261–62.

116. The notes of a Hungars vestry meeting in March 1859 record a letter informing the church that it had lost its suit when the Court of Appeals "did on the 14th of February last regards the land in force render a verdict in favor of the Overseers of the Poor and adverse to the Church." Hungars Parish, Northampton Country, Vestry Book (1812–1938), 197 (quoted in Stitt, "The Will of Stephen Charlton," 275). The opinion of the court apparently was not reported. Although we may never know the reasoning of the judges, it seems that Hungars never established that a residuary legatee from the original donation (made in the will of Stephen Charlton in 1654) could in fact be located but simply relied on the existence of a reversionary clause in the will.

117. Parts of the glebe were sold in the early 1870s. The central "manor" section, which included more than 400 acres and the glebe house, was sold in 1876. The house is now a Virginia historic landmark, even though experts disagree on its age. Ralph T. Whitelaw, *Virginia's Eastern Shore: A History of Northampton and Accomack Counties*, 2 vols. (Richmond: Virginia Historical Society, 1951), 1:431–32.

2

"It cant be cald stealin'"

Customary Law among Civil War Soldiers

THOMAS C. MACKEY

Introduction and Problems

Scholars of the history of the law in the nineteenth-century United
States have argued that a "legal culture," a remembered and applied
customary law, exists embedded in the general culture and society.[1] To
unearth and recover this customary law, legal scholars must immerse
themselves in the rich archival resources. In his own work and by example through his teaching and mentoring of students and scholars, especially as founder of the New York University Law School's Legal History
Colloquium, William E. Nelson has issued a fundamental injunction
to "go to the sources, go to the sources, go to the sources" that reso-
nates throughout the contemporary scholarship in United States legal
history.[2]

To plumb this idea of a customary law existing among average nineteenth-century people, legal historians analyzed the role of custom in
Anglo-American history in many different times and places. From large
overviews of custom to more specialized studies of popular politics and
criminal law in the Revolutionary era, to examining how popularly held
understandings of customary rights explain the bargaining and conflict
between perceived social norms regarding pig keeping in antebellum
New York City, these scholars have shown that custom and customary law constitute key aspects of United States legal history that most
scholars have neglected in favor of studying forms of law and lawmaking.[3] Understandably, law-on-the-books constitutes the major focus of
scholarly work in the field; however, law-in-action (or law-as-applied)

also requires study and interpretation.[4] Thus, an important historical question suggests itself: Where else might legal/historical investigators search in the borderlands of law and custom in the nineteenth century when people needed to develop and use customary law in reaction to their changed circumstances? Civil War armies constitute one possible answer.

During the U.S. Civil War, millions of men volunteered or were drafted, left their homes and their localities (often for the first time), and found themselves surrounded by the new routines and disciplines of the army, controlled by military law. Civil War soldiers entered the army, an institution governed by many rules and possessing at least formal coercive authority over them. These soldiers found themselves and their daily lives organized and disciplined in new and not always welcomed, or seemingly rational, ways. Then, in time, some soldiers found themselves in areas of combat where the restraints of civil and even military law had loosened while they were being ordered or allowed by necessity to behave in ways that back home, they knew, would have given rise to civil action and even perhaps even to criminal prosecution. Not surprisingly, the men reacted to these new disciplines and opportunities, such as taking the property of civilians (what many people in the era politely called "foraging"), in a variety of ways. To make sense of this foreign world of the military, sometimes governed by military law and sometimes governed by no identifiable law, the soldiers justified their actions in letters they sent home explaining what they had done and why they had acted in ways that might have been approved under the laws of war but that normal civilian law would not allow.[5]

The rich manuscript resources and the published primary sources of Civil War soldiers' letters and diaries reveal a pattern, subtle but present, among the soldiers that can be described as a customary common law of soldier behavior. Although not every soldier felt the need to explain himself and his behaviors to those back home, enough soldiers did explain why and how they broke rules that used to govern them back home—and would govern them again when they returned home. Those explanations, in that historical context, in turn raise the question of how those men in the ranks (and sometimes including officers) made sense of and reconciled such behavior as stealing that, on the home front, would have been illegal but that in the midst of a war zone were legal and perhaps even necessary, or even mandated by orders from higher military authority. One possible answer is that a customary law emerged among the soldiers that both guided and explained their behaviors. Soldiers adopted and adapted custom and necessity to their new strange environments; in turn, custom and necessity helped to explain and justify their behaviors within the military and wartime contexts. In this manner, the evidence explored in this essay suggests that more was at work with the men, their actions, and their explanations of their actions than mere self-preservation. No doubt at times men on both sides in extreme situations acted from a sense of self-preservation, but those times were few and far between: The more common actions they described in their letters find justification on other grounds.

Civil War officers on both sides fretted that their men possessed little respect for military law. Civil War soldiers created new communities, new rules, new customs, and new traditions within their units during their service in uniform. Within this context of military experiences, the men developed their own subculture of legal values that existed parallel to military law and that, at least at times, operated outside of the control of military law and their officers. Soldiers explained their social behaviors in legalist terms and then used those explanations to craft a self-justifying "rule of law," a common law of soldiers that, they insisted, did not violate military law-on-the-books. Identifying the presence of and analyzing the significance of this informal, in-dwelling, customary law is the focus of this study.[6]

Sources and Approach

Considering the available sources reveals problems for the researcher. Examining the evidence, it becomes clear that the social behaviors being analyzed are "extralegal." The working hypothesis is that customary law existed alongside formal military law and outside the normal civil and criminal law. Men in the ranks of all the armies had to re-create communities and explain their behavior within their companies and regiments based on civilian life experiences and in reaction to wartime contexts. Men in the ranks had to make sense both of the destruction of property in war and of their own behaviors, which drove them to act in manners that in their civilian lives would have been at least immoral, if not illegal. Volunteering for and then being socialized into a well-ordered military community, the men created and applied their extralegal customary law standards to explain and justify the confusing world of war and the surrounding military environment.[7]

Those choices made by the men in the ranks did indeed constitute a form of customary law, but we can account for that form of law-in-action in a different way by understanding the choices the soldiers made as a conflict-of-laws conundrum. Soldiers faced a tension between competing valid normative orders—the civilian laws they knew and grew up with in their localities at home *and* the new military law of discipline of federal service. As a result, those men made a choice-of-law decision about which of the laws to apply and to live by in governing and explaining their behavior. In a sense, this new "law," military law, forced the soldiers to choose between conflicting bodies of law—civilian norms and military norms.[8] What resulted was a common law of soldiering whereby the soldiers navigated an uncharted world of competing laws in conflict. Within that legal world, they created their own resolutions of the legal conundrums they faced, supplemented by justifying arguments for the resolutions they developed. While the traditional schematic dichotomy of law-in-books versus law-in-action helps to makes sense of the behavior of the men in the ranks, the complexities of choosing between competing and conflicting bodies of law challenged soldiers to seek new and creative explanations for their actions, and this understanding of what they were doing as reasoning legal actors better explains their actions and the justifications they devised for those actions. A more nuanced consideration of the rich evidence before us suggests that the soldiers grappled with and, in time, resolved their conflict-of-laws issues in unexpected ways. We can explore and assess the nature of this conflict-of-laws and the soldiers' reasoning about how to solve the various examples of that conflict through analyzing the primary sources that these soldiers have left for us.

And what amazing sources exist. In fact, in this inquiry the problem is not the usual historian's problem of too few sources but rather of too many sources. Most mid-nineteenth-century American men, and women, wrote, and they wrote a lot. The surviving document base of Civil War letters and diaries from both officers and enlisted men (who generated more interesting and valuable sources for this inquiry) is frankly overwhelming. Every library and archive has its own treasure-trove of Civil War letters and diaries—from the Library of Congress and the National Archives; to online databanks; to state libraries and archives; to the U.S. Army's archive at Carlisle Barracks in Carlisle, Pennsylvania; to the most humble local or county archive (which is open to researchers when the local librarian or archivist damn well feels like it); to letters and diaries still in private hands. When this vast array of unpublished documents is added to the mountain of published primary sources, the depth and breadth of the sources available for research makes the Civil War perhaps the closely and thoroughly documented war in human history.[9]

Social anthropologists have noted the existence and application of customary law within subcultures and communities on the margins of the mainstream. For example, New York City Jewish diamond merchants constitute a small subgroup of a small group of Hasidic Jews living and working in New York City. These merchants carry on their businesses and their way of life by reference to a set of informal customary rules adopted from Jewish religious texts and practical business needs. Both the social foundation of law within that community and the agreement to live and work by those unspoken but understood rules govern the business of the diamond trade. As Renée Rose Shield points out, "The social foundation [of their community and customary law] allows business to happen and makes business pleasurable."[10] Using criminological techniques, other scholars have identified this same phenomenon of a customary law existing outside of the normal channels of law and society in business organizations.[11]

Further, and closer to the subject of the present inquiry, historians studying the lives and cultures of soldiers of the Civil War have noticed that the men in the ranks brought their cultural assumptions about social status into the military with them.[12] For example, early in the war, men elected their company's officers; an analysis of these elections suggests that a symbiotic relationship existed between the men and their officers that shaped their understanding of "leadership" and their military experience. Thus, whereas military manuals and standards described how the relationship between officers and enlisted personnel relationship ought to look, the lived reality within units in general and the individual soldier's relationship with his officers in particular constituted a different, at times even vastly different, reality.[13]

Another issue arising from the sources is the relevance of military law to this inquiry. During the Civil War, the Articles of War controlled the actions of the armies and the soldiers within the armies, at least formally. In fact, during the war the Union adopted military law reform: on April 23, 1863, President Abraham Lincoln promulgated as General Order 100 the so-called "Lieber Code," named for its author, the German-born jurist Francis Lieber.[14] Organized into 157 articles and ten sections, the Lieber Code clarified the application of martial law to the United States and provided guidance on definitions and procedures. Lieber sought to bring the formal U.S. military law better in line with the international law of war.[15] In particular, the Lieber Code defined issues such as "military necessity" and the respect that armies and soldiers should provide to the enemy's property. For example, Section II, Article 44 of the Lieber Code stated:

> All wanton violence committed against persons in the invaded country, all destruction of property not commanded by the authorized officer, all robbery, all pillage or sacking, even after taking a place by main force, all rape, wounding, maiming, or killing of such inhabitants, are prohibited under penalty of death, or such other severe punishment as may seem adequate for the gravity of the offences.
>
> A soldier, officer or private, in the act of committing such violence, and disobeying a superior ordering him to abstain from it, may be lawfully killed on the spot by such superior.[16]

Although this section would appear to control—and to prohibit—many of the actions and social behaviors described in this study, it would be a mistake to equate these administrative, black-letter guidelines (law-on-the-books) with the actual, in-the-field behavior of soldiers and officers (customary choice of law-in-action). To be sure, the Lieber Code deservedly continues to draw the attention of scholars, but to gauge the nature and extent of an embedded customary law among Civil War soldiers, the Lieber Code and the Articles of War do not explain or account for such behaviors.

As always, then, when considering gaps and contradictions between civilian and military law-on-the-books and the choice of law-in-action in the lives of Civil War soldiers, the researcher must turn away from the formal rules of law, international rules of law, and the admittedly important reforms to military and martial law during the Civil War. Rather, this inquiry must explain and analyze how soldiers in the ranks reacted to the new circumstance of wartime and their new status as soldiers. As a consequence, the historian seeking to explain these soldiers' actions and explanations must consider and weigh the evidence of the behaviors of ordinary soldiers against the backdrop of the larger cultural norms of their day.

The Articles of War of 1806, which governed soldiers on both sides during the Civil War until April 1863, proved useful for the internal governance of the U.S. armies and their Confederate counterparts, but the behaviors and values of interest existed beyond the reach of the formal code of military law. Even though the enlisted men and the officers heard the Articles of War read to them at their enlistment (as required by Article 10) or at other formal occasions, they remembered nothing of the document, found it irrelevant to their situations, chose not to mention it in letters home, or ignored it in favor of ideas of due process and property rights that they carried with them into the military and developed among themselves within their units.[17]

Like the Lieber Code, black-letter military law on its face appeared to control the behavior of the soldiers in the new situations into which the war plunged them. For example, Article 54 of the Articles of War read:

> All officers and soldiers are to behave themselves orderly in quarters, and on their march; and whosoever shall commit any waste or spoil, either in walks of trees, parks, warrens, fish ponds, houses, or gardens, cornfields, enclosures of meadows, or shall maliciously destroy any property whatsoever, belonging to the inhabitants of the United States, unless by order of the then commander in chief of the armies of the said states, shall (besides such penalties as they are liable to by law) be punished according to the nature and degree of the offense, by the judgment of a regimental or general court martial.

And Article 58 held:

> All public stores taken in the enemy's camp, towns, forts, or magazines, whether of artillery, ammunition, clothing, forage or provisions, shall be

secured for the service of the United States; for the neglect of which the commanding officer is to be answerable.[18]

Both of these provisions governed the activity usually called "foraging." Soldiers on both sides developed and used "foraging" as a catch-all word to denote and explain their taking of other people's property, a crime in normal peacetime circumstances. These provisions of the Articles of War allowed and justified such military takings. The doctrine of "military necessity," defined and described in Francis Lieber's 1863 Code, specifically in General Order 100, consisted of "the necessity of those measures which are indispensable for securing the ends of the war, and which are lawful according to the modern law and usages of war."[19] Thus, some military law doctrines and codified provisions provided for and justified foraging. Nor was this doctrine of military necessity born new into the world during the U.S. Civil War. As early as 1758, the legal writer and political theorist Emmerich de Vattel drew a distinction between committing "waste" on an enemy's land and the harsher treatment of "ravaging" the land. Whereas normal military operation might "waste" the enemy's land and property, armies (including, of course, soldiers in the armies) pursued the "ravaging" of the land and the enemy's property not just as part of military operations but in furtherance of a policy of a punitive, hard war. Union General William Tecumseh Sherman's 1864 "march to the sea" from Atlanta to Savannah exemplifies "ravaging" and not merely "wasting" an enemy's land and property.[20] And yet in this mix of military law, military discipline, and law codes, soldiers in ranks and even their officers neither made nor invoked any of these arguments. As the sources illustrate, soldiers knew and acted on "military necessity," but they did so as responses to their experiences of material deprivation, and they justified their actions on equally valid customary law grounds rather than by invoking black-letter military law and codes of military behavior.

When these sources are read with the bent and predisposition of a legal historian (a trait shared by all students and scholars who have been lucky enough to take part in William E. Nelson's New York University School of Law Legal History Colloquium), patterns emerge. For example, not only did issues of foraging give rise to other issues finding resolution within the realm of soldiers' customary law; that customary law expanded its reach to cover and provide resolutions to other issues concerning property and legal behavior in wartime. Men in the ranks on both sides of the conflict often disciplined wayward colleagues themselves even though by doing so they did not follow the rules set down in military law. They oversaw and protected one another's private property. They distinguished between loyal and disloyal property as they advanced into war zones, and they occasionally established "courts" in their companies, regiments, and prisoner-of-war camps to resolve conflicts arising under soldiers' customary law.

These extralegal social behaviors by Civil War soldiers suggest that something more than military versus civilian law was at work among these nineteenth-century people; they faced a conflict of valid, competing bodies of law, and they had to make hard choices and craft persuasive arguments (at least to themselves) to explain and justify their behavior as soldiers. This essay samples the sources while making a few suggestions about the presence and nature of customary law among Civil War soldiers. Though these soldiers may have written their letters with the thought that posterity might read them, they could not have expected that their letters would be evidence for legal historians. Because this evidence was written for that single unique moment in the lives of these almost-forgotten men, it fits the category described by the great French historian Marc Bloch in his classic work *The Historian's Craft* as "the evidence of witnesses in spite of themselves."[21] Always keeping these larger evidentiary issues in mind, allowing the evidence to speak constitutes the next task.

Some Evidence

On Thursday morning, September 3, 1863, near Gallatin, Tennessee, Private Reuben Lamphear, Company F, Second Minnesota Volunteer Infantry Regiment, finished his breakfast. He then sat down and wrote a letter to his sister, Eliza.[22] "I had a pretty good breakfast this morning, better than I get every day," he started; "it consisted of sweet potatoes, green corn, and soft bread, with plenty of fresh hog to make it relish good." Lamphear then shifted into using normal military slang in the Union Army writing, "[A]ll of this good living was foraged from our sesech neighbors that live about hear accept the soft bread, that was furnished us by uncle Sam." "Sesech" became the shorthand term used by northern and midwestern soldiers and civilians alike during the war to refer to Southerners, the secessionists. On the other hand, both sides used the words "forage" and "foraging" to describe living off the resources of the land. Men in both armies and all theaters of action found themselves poorly provisioned by their state and central governments, Union as well as Confederate, so the men turned to foraging along their routes of marches, in particular, for the food and provisions they needed, but sometimes for other kinds and descriptions of property. "Foraging" became a catch-all phrase justifying a wide variety of social behaviors—from hungry men helping themselves to the bounty of the land and informally confiscating from the enemy, to Union soldiers' either freeing slaves, the South's peculiar property (from most Union soldiers' point of view), or stealing the South's most valuable property (from the Southerners' point of view). Thus, Lamphear participated in an age-old activity by having his foraged breakfast that morning, and although most soldiers did not reflect on their foraging activities, Lamphear did.

Bragging a bit to his sister, Lamphear continued, "[T]his tennerssee rally is the best Country we have bin in for foraging in a long time, and you ought to see the yankee hirelings[23] as the Rebs call us, come into Camp with back loads of good things, such as apples, peaches, potatoes, Green corn, fresh pork, and once in a while a good fat chicken is found among the verialy." He then turned philosophical: "Soldiers are curious fellows, they like a good meal once in a while as well as any boddy, and if the Country affords any thing good to eat they are bound to have it." Lamphear suggested that the new and different status of being a soldier changed his view of the land's bounty around him; soldiers are "curious fellows" and if they happen upon food, then (regardless of ownership) "they are bound to have [the food]." In this case, opportunity created need, and need combined with the needy person's status of soldier to create opportunity.

Lamphear explained further to his sister about his foraging, "[I]t cant be cald stealin' as I see, for they had just as soon take it right before the owners fase and eyes as behind his back." To Lamphear, taking foodstuffs did not rise to the level of stealing. Lamphear's special pleading tacitly acknowledged his understanding that, in normal circumstances, his behavior would most definitely be a crime; but, for soldiers in wartime and in a war zone, the lines of appropriate and inappropriate personal behavior blurred. In his defense, Lamphear wrote that at least this form of taking was done in public, before the owner. Lamphear argued that he was not stealing or foraging food in the dead of night like a thief but in the open before the owner's face. His status as a soldier, his hunger, and his open and public takings combined to justify his actions, which society might otherwise consider immoral if not at least illegal.

In his next sentence, Lamphear shifted his argument again, this time enlarging his focus to encompass larger political ends justifying his foraging. He wrote, "[T]he poor miserable Reb thinks it rather hard to have his stuff all eat up so by the Yankees, but who is to blame for it but himself. He helpt to bring on this destructive war and ought to suffer the consequences." Lamphear's foraging also could not be called stealing, he insisted, because his foraging hurt the enemy who had brought the scourge of war (and hungry Minnesota soldiers) into this Tennessee locality, county, and state.

Thus, Lamphear's arguments suggest that something as routine among soldiers in the Civil War as foraging achieved an array of personal and military goals: Foraging fed the hungry, foraging supported their cause, foraging hurt the enemy's cause, foraging deprived the enemy of resources, and foraging by Union soldiers in Tennessee occurred not because someone like Lamphear was a thief but rather because Tennesseans had proven their disloyalty to the Union by their having supported secession. Therefore, part of the price to be paid for supporting secession was an invading hungry Union army and the consequent loss of property to foraging soldiers. Lamphear assuaged his conscience by linking his foraging to the larger political and national cause for which he fought. Foraging in time of war was not stealing, he reasoned; it was punishment to the disloyal civilians who supported secession. Given Lamphear's historical context in an intensely Protestant world that stigmatized such behaviors as stealing, wartime foraging provided a personal and an extralegal mechanism for him to deny plausibly that he and his comrades stole food; instead, they pursued the war's goals through means other than combat. This letter suggests that more than just religious concern about stealing existed in the minds of the soldiers such as Lamphear; it suggests that something more than "military necessity" existed in the thinking of among at least some Union soldiers; finally, it suggests the existence of a customary law's shaping and channeling his explanation of his behavior.

Broadening this analysis, consider the following statements by David Wyatt Aikens, Adjutant, Seventh South Carolina Volunteer Infantry Regiment, Kershaw's Brigade, on June 28, 1863.[24] To establish the context, recall that the Army of Northern Virginia (ANV) made two great raids northward: the first in September 1862 into Maryland, and the second in late June and July 1863 through Maryland into Pennsylvania. To be sure, both raids have drawn enormous historical and popular scholarship, but what is of interest here is the experience of the Southern men who made the raid. As an officer, Aikens reported home the Army of Northern Virginia's official policy, in particular its orders to the soldiers taking part in the raid to behave themselves. Aikens assured the people back home, "The Genl is very guarded in his advance & allows no deprivations to be committed, not even a chicken to be taken unless paid for. He takes corn, flour, cattle, horses & everything that the army needs, but pays for everything to [in] Confed money." Aikens reported that soldiers issued receipts to civilians for goods taken along the invasion route "so the Yankee may present this receipt to Lincoln's Govt as a claim for damages." This process followed the guidelines described in Article 38 of Lieber's Code, which held that "private property, unless forfeited by crimes or by offenses of the owner, can be seized only by way of military necessity, for the support or other benefit of the army or of the United States. If the owner has not fled, the commanding officer will cause receipts to be given, which may serve the spoliated [sic] owner to obtain indemnity."[25] Though in this example Aikens served in the so-called Confederate army, both Union and Confederate armies adopted the same process for dealing with injured civilians. The Army of Northern Virginia's invasion of the North provided General Robert E. Lee's men a chance to live off and forage among the people in the states of Maryland and Pennsylvania.

Still, Lee understood that risks existed in authorizing Confederate soldiers to take what they wanted and needed. Aikens mentioned a general statement released by Lee to his forces congratulating them on their good behavior on the march; Lee was offering them incentives for continuing to behave themselves. As related by Aikens, Lee "told them he had come here [Pennsylvania] to fight armed men & not to plunder, & frighten women & children." On July 1–3, 1863, Lee's Army of Northern Virginia and the Union Army of the Potomac found each other at the crossroads village of Gettysburg, Pennsylvania, where, it turned out, Lee found his match in the armed men he had come to fight.

Although Lee and his staff stuck to the official line of the ANV, the experience on the ground was quite different. Officers could not be everywhere all the time, and Lee's raid through Maryland and into Pennsylvania proved too tempting for many Southern soldiers. Instead of just wasting the land and the enemy's property, they decided that the time had come both to feed themselves and to punish Northern civilians for their support of the war. Given the right circumstance, Southern forces could "ravage" the land and the property of their enemies just as well as Union forces could ravage the South. For example, Heath James Christian, Private, Company D, Third Virginia Volunteer Cavalry Regiment, wrote to his father on July 13, 1863, on Lee's retreat from Pennsylvania after Gettysburg, "They would not allow us to pillage in Penna but told us if the people would not take Confederate money to press what we wanted. I have not spent a cent since I left Va. . . . ."[26] So, too, Captain Florence McCarthy, Thomas Artillery Battery, ANV, wrote to his sister, Jane Elizabeth McCarthy, on the retreat from Pennsylvania relating news from the Gettysburg campaign.[27] In particular, McCarthy assessed for his sister some of the people whom he encountered on the way back south: "Some of the Pennsylvania people in town showed some spirit. One old woman beat out our men out of her garden with a stick. A girl in Chambersburg took water and broom and washed the pavement where our men had laid their haversacks." It would seem at least that a couple of the Dutch (the Deutsch, or German Pennsylvanians) cared not at all for the Southern invaders, and McCarthy returned their dislike in full measure: "But as a general thing they [the Pennsylvanians] are the most cringing mean-spirited people on earth. . . . They will do anything to save property and hides. The woman are all gross and sinewy. The men speak of them invariably as the women, and say they have no ladies here,—they are all women. The women call them the men." On this point of gender differentiation, even though they all spoke one language, English, the Southern invaders and their Pennsylvania "hosts" communicated not in the slightest.

McCarthy reported further, "Our men have strict orders to take nothing without paying, but they do just as they please, which is not a twentieth part as bad as [what] they [the Yankees] did in Virginia. The fences chickens hogs and vegetables are being consumed rapidly. The crops in some places will be ruined by camps and by stock [Confederate horses], but we have not hurt them enough to talk about. All their public property has been destroyed that we could destroy." For public consumption and following the laws of war, Lee and his officer corps saw the need to reject foraging. They urged the use of Southern scrip to "pay" for damages and costs, but the soldiers on the ground saw the Pennsylvania raid in a different light—it was an opportunity to take the war (and not just those aspects of the war justified by military necessity) to the Northern people and to do to Pennsylvanians what Union forces had done to Virginia for more than two years. Further, Southern soldiers made the same arguments to justify their foraging, wasting, and ravaging that Union soldiers made to justify their actions. This evidence suggests not that there were separate Northern and Southern legal views on the sanctity of property but rather the presence of a U.S. customary law's taking shape visibly in these soldiers' letters, Union and Confederate, North and South. Such "evidence of witnesses in spite of themselves," in the words of Marc Bloch, suggests both that these men were applying customary law and that they all partook of a general, shared customary legal culture.[28]

Out west, this same pattern can be discerned. On May 31, 1862, Peter Warden of the 3rd Volunteer Illinois Cavalry wrote to his aunt about his actions in Arkansas. He reassured her that no large force of Confederates existed in the area, but "our foragers are some times attacked and serious injury done to them by bands of guerrillas who make it a rule to take no prisoners." He claimed further that nearly a company of foragers had been killed in the region, some of the men shot more than once. Expressing his indignation at the civilians' killing of soldiers, Warden warned, "If the people of this country intend to carry a guerrilla war fare it will be the worse for them selves for Our enraged soldiers will burn and destroy everything they can lay their hands on." Perhaps catching himself in mid-argument, Warden reassured his aunt, "which is however contrary to orders of our generals." Warden saw and knew that the Union army's presence caused hardship for the local population: "There

is a great deal of suffering here on the part of the citizens cause by taking everything they have to subsist on. [T]his is not done according to
orders, but the boys will go out and take what ever they can get in the
eating line and in some instances do not leave women and children
enough to eat for a week and [no] prospect of getting more until a new
harvest which you [know] is good ways of[f] yet."[29] Foraging and takings held risks for all parties.

Yet, the process of foraging for food to feed the soldiers could and
did become routine. For example, John Price Kempner, Quarter Master Sergeant, Company I, 6th Pennsylvania Volunteer Cavalry, Rush's
Lancers, kept a diary in which each day he recorded a sentence or two
describing his activities. His diary entries make clear that foraging had
become a normal part of his duties. On May 21, 1862, he recorded, "In
camp all day, at the same old place [Fredericksburg]. Was out foraging. Another warm past time, good and roads splendid." On May 23:
". . . This part of the country is beautiful and the land under cultivation.
Foraged for corn which we found in abundance." On September 17, he
noted, ". . . Up late last night writing. Out foraging in the afternoon.
Have drawn no rations for 8 days." On September 28, Kempner wrote,
". . . Raining in showers all day. Cummings out foraging and brought
in a porker weighing about 250." On October 24, Kempner wrote,
". . . Teams out foraging brought in a good load of hay corn and eatable."
Three days later, he noted the unfortunate news that "7 Hd. Qrs Teams
were captured yesterday foraging with Co. of Inf. as guards."[30] By 1862,
at least one soldier of the Union Army of the Potomac had become so
accustomed to foraging off the land and from the local Virginia populations that his behavior warranted a mention, but only a brief mention,
and then only when linked to something larger like losing the head-
quarters' teams.

Soldiers coined euphemisms to describe their actions and to try to
hide those actions from their own officers. For example, on August
12, 1862, near Baton Rouge, Louisiana, Private John S. Jackman, Company B, Ninth Kentucky Volunteer Infantry Regiment (Confederate,
Orphan's Brigade), wrote in his diary, "This morning Charlie A. of our
Company and Sam S., of the 4th., killed a 'bear' in the swamp, and Bil-
lie A. and Gus M., having gone to a house and had bread cooked, we
had a feast."[31] The editor of the diary, William C. Davis, explained that

a "'bear' in soldier parlance usually meant a farmer's pig." Davis continued, "Forbidden to steal livestock from Confederate civilians, hungry soldiers often killed, cooked, and ate their prey on the spot, euphemistically referring to it as 'bear' meat if an officer enquired."[32] It is doubtful that this tactic fooled any of their officers for long, if at all. By June 4, 1864, near Dallas, Georgia, Jackman described killing "a large pet pig" of a Confederate family. He and his comrades had started the process of scalding the pig when the "old lady" caught them and reported them to their captain. With the woman present, the captain had the men arrested and promised her that he would inform the general. But, as soon as she had left, the captain turned the men loose "and [they] went on with their cooking. Part of the meat, after being cooked, went into Captain S's haversack, and it is not likely that the 'bear hunters' will be reported."[33] Men and officers participated in this shared world of informally appropriated property, and they could manipulate the formal rules of reporting to serve their own ends—such as supper.

A few more examples are in order. On October 18, 1862, Private William Wiley, Company F, Seventy-seventh Illinois Volunteer Infantry Regiment, described in his diary an encounter that he witnessed as his unit moved south from Covington, Kentucky. He wrote, "We camped on a farm belonging to a Dr. who we were told was no neutral but a full-fledged reb and away with the rebel army. So the boys concluded during the night that it was of their duty at least to confiscate his property such of it at least as suited their purpose best." As Wiley recounted, the soldiers were combining personal need with patriotism by punishing the enemy for disloyalty. Wiley concluded, "So that morning such things as hogs sheep chickens honey had become rather scarce about that ranch."[34] In this instance, Wiley raised foraging to a military duty as an explanation for his and his unit's actions.

On December 15, 1862, Captain John W. Ames, Eleventh United States Infantry, wrote to his mother from a curbstone in Fredericksburg, Virginia.[35] Union forces had crossed the Rappahannock River on pontoon bridges and had tried to take the Confederate positions on Marye's Heights. In doing so, Union forces hoped to turn the Confederates' right flank (the Union's left flank) in a coordinated attack, but nothing went as planned. Despite repeated attacks up the hill at Marye's Heights, the Confederates repulsed every Union charge, inflicting heavy losses on the attackers, whereas the Union flanking attack started late, was poorly coordinated, and quickly sputtered to a halt. In the meantime, Union forces occupied the town of Fredericksburg and proceeded to sack the town. As Ames put it, ". . . the town [is] burning in one or two places, but from our looking it seemed hardly injured, as the spires and roofs looked whole enough. But there was great pillage and sack by our troops, I believe, injuring the town far more than the fires and the shells." While he waxed indignant about a lot of what he saw in the military and in Virginia, Ames gave only casual mentioned to the sacking of Fredericksburg. In an interesting sidelight on the losses that Fredericksburg suffered, the Virginia Historical Society has a file dealing with liberated, but returned, books from the Civil War. After the war, some of the men who looted Fredericksburg began to feel guilty about keeping the books they had picked up there, and so they sent those books to the Virginia Historical Society to return to the their rightful owners. On the flyleaf of one of these "liberated" books John A. Thompkins wrote, "On the 12th of Dec 1862 the Army of the Potomac crossed the Rappahannock, occupied Fredericksburg, and—captured this book."[36] Having evidence that the troops took books was not surprising, but trying to return the book—stolen property—is surprising.[37]

Albert Ballard Smith of the Ninth Kentucky Cavalry (Confederate) fled south before Sherman and the Union Army of the Tennessee from the 1862 battle of Perryville, Kentucky. Through the Tulahoma campaign, the Atlanta campaign, and while he was fleeing from Sherman and his "hirelings" into Georgia and, in time, the Carolinas, Smith always maintained his faith in the Southern cause. On January 20, 1865, he wrote to his wife, Anna Tarlton Shrader, commenting on the war, "The people of the south are different in regard to property to what they were in the beginning of the war. They [torn: consider?] property as nothing at present. Nearly all are willing to sacrifice their last dollars so they gain their independence."[38] Smith knew that the war had caused hardships on the home front: "[M]any ladies who have never known anything but to sit in the parlor and entertain company are now wearing their homespun dresses and knit and sew in as fine spirits as though they had been accustomed to it all their lives. Such a people can never be subjugated." Though he was wrong about not being subjugated, Smith returned in his letter to an earlier statement about having a chicken dinner; he explained, "I guess you will think from the chickens we get that there is something wrong. Tis true that many we get are not paid for but we know the Yankees would get them if we did not therefore I do not think there was any harm in taking them." Here again can be found a soldier explaining stealing—although, yes, he did not pay for the chickens, the enemy would have gotten them, so to deny the enemy the chickens by eating them himself constituted a correct and even a patriotic act. Instead of the red light of untouchable private property, the military situation had created and allowed Smith to argue plausibly the green light of an acceptable taking; military and personal necessity created social and legal exceptions to conventional legal rules.

Occasionally soldiers wrote of actions that were illegal by any standard—and did so in chilling ways. For example, on January 20, 1863, in a letter to his wife, Edward J. Seaman, Company F, Tenth New Jersey Volunteer Infantry Regiment, recounted his time in and around Charleston, South Carolina, during the previous summer. Like many enlisted personnel, then and now, Seaman disliked his officers. But Seaman disliked officers a lot more than most of his uniformed colleagues did. He wrote, ". . . on Sunday the 15th of last June we had our cartridges dealt out to us for the advance to Charleston the next morning and the Lieutenant of camp K dealt out one that laid him low on James Island he was hated by the whole regt and I am sure if this regt should ever go in the field there wold not one half of the officers ever come out alive for if they were not killed by the enemy they would be by their own men for after the first fire the ranks is sure to break and before they can rally them again we can shoot who we see fit."[39] Military authorities frowned upon soldiers' shooting officers, as did the Articles of War, not to mention the criminal law in the civilian world. This account of not-so-friendly fire raises questions about relationships between soldiers and officers in Civil War armies (a topic needing work), but this account also suggests Seaman understood that the murder of unpopular officers could occur; shooting an officer during a fire fight constituted a type of self-help to rid a company or a regiment of unpopular officers. This purging of unpopular officers, though murder, could be accomplished in the midst of battle without risking punishment for the crime. In this admittedly extreme case, combat created opportunity for extralegal behavior by soldiers that most officers hoped would not become a common-law custom of enlisted men.

On the other side of the coin from the darkness of military murder, many instances of humor appear in the sources. For example, on January 13, 1863, Marcus Woodcock, First Corporal, Company H, Ninth Kentucky Infantry (Union), defended foraging by combining two justifications—hunger of the soldiers and the political. He wrote, "On the 11th we had a general feast in No. 2 on fowls of various description which the foragers had seized in the farm yards out in the country by authority of the famous Emancipation Proclamation. . . ."[40] In other words, Woodcock and his comrades had liberated Confederate chickens from their Southern bondage to serve the Union cause—and did so in all likelihood with biscuits and gravy. Like other Union commanders, the Union commander in the western theatre, Major General Don Carlos Buell, had issued orders to protect civilian property, yet soldiers did not always follow his or similar orders. One evening, a soldier walked into camp carrying a quarter of mutton. He walked up to his captain saying, "I do respect General Buell's order, but darn me if a rebel sheep shall butt me!"[41] In this fashion, rebel sheep entered the Union larder.

And consider the good fortune of Thomas W. Parson, Commissary Sergeant, Fourteenth Kentucky Cavalry (Union). In May 1862, he had spent the day on a long march in north central Kentucky chasing guerrillas in what the military historian Clay Mountcastle has labeled the punitive war between Confederate guerrillas and Union reprisals.[42] Outside Augusta, Kentucky, Parson topped a hill and saw the men in his company breaking ranks and running to a small outbuilding on a nearby knob. When he asked what had drawn the attention of the men, someone told him that they had found a winepress. As Parson related this episode, "I was very tired and almost famished for want of water," but somehow he found the energy to climb the little hill "and found a large vat of newly pressed wine." He continued, "I loosened my tin cup from my haversack and filled it and drank it off, and then half filled it again." He also admitted that he filled his canteen from the vat. And then, for soldiers, he did something seldom discussed in the letters, diaries, and memoirs under analysis: Parson claims to have offered to pay for the wine he took. "[T]aking some money out of my pocket [I] offered to pay," he related, "but the proprietor, who was a foreigner, shook his head and said 'No no monish to-day.'" Parson insisted, saying, "[Y]ou cannot afford this we are drinking all of your wine. He repeated himself, 'No no monish to-day.'"[43] Why in this instance did the civilian refuse the payment offered by Parson? Perhaps this "foreigner" may have carried out a quick cost-benefit analysis; that is, perhaps he decided that it was better to lose a vat of wine to the troops rather than risk their decision to forage the rest of his farm and stores. This intoxicating encounter suggests another context where in wartime the line separating appropriate from inappropriate takings blurs.

Informal retribution against guerrillas and their local supporters could be quick and harsh. On October 4, 1862, Quarter Master Sergeant John Price Kempner recorded one such action in his diary: ". . . Lt. Meigs was shot last night by guirillas embalmed today . . . Up late. To retaliate for the death of Lt. Meigs the buildings near Harrisonburg were burned for miles around."[44] Not paying for wine, taking hogs, burning property, appropriating foodstuffs—all of these actions occurred outside any of the normal channels of military and civilian law.

Conclusion

Out of the ordinary, unexpected, engaging, and absorbing, this "evidence of witnesses in spite of themselves" from Civil War soldiers may not prove the existence of a customary law among Civil War soldiers, but it does suggest the existence of such a customary law, of choices made between conflicting bodies of law, among the men in the ranks. Not just overwhelming Protestant and religious values, but legal values of right and wrong, of owned and not owned, and appropriate and inappropriate behavior, permeated the soldiers' world.[45] Military law shaped their world as well, but military law shaped their behaviors in limited fashions. In the lived experience of military life in Civil War armies, the men carried their civilian legal values into military service and adapted those legal and cultural values to the new circumstances they confronted—both limited by military law and allowed by military "necessity." A conflict of legitimate legal values confronted the soldiers: civilian and military. As a result, the soldiers made choices to resolve that conflict, and in the process of resolution the soldiers created their own cultural elbow room for taking the actions they had to take as soldiers while explaining their actions to themselves and to others through the world of a soldiers' common law. Thus, they created code words in their subculture for justifying and explaining their behaviors, words such as "foraging" and "bears." They heard their officers instruct them on how to act, and then they ignored those instructions. Their behaviors, which in nonwartime situations would make them civilly liable for damages or criminally liable for punishment, took on a different character in war; indeed, some soldiers cloaked these legal remedies with humor, thereby obscuring the meaning and effect of their actions. Civil War soldiers created their own subculture governed by their own rules of customary law separate and distinct from formal military law. Yet their efforts to explain and justify their actions exhibit a lawmindedness, a sense of a customary chosen law-in-action, that existed within the soldiers' ranks. The men sought a balance between constraint (in the form of competing normative orders—cultural values, civilian law, and military law—and discretion of action in the unusual situation of civil war. Troops had to follow the rules of war and the black-letter rules governing armies, but they also carved out space enough to act against the enemy and to act in their own personal self-interest. This suggestive evidence presented and analyzed in this short study supports the existence of an in-dwelling legal culture; if anything, it supports the presence and importance of customary law assisting these men, Americans all, to understand and explain the unusual and disquieting circumstances of life in the military during wartime. "It cant be cald stealin'" because, given their historical contexts, their needs, their special pleadings, and the larger legal and political goals of the war, the ordinary rules of civil society and even military law did not apply neatly. Within that messy historical context, the men created a self-justifying set of rules and explanation of those rules, resolved their conflict-of-laws problems, and created a soldiers' world of customary law for survival in the ranks in wartime. These extant testimonies about those lost worlds and values offer historians a chance to glimpse the unspoken and internalized legal values and lawmindedness of that generation of Americans. Stealing—perhaps, perhaps not; intriguing, absolutely.

NOTES

1. John Phillip Reid, *Law for the Elephant: Property and Social Behavior on the Over-land Trail* (San Marino, Calif.: The Huntington Library Press, 1980). See also the standard textbook in the field of United States legal history as evidence of the acceptance in the field of the idea of a legal culture; Kermit L. Hall and Peter Karsten, *The Magic Mirror: Law in American History*, 2nd (New York: Oxford University Press, 2009), 141. I have not altered or corrected any quoted source as to grammar, spelling, or punctuation.

2. William E. Nelson, *Americanization of the Common Law: The Impact of Legal Change on Massachusetts Society, 1760–1830* (Cambridge, Mass.: Harvard University Press, 1975); William E. Nelson, *The Common Law in Colonial America: Volume 1, The Chesapeake and New England, 1607–1660* (New York: Oxford University Press, 2008); William E. Nelson, *Dispute and Conflict Resolution in Plymouth County, Massachusetts, 1725–1825* (Chapel Hill: University of North Carolina Press, 1981); William E. Nelson, *Fighting for the City: A History of the New York City Corporation Counsel* (New York: New York Law Journal in association with the Law Department and the Mayor's Fund to Advance New York City, 2008); William E. Nelson, *The Legalist Reformation: Law, Politics, and Ideology in New York, 1920–1980* (Chapel Hill: University of North Carolina Press, 2001); William E. Nelson, *The Roots of American Bureaucracy, 1830–1900* (Cambridge, Mass.: Harvard University Press, 1982).

3. For the best modern overview of custom and law, see David J. Bederman, *Custom as a Source of Law* (New York: Cambridge University Press, 2010). On customary law and criminal justice in the era of the American Revolution, see Steven Wilf, *Law's Imagined Republic: Popular Politics and Criminal Justice in Revolutionary America* (New York: Cambridge University Press, 2010). On the "right" to keep pigs in New York City, see Hendrik Hartog's now-classic article "Pigs and Positivism," *Wisconsin Law Review* (1985): 899–935.

4. For examples of the law-in-action scholarship, see the major works of William E. Nelson, cited in note 2 above. Other recent important work in the field plumbing the borderlands of law and custom includes: Laura F. Edwards, *The People and Their Peace: Legal Culture and the Transformation of Inequality in the Post-Revolutionary South* (Chapel Hill: University of North Carolina Press, 2009); Lisa Ford, *Settler Sovereignty: Jurisdiction and Indigenous People in America and Australia, 1788–1836* (Cambridge, Mass.: Harvard University Press, 2010); Lawrence M. Friedman, *American Law in the 20th Century* (New Haven, Conn.: Yale University Press, 2002); Christopher Tomlins, *Freedom Bound: Law, Labor, and Civic Identity in Colonizing English America, 1580–1865* (New York: Cambridge University Press, 2010).

5. This issue of the context of wartime changed how the administration of Abraham Lincoln conceived of and acted toward the property of disloyal Southerners. For the best recent interpretation of Lincoln and the law of war, see Burrus M. Carnahan, *Lincoln on Trial: Southern Civilians and the Law of War* (Lexington: University Press of Kentucky, 2010). See also Daniel W. Hamilton,

The Limits of Sovereignty: Property Confiscation in the Union and the Confederacy during the Civil War (Chicago: University of Chicago Press, 2007).

6. A large literature exists on military law and the history of military law in the United States. Jonathan Lurie's works are good places to start to understand military law. See Jonathan Lurie, *Arming Military Justice* (Princeton, N.J.: Princeton University Press, 1992); *Military Justice in America: The U.S. Court of Appeals for the Armed Forces, 1775–1980* (Lawrence: University Press of Kansas, 2001); *Pursuing Military Justice: The History of the United States Court of Appeals for the Armed Forces, 1951–1980* (Princeton, N.J.: Princeton University Press, 1998).

7. William E. Nelson made a similar point regarding the American colonists who had lived quite happily as British subjects until the colonial crisis. Once the colonial crisis started, colonials became aware of the conflict-of-laws problems they faced with and within the Empire and became aware that they faced a division-of-powers issues (a federalism issue) within and between each colony. See William E. Nelson, "The American Revolution and the Emergence of Modern Doctrines of Federalism and Conflict of Laws," in Daniel R. Coquillette, ed., *Law in Colonial Massachusetts, 1630–1800: A Conference Held 6 and 7 November 1981 by The Colonial Society of Massachusetts* (Boston: The Society; [Charlottesville]: Distributed by the University Press of Virginia, 1984), 419–67.

8. As far as can be determined, all sources come from men who volunteered for service in the Civil War armies. Both sides conscripted (drafted) men, but none of the sources employed come from conscripts.

9. For a quick sampling of the published primary sources, see Gregory Acken, ed., *Inside the Army of the Potomac: The Civil War Experience of Captain Francis Adams Donaldson* (Mechanicsville, Pa.: Stackpole Books, 1998); Stephen E. Ambrose, ed., *A Wisconsin Boy in Dixie: Civil War Letters of James K. Newton* (Madison: University of Wisconsin Press, 1961); George Montgomery, ed., *Georgia Sharpshooter: The Civil War Diary and Letters of William Rhadamanthus Montgomery* (Macon, Ga.: Mercer University Press, 1997); Lance Herdegen and Sherry Murphy, eds., *Four Years with the Iron Brigade: The Civil War Journal of William Ray, Company F, Seventh Wisconsin Volunteers* (Cambridge, Mass.: Da Capo Press, 2002); Jeffrey C. Lowe and Sam Hodges, eds., *Letters to Amanda: The Civil War Letters of Marion Hill Fitzpatrick, Army of Northern Virginia* (Macon, Ga.: Mercer University Press, 1998); Cynthia DeHaven Pitcock and Bill J. Gurley, eds., *I Acted from Principle: The Civil War Diary of Dr. William M. McPheeters, Confederate Surgeon in the Trans-Mississippi* (Fayetteville: University of Arkansas Press, 2002); Steven Raab, ed., *With the 3rd Wisconsin Badgers: The Living Experience of the Civil War Through the Journals of Van R. Willard* (Mechanicsville, Pa.: Stackpole Books, 1999); Emil and Ruth Rosenblatt, eds., *Hard Marching Every Day: The Civil War Letters of Private Wilbur Fisk, 1861–1865* (Lawrence: University Press of Kansas, 1992); Daniel E. Sutherland, ed., *Reminiscences of a Private: William E. Bevens of the First Arkansas Infantry, C.S.A.* (Fayetteville: University of Arkansas Press, 1992); F. Jay Taylor, ed., *Reluctant Rebel: The Secret Diary of Robert Patrick, 1861–1865* (Baton Rouge:

Louisiana State University Press, 1959 [1987]); Richard Trimble, ed., *Brothers 'Til Death: The Civil War Letters of William, Thomas, and Maggie Jones, 1861–1865: Irish Soldiers in the 48th New York Volunteer Regiment* (Macon, Ga.: Mercer University Press, 2000); Sam R. Watkins, *"Co. Aytch": A Side Show of the Big Show* (New York: Collier Books, 1962).

10. Renée Rose Shield, *Diamond Stories: Enduring Change on 47th Street* (Ithaca, N.Y.: Cornell University Press, 2002), 209. Thanks to Professor Morton J. Horwitz for suggesting this parallel and for bringing this book to my attention.

11. Joseph Heath, "Business Ethics and Moral Motivation: A Criminological Perspective," *Journal of Business Ethics* 83 (December 2008): 595–614. Thanks to Professor James A. Wooten for suggesting this parallel and for bringing this article to my attention.

12. For general histories of Civil War soldiers and their experiences, see Michael Barton, *Goodmen: The Character of Civil War Soldiers* (University Park: Penn State University Press, 1981); Michael Barton and Larry M. Logue, *The Civil War Soldier: A Historical Reader* (New York: New York University Press, 2002); Larry J. Daniel, *Soldiering in the Army of Tennessee: A Portrait of Life in a Confederate Army* (Chapel Hill: University of North Carolina Press, 1991); Earl J. Hess, *The Union Soldier in Battle: Enduring the Ordeal of Combat* (Lawrence: University Press of Kansas, 1997); Gerald F. Linderman, *Embattled Courage: The Experience of Combat in the American Civil War* (New York: Free Press, 1987); James M. McPherson, *For Cause and Comrades: Why Men Fought in the Civil War* (New York: Oxford University Press, 1997); James M. McPherson, *What They Fought for, 1861–1865* (Baton Rouge: Louisiana State University Press, 1994); Reid Mitchell, *Civil War Soldiers: Their Expectations and Their Experiences* (New York: Viking Press, 1988); J. Tracy Power, *Lee's Miserables: Life in the Army of Northern Virginia from the Wilderness to Appomattox* (Chapel Hill: University of North Carolina Press, 1998); James I. Robertson Jr., *Soldiers Blue and Gray* (Columbia: University of South Carolina Press, 1988); Aaron Sheehan-Dean, ed., *The View from the Ground: Experiences of Civil War Soldiers* (Lexington: University Press of Kentucky, 2007); Bell Irvin Wiley, *The Life of Johnny Reb: The Common Soldier of the Confederacy* (Indianapolis: Bobbs-Merrill, 1942); Bell Irvin Wiley, *The Life of Billy Yank: The Common Soldier of the Union* (Indianapolis: Bobbs-Merrill, 1952); Steven E. Woodworth, ed., *The Loyal, True, and Brave: America's Civil War Soldiers* (Wilmington, Del.: Scholarly Resources, 2002).

13. Typical of this work describing these relationships is Charles E. Brooks, "The Social and Cultural Dynamics of Soldiering in Hood's Texas Brigade," *Journal of Southern History* 67 (August 2001): 535–72.

14. United States War Department, *The War of the Rebellion: A Compilation of the Official Record of the Union and Confederate Armies* (Washington, D.C.: Government Printing Office, 1899), Series III, Vol., 3, 148–64. Hereinafter cited as *OR*. Originally issued as General Order No. 100, Adjutant General's Office, April 24, 1863.

15. On Lieber, see Frank Freidel, *Francis Lieber, Nineteenth Century Liberal* (Baton Rouge: Louisiana State University Press, 1947). For recent work on the Lieber Code, see

Burrus M. Carnahan, "Lincoln, Lieber, and Laws of War: The Origins and Limits of the Principle of Military Necessity," *American Journal of International Law* 92 (April 1998): 213; Richard S. Hartigan, "Lieber's Code and the Law of War," *The Army Lawyer* 9 (1983): 43; Susan Posner and Elizabeth R. Varon, "United States v. Steinmetz: The Legal Legacy of the Civil War Revisited," *Alabama Law Review* 46 (Spring 1995): 725. John Fabian Witt, *Lincoln's Code: The Laws of War in American History* (New York: Free Press, 2012), appeared too late for me to use it in preparing this essay.

16. *OR*, General Order 100, Section II, Art. 44.

17. "An Act for establishing Rules and Articles for the government of the Armies of the United States," *United States Statutes at Large* 2 (1806): 359–72.

18. *Ibid.*, 366.

19. *OR*, General Order 100, Sec. I, Art. 14.

20. See Book 3, Chapter 9, "Waste and Destruction," and "Ravaging and burning" in Emmerich de Vattel, *Le Droit des Gens: Ou, principles de la Loi Naturelle, Appliqué à la Conduite & aux Affaires des nations & des Souverains* (Londres: [s.n.], 1758); *The Law of Nations, or, Principles of the Law of Nature: Applied to the Affairs of Nations and Sovereigns: A Work Tending to Display the True Interest of Powers* (Northampton, Mass.: Printed by T. M. Pomroy and S. & E. Butler, 1805). Burrus M. Carnahan made this important distinction and point; see Carnahan, *Lincoln on Trial*, 87; n.3, 142, n.41, 145.

    For the best treatment of the "march to the sea" that also is sensitive to the issue of property confiscation, wasting, and ravaging, see Joseph T. Glatthaar, *The March to the Sea and Beyond: Sherman's Troops in the Savannah and Carolinas Campaigns* (New York: New York University Press, 1986).

21. Marc Bloch, *The Historian's Craft* (New York: Vintage, 1953), 61.

22. Reuben Lamphear to Eliza, September 3, 1863, Reuben Lamphear Papers, "Lamphear 1863" Folder, Special Collections, Hoskins Library, University of Tennessee, Knoxville, Knoxville, Tennessee.

23. Southerners often criticized Union Army soldiers, labeling them as "hirelings," because so many of the troops of the Union were first- or second-generation immigrants. By referring to the Union soldiers as hirelings, Southerners hoped to stain the Union forces as un-American (as opposed to Southerners, who fought in the defense of their homeland), and Southerners sought to analogize Union soldiers to the much hated "Hessians" of the American Revolution (German foreign forces employed and deployed by the British to fight George Washington and his Continental Army, often mischaracterized as mercenaries).

24. David Wyatt Aiken to wife, June 28, 1863, David Wyatt Aiken Papers, South Caroliniana Library, University of South Carolina, Columbia, South Carolina.

25. Lieber Code, Section II, Article 38.

26. Heath James Christian to "Dear Father," July 13, 1863, Christian Family Papers, Virginia Historical Society, Richmond, Virginia.

27. Florence McCarthy to "Dear Sister," July 10, 1863, McCarthy Family Papers, Virginia Historical Society, Richmond, Virginia.

28. Bloch, *The Historian's Craft*, 61.
29. Peter Warden to aunt, May 31, 1862, Vreeland-Warden Papers, Peter Warden 3rd Illinois Cavalry File, U.S. Army Military History Institute, Carlisle Barracks, Carlisle, Pennsylvania.
30. Diary, pages 6–19, John Price Kempner Papers, Virginia Historical Society.
31. William C. Davis, ed., *Diary of a Confederate Soldier: John S. Jackman of the Orphan Brigade* (Columbia: University of South Carolina Press, 1990), 54.
32. *Ibid.*, footnote 17. Jackman used the word "bear" for pig again on May 24, 1864, 129.
33. Davis, *Diary of a Confederate*, 136. Davis identifies the officer as Captain Thomas Steele Jr., Company E, 4th Kentucky (CSA).
34. Terrence J. Winschel, ed., *The Civil War Diary of a Common Soldier: William Wiley of the 77th Illinois Infantry* (Baton Rouge: Louisiana State University Press, 2001), 16.
35. John W. Ames to Mother, December 15, 1862, John W. Ames Papers, Carlisle Barracks, United States Army Military History Institute, Carlisle, Pennsylvania.
36. "Liberated Books," Horace Smith, *Gaieties and Gravities* (New York: D. Appleton & Company, 1852), together with letter dated October 12, 1900, returning book to Virginia from Major Douglas H. Thomas, "Liberated Books," Virginia Historical Society, Richmond, Virginia.
37. For the best analysis of the Fredericksburg campaign, see George C. Rable, *Fredericksburg! Fredericksburg!* (Chapel Hill: University of North Carolina Press, 2002).
38. Albert Ballard Smith to Anna [Tarlton Shrader] Smith, January 25, 1865, in the private collection of Margaret Ward Bromley, Louisville, Kentucky. Letter used with the permission of Mrs. Bromley, and with thanks to her for access to this letter.
39. Edward J. Seaman to wife, January 20, 1863, Grist Mill Collection folder, "War," Vol. 1, American Revolution to 1920, Bryant Local History Reading Room, Roslyn Public Library, Roslyn, New York.
40. Marcus Woodcock, *A Southern Boy in Blue: The Memoir of Marcus Woodcock, 9th Kentucky Infantry (U.S.A.)*, ed. Kenneth W. Noe (Knoxville: University of Tennessee Press, 1996), 143.
41. Thomas J. Wright, *History of the Eighth Regiment Kentucky Volunteer Infantry* (St. Joseph, Mo.: St. Joseph Steam Printing Co., 1880), 40.
42. Clay Mountcastle, *Punitive War: Confederate Guerrillas and Union Reprisals* (Lawrence: University Press of Kansas, 2009).
43. Thomas W. Parsons, *Incidents & Experiences in the Life of Thomas W. Parsons, From 1826 to 1900*, ed. Frank Furlong Mathias (Lexington: University Press of Kentucky, 1975), 105.
44. Diary, page 17, John Price Kempner Papers, Virginia Historical Society.
45. On how thoroughly religion affected the lives of Civil War soldiers, see the important study by George C. Rable, *God's Almost Chosen People: A Religious History of the Civil War* (Chapel Hill: University of North Carolina Press, 2010).

3

Debating the Fourteenth Amendment

The Promise and Perils of Using Congressional Sources

DANIEL W. HAMILTON

William E. Nelson's groundbreaking book *The Fourteenth Amend-ment*[1] is important on two main fronts. First, the book's value lies in the new historical findings that Nelson uncovers after exhaustive archival research into the politics and the antebellum precedents for the Four-teenth Amendment. Second, the book remains innovative in its use of historical evidence, particularly the congressional debates of the Thirty-eighth, Thirty-ninth, and Fortieth Congresses. Of course, Nelson is one of many historians who have used these debates. His innovation was not that he brought them back but rather that he reframed their use, helping to change the questions that we ask of them, interrogating these landmark debates for what they teach us about the constitutional and legal history of the Civil War and Reconstruction in a new way. Using Nelson's book as a starting point, this essay focuses on the use of congressional sources in writing the constitutional history of the Four-teenth Amendment, on their limits and their possibilities; more gener-ally, it will consider the evidence we work with as historians and the relationship between our sources and our interpretations. The central question, which is highlighted in Nelson's book and remains with us, is how we can best use these congressional sources to do constitutional history rather than contemporary constitutional law.

As it set out to do, Nelson's book did break an impasse in Four-teenth Amendment scholarship in a way that energized the field. At the time the book came out in 1988, constitutional history was somewhat moribund while legal history was taking a decisive turn to private law, in landmark work by such scholars as Lawrence M. Friedman and Morton J. Horwitz, and of course Nelson himself.[2] The historian Michael Vorenberg reports that the American Society for Legal History even considered making the theme of its 1980 conference "Is Constitutional History Dead?"[3] The central questions of earlier work on the constitutional history of Reconstruction and the Fourteenth Amendment had largely played themselves out, and as Vorenberg notes of the period, "with stalemate came staleness."[4]

By the end of the 1980s, the constitutional history of Reconstruction had largely reached a scholarly dead end within the larger field of legal history, as one question was asked over and over: What did the framers of the Fourteenth Amendment intend? I want to be very clear that I am not criticizing the use of the debates and the words of individual legislators as historical evidence. Just as we pay extraordinary attention to the First Congress to explore competing understandings of the meaning of the Constitution and the Bill of Rights in the late eighteenth century, so we turn to a different set of framers when examining how the Thirty-seventh, Thirty-eighth, Thirty-ninth, and Fortieth congresses debated the meaning of the Thirteenth, Fourteenth, and Fifteenth amendments. Yet much of the use of the debates over the Fourteenth Amendment amounted then to first-rate historical work (carefully grounded in a wide reading of primary sources) that was driven by an essentially ahistorical premise, resulting in a rampant presentist use of the debates to provide definitive constitutional answers to contemporary disputes.[5]

Though the question driving that scholarship—what did the framers intend?—was of course a species of Fourteenth Amendment originalism, we must break down that originalism into its component categories: originalism as practiced by lawyers and judges, distinct from a kind of originalism practiced by historians and legal and constitutional scholars. In both varieties, the congressional debates were central. Lawyers and judges turned to the debates, and turn to them still, to try to find the definitive content of the famous phrases "equal protection of the laws," "due process," and "privileges and immunities" to resolve current constitutional litigation. Nelson condemned this use of the history of the Fourteenth Amendment, which had "transformed the judicial search for framers' intentions into a sort of game, in which judges search for historical tidbits to support preconceived positions grounded in contemporary policy choices." Yet "virtually everyone who plays this interpretivist game knows that specific intentions compelling judges to reach a particular result rarely exist in Fourteenth Amendment cases."[6] In this pursuit, their use of the debates was prone to all the historical sins of originalism in interpreting the Constitution, in particular looking to the past to find your friends. Yet it might be fair to say that the Fourteenth Amendment was, and may still be, the most sinful spot on the originalist map.[7]

What's more surprising was the way that constitutional historians in the middle 1980s had tracked this instrumentalist search for original intent in their research. As Nelson put it, "[H]istorians have been engaging in a debate [over the Fourteenth Amendment] which parallels that of the lawyers."[8] The questions that scholars asked were distinct from law office history in that generally they were asking more sophisticated questions and including a wider range of historical actors. Yet, at the same time, they regularly sought answers that imposed modern legal questions on the Reconstruction Congress. Did the framers of the Fourteenth Amendment intend to apply the Bill of Rights to the states? Did they intend to prohibit private discrimination or only state action? Did they intend to prohibit racial segregation? Congressional leaders certainly considered these questions, but they never reached anything like resolution, and the framers had and expressed no generalizable intent as to how the Fourteenth Amendment would apply to these questions.

Scholars turning to the debates to find answers to these questions, however rich their source base, at the time were reflecting a presentist obsession with nailing down once and for all the goals of the amendment's framers to answer some of the burning questions of their time. Given that it was heading down this road, much of the work of that era resembles legal briefs, at once sophisticated but still asking questions pulling the amendment and its origins into the present. Were the framers, by our lights, essentially liberal or conservative? Did they intend the Fourteenth Amendment to be read narrowly or broadly? There are major books on both sides of this question, and it is possible to line up very important work on both sides of the ledger. Yet the demand that the framers answer modern questions drained the field of vital ambiguity and contingency. By the time of the publication of Nelson's book, we were at a frustrating draw, or, as Nelson put it: "[H]istorical scholarship on the adoption of the Fourteenth Amendment is now at an impasse."[9]

In his book, therefore, Nelson mounted a frontal assault on originalist uses of the congressional debates surrounding the Fourteenth Amendment, providing a necessary corrective. With a bracing and challenging declaration of a pox on both their houses, Nelson set forth a devastating critique of lawyers and scholars for using congressional debates in a way that ultimately "impoverished our understanding of constitutional history."[10] When we turn to congressional debates, we cannot go looking for intent of either stripe—the lawyerly or the scholarly—because we will find it. By this I do not mean to suggest that the quest for intent will lead researchers to invent it where it does not exist. Rather, my claim is that the search for intent is largely ahistorical and can too easily obscure multiple intents on the part of multiple historical actors. We must "turn instead to identifying the meaning which the amendment had for its proponents."[11] Nelson's book issued a clarion call to re-historicize the use of congressional debates. Once we are free of the need to answer to the present, we are free to make a genuine effort to understand the debates in their historical context, and thus to make available to historians a much richer use of this source base.

One central accomplishment of Nelson's book, then, is to show us that we cannot find the intent of the framers in the congressional debates, understood in a presentist sense, and to insist that we stop looking. But if we know what we *won't* find, what is it that we *will* find when we interrogate the debates over the Fourteenth Amendment? First and foremost, Nelson shows, we find a new emphasis on the tracing and elaboration of legal ideology. The congressional conflicts over the Fourteenth Amendment "existed on a conceptual level different from the doctrinal level on which most scholars have examined it." The framers simply were not asking the doctrinal questions that the originalist literature would have us ask them. Instead, Nelson's book seeks to trace the ideas that drove the creation of the Fourteenth Amendment, and in his book we find first and foremost what Nelson calls "principles of equality, individual rights, and local self-rule." He identifies and analyzes "a popular ideology of liberty and equality" in antebellum America linking "ideas about rights derived from natural law and republican society."[12] These were contested concepts, of course, and there were distinct Northern and Southern, Democratic and Republican commitments to these ideas. In particular, Nelson shows how differing conceptions of equality held by North and South clashed in the decades before the Civil War and were brought to bear on debates over the Fourteenth Amendment. In this connection, one of his chapter titles is especially illuminating of the originality and historical focus of his enterprise: "Ideas of Liberty and Equality in Antebellum America."[13]

My purpose here, in considering Nelson's argument, is to highlight the link that it draws between methodology and ideology. Where previous scholars by and large attempted to reach a definitive understanding of a particular doctrinal dispute in our time through resort to the congressional debates from the time of the amendment's origins, Nelson instead used the debates to reveal high-stakes ideological conflict contextualized within a crucial moment in American legal and constitutional thought. What was groundbreaking, in Nelson's use of Reconstruction congressional debates, was his emphasis on the conceptual heart of the debates, his stress on the centrality to those debates of disputes over legal ideas, driven primarily neither by political nor economic self-interest nor by an attempt to locate doctrinal disputes that track our own. In this way, Nelson's focus on the constitutive power of ideas reveals something similar to what Robert Gordon has called "legal history as the history of legal consciousness" or "law as legitimating ideology."[14]

Both Gordon and Nelson are interested in what Gordon describes as legal history that "can be told without reference to pressures of immediate interest." Gordon is interested primarily in the ways that we can mine legal ideas in case law and treatises, whereas Nelson shows how we can mine legal ideas in constitutional debates as well. Both bodies of sources are, in Gordon's words, "among the richest artifacts of a society's legal consciousness" in that they are both "rationalized and elaborated legal products" containing "an exceptionally refined and concentrated version of legal consciousness."[15]

The congressional debates surrounding the Fourteenth Amendment are exceptionally valuable for what they reveal about mid-nineteenth-century legal ideology, and by mining congressional debates we produce a legal and constitutional history with its dominant focus on the arguments of legislators, and not solely on cases, courts, or litigation. Congressional debates are not important only when they make it into court and are not essentially preludes to *The Slaughterhouse Cases* (1873) or the *Civil Rights Cases* (1883) or *Lochner v. New York* (1906), and we ought not read them primarily with an eye to future great cases.[16]

Of course, this is not to say that there is not great work on the legal and constitutional history of the Civil War that focuses primarily on courts.[17] Neither is it to say that there are not legal historians of the period who rely primarily on congressional sources and not on courts as their dominant source base. Indeed, in this era, and in particular before the Civil War, many of the leading constitutional questions were not, with the great exception of *Dred Scott*, fought out in the courts, and congressional debates are often the starting point for legal research. Nonetheless, Nelson's use of these sources was an innovative and important assertion of the independent value of congressional debates for what they reveal about congressional thought—and, by implication, American thought—in the Civil War and Reconstruction. Indeed we can best understand Nelson's reliance on sources of congressional debate, and his focus on Congress first and courts second, as presenting a methodological argument.

This methodological argument bears greater scrutiny. To my mind, what is still somewhat lacking in Nelson's treatment is explicit attention to the need to test for ideological commitment within political debate. Although, following Nelson, I acknowledged at the outset its unquestioned value, I argue further that the congressional source base generates its own methodological and empirical questions—questions that every scholar of the period must confront. Do speeches made by politicians reveal deep and significant ideological divisions, or do they present nothing more than shallow rhetoric primarily serving pressing strategic or tactical interests? Can they be both at once? The clear answer is yes, they can be both at once; indeed, we must almost always understand them as being both at once. Those who were carrying on these debates were working politicians, and thus, even in the midst of principled ideological discourse, we simultaneously find competing demands of party and faction, of region and popular opinion.

One chief benefit of considering Congress is that it is in Congress where the immediate stakes are high, where much depends on the

outcome, and representatives and senators knew it. For too long, scholars have treated congressional debates primarily either as the source of
intent, as discussed above, or as a mere mask for self-interest, window
dressing that masked underlying high-stakes political struggles. It was
necessary, for the most part, to follow the money, to identify whose ox
was being gored, on the grounds that such inquiries in and of themselves will explain partisan politicians' ideological statements and
commitments. By rejecting this reductionist construct, Nelson's book
revitalized the examination of speeches and debates of legislators to
highlight what they revealed about ideologies and legal thought in the
wake of the Civil War. To his great credit, Nelson helped to take the
exclusive focus away from the traditional close analysis of voting patterns and political faction as the chief way of studying Congress and its
treatment of the amendment.[18] Nelson instead put the emphasis on the
words of legislators, using their speeches and debates as a starting point
for serious contextual analysis of the historical rather than the modern
meaning of the Fourteenth Amendment.

Yet if Nelson's book is an antidote to the excesses of presentist originalist scholarship by legal scholars and historians alike, it goes too far
in the other direction. In place of self-interest driving ideology, we have
ideology standing alone, or at least without being put into sufficient
political context. We still have, in the decades since Nelson's landmark
book, a dichotomy in the use of these sources, but it is a new dichotomy.
Some historical work considers congressional sources as a window into
politics; other historical work relies on these same sources as a window
into legal and constitutional thought. Both are of course valuable, but
they exist in parallel, not in dialogue. As we were at the time of Nelson's
book, we remain at something of an impasse.

Legislators, even those debating changing the Constitution, never
ceased to be politicians, and we must take their political imperatives
as seriously as we take their ideological commitments. We still must
ask, to what extent did demands of party or region drive the actions
of legislators, blurring or even eclipsing their legal arguments? Should
we try to separate political imperatives from legal and constitutional
arguments? How are we to understand and make clear the interaction
between them? Of course, we ask these questions of the judges whom
we study, but we ought to ask these questions with a new intensity in

considering the words and votes of working politicians in a deeply partisan era. Congress was not an Athenian debating society. We regularly debate the extent of the law/politics distinction in courts. What do we do when, as in congressional debates over amending the Constitution, there actually is no law/politics distinction?

Looking inside institutions, we must acknowledge that a legislator's speech, or a judge's opinion, was at once conceptual, political, and shaped by institutional traditions. We must remember that the questions that Congress faced never were bloodless, disembodied abstractions but instead formed the threshold issues that legislators debated in considering whether to alter fundamentally the relationships among the federal government, the states, and the American people. The story of the creation of the Fourteenth Amendment was at all times the story of a particular piece of legislation, even though it ultimately would transcend the character of legislation by becoming part of the Constitution, the nation's fundamental law, and thereafter form part of the standard for assessing the constitutionality of ordinary legislation. Thus, demands of public opinion, machinations of party politics, and competing institutional claims all came to bear on the congressional debates over the amendment. Of course Congress was not a hermetically sealed body, and its members were interacting with a constellation of other political actors, including the president and his cabinet, lawyers, academic writers, newspaper editors, and their constituents, all of them trying to shape policy.

It is precisely this interaction that is potentially the most fruitful focus of future historical study. Thankfully, we are long past the point when historians distinguished sharply between intellectual history and on-the-ground social and political history.[19] More and more, the work of historians reveals the artificiality of once-standard dichotomies dividing ideas and interests, theory and practice. Intellectual history is shaped at all levels of society, and ideas are themselves both causes and effects. This is certainly true in the story of the creation of the Fourteenth Amendment, where ideas and political processes are entangled to the point that we could not separate the two even if we wanted to do so. The debate over the Fourteenth Amendment lived, as many legal debates do, in the middle ground between high theory and social practice and was shaped by doctrine and political machinations alike.[20]

Debates over the amendment were no less intellectually significant because they took place among legislators and not professional intellectuals, nor because the stakes were so high.

The next crucial step in historians' use of congressional sources is to seek a better integration of the competing conceptions of the meanings of congressional debate. Highlighting tensions between political expediency and ideological commitment is one of the chief values of considering congressional debates as part of the elaboration of constitutional thought. It is in Congress where the ideological rubber hits the road, so to speak, where legislators must explain and debate and act upon their ideological commitments. Debates in Congress were not debates about writing a treatise on the Constitution but, particularly in the case of the congressional debates of the Fortieth Congress, a debate over how the Constitution itself should be fundamentally rewritten. If we are accustomed to looking to legal treatises for the elaboration of legal ideology, a kind of ideology in books, we should look to congressional debates to find constitutional and legal ideology in action.[21]

To be sure, exploring the motivations of historical actors is a complex and highly theorized field, and in this short space I wish mostly to be suggestive about potential directions of research that leave room for both political self-interest and ideological commitment. Legal ideas are shaped at all levels of society, and legal ideas themselves are both effects and causes, strategic and autonomous.[22] Yet even as we move beyond the easy and false dichotomy between "ideas" and "interest," we can test the power of ideology and the "restraining power" of ideology in given cases. That is, if we identify manifest political self-interest of a single legislator or a group of legislators in a given debate (for example, the anticipated position of New England abolitionists or fire-eaters from South Carolina), it is most often the case that strategy and ideology align, that legislators speak and vote in alignment with these anticipated positions.

At some points in constitutional and political debate, however, they act out of alignment with, or even in opposition to, their clear political self-interest. It is at such times, with politicians acting against their interests, that the pulls of party and faction and region and public opinion do not drive behavior and that that the role of ideology comes into high relief. It is in these cases that ideology "holds," that ideological commitments are determinants, and that they transcend the demands of party and region.[23]

It is when the New England abolitionist or the Southern sympathizer from a border state speaks or votes against his self-interest in a debate over the Fourteenth Amendment, in deference to a legal or constitutional commitment, that we see the restraining power of ideology. This is not to say, of course, that those acting in line with their political commitments are not also driven by ideology to some extent—only that in those cases, in most instances, ideological commitment and political commitments line up in unsurprising ways. It is at those times when a political commitment is potentially costly to a legislator, when once again the ideological rubber hits the road. At such times, we can better assess the relative power of political imperatives and of ideological commitments in driving the behavior of legislators. In Nelson's book, ideological commitments—what he calls commitments to concepts of equality and justice—rightly pervade his interpretation of the Fourteenth Amendment's origins. The question he leaves unanswered is: How do these conceptual commitments interact with political commitments? It is in studying congressional debates that we can test those interactions and that we can also identify the extent to which ideology drives as well as restrains political actors and legal change.

This ideology also appears, of course, in the content of the debates, and also in the elaboration of institutional power that is a necessary consequence of the debates. The study of such institutions as Congress and of that institution's conception of the boundaries of its authority necessarily touches on ideological arguments about the legitimate exercise of power. As Christine Desan notes in her work on eighteenth-century Anglo-American legal history, ideological battles are not fought out as ethereal contests of visions. Desan reminds us that power is always necessarily mediated through specific institutional channels and that the decision on where to ground power is an integral part of ideological conflict. Indeed, boundaries between institutions are fluid and contested along ideological lines.[24]

By assigning power to state or federal government, or by assigning power to one branch or another, Congress made ideological choices as revealing as those disclosed by the language of debate. Put simply, the ideological debate and the institutional debate are inseparable, and we see this connection in high relief within congressional debates that reallocate constitutional power. To call some powers "state" and others "federal" is itself an ideological act with profound consequences, both practical and theoretical. The argument that certain powers are the province of the judiciary and others of the legislature is just that—an argument, and one that has changed dramatically over the course of American history. This was certainly the case with the debates over the Fourteenth Amendment.

The debates over the Fourteenth Amendment are a case study of the ways that lawyers and legislators in mid-nineteenth-century America negotiated the autonomy of law and ideology. These negotiations had radically different outcomes in different places and between different historical actors. Law and ideology are neither wholly autonomous nor the mere reflections of interest-group politics or class divisions. Lawyers and legislators grappling with the amendment were not solely result-oriented, but neither, generally, were they bound exclusively to rigid ideological and legal commitments. Law and ideology are, in the famous formulation, relatively autonomous, or a mixture of largely independent legal ideas and responses to external political and social pressures.[25] Yet even this "relative autonomy" is not fixed but instead remains historically contingent. In confronting a fundamental change to the Constitution, legislators debating the Fourteenth Amendment struck very different balances between the opportunistic use of legal theory and the maintenance of ideological and legal autonomy. It is to understand better the amalgam of politics and ideology surrounding the creation of the Fourteenth Amendment that we need to return to the work of the legislators themselves. Nelson's book provided insight into how to interrogate congressional debates on their own terms. We need now to interrogate them some more.

NOTES

1. William E. Nelson, *The Fourteenth Amendment: From Political Principle to Judicial Doctrine* (Cambridge, Mass.: Harvard University Press, 1988).

2. Morton J. Horwitz, *The Transformation of American Law, 1780–1860* (Cambridge, Mass.: Harvard University Press, 1977; reprint, New York: Oxford University Press, 1992); Lawrence M. Friedman, *A History of American Law* (New York: Simon and Schuster, 1973; 2d edition, 1985; 3d edition, 2005); William E. Nelson, *Americanization of the Common Law: The Impact of Legal Change on Massachusetts, 1760–1830* (Cambridge, Mass.: Harvard University Press; reprint, with new introduction, Athens: University of Georgia Press, 1994).

3. Michael Vorenberg, "Reconstruction as a Constitutional Crisis," in Thomas Brown, ed., *Reconstructions: New Perspectives on the Postbellum United States* (New York: Oxford University Press, 2006), 141–71 (quote at 146). Vorenberg cites Harry Scheiber's assessment that there was in the early 1980s "a serious erosion of concern with constitutional law and history in the training of both undergraduate and graduate students." Harry N. Scheiber, "American Constitutional History and the New Legal History: Complementary Themes in Two Modes," *Journal of American History* 68:2 (September 1981): 337–50 (quote at 339).

4. Vorenberg, "Reconstruction as a Constitutional Crisis," 146.

5. Nelson correctly cites, among other important work, Judith A. Baer, *Equality Under the Constitution: Reclaiming the Fourteenth Amendment* (Ithaca, N.Y.: Cornell University Press, 1983); Michael Kent Curtis, *No State Shall Abridge: The Fourteenth Amendment and the Bill of Rights* (Durham, N.C.: Duke University Press, 1986); Michael P. Zuckert, "Congressional Power under the Fourteenth Amendment—The Original Understanding of Section Five," *Constitutional Commentary*, 3:1 (Winter 1986): 123–56; and Raoul Berger, *Government by Judiciary: The Transformation of the Fourteenth Amendment* (Cambridge, Mass.: Harvard University Press, 1977; reprint, Indianapolis: Liberty Fund, Inc., 1997).

6. Nelson, *Fourteenth Amendment*, 5.

7. It is of course the case that there are several different species of originalism, some quite concerned with historical fidelity and attentive to historical questions. Still, it is my understanding that, as Edward A. Purcell Jr. has written elsewhere in his excellent analysis of originalism and federalism, the interpretation of most constitutional text is "intrinsically elastic, dynamic and underdetermined" and makes most constitutional disagreements—"insofar as Americans sought to settle them by reference to some 'original' constitutional meaning or understanding—inherently unresolvable." Edward A. Purcell Jr., *Originalism, Federalism and the American Constitutional Enterprise* (New Haven, Conn.: Yale University Press, 2007), 6.

8. Nelson, *Fourteenth Amendment*, 2.

9. *Ibid.*, 4.

10. *Ibid.*, 5.

11. *Ibid.*, 6.

12. Nelson, *The Fourteenth Amendment*, at 13.

13. *Ibid.*, Chapter II.

14. Robert W. Gordon, "Critical Legal Histories," *Stanford Law Review* 36:1&2 (January 1984): 57–125.

15. *Id.*, 120.

16. 83 U.S. (16 Wall.) 36 (1873); 109 U.S. 3 (1883); 198 U.S. 45 (1905).

17. See, for example, Robert J. Kaczorowski, *The Politics of Judicial Interpretation: The Federal Courts, Department of Justice, and Civil Rights* (Dobbs Ferry, N.Y.: Oceana Publications, 1985; reprint, New York: Fordham University Press, 2004).

18. For example, David Herbert Donald, *The Politics of Reconstruction, 1863–1867* (Cambridge, Mass.: Harvard University Press; reprint, with new introduction, 1984).

19. "It is as rare now to find intellectual historians confining their analysis to the narrow explication of a few texts written by intellectuals, as it is to find social historians providing quantitative descriptions of ordinary people without interpreting their meaning and significance. Intellectual historians now trace the movement of ideas and values across different domains, from religion to popular culture, from race to politics, from gender to economy, as well as among those who made it their business to write books and scholarly articles. Intellectual history is now merging with other fields ranging from the history of ethnicity to the history of law." James T., Kloppenberg, "Intellectual History, Democracy and the Culture of Irony" in Melvyn Stokes, ed., *The State of American History* (Oxford: Berg, 2002), 199–222 (quote at 203–4). See also Jennifer Nedelsky, *Private Property and the Limits of American Constitutionalism: The Madisonian Framework and Its Legacy* (Chicago: University of Chicago Press, 1990), for a historical account stressing the intellectual importance of the arguments of political actors.

20. For three examples of constitutional history that seamlessly weave together political theory and power politics in the Civil War era, see Heather Cox Richardson, *The Greatest Nation of the Earth: Republican Economic Policies During the Civil War* (Cambridge, Mass.: Harvard University Press, 1997); Michael Vorenberg, *Final Freedom: The Civil War, the Abolition of Slavery and the Thirteenth Amendment* (Cambridge and New York: Cambridge University Press, 2001); and Michael Les Benedict, *A Compromise of Principle: Congressional Republicans and Reconstruction* (New York: W. W. Norton & Co., 1974).

    The classic work exploring the legal and constitutional dimensions of Reconstruction remains Harold M. Hyman and William M. Wiecek, *Equal Justice Under Law: Constitutional Development, 1835–1875* (New York: Harper & Row, 1982). Hyman's and Wiecek's book remains the model for a kind of legal-constitutional history of the Civil War and Reconstruction that considers the war and its aftermath on its own historical terms. See also Harold M. Hyman, *A More Perfect Union: The Impact of the Civil War and Reconstruction on the Constitution* (New York: Alfred A. Knopf, 1973).

    Eric Foner's landmark work, although less focused on legal and constitutional questions, explores the ideological core of Reconstruction-era political debate. See Eric Foner, *Reconstruction: America's Unfinished Revolution* (New York: Harper & Row, 1988); Eric Foner, *Politics and Ideology in the Age of the Civil War* (New York: Oxford University Press, 1980).

21. For a classic illustration of the turn to treatises to mine shifts in legal ideology, see Morton J. Horwitz, *The Transformation of American Law, 1870–1960: The Crisis of Legal Orthodoxy* (New York: Oxford University Press, 1992).

22. See James T. Kloppenberg, "Premature Requiem: Republicanism in American History," in James T. Kloppenberg, *The Virtues of Liberalism* (New York: Oxford University Press, 1998), 59–70 (quote at 61): "We must appreciate that both the instrumental and constitutive dimensions of language are inescapable. It is true that we do things with words, but what we do when we speak or write cannot be reduced simply to self-interest. Our projects as individuals and members of various communities are not entirely our own but rather emerge through the interaction of our minds with our cultural environments, and those projects frequently assume an importance for us that transcends calculation of personal advantage."

23. For an example of how legislators mediated between legal ideas and party politics in the case of property confiscation during the Civil War, see Daniel W. Hamilton, *The Limits of Sovereignty: Property Confiscation in the Union and the Confederacy during the Civil War* (Chicago: University of Chicago Press, 2007). See also Richardson, *The Greatest Nation of the Earth*, and Vorenberg, *Final Freedom*.

24. See generally Christine A. Desan, "The Constitutional Commitment to Legislative Adjudication in the Early American Tradition," *Harvard Law Review* 111:6 (April 1998): 1381–503.

25. The insight that law was "relatively autonomous"—neither a political tool, nor a self-enclosed system, but both to different degrees at different times—is one of the chief achievements of the critical legal studies movement. For a wonderful discussion of the historiography of legal analysis, and a persuasive assertion that the most fruitful area of legal historical study is the interaction of internal doctrine and external pressure, see Gordon, "Critical Legal Histories."

II

Law and Social Regulation

4

Was the Warning of Strangers Unique to Colonial New England?

CORNELIA H. DAYTON AND SHARON V. SALINGER

Our story begins with the wintry day in 1765 on which an obscure Bostonian, Robert Love, entered the ranks of minor officialdom. The setting was the Selectmen's Chamber on the second floor of Faneuil Hall. At the age of sixty-five, Love was sworn in to a part-time position that had no name. He would be remunerated for the activity that New Englanders called warning strangers (thus, we refer below to Love and other "warners"). The town clerk read aloud Love's formal orders: "You [are] to make enquiry after all Strangers, and other Persons who shall hereafter come into the Town and reside here that are not Inhabitants, and all such of them as you shall apprehend are in low Circumstances you are immediately to warn to depart this Town in (14) fourteen Days, or [to] give security to the satisfaction of the Selectmen." For the next nine years, Robert Love, a trader in ribbons and horsehair and a retailer (with his wife) of small drams from their rented house, would search the streets, tenements, and taverns of the peninsular town and among its roughly 16,000 residents, warning more than 4,000 individuals. Love was so good at identifying newcomers that four years into his service, the town dismissed the two other men appointed to the same task, retaining and salarying Love at £40 per year.[1]

What was this warning practice, considered by many scholars to have been peculiar to New England towns? In terms of modern law categories, the practice would map onto a mélange of municipal, administrative, immigration, and welfare law. Early moderns would have categorized it as part of the settlement laws by which every British subject had a legal place of inhabitancy—a parish, manor, or borough in which he or she was entitled to receive poor relief. In Massachusetts and neighboring Puritan-inflected colonies, the legal gesture of warning functioned as a bar to a newcomer's receiving inhabitancy. Thus the town issuing the warning could be assured that it never would be liable to relieve the stranger should he or she become indigent. At its core, the warning system protected local taxpayers from the uncontrolled poor support costs that could result from influxes of newcomers.

Instructed to warn especially those who appeared to fall into the description of "low circumstances"—a phrase similar to one common in England at the time, "likely to be chargeable"—Love assessed new residents of Boston by sizing up their clothing, shoes, baggage, hands, and faces and by interviewing them about their work and future plans. Like many of the constables, beadles, and other searchers appointed in England and New England localities to monitor people on the move, he chose to warn not just beggars and those in tattered clothing but a broad range of middling people. Bostonians were all too aware that a range of misfortunes—serious injury, prolonged sickness, an economic downturn—could cause working people to need temporary relief.[2] To take legal effect, the warning had to be proclaimed orally ("I warn you in His Majesty's Name to depart the town of Boston in 14 days"), with a written version lodged in court. To this end, Love kept notarial-style logbooks, and every month he copied his warnings onto pre-prepared warrants for return to the Suffolk County Court of General Sessions.[3]

"Warning out" has long been familiar to both antiquarians and modern scholars of the region. In a now-classic study published in 1911, Josiah Henry Benton summarized the laws relating to the practice in each New England colony. He also chronicled how implementation of those laws varied from place to place, presenting extracts from published town records.[4] More recently, such social and legal historians as Gary B. Nash and Douglas Lamar Jones have tended to equate those warned with the transient poor. Over the decades, the practice has been depicted as an irrational deterrent to labor and a cruel gesture rooted in Puritan insularity.[5] In the larger study from which this essay is drawn, we mine Love's previously unnoticed records to revisit the warning process, to investigate its legal origins, and to illuminate what set people in motion in the British Atlantic world.[6]

The leatherbound logbook of Robert Love covering the first twenty months of his service as warner had been resting in its cherry-red clam-shell box in the collections of the Massachusetts Historical Society since 1840. Yet historians interested in warning out had not known of its existence. Instead, they used the Warning Book covering the years 1745 to 1770 that survives in the records of the Boston overseers of the poor. This folio ledger contains an alphabetical listing of warned strangers in the elegant hand of longtime town clerk William Cooper. He compiled the data from the warrants that warners returned to him, arranging the essential information into columns. The ledger allows counting of persons warned out and mapping where they were last from, but not much more.[7]

Of the sixteen or so men who had been appointed to warn strangers in Boston since the 1690s, Robert Love stands out as a conscientious record keeper. Whereas almost all of his predecessors wrote down minimal information (household head's name and place last from), Love noted where and with whom newcomers were lodging in Boston, the method by which they had come to town (by sea, land, or wagon), and, in some cases, additional particulars ("a goldsmith" by trade, "Clothed in rags," "she is an Indin Womon," "he Wants a pasage to England"). Equally important, in contrast to the town clerk's resort to a cursory accounting of families ("Steel[,] Henry[,] Wife & 2 Children"), Love recorded the name of every spouse, child, and other person arriving in Boston as member of a kin group. The warner's thoroughness is further demonstrated by his copying his logbook entries verbatim onto the warrants that he was required to submit to court.[8] They survive in the Suffolk Files collection at the Massachusetts State Archives, permitting us access (given that Love's logbooks for 1768–74 have not surfaced) to extraordinary details on those warned over nine years and two months.[9]

Our findings challenge the conventional portrait of warning in New England as a harsh, exclusionary measure reflecting Puritans' aversion to "others" and their desire for homogeneity.[10] Four features of the system flatly contradict the notion that warning entailed exclusion and the denial of charity. First, newcomers were not barred or removed from the town by the warning itself. During Love's years as a warner, only thirty physical removals by warrant occurred out of the 2,400-plus parties warned.[11] Second, warning did not mean that one was excluded from the civic and economic life of the town. A person under warning could find employment, rent lodgings, purchase land, transact business, become a church member, get married, raise a family, pay taxes, die, get buried, and even vote (if qualified).[12]

Third, the largest proportion of Boston's warned should not be considered transients. Our research shows that they were youths, equally divided between female and male, aged fifteen to twenty-four, who had yeoman fathers and had grown up in nearby towns. Thus, they were firmly rooted in middling, propertied New England families. They came to Boston not as genuine strangers but as participants in the familiar cycles of a regional labor market—the men to train or work with a tradesman, the women to "go to Servis." Many arrived in Boston to fulfill work stints that had been arranged in advance; within a few years they can be traced returning to their natal towns, marrying, and often moving on from there to frontier towns.

Fourth, even though the warning saved the *town* of Boston harmless from future poor relief expenditure, the polity of Massachusetts Bay Colony generously extended relief to strangers and migrants in need. Love's descriptions indicate that 20 percent of those whom he warned were visibly needy: ragged in clothes, befogged of mind, begging, strolling, or disabled. But were they forced out of town? Rarely. Several times a month, the selectmen and overseers authorized almshouse admission for ailing workers or newcomers whose place of settlement was outside the Bay Colony. Boston's almshouse could accommodate as many as 260 souls, and it was one of the few that existed in the region. It functioned as a medical dispensary, shelter, and lying-in hospital wrapped into one. Massachusetts had long since worked out a system by which the province's taxpayers paid for the relief and medical care of these "strangers." In a move replicated by no colonies outside New England, Massachusetts devoted a sizable chunk of its annual revenues to cover this expense. Towns routinely applied for reimbursement from what was known as "the Province account," and Boston was by far the largest recipient of such monies.[13]

Given these attributes of the system, we argue that warning was at its essence a registration system for those on the move. It allowed labor to flow into the port town, but it also protected the town's budget from explosive relief costs. We can also think of it as a crucial prop in a unique dual-accounting system. Warning "strangers" was the mechanism by which the cost of aiding those in need—whose settlement was elsewhere—was shifted from Boston's taxpayers to the province as a whole. Without recording the origins of newcomers, "cities could do [little] to prevent strangers from coming in to live off the poor rates." These are the words of Carl Bridenbaugh, one of the few historians to come close to capturing the crucial link between the Bay Colony's province account and the effort that its towns put into warning. Describing the decade before the Revolution, Bridenbaugh asserted that Boston, "basing its policy upon more than a century of successful experience, . . . continued to lead [the major port towns] in public benevolence. . . . [T]he *province* boarded *its poor* in the Boston Alms House" such that "the town was spared responsibility for poor immigrants, for the city officials carefully investigated all strangers to prevent their becoming a charge on the rates." "The burden of the poor" was handled "efficiently and humanely," we argue, extending Bridenbaugh's conclusion, because of legislators' vision of how a godly government extended Christian charity and because of taxpayers' willingness to pay two types of poor rates.[14]

Once the internal logic and workings of the warning system are apparent, these questions come to the fore: To what degree were its creators borrowing from English traditions? How much were they innovating? Can warning be explained by the distinctive impulses of Puritan jurisprudence? Given its effectiveness, why would it not have been used in colonies south of New England? In his recent exploration of regional variation in the "legal orders" of England's seventeenth-century North American colonies, William E. Nelson argues that that Puritan concepts of law "compelled leaders to act . . . in pursuit of public-regarding principle" and that "concern for those in positions of deprivation was . . . great."[15] The province poor account paired with the warning of strangers reflects one of the workings-out of these principles. But although we would agree that much about the system was Puritan, its origins lie in the wider swath of reformist impulses concerning the ordering of towns and the provision of poor relief that can be seen across Europe in the late sixteenth and early seventeenth centuries.[16]

In the rest of this essay, we sketch what we see as the ideological origins of Massachusetts's welfare regime and the English legal origins of the warning of strangers. Concluding that warning had precedent in an obscure English writ, we then report on our hunt to determine whether other British jurisdictions in the New World ever used the warning mechanism or a system akin to the province poor account. How did other cities cope with relieving strangers, given that urban leaders everywhere were concerned to be seen as beneficent and civic-minded?

*　　*　　*

Josiah Henry Benton, for whom the charm of historical study lay in tracing continuities, argued that the concept of settlement reached back to Saxon England and even further—to ancient German customs and "the remote villages of the Aryan East." Benton cited evidence that the Teutonic village communities of England followed the rule that if a "stranger remained . . . without challenge" and without being removed for "twelve months, he was from thenceforth allowed to dwell in peace and security."[17] How long such a one-year residency requirement lasted past the Norman invasion of England in 1066 and into the medieval period is not clear. In the late 1400s, we find in ecclesiastical court records rare deployments of the verb "monuit" (Latin for "warn") as a command to depart. The context was not that of strangers intruding into a parish but sinners convicted of serious crimes (sorcery, adultery) and punished partly by being banished from the parish.[18]

As early as the 1520s, Christian humanists such as Erasmus were urging deep change in addressing the problem of poverty. They argued that poor relief should be overseen by secular authorities and not be left to the Church and monasteries. For relief to be adequate and to reach those in need, its delivery must be rationalized. An influential plan for Bruges circulated by the Spanish humanist Juan Luis Vives proposed that officials canvass the city to understand the various categories of poor within the walls and then establish discrete institutions and methods of aid for each. The Catholics and Protestants who embraced these changes were convinced that a disciplined and rational approach to poor relief would lead to one of their vaunted goals for godly governance on earth—effective stewardship.[19]

In England, the quest to put into operation on the local and municipal level what Steve Hindle has termed effective welfare regimes first appeared in the 1570s in such towns as Norwich and Ipswich. Municipal leaders began by taking a detailed, parish-by-parish census of the poor and working poor, listing "the name, age, occupation and dwelling of every man, woman and child." The next steps included sending small numbers away to their places of legal settlement, ordering incorrigible idlers into a newly established workhouse, placing youths with masters, reestablishing a small orphanage, and dividing the city into wards for better local oversight of the needy. Several additional planks of this godly approach to reforming poor relief were pursued in Norwich: increasing the amounts that could go to individual recipients, organizing a well-run workhouse, forbidding begging altogether, and strictly enforcing settlement regulations.[20] Norwich officials were adopting a particular logic: Only by rigorously patrolling the town to remove those who did not belong could officials offer generous and systematic relief to the town's poor.[21]

Although Anglican leaders numbered among those advocating these innovative improvements at the local level in advance of parliamentary action, puritans brought a particular religious conviction to their effort to impose a "culture of discipline" on the urban landscape. Evangelical Protestants were convinced that if secular and ministerial officers established a program of godly reforms, turning their jurisdictions into "second Genevas," then, as one cleric wrote, God would watch over them "in special manner" and ensure that they would "escape . . . many dangers." Besides systematizing the delivery of relief, reforms that signaled a godly city included providing education for young people, punishing vice, eliminating disorderly alehouses, and providing for clean water and swept streets.[22]

Whether cities and parishes took an early initiative or were jarred into action by the laws that made poor rates compulsory, they directed new attention to the monitoring of in-migrants. Localities turned to four methods, none of which yet had statutory backing. One was the interview with local officials. For example, in Leicester starting in 1562, "no stranger could be admitted as a tenant" until he was examined by the mayor and the ward's aldermen to discover "from when he comyth & what honest behavior such forren person(s) be of."[23] To get newcomers before the aldermen, however, officials usually had to search them out—a second mechanism in the parish's new toolkit. Thus we find references to "searchers"—men whose task resembled that of Boston's Robert Love. Ipswich was very early to adopt this procedure, setting a compulsory poor rate and instructing the bailiffs in 1557 to "order searchers for new commers into the Towne, and idle persons and vagabonds." By the 1580s, it was the town's constables in each ward who were to "make search every month for needy, impotent and vagrant p'sons, and therof make certifficate that they may be settled according to law."[24] In the Surrey parish of St. Savior, Southwark, in 1606 two men were paid twenty shillings to be "surveyore[s] of Inmates" for the year.[25]

Besides searching for newcomers and interviewing them, some towns used a third mechanism to minimize the poor rolls: They gave newcomers who were not abjectly indigent the chance to give security (in the form of a bond) that they would not become chargeable.[26] A fourth approach entailed fining landlords who entertained or rented to lodgers for more than seven days without notifying town leaders.[27] All of these mechanisms—searching, interviewing, demanding security from strangers, and putting restrictions on landlords—became elements of New England's warning-out system.

With a string of statutes starting with the Settlement Act of 1662, Parliament laid down a national set of policies for the monitoring and removal of intruders. These statutes introduced both the certificate (a sort of worker passport) and an enumeration of ways in which one could gain settlement in a new parish—by paying taxes, holding office, and paying more than £10 in annual rent, for example. From 1685 onward, one could no longer gain inhabitancy by residing in a place for a certain time without detection. And yet, as Norma Landau has shown, parishes continued to monitor migrants, conducting "prudential" examinations so that their places of settlement would be on record should they ever need relief.[28]

Taken together, the set of statutory and local practices in place by the early 1700s in England took cognizance of at least several types of people on the move—including servants contracted for one year, demobilized soldiers, and certificate holders. In other words, the measures constituted an interlocking complex, the regulatory details of which often emerged from litigation between parishes. The ins and outs of settlement law—when a person was removable, what writ must be used, when children's settlement followed their parents', and so forth—took up 230 pages in the eleventh edition of Richard Burn's much-relied-upon JP manual, published in 1769.[29]

How did the system forged by Massachusetts's Puritan leaders square with that of their English forebearers and counterparts? In contrast to England's complicated regulatory matrix, Massachusetts adopted a single law (in 1692) and a single registration system (warning) to encompass the diverse types of mobile people. We argue that the Bay Colony's approach was to forge a capacious, flexible instrument—warning—that would address the intertwined issues of settlement and poor relief in the North American setting. Legislators built on reform ideas and on seventeenth-century English practices while introducing several unique features. One such feature, as we have seen, was the province account—a truly radical commitment by the central state to extend alms and relief to incoming strangers and sojourners. A second innovation was the 1692 provision that the verbal warning to depart was sufficient in and of itself to block the warned person from gaining settlement.[30] Thus when forty-year-old James Miller walked all the way "by land" from New York to Boston in autumn 1767 and was warned on the very day he entered the port town, he encountered one of those legal fictions that law professors love to write about. The language of the warning made it sound as if King George himself had commanded Miller, "poorly and Not Well in health," to "depart the town of Boston." But given that Massachusetts had decoupled immediate physical removal from warning, warned persons could stay unless they became troublesome.[31]

Boston's warning was quite similar to English parishes' practices of examining incomers and using prudential examinations as insurance in case the new arrival at some point became indigent. However, the word "warn," in its specialized meaning of regulating in-migration, was not used in prudential examinations. Indeed, warning is absent from a range of key English legal sources. It appears in neither parliamentary legislation nor English dictionaries of the period. It is mentioned in only one of the many legal manuals or formbooks published in the seventeenth and eighteenth centuries to help parish officers and justices of the peace understand the statute and case law pertaining to the poor. The exception is Richard Kilburne's book *Choice Presidents* [*sic* for Precedents], which included "a warrant to warn one to depart out of a Parish . . . or to give sufficient security to indempnifie the Parish."[32]

Kilburne's sample warrant gives us the clue that warning-to-depart was not unknown in local English practice.

The verb "warn" and the use of the warning warrant crop up occasionally in English parish and town records. An early example is from Ipswich in East Anglia, a region of Puritan strength from which many early-seventeenth-century New England settlers came. By a December 10, 1578, order, "searches shall be made forthwith [by Constables] for new Commers, . . . and to . . . warne new Commers to depart the Towne."[33] Landau reports from her research that the warning warrant was used in some parishes in the seventeenth century; by the early eighteenth century, it had largely disappeared.[34] Thus, the main lesson about terminology is that English officials inquiring into settlement and ordering removals almost never relied on the language of warning. Yet New Englanders formulating their own policies toward intruders and strangers starting in the 1670s knew the term and understood its utility. They would expand its use so that it became their chief instrument for monitoring immigration and protecting community resources.

*   *   *

Given that the warning writ was available to New Englanders, it could have been appropriated by other British Atlantic jurisdictions as well.[35] Commentators on the warnings used by towns all over New England have long assumed it was not to be found outside the region, but is this assumption accurate? A search of the printed volumes of the minutes of the Philadelphia Common Council and the New York City Mayor's Court does not turn up the word "warn" in the context of regulating strangers. Historians well versed in the surviving records for eighteenth-century Philadelphia and the lives of the working poor could not recall seeing such usage. In the eighteenth century, faced with ever-mounting influxes of sojourners and migrants from overseas, authorities in these cities admitted strangers in distress to their overcrowded almshouses and frequently begged their provincial legislatures to help cover the costs. One 1763 Philadelphia petition revealed that "into rooms but ten or eleven Feet square . . . [we] have been obliged to crowd five or six Beds" in addition to housing some of the needy in a nearby church. Neither government responded by instituting a regularized, well-advertised dual town-and-province accounting system like that of Massachusetts. City authorities took what small steps they could: As in Boston, at times they removed pregnant women to their last places of settlement in the colony and paid the passage to England of some indigents.[36] And yet the question remains: Did they really eschew warning as a mechanism to "save the town harmless," and if so, why?

If mid-Atlantic and southern colonial jurisdictions ever used warning as the first legal step in removing a pauper whose settlement was contested, the most likely place to find a record of it would be in file papers of the quarterly sessions courts. For Philadelphia County, the loose papers do not survive.[37] However, the county just to the west—Chester—has extraordinarily well-preserved court and township records. Warning was not easy to find. Surviving township books and financial accounts chronicle poor relief disbursements and efforts to remove nonsettled paupers but omit the vocabulary of warning.[38] At the magnificent Chester County Archives, where archivists have invested considerable time in arranging loose papers by subject, we were directed to a box of papers that had been filed with the county sessions court relating to litigation between townships over pauper support. This is the most likely type of case to include a reference to warning, given that localities needed to show exactly how they had dealt with paupers who, they believed, had settlement elsewhere in the province. Here, embedded in the requests and appeals of overseers of the poor, was the occasional use of the verb "warn."

Joseph Nicklin recalled how the overseers of Concord, Pennsylvania, of whom he was one, responded to an elderly woman in 1726:

> there came one meagat Power to reside among us & wee finding that She was a transient person & being very old no viseble estate to support her wee according to a late act of assambly requiring to prevent any parson clandestinely setling among us wee as our duty required went to ye sd margreat power & desired hir to give security for ye Indaminfing ye town which refusing to do wee warned her for to depart & declered to her that unless She would give the Security aforsd She Should not have any Settlement here.[39]

The phrase "warned her [or him] for to depart" appeared four more times in contested pauper settlement cases—in 1730, 1741, 1748, and

1752. Warning was not an iconoclastic choice by local officials in one township. The phrase was also used by overseers of Ridley, Thornbury, Middletown, Chichester, and Easton.[40]

In Chester County, the warning of strangers did occur, but in a limited and local way. Associated with removal, the verb "warn" crops up only in two genres of documents: overseers' testimony and removal orders by justices of the peace responding to overseers' complaints. Even in these, it is often absent. By the 1760s, it appears not at all. Interestingly, the settlement examinations of "poor and Impotent" persons (long narratives of the many moves they made within the province) that survive do not refer to the experience of being warned.[41] The word is not to be found in the docket books of the Court of Quarter Sessions where outcomes in these cases are summarized. Nor do warning warrants (like those of Robert Love and other warners of Massachusetts) appear in the surviving court file papers, as far as our searches have revealed. It is little wonder, then, that most previous researchers could not recall seeing warning in Pennsylvania records or poor relief records: Such usage either was not present or it was so rare and obscure as not to be noticeable.

When Chester County overseers referred to legislation, they invoked the 1718 and 1734 amendments to "An Act for the Relief of the Poor" passed by the provincial legislature in 1705. The first measure adopted contemporary parliamentary definitions of how newcomers could gain settlement in a township (by serving there for one year, holding office, paying certain taxes, leasing for at least £5 per year, or giving security). Without using the language of warning, the statute also spelled out the process by which an unsettled person likely to become chargeable could be "required by the overseers . . . to return from whence they came" and so ordered by warrant signed by two justices of the peace. The 1734 amendment borrowed even more heavily from British statute law by introducing a certificate system and requiring incomers (except "mariners and other healthy persons, coming directly from Europe") to notify the town within days of arriving.[42] Pennsylvania's legislative incorporation of English settlement law (along with Rhode Island's in 1748 and New York's in 1773) throws into sharp relief Massachusetts's embrace of an alternative system of monitoring strangers—one focusing on warning.[43]

Given that warning was used occasionally in the parlance of settlement and removal in Chester County, it is likely that overseers of the poor and justices of the peace resorted to it at times in other parts of British America. In New York, eastern Long Island communities founded by Puritans adopted the warning practice, but other townships seem not to have done so. In New Jersey, warning is not mentioned in the sample of township books or appellate pauper support cases that we have examined or inquired about.[44] Historians' accounts of poor relief administration and authorities' often-lax attention to settlement law in Maryland, Virginia, and North and South Carolina omit references to warning.[45] Where relief was dispensed at the town or township level, county commissioners' records call out for further study. We have found a few references to counties' covering expenses such as boarding and medical care for individuals in great distress who lacked local legal settlement. In other words, a unit of government larger than the town or township sometimes acknowledged an obligation to devote part of its tax revenue on an ad hoc basis to relief to the nonsettled poor.[46] But it appears that, in contrast to Massachusetts (where in the late 1760s the province treasurer paid out £800–£1000 sterling annually in charges to the province poor account), such relief to strangers in colonies outside New England entailed neither large annual expenditures nor a well-established, routine process.[47]

What we know so far allows us to posit that warning was either nearly invisible or in disuse in the legal order and welfare regimes of colonies outside New England. Why? It is not that officials in the mid-Atlantic or South were less motivated by Christian charity than were their more northerly counterparts.[48] Officials in the cities of New York and Philadelphia would have welcomed a system such as Massachusetts's province account, and it might have led them to adopt a registration system including the warning warrant that would indicate which set of funds—municipal or provincial—was to cover the needs of which needy person. However, the political will was lacking in Pennsylvania and New York, where assemblymen representing rural interior townships rejected pleas from the cities for help in paying relief for desperately needy newcomers who had settlement elsewhere.[49] Furthermore, less independent-minded in their jurisprudence than New England colonies with Puritan roots, the middle colonies hewed to the post-1685

English approach to settlement, which entailed scant use of the warning of strangers.[50]

Further research is needed to determine to what extent provincial treasurers outside New England paid for the care of travelers in distress and passage out of the colony when it was requested. Some colonies may have had a system akin to the Bay Colony's province poor account without calling it such. South Carolina, for example, with its smaller population and dependence on an enslaved labor force, came up with an alternate way to provide for both strangers of free status and those whites considered to be among the town and colony poor. Wealthy St. Philip's Parish in Charleston shouldered the costs of aiding, housing in the workhouse, or sending homeward many disabled sailors, back-country settlers fleeing Indian raids, and other nonresidents. Only occasionally did the assembly reimburse the parish, besides its assuming responsibility for the large maintenance bills for exiled Acadians. Like Charleston's, rural South Carolina parishes ignored the 1712 law that would have allowed them to remove the nonsettled to their places of inhabitancy.[51]

Our account suggests that Massachusetts was generous in that it provided significant aid to both the town poor and sojourning strangers. Yet scholars have shown that the out-relief (aid given to people living on their own, not in almshouses) extended by Boston and other New England towns to the town's poor—typically consisting of firewood and small cash payments—was not designed to cover living expenses. Annual per capita outlays were higher for those disabled and elderly poor who received pensions or who were boarded with independent householders, given the more involved care they needed.[52] Historians of poor relief in the southern colonies argue that the amount and extent of poor relief given to white residents were greater than in the north, comprising "a reasonable standard of living rather than merely subsistence" and marking off an entitlement denied to persons of color. Pensioners in the wealthy South Carolina port of Charles Town received on average 8 sh., 7 d. per month (which exceeded the estimated cost of food by 3 shillings), whereas their counterparts in Boston and Philadelphia received between 4 and 6 shillings monthly, less than what an individual would pay for food. Concluding from such comparisons, as some scholars do, that in the north authorities' major concern was "reducing expenses" and taxes, not relieving want and suffering as it was in the South, is misguided, however.[53] Rather, the variations in levels of relief and systems of assessing who received relief beg a multitude of questions. We need additional research on welfare mechanisms in specific localities. The modest geographical comparisons made in this essay suggest too that we need a more fine-tuned synthesis, acknowledging the ubiquity of stated principles of Christian charity and civic humanism and rethinking the meanings of generosity in an era when slaves as a group experienced the most entrenched impoverishment, "poor" Indians were not consistently seen as belonging to English towns, arguments based on human rights were emergent, and taxation schemas that raised relief chiefly for the white poor varied greatly.[54]

*   *   *

In the final analysis, New England emerges with a distinctive profile. All British American mainland ports at the mid–eighteenth century had rapidly growing Euro-American populations along with dramatic in-migration and thus struggled with distinguishing poor relief for residents from that for strangers. What stands out is how long a major port town, Robert Love's Boston, and set of colonies, Massachusetts and most of its neighbors, adhered to the effort required for monitoring newcomers as an aspect of what they saw as the best means of extending Christian charity to the deserving poor, both local and foreign. The Massachusetts model elevated the obscure English warning warrant to a highly visible practice because it proved flexible enough to save the towns from extraordinary charges for all manner of sojourners (such as travelers, beggars, casual workers, migrating families, and unwed mothers) while not discouraging the flow of labor. In Boston, we should emphasize, warning strangers joined other rituals of perambulation and surveillance (such as the night watch, the yearly walk of the town bounds, and the gentlemen's annual visitations of the schools and almshouse), working to reassure town leaders and town residents that even Massachusetts's largest town was a well-disciplined "godly city."

Was the warning system "Puritan"? Yes and no. We can explain its impetus and its staying power by religious and civic commitments of the Puritan-minded men and women who founded and provided leadership for most of the New England colonies. But the ideas behind the system were not uniquely Puritan. In adopting a system of closely monitoring migrants, New England settlers were following the same logic that by the early seventeenth century had found widespread approval among English elites and local leaders—Puritan and non-Puritan alike.[55] As Paul A. Slack has written, the individual elements that "godly" reformers put into place were not particularly new. Rather, it was the desire and will to adopt the entire package systematically that distinguished towns aspiring to "godly" governance. Adding searchers, assigning overseers of the poor to wards, and requiring regular written reporting entailed not only a concerted municipal commitment of resources but also hours of time invested by individual volunteers or paid townsmen. In England, Slack argues, many towns "fell far short of the ideal," and by the 1640s most had abandoned any comprehensive program.[56]

As a warner who walked the streets almost daily and identified up to 420 "strangers" per year, Robert Love epitomizes this "constant supervision" that early modern visionaries knew was requisite to maintain their well-ordered towns. Whereas the vision of the "godly citie" was introduced differently and often fitfully elsewhere in the British empire, New England jurisdictions such as Boston throughout the eighteenth century continually renewed their designs for patrolling, guarding, and disciplining the urban landscape.[57]

NOTES

1. *A Report of the Record Commissioners of the City of Boston Containing the Selectmen's Minutes from 1764 through 1768* (Boston, 1889) [hereafter *BTR* for Boston Town Records], XX: 130. Initially, Love was paid through an incentive system, with each of the three warners paid "in proportion to the Number of Persons each." In the first two years under this system, Love took home nearly two-thirds of the allotted sum. From September 1768 until a month before his death in April 1774, Love served as the sole warner; *BTR*, XX: 139, XXIII: 11, 32, 141.

2. For variations in authorities' decisions on whom to warn, see Josiah Henry Benton, *Warning Out in New England, 1656–1817* (Boston: W. B. Clarke Company, 1911; reprint, Bowie, Md.: Heritage Books, 1992), 55–62, and Douglas Lamar Jones, "The Transformation of the Law of Poverty in Eighteenth-Century Massachusetts," in *Law in Colonial Massachusetts, 1630–1800*, ed. Daniel Coquillette (Boston: The Colonial Society of Massachusetts, 1984), 181. For the logic and persistence of regulating migrants in England, see Norma Landau, "The Laws of

Settlement and the Surveillance of Immigration in Eighteenth-Century Kent," *Continuity and Change* 3:3 (1988), 394–420.

3. The average number of parties (solo travelers and kin groups) warned by Love per year from 1765 through 1773 was 265. Warning peaked in Boston in 1767 and 1768; in those years Love warned 324 and 326, respectively. On average, 73 percent of the warned strangers were noted to be solo arrivals.

4. Benton is largely accurate, but he omitted an important Massachusetts statute enacted in 1767.

5. Unfortunately, misimpressions of how warning worked continue to inform the syntheses and textbooks geared to social work professionals. See Phyllis J. Day, *A New History of Social Welfare*, 6th ed. (Boston: Pearson/Allyn & Bacon, 2009), 147; Mimi Abramovitz, *Regulating the Lives of Women: Social Welfare Policy from Colonial Times to the Present*, rev. ed. (Boston: South End Press, 1996), 79–83, 99, and the discussion in Michael Dane Byrd, "White Poor and Poor Relief in Charles Town, 1725–1775: A Prosopography" (Ph.D. diss., University of South Carolina, 2005), 276–300.

6. Cornelia H. Dayton and Sharon V. Salinger, *Warning Out: Robert Love Searches for Strangers in Pre-Revolutionary Boston* (Philadelphia: University of Pennsylvania Press, forthcoming).

7. The column headings are: Persons Warned, Time when, By Whom, Towns they came from, Time they have been here. "Warning Book from Jan. 4, 1745 to 1770," Records of the Boston Overseers of the Poor, Box 1, Folder 3, Massachusetts Historical Society (hereafter MHS).

8. Born in County Antrim to Ulster Scots, Love had possibly imbibed the Scottish notarial tradition according to which it would not be odd for the scrivener to repeat the line "warned in his Majesty's Name to depart the town of Boston in 14 days" in every entry and every copy made.

9. Twenty-six warrants appear to be missing from the 200-plus survivals (Love submitted a warrant two to three times a month); for almost all of those dates, we can reconstruct Love's warnings using the Warning Book, but without the richer details. Love also made a copy each month (on larger sheets of paper, folded) for the Overseers of the Poor; the run for 1767 exists (Records of the Boston Overseers of the Poor, Loose papers, Box 4, MsBosW2, Boston Public Library; we thank Ruth Herndon for drawing our attention to this source). Because the overseers authorized almshouse admissions for many newcomers to town, they needed the warning records to identify which relief recipients would be charged to the town of Boston, which to other towns in Massachusetts, and which to the province treasury. The province's shouldering of responsibility for offering relief to those with settlement outside of Massachusetts is discussed below. For selectmen's orders that warnings be copied for the overseers, see *BTR*, XIX: 43, 130.

10. For recent examples, see J. H. Elliott, *Empires of the Atlantic: Britain and Spain in America, 1492–1830* (New Haven, Conn.: Yale University Press, 2006), 263

("Poor law legislation in Massachusetts was even harsher than its English origi-nal. Stern measures were taken to . . . 'warn out' unwanted paupers"), and Gary B. Nash, "Poverty and Politics in Early American History," in *Down and Out in Early America*, ed. Billy G. Smith (University Park: The Pennsylvania State University Press, 2004), 4 (the midcentury "influx of poor people"—"transients warned out"—pressured town officials to "enforce more rigorously the resi-dency laws that cut poor relief off from transients who took to the road").

11. We identified removal orders and warrants by combing the selectmen minutes, sessions court papers, and the 1745–70 Warning Book. Towns had the option of following up a warning with a warrant from a single justice of the peace order-ing the removal of any stranger who lingered fourteen days after being warned and failed to offer security. Constables carried out the order by escorting the named person(s) to the town border or delivering them to the selectmen in the town where they were believed to have legal settlement. As in England, localities mostly avoided the costly business of removing (on average, several pounds), reserving it mostly for young married couples with children and "dis-orderly" or frequently pregnant single women. See E. M. Hampson, *The Treat-ment of Poverty in Cambridgeshire, 1597–1834* (Cambridge: Cambridge University Press, 1934), 137, and James Stephen Taylor, "The Impact of Pauper Settlement, 1691–1834," *Past and Present* 73 (Nov. 1976): 62.

12. Benton, *Warning Out*, 116; Lawrence M. Friedman, *A History of American Law*, 2d ed. (New York: Simon and Schuster, 1985), 90 (warning out "was not a sentence of banishment, but a disclaimer of responsibility"); Gary B. Nash, *The Urban Crucible: Social Change, Political Consciousness, and the Origins of the American Revolution* (Cambridge, Mass.: Harvard University Press, 1979), 185. William Pencak, like us, traced some of those warned in the 1760s to the Boston roll of one of the few surviving provincial tax evaluations, that of 1771, showing that they stayed in Boston; *War, Politics, and Revolution in Provincial Massachu-setts* (Boston: Northeastern University Press, 1981), 202.

13. Several strangers arriving from outside the colony told Love when he warned them on their first day in town that they wanted "to git into the" almshouse, indicating that information circulated afar about the province's policy. The province poor account's origins lay in relief given to white settlers burned out in King Philip's War and in legislative provisions from 1701 onward. See Robert W. Kelso, *The History of Public Poor Relief in Massachusetts, 1620–1920* (Boston: Houghton Mifflin, 1922), 121–23, and Stephen Edward Wiberly Jr., "Four Cities: Public Poor Relief in Urban America, 1700–1775" (Ph.D. dissertation, Yale Uni-versity, 1975), 54–55, 208. For early references to the province account, see *The Acts and Resolves, Public and Private, of the Province of the Massachusetts Bay . . .* 21 vols. (Boston: Wright and Potter, 1869–1922), I, 451–53, 469; IX, 47, 474 [here-after, *Acts and Resolves*]; BTR, XV: 17.

14. *Cities in Revolt: Urban Life in America, 1745–1776* (New York: Alfred A. Knopf, 1955), 319–20 (emphasis added); see also 123. Technically, there was no separate

province poor rate; taxpayers were contributing to the province poor account by paying their province tax. Without mentioning them in statutes, starting in the 1680s Massachusetts towns occasionally issued certificates indemnifying another town for charges arising from a specific individual who had moved there; for early examples, see *BTR*, VII: 148, 149, 170, 182, 188–89, 199, and for a typical town-to-town negotiation that produced certificates, see *BTR*, XIII: 294–95, 312–13, 317.

15. *The Common Law in Colonial America*, Vol. I: *The Chesapeake and New England, 1607–1660* (New York: Oxford University Press, 2008), 7, 65, 59. Nelson points to a 1640 Salem case in which "one defendant was sentenced to time in the stocks for 'being uncharitable to a poor man in distress'" (59). For additional commentary on Puritan jurisprudence, see Cornelia H. Dayton, *Women before the Bar: Gender, Law, and Society in Connecticut, 1639–1789* (Chapel Hill: Omohundro Institute of Early American History and Culture and University of North Carolina Press, 1995), 27–34.

16. In a study of Massachusetts town governance, Barry Levy draws similar conclusions about the reformist influence of civic humanism; however, he too often equates warning with physical removal and mistakenly asserts that no province poor account existed before 1793; *Town Born: The Political Economy of New England from Its Founding to the Revolution* (Philadelphia: University of Pennsylvania Press, 2009), esp. 17–34, 108–10, 293.

17. Benton, *Warning Out*, 4–5, quoting Francis Palgrave, *Rise and Progress of the English Commonwealth* (London, 1832), Part I, 83, on the laws of the Salic Franks. Taylor similarly believes that the earliest settlement restrictions can be seen "in the laws of Anglo-Saxon kings" and seventh-century practices of hospitality to travelers; these were cited also by the seventeenth-century treatise writer Michael Dalton; see Taylor, "Impact of Pauper Settlement," 47–48. Several institutional historians of the late nineteenth and early twentieth centuries shared an obsession with the Saxon English roots of "our race"; see Charles Howard Shinn, *Mining Camps: A Study in American Frontier Government* (New York: Charles Scribner's Sons, 1885), 2–3, 8, 22–23; and Herbert Baxter Adams, *The Germanic Origin of New England Towns*, Johns Hopkins University Studies in Historical and Political Science II (Baltimore: N. Murray, 1882).

18. Ex officio c. D. Thomas Morgan, chaplain of Eastchurch (Canterbury 1492), KAO, Act book P.R.C. 3.1, f.26: "Postea judex decrevit et monuit predictum dominum Thomam quod amoveat se ab ista jurisdictione citra festum Michaelis." [Translation: "Afterwards, the judge decreed and warned the aforesaid Master Thomas that he remove himself from that very jurisdiction before the feast of (Saint) Michael."] Richard Helmholz, personal communication, February 5, 2007, enclosing his transcription of five cases. In the four other cases, a verb such as "recedat" was used instead of "monuit." Thanks to Professor Helmholz, and to Professor Alan Ward for translation.

19. Margo Todd, *Christian Humanism and the Puritan Social Order* (New York: Cambridge University Press, 1987), 137–41, 145–46; and Bronislaw Geremek,

Poverty: A History, trans. Agnieszka Kolakowska (Cambridge, Mass.: Blackwell, 1994), 136–41, 186–96. Elements of the Bruges plan, and one implemented in Ypres, included prohibiting begging, setting the able poor to work, and cajoling propertied city residents into contributing to a poor fund. Accounts of both schemes were translated and published in England, thus shaping early legislation and discussions about how to address poverty.

20. On Norwich's reorganization of poor relief in 1570–71, see E. M. Leonard, *The Early History of English Poor Relief* (Cambridge: Cambridge University Press, 1900), 103–7, and the documents in Appendices II and III. Leonard notes that the system worked for about ten years in the utopian way that its creators had hoped for, and that their pride in providing better for the town's poor and in saving money in overall expenses comes through clearly in the mayor's books and other records.

21. William Hunt, *The Puritan Moment: The Coming of Revolution in an English County* (Cambridge, Mass.: Harvard University Press, 1983), 79–84, 252; Leonard, *Early History of English Poor Relief*, 297; Marjorie K. McIntosh, "Local Responses to the Poor in Late Medieval and Tudor England," *Continuity and Change* 3 (Aug. 1988), 211. Most of these authors stress the Puritan or radical Protestant impulse behind parish-initiated reform. For a particularly revealing vision, see Steve Hindle's analysis of the memorandum book left by Alexander Strange, vicar of Layston: "Exclusion Crises: Poverty, Migration and Parochial Responsibility in English Rural Communities, c. 1560–1660," *Rural History* 7: 2 (1996), 131–38.

22. Robert Jenison, *The Cities Safetie . . .* (London, 1630), 11, 29, quoted in Paul Slack, *From Reformation to Improvement: Public Welfare in Early Modern England* (Oxford: Clarendon Press, 1999), 29; see also 30–31. On Geneva as a model, see Hunt, *Puritan Moment*, 83–84, 252. On Geneva's policies toward the poor, see Robert M. Kingdon, "Social Welfare in Calvin's Geneva," *American Historical Review* 76 (Feb. 1971), 50–69; William C. Innes and Susan Cembalisty-Innes, *Social Concern in Calvin's Geneva* (Allison Park, Penn.: Pickwick Publications, 1983); and Jeannine E. Olson, *Calvin and Social Welfare: Deacons and the 'Bourse Francaise'* (Selinsgrove, Penn.: Susquehanna University Press, 1989). For an interpretation that does not stress the role of "the godly," see Anthony Fletcher, *Reform in the Provinces: The Government of Stuart England* (New Haven, Conn.: Yale University Press, 1986), 351–73. For Anglican involvement, see Marjorie K. McIntosh, "Networks of Care in Elizabethan Towns: The Example of Hadleigh, Suffolk," in Peregrine Horden and Richard Smith, eds., *The Locus of Care: Families, Communities, Institutions, and the Provision of Welfare since Antiquity* (New York: Routledge, 1998), 75–76.

23. Philip Styles, "The Evolution of the Law of Settlement," in Styles, *Studies in Seventeenth Century West Midlands History* (Kineton, Eng.: Roundwood Press, 1978), 178, 182.

24. Leonard, *Early History of English Poor Relief*, 108; Nathaniel Bacon, *The Annalls of Ipswich. The Lawes Customes and Government of the Same. Collected out of the Records Bookes and Writings of that Towne*, ed. William H. Richardson (Ipswich, Eng., 1884), 249, 319, 337, 351 (ordering weekly searches, February 1587). What

happened to the non-inhabitants who were found is not clear, but on May 17, 1599, "A fforrainer, his wife and children, [were] ordered to depart the Towne" (398). For searches by ward ordered by the common council of London in 1574, see Leonard, *Early History of English Poor Relief*, 307.

25. Helen Raine, "Christopher Fawsett Against the Inmates: An Aspect of Poor Law Administration in the Early Seventeenth Century," *Surrey Archaeological Collections* 66 (1969), 79–85.

26. McIntosh offers the example of Bury St. Edmunds, which conducted periodic checks of each ward for families likely to be chargeable—and expelled them (forty-three in the month of January 1571) if a townsman did not come forward to post bond that they would never be chargeable. In the late 1500s, "the chief worry concerning poor outsiders was that they might remain in the community for the three years which entitled them to relief"; "Local Responses to the Poor," 232–33. For an analysis of the amounts demanded in these bonds, to whom they applied, and how long they lasted, see Styles, "Evolution of the Law of Settlement," 181–84. For regular searches and demands for security in St. Albans and the borough of Stratford, see Leonard, *Early History of English Poor Relief*, 108–9, and Styles, "Evolution of the Law of Settlement," 178–79.

27. Styles, "Evolution of the Law of Settlement," 178–81. Styles points out (181) that many of these methods were attempts to get around the patent fact that, before 1662, town officials could not legally order removals except under the vagrancy laws. Placing the burden on the landlord rather than on the inmate preserved "the common law right to freedom of movement of all who could not be classed as rogues and vagabonds" (177–78). When parish officials became aggressive about ordering removals, many of these were in fact illegal, and a tussle between local officials and supervising JPs ensued, especially in the 1630s to 1650s (185). See also Fletcher, *Reform in the Provinces*, 202–4.

28. Norma Landau, "Who Was Subjected to the Laws of Settlement? Procedure under the Settlement Laws in Eighteenth-Century England," *Agricultural History Review* 43:2 (1995), 139–59, and *idem*, "The Application of the Laws of Settlement in Eighteenth-Century England," Working Paper Series No. 67, Agricultural History Center, University of California, Davis, June 1992. For a succinct summary of the late-seventeenth-century acts, see Paul Slack, *Poverty and Policy in Tudor and Stuart England* (New York: Longman, 1988), 194–95.

29. Richard Burn, *The Justice of the Peace and Parish Officer* . . . 11th ed., Vol. 3 (London, 1769), 285–515. Other groups monitored under English laws were householders renting for under £10 a year, apprentices, and vagrants.

30. Before 1685, English parishes in many instances had to remove the incomer to block settlement by residency. After that date, newcomers not qualified for settlement were required to give notice of their presence within days of arrival, and only if they did so (and few migrants did) did the "residency" clock start. Pennsylvania adopted this notice rule in 1734, but Massachusetts waited until 1767 to do so, and yet, for reasons we offer below, towns continued to warn (that is, register) strangers.

31. Miller was warned on November 2 (Suffolk File 88037, Massachusetts State Archives). The next day, he was admitted to the almshouse on the province account; he died there six days later; the almshouse keeper estimated his age as forty; *The Eighteenth-Century Records of the Boston Overseers of the Poor*, Eric Nellis and Anne Decker Cecere, eds. (Boston: The Colonial Society of Massachusetts, 2007), 185, 297.

32. [Richard Kilburne,] *Choice Presidents Upon all Acts of Parliament, Relating to the Office and Duty of a Justice of the Peace . . .* 5th ed. (London, 1694), 385–86. Warning in this sense is not found in Burn, *Justice of the Peace and Parish Officer*. We have also searched in the removal orders in *[Warwickshire] Quarter Sessions Order Books . . .*, S. C. Ratcliff and H. C. Johnson, eds., Vols. 2 and 3 (Warwick: L. E. Stephens, 1935–39); and *Records of the Borough of Leicester*, ed. Mary Bateson, revised by W. H. Stevenson and J. E. Stocks, Vol. 3 (London: C. J. Clay, 1905); and consulted legal compendia such as the 1635, 1677, and 1742 London editions of Michael Dalton, *The Country Justice . . .* ; Edmund Bott, *Decisions of the Court of King's Bench upon the Laws Relating to the Poor. Originally published by Edmund Bott, Esq. . . . Now Revised, Corrected, and Considerably Enlarged. . . . The Third Edition . . .* by Francis Const, 2 vols. (London, 1793); and James Burrow, *A Series of the Decisions of the Court of King's Bench upon Settlement Cases from the Death of Lord Raymond in March 1732*, 2 vols. (London, 1768).

33. Bacon, *Annalls of Ipswich*, 319. Bacon was elected Recorder of Ipswich in 1642 and later became an MP, Judge of the High Court of Admiralty, and a master of the Court of Requests (*ibid.*, ii). "Warned out" or "warned away" appears twice with regard to being ordered to leave a lodging-place (versus a parish); see Hindle, "Exclusion Crises," 146 n.60, quoting a 1646 usage in the Hertfordshire County Records, V, 382; and Raine, "Christopher Fawsett Against the Inmates," 84. We conducted our search for the language of warning in the secondary literature on local British history and in printed parish records in the collections of the Huntington Library, San Marino, California, in summer 2002.

34. Styles, "Evolution," 199; Landau, personal communication, September 29, 2006. In Massachusetts, the practice of "returning" the names of strangers "and their qualities" to a court is first mentioned in a June 1650 law (quoted in Benton, *Warning Out*, 47). In 1671, Boston selectmen began ordering that the names of strangers who remained in Boston despite not having been admitted as inhabitants of the town or colony be returned to the county court (*BTR*, VII: 58–128, *passim*).

35. Rhode Island used warning to end a nonsettled resident's stay rather than a marker of nonsettlement upon the person's arrival; see Ruth Wallis Herndon, *Unwelcome Americans: Living on the Margin in Early New England* (Philadelphia: University of Pennsylvania Press, 2001), 4–15.

36. The 1763 petition is quoted in Nash, *Urban Crucible*, 255; see also 327. See also Wiberly, "Four Cities," 48–49, and Robert E. Cray Jr., *Paupers and Poor Relief in New York City and Its Rural Environs, 1700–1830* (Philadelphia: Temple University Press, 1988), 73.

37. The extant quarter sessions docket books for Philadelphia County contain many JP removal orders appealed and quashed, but these lack the level of detail that might include references to warning (Dockets, 1753–60, 1773–80, Philadelphia City Archives). William E. Nelson shared with us his notes on the docket books for Northampton, Lancaster, and York counties in Pennsylvania: these contain litigation over removal orders, but no language of warning; personal communication, October 27, 2010.

38. We are grateful to the legal historian Holly Brewer for alerting us that she had seen warning mentioned in Chester County records. See Brewer, *By Birth or Consent: Children, Law, and the Anglo-American Revolution in Authority* (Chapel Hill: University of North Carolina Press for the Omohundro Institute of Early American History and Culture, 2005), 257n45. East Bradford Township Book, MS 76209; West Bradford Township Accounts, MS 76214; East Caln Township, Accounts of the Poor, 1735–1757, MS 13524; and Goshen Township Account book, 1718–1869, Chester County Historical Society.

39. Testimony of Joseph Nicklin, in Folder on Margaret Power, Chester County Court of Quarter Sessions, Clerk of Courts, Overseer of the Poor Petitions, 1722–1798, Chester County Archives [hereafter, CCA]. In the same document, two overseers who served in 1727 signed a similar statement that under their watch Powers "was warned to go out of the" township. A fragmentary parchment pertaining to the case also notes that Powers, originally from Ireland, had been "by the successive Overseers [of Concord] legally warned out."

40. The cases of William Evans, Ann Worrilaw, Ann Noys, Elizabeth Knight, and Mary Massia, *ibid.* In Worrilaw's case, the Thornbury overseers contended that their counterparts in Edgmont failed to warn her, which was one of the reasons why her legal settlement was there. Because of time constraints, we were not able to read all petitions in the box, which are arranged alphabetically by the pauper's name. Working from the docket book, we read almost all cases from the 1720s–1750s and several from the 1760s.

41. Examinations of Ann Noys [1748]; Anne Dodd, 1766; and others, *ibid.*

42. *A Compilation of the Laws of the State of Pennsylvania, Relative to the Poor from the Year 1700, to 1795, Inclusive* (Philadelphia, 1796). Bridenbaugh (*Cities in Revolt*, 123) refers to "a careful registration system" worked out in Pennsylvania in the 1730s that he infers was allowed to lapse. He may have been referring to Section 7 of the 1734 supplemental act, by which overseers were to deliver to a JP "a fair duplicate" of their rates for the poor and "fair and true lists of the poor . . . [with pertinent] certificates and notices," and, further, to keep these details in in a book to "be delivered" to their successors in office (*Compilation*, 27–28).

43. Massachusetts never incorporated the English options of office-holding, paying taxes, or renting as ways of gaining settlement. It hewed closely to the rule of townsmen giving positive consent. Otherwise, one gained settlement by being born in a town (until 1767), residing for one year without being warned (also until 1767), opting to stay in the town where one had served out one's

apprenticeship, and (for a woman) marrying a legal inhabitant. See *Acts and Resolves*, I: 451–52, II: 994–95. It is significant that the Boston editors of a pirated version of Burn's JP manual left out the long section on settlement law and explained that they omitted sections discussing "acts of the British Parliament, which can never have any relation to this colony"; *An Abridgment of Burn's Justice of the Peace and Parish Officer, To Which Is Added an Appendix . . .* (Boston: Printed for Joseph Greenleaf, 1773). South Carolina was another outlier; its 1712 law stipulated only one pathway to settlement—peaceable residence for three months without removal (extended to twelve months in 1768); Nicholas Trott, *The Laws of the Province of South Carolina*, 2 vols. (Charleston, 1736), I: 270–75.

44. Cray, *Paupers and Poor Relief in New York City*, 55. Beyond querying experts who have studied colonial New York records, we have not checked whether loose papers survive for early sessions courts in Suffolk, Westchester, or Albany counties. Jean R. Soderlund, "The Delaware Indians and Poverty in Colonial New Jersey," in *Down and Out in Early America*, 289–311; John A. Grigg, "'Ye relief of ye poor of sd towne': Poverty and Localism in Eighteenth-Century New Jersey," *New Jersey History* 125:2 (2010), 23–35; Nottingham Township Minute Book, published in *Proceedings of the New Jersey Historical Society* 58 (1940): 22–44.

45. Zachary Ryan Calo, "From Poor Relief to the Poorhouse: The Response to Poverty in Prince George's County, 1710–1770," *Maryland Historical Magazine* 93 (Winter 1998): 393–427; John K. Nelson, *A Blessed Company: Parishes, Parsons, and Parishioners in Anglican Virginia, 1690–1776* (Chapel Hill: University of North Carolina Press, 2001), 70–83; Alan D. Watson, "Public Poor Relief in Colonial North Carolina," *North Carolina Historical Review* 54 (October 1977): 347–66; Tim Lockley, "Rural Poor Relief in Colonial South Carolina," *The Historical Journal* 48 (December 2005), 955–76.

46. See the February 1724 case of Elizabeth Roost, Chester County Court of Quarter Sessions, Clerk of Courts, Dockets, Vol. for 1723–1733, and the February 1748 ruling in the case of Jane Andrews, Overseer of the Poor Petitions, 1722–1798, CCA; and Grigg, "Poverty and Localism in New Jersey," 33, for a case involving "an old Indian" who evidently was not accounted a legal inhabitant. Similarly, in Massachusetts, towns such as Natick, where Indians had much earlier been gathered by English missionaries to reside in a "praying town," refused to consider Indians as the town poor and instead charged the province account; Jean M. O'Brien, *Dispossession by Degrees: Indian Land and Identity in Natick, Massachusetts, 1650–1790* (New York: Cambridge University Press, 1997), 193–98.

47. Province Treasury records for 1768–69 and 1769–70, Mass. Archives 125: 340–59, 363–92, Massachusetts State Archives, Boston. In both years, the payments for the province poor constituted about 10 percent of all appropriations.

48. See Timothy James Lockley, *Welfare and Charity in the Antebellum South* (Gainesville: University Press of Florida, 2007), 6; Virginia Bernhard, "Poverty and the Social Order in Seventeenth-Century Virginia," *Virginia Magazine of History and Biography* 85 (April 1977), 152–55. On changing views among Boston

clergymen, see J. Richard Olivas, "'God Helps Those Who Help Themselves': Religious Explanations of Poverty in Colonial Massachusetts, 1630–1776," in *Down and Out in Early America*, 262–88.

49. For examples of such pleas, see Nash, *Urban Crucible*, 255, 327; for the burden of supporting nonresident paupers in the New York city almshouse, see Cray, *Paupers and Poor Relief*, 73.

50. Beyond Pennsylvania's 1718 and 1734 statutes, New Jersey enacted a settlement law in 1754; New York did so belatedly in 1773, and Delaware in 1775. In the South, only South Carolina passed a comprehensive poor law before the 1760s.

51. See Byrd, "White Poor and Poor Relief in Charles Town," Chap. 8, and Lockley, "Rural Poor Relief." Similarly, Philadelphia overseers paid the passages of more than 200 nonsettled poor from 1768 to 1775 (years for which their minutes survive); Wiberly, "Four Cities," 48–56.

52. For different perspectives on why costs were higher for those boarded versus those on outrelief, see Calo, "Response to Poverty in Prince George's County," 398–400, and Geoffrey Guest, "The Boarding of the Dependent Poor in Colonial America," *Social Service Review* 63 (March 1989), 92–112. In midcentury Massachusetts, annual pensions to incapacitated veterans ranged from £3–5; *Acts and Resolves*, XI–XVI, passim. Such former provincial soldiers often received up to £100 in compensation for medical bills and upkeep before the granting of a pension; Casey Green, "Valuing the Body: Contractual Obligations and Disabled Veterans' Petitions in Colonial Massachusetts, 1727–1755," unpublished graduate research seminar paper, University of Connecticut, Spring 2010.

53. For North–South comparisons, see Lockley, *Welfare and Charity in the Antebellum South*, 5–12 (quoted phrase, 6); and Wiberly, "Four Cities," 157–58. Differences in regional practices are often overstated: As in Charleston, recipients in Massachusetts sometimes received public support for decades. For parish levies and relief to whites in Virginia, see Nelson, *A Blessed Company*, 43–47, 70–84.

54. For the point that poor relief analyses cannot ignore wider contexts of immiseration, see Philip D. Morgan, "Slaves and Poverty," in *Down and Out in Early America,* 93–96. For a comparison between Massachusetts's "sophisticated" and democratically based province tax system with those of Virginia and other colonies, see Robin L. Einhorn, *American Taxation, American Slavery* (Chicago: University of Chicago Press, 2006), Part I.

55. For more on this debate, see Margaret Spufford, "Puritanism and Social Control?" in Anthony Fletcher and John Stevenson, eds., *Order and Disorder in Early Modern England* (New York: Cambridge University Press, 1985), 41–57; Todd, *Christian Humanism*, Chap. 5; and Paul A. Fideler, "Introduction [to Symposium on the Study of the Early Modern Poor and Poverty Relief]: Impressions of a Century of Historiography," *Albion* 32 (Autumn 2000), 381–407.

56. Slack, *From Reformation to Improvement*, 46–52 (quote on 49).

57. *Ibid.*, 50–52.

5

Ambiguities of Free Labor Revisited

The Convict Labor Question in Progressive-Era New York

BARRY CUSHMAN

Professor William E. Nelson was among the first scholars to identify the connections between antebellum free-labor ideology and late-nineteenth- and early-twentieth-century substantive due process. The article in which he did so was published in the *Harvard Law Review* in January 1974, back when Nelson was still a young Assistant Professor of Law at the University of Pennsylvania. Professor Nelson showed that the antebellum period's "jurisprudence of antislavery" was characterized by recognition of rights of property and contract, and of the rights to free trade and to immunity from class legislation, as among "the core rights to which all men were inherently entitled."[1] He went on to elaborate the ways in which antislavery jurists ascending to the bench in the postbellum era brought these ideas to bear in their interpretations of Section 1 of the Fourteenth Amendment, with such doctrines as liberty of contract and the prohibition on class legislation.[2]

With an observation on which he would later elaborate in illuminating detail in his prizewinning book on the Fourteenth Amendment,[3] however, Professor Nelson warned that "human rights concepts . . . are of no help in deciding the great mass of cases in which two or more possible results are equally consistent with men's enjoyment of their 'natural rights.'"[4] This essay brings that insight into the ambiguities of the Fourteenth Amendment to bear on a central issue confronting liberal reformers in the late nineteenth and early twentieth centuries: convict labor. Throughout the nineteenth century, organized workers had agitated for reform of the system of prison labor, contending that prison-made goods competed unfairly with goods produced in the private economy. They viewed convict labor as a species of slave labor that threatened to degrade free laborers, impeding their capacity to acquire capital and to enjoy the upward social mobility that free-labor ideology promised to industrious, disciplined workmen. Professor Nelson's native New York became a leader in this reform effort. The legislature abolished various objectionable forms of convict labor and prohibited the sale on the private market of goods manufactured in its prisons. Convict-made goods produced in other states, however, continued to offer competition with products produced by free labor in New York, and the New York statutes regulating the sale of these out-of-state goods raised contentious issues under both the Dormant Commerce Clause and the Fourteenth Amendment. As Professor Nelson pointed out in his 1974 article, late-nineteenth-century jurists viewed the inherent right of freedom of contract as embracing "the right to use and dispose of property." "Every man . . . had a 'natural right to sell or keep his commodities as best suit[ed] his own purpose.'" "[T]he right to use and dispose of property was viewed as a necessary consequence of the right to acquire and hold it."[5] The question presented under the Fourteenth Amendment was whether New York's effort to protect its free laborers deprived the owner of convict-made goods of property rights without due process or denied him equal protection of the laws. Put another way, the question was whether free-labor ideology operated not only as a source of rights, protecting the individual from interferences with his Fourteenth Amendment liberty and property interests, but also as a source of power, underwriting state regulation of privately owned goods. That question ultimately would be answered in the affirmative, but only after a half-century of contentious debate over the ambiguous legacy of free-labor ideology.

*   *   *

Throughout the nineteenth century, New York State had been a national leader in the effort to reform state penitentiaries.[6] As one scholar has put it, "Pre-eminent among the northern industrial states, New York conducted more investigations, tried more laws, and expended more effort in the pursuit of a solution to the competition of convict labor than any other."[7] "Situated at the center of much of labor's political agitation, this state experienced from the first the full gamut of forces playing around the problem. It devised the legislation that formed the basis for much of the discussion and practice of its neighbors in succeeding years."[8] The principal target of labor leaders and prison reformers was the contract labor system, under which private employers would provide machinery and supervise inmates in the production of goods to be sold on the open market. Workers "continually denounced the system as unfair competition and an affront to their dignity as free laborers."[9] By the decade of the 1880s, this campaign began to bear fruit. As *The Nation* would later recount the story, in 1883

> the professional friends of labor started the cry that this contract convict labor was injuring honest workingmen by reducing the price of commodities, and consequently reducing wages. It was an old cry revived in new form. . . . It was made in the Legislature of 1883, when the fear of the labor vote was especially aggravated, and the result was that a bill was passed providing for submitting to the people the question of abolishing the system.[10]

In what the New York Commissioner of Labor described as "the largest vote total recorded in New York history on 'any proposition ever submitted to the people of the State,'" voters favored abolition by a margin of 405,882 to 266,966.[11] In the spring of 1884 the state legislature complied with this mandate by enacting a statute prohibiting the renewal of existing contracts. Superintendent of Prisons Isaac V. Baker Jr. was instructed henceforth to operate the prisons on the "public account" system, under which goods produced by inmates would be sold on the open market only by the state on its own account.[12]

As the existing contracts expired, however, the wardens found themselves deprived of the staff, machinery, raw materials, and capital necessary to make the transition. As a consequence, "unemployment in the prisons soared."[13] The situation at Auburn was "desperate," while the warden at Elmira "was almost at his wit's end."[14] In 1886, the legislature responded by permitting employment of convicts under both the public account and the "piece-price" system, under which private employers would provide machinery and raw materials, but the inmates would manufacture products under the direction and supervision of prison officials instead of private parties.[15] In 1888 the legislature disregarded the advice of the Prison Labor Commission and again shifted gears with the enactment of the Yates Law, which prohibited both contract labor and piece-price arrangements, and abolished "all manufacture that used motive-power machinery. Only production by hand labor was allowed, and then only for the use of state institutions." The Yates Law, as one scholar observed, "succeeded in disjointing" the State's "entire prison system." "Immediately the recent surpluses were exchanged for enormous deficits. . . ."[16] The legislature quickly backtracked the following year by enacting the Fassett Law, which prohibited contract labor but authorized use of both the piece-price and public account systems. The statute further limited the number of prisoners working in any particular industry to 5 percent of the number of free workers in the state working in that industry.[17]

In 1894, with the country in the grip of a severe economic downturn, the voters of New York adopted an amendment to the state constitution mandating the "state-use" system of convict labor. Under the terms of the amendment, the state was forbidden after January 1, 1897, to hire out the labor of its convicts to private parties, and goods made by convicts in state institutions could be disposed of only to the state and its political subdivisions, and not placed on the private market.[18] No one doubted that the state possessed the authority so to restrict the sale of goods produced in its own prisons. Whether New York could regulate the private market in goods produced in the prisons of other states and then shipped into the Empire State, however, was another matter. In *Leisy v. Hardin*, decided in 1890, the U.S. Supreme Court had held that the Dormant Commerce Clause prohibited states from regulating the sale of alcohol shipped into a dry state from a wet state, so long as the booze remained in its original package.[19] Congress lifted this Dormant Commerce Clause disability with the Wilson Act the following year.[20] The statute, which allowed states to regulate liquor in its original package upon arrival and delivery in the state of destination, was upheld by the Supreme Court in *In re Rahrer*.[21] Reformers recognized a cognate problem with respect to convict-made goods, and the success of this strategy of "divesting" liquor of its interstate character prompted a decades-long effort to secure a comparable bill for the products of prison labor.

In fact, federal efforts to regulate interstate commerce in prison-made goods had begun in 1888. In March of that year the Court had handed down a decision foreshadowing *Leisy*,[22] and that May Representative John Joseph O'Neill (D–MO) introduced "A bill to protect free labor and the industries in which it is employed from the injurious effects of convict labor by confining the sale of goods, wares, and merchandise manufactured by convict labor to the State in which they are produced."[23] In other words, the bill forbade interstate shipment of prison-made products. The bill never came to a vote, but the remarks of Stephen V. White (R–NY) during the floor debates foreshadowed the difficulties that members of the state's judiciary would experience when grappling with the constitutional issues presented by statutes regulating the sale of convict-made goods. White professed deep sympathy with the objective of protecting "American free labor from competition with foreign pauper and domestic convict labor." But he was convinced that the O'Neill bill was unconstitutional. "The State which properly punishes its criminals can properly employ them at labor, and the product of that labor is property of equal dignity and consideration under the Constitution with any other product of man's labor," White argued.

> If Congress, under its authority to regulate commerce between the States, can prevent all commerce between the States in the product of prison labor, it can prevent all commerce in the product of our farm labor or that of our paid operators in factories. If the proposition were before us to prevent absolutely the shipment of wheat from one State to another, or of cotton goods from one State to another, I believe we would all agree that we did not have such power of prohibition under the power of regulation of commerce.

If Congress could "prohibit goods manufactured by one establishment from transshipment we can in like manner prohibit goods from all establishments." White believed that "adequate relief" could "be had through the action of the States, whose Legislatures have undoubted right to direct that their own convict labor should not be permitted to compete with American labor." But he regretfully concluded that the O'Neill bill was "unconstitutional because it prevents commerce instead of regulating it, and because it takes lawful property from its owner without due process of law."[24] Dealers in convict-made merchandise acquired lawful property rights in those goods, and the protection of the interests of free labor did not justify governmental abridgement of those rights.

A similar question would come to the New York Court of Appeals in 1898. In 1896 the New York legislature enacted a statute making it a misdemeanor to sell or expose for sale goods made in any prison without attaching to them a label disclosing them to be "Convict-Made" and revealing the name of the prison in which they had been produced.[25] The state regime thus prohibited the sale of convict-made goods produced in New York and required the labeling of convict-made goods produced outside the state. Samuel K. Hawkins was charged with offering for sale a scrub brush produced in an Ohio prison without the label required by the statute. In October 1898 a sharply divided New York Court of Appeals held that the statute violated the dormant Commerce Clause.[26] Three of the court's seven judges dissented from the judgment: Republicans Edward T. Bartlett and Albert Haight, and Chief Judge and future Democratic presidential nominee Alton B. Parker. Bartlett wrote a lengthy dissent; Parker added a brief memorandum concurring with Bartlett.

Bartlett contended that the statute did not violate the Commerce Clause because it was a legitimate exercise of the state's police power "to promote the public welfare and prosperity" by implementing "the deliberate policy of this state that free labor shall be protected from disastrous competition with the convict system, which pays to the workman no wages, and therefore finds little difficulty in supplanting the wage earner in the public markets." It was "self-evident that the protection of free labor from competition with convict-made goods in our domestic markets" would "promote the public welfare and prosperity." A statute that had as its "purpose, in pursuance of an enlightened public policy, to promote and protect the interests of free labor as against convict labor" was surely not "beyond the power of a sovereign state to enact." It was "most fitting," Bartlett concluded, "that the state should protect its citizens, and the interests of free labor."[27]

The opinion for the majority was written by Democrat Denis O'Brien, who maintained that the statute was "in conflict with the commerce clause of the federal constitution."[28] This judgment confirmed that of a 4–1 decision of the Appellate Division's Third Department, which had concluded that the statute could not "be sustained as a valid exercise of the police power of the state" and therefore "must be condemned as a violation" of "the interstate commerce provision of the national constitution."[29] Much of Republican Justice John R. Putnam's reasoning for the Appellate Division would be echoed in O'Brien's opinion. Putnam explained that it had not been alleged in the Hawkins indictment "that the brush was not a good one; was not the same, in all regards, as that made by other than convict labor."[30] Nor was it "claimed to have been an inferior or deceptive article." It was "an ordinary merchantable scrub brush."[31] It was not an article "clearly injurious to the lives, health, or welfare of the people."[32] Such a "merchantable article"[33] was "an article of commerce,"[34] and "the police power of a state only extends to property which does not belong to commerce."[35] Because Hawkins's scrub brush was not an outlaw of commerce, the "burden" placed upon its sale by the New York statute offended the Dormant Commerce Clause.[36]

O'Brien followed Putnam in rejecting the claim that the statute constituted a legitimate exercise of the state's police power. It was "not claimed that there is any difference in the quality of this scrubbing brush when compared with one of the same grade or character made outside the prisons." Nor was there any "pretense that the act was passed to suppress any fraudulent practice." The sole "purpose of the law was to promote the welfare of the laboring classes by suppressing, in some measure, the sale of prison-made goods."[37] O'Brien insisted that protecting the interests of free laborers in New York was not a police power objective that could justify the statute's regulation of interstate commerce. New York could not "by hostile legislation drive the cheaper-made goods out of its markets, even though such legislation would increase the wages of its own workmen. Trade and commerce between the states must be left free."[38] "A citizen of this state who happens to buy goods made in a prison in Ohio has the right to put them upon the market here on their own merits," O'Brien insisted, "and if this right is restricted by penal law, while the same goods made in factories are untouched, such a law is a restriction upon the freedom of commerce, and the objection to it is not removed by the fact that it may have been enacted in the guise of a police regulation."[39]

This holding that the labeling regulation was not within the state's police power to enact might be taken to have implications for its status under the Fourteenth Amendment. In its discussion of the Dormant Commerce Clause issue, the Appellate Division had occasionally made brief statements suggesting that Fourteenth Amendment concerns were implicated.[40] That court had opined that Hawkins's "merchantable scrub brush" was "property owned by the defendant, and which he had a right to own, possess, and dispose of without any restrictions whatever."[41] The court had rested its decision on the Dormant Commerce Clause alone, but its language suggested the possibility that its judgment might also rest on the Due Process Clause.

But the fact that a police power rationale did not pass muster under the Dormant Commerce Clause did not necessarily imply that it would not suffice to support state regulation under the Fourteenth Amendment. *Leisy* prohibited regulation of sales of out-of-state liquor in its original package, but the states clearly possessed power to prohibit the sale of alcohol over which they had jurisdiction.[42] Similarly, *Schollenberger v. Pennsylvania*[43] held that the Dormant Commerce Clause prevented the state from regulating original-package sales of oleomargarine, but the state was otherwise free to prohibit local sales of the product.[44] The Court of Appeals' holding under the Dormant Commerce Clause therefore left open the question of whether the statute requiring that convict-made goods be labeled would be constitutional were the Dormant Commerce Clause disability removed by congressional action, or were the prison-made product no longer in its original package.

It was to this question that O'Brien next turned. O'Brien concluded that the New York labeling statute deprived Hawkins of his property without due process of law. "The scrubbing brush in question was beyond all doubt an article of property in which the defendant could lawfully deal," O'Brien insisted. Yet the statute forbade him to sell it "except upon the condition that he shall attach to it a badge of inferiority which diminishes the value and impairs its selling qualities." "A law which interferes with the property by depriving the owner of the profitable and free use of it, or hampers him in the application of it for the purposes of trade or commerce, or imposes conditions upon the right to hold or sell it, may seriously impair its value, against which the Constitution is a protection." It was not "essential to the public welfare" that purchasers be informed of "the origin of every article of property which is the subject of sale, trade, or commerce." And even if it were, such a law "could be effective only when applied to all property alike, and not limited to articles made in certain places and by a certain class of workmen." There was "nothing in the character or effect of prison labor to justify" legislation requiring the owner of a prison-made scrubbing brush "to label it with the history of its origin and to indicate the place where it was made and the class of workmen that produced it."[45]

The statute was thus simply an effort "to regulate the price of labor" by depressing the market demand for goods "made by one class of workmen"—convict laborers—and thereby to enhance "the price of goods made by another class." O'Brien asserted that no court had ever invoked the police power to justify such a statute, and with good reason. For if "the wages of labor in a few factories producing goods such as are also made in prisons may be regulated by the police power," then there was "no reason why that power may not be used to regulate the rewards of labor in any other field of human exertion." O'Brien proceeded to spin out a parade of objectionable class legislation that might follow:

> Why not give the workman who has a large family to support some advantage over the one who has no family at all? Why not give to the old and feeble a helping hand by legislation against the competition of the young and the strong? Why not give to the women, the weaker sex, who are often the victims of improvidence and want, a preference by statute over the men? Why confine such legislation to scrubbing brushes and like articles made in prisons, when multitudes of men engaged in farming, mercantile pursuits, and almost every vocation in life are struggling against competition?

If the New York labeling statute were a valid exercise of the police power, O'Brien could see no reason why the legislature might not "interfere" in each of these instances "to help those who need help at the expense of those who do not."[46] O'Brien concluded that the merchant or dealer "may buy his goods where he can obtain them to his best advantage." Any "restriction upon his freedom of action in this respect by State law" was "an invasion of his right of liberty." The statute interfered with "the right to acquire, possess, and dispose of property and with the liberty of the individuals to earn a living" by dealing in convict-made goods.[47]

O'Brien's opinion thus expressly embraced the view that the application of New York's labeling statute to prison-made goods produced outside the state deprived their owner of liberty and property without due process. But no other member of the Court of Appeals joined that portion of O'Brien's opinion. Chief Judge Parker and Judges Bartlett and Haight regarded the statute as "well within the police power of the state,"[48] while Judges Gray, Martin, and Vann concurred in the judgment solely "upon the ground that the statute conflicts with and is repugnant to the commerce clause of the federal constitution."[49] Six of the seven judges of the New York Court of Appeals either expressly rejected or refused to embrace O'Brien's view on the due process issue.

The New York appellate courts would not revisit this issue until 1910. *People ex rel. Phillips v. Raynes*[50] involved a statute requiring anyone displaying convict-made goods for sale to pay an annual license fee of $500 and to display that license prominently in his place of business.[51] The statute did not implicate the Dormant Commerce Clause because the goods in question had lost their character as interstate commerce and become part of the general merchandise of the state.[52] The sole question considered by the court, therefore, was whether the license tax violated the Fourteenth Amendment.

Republican New York state Attorney General Edward R. O'Malley defended the statute as a legitimate exercise of the state's police power and the classification as reasonable.[53] O'Malley emphasized that O'Brien had been the only member of the *Hawkins* court to embrace the view that the labeling statute there involved violated the Fourteenth Amendment, and much of his brief amounted to a rebuttal of that portion of O'Brien's opinion.[54] The history of New York legislation regulating convict labor demonstrated "a long-continued recognition by the legislature and the people of the State that a clear distinction exists economically between goods made by convicts and those manufactured by free labor and in free institutions." Convict-made goods were "dangerous to the free manufacture of similar goods." They differed from goods manufactured by free labor "not merely in that they have a different origin" but more "fundamentally in that they are virtually a product of slave labor." Therefore, "under the police power of the State the dealing in such goods should be limited and restricted for the protection of the labor of our free citizens and the capital invested in our free industries."[55] This was necessary "to promote the public welfare and prosperity" and to protect "free labor and free capital from unfair," "ruinous competition" with cheaply manufactured prison goods.[56] It was also necessary to protect the consuming public, many of whom "prefer to buy goods made by free labor and would not purchase prison-made goods if they knew where they were made."[57] The statute's protection was therefore "not merely to the laboring classes, but to the entire community, by protecting both the manufacturing industries and the wage earners." It was "not an effort to suppress the price of a certain class of labor, but to prevent goods made by convict or slave labor from competing on unequal terms without disclosing their origin." The statute sought only to compel convict-made goods "to stand before the community on their own merits and with their origin disclosed and to prevent dealers in them from having an undue advantage over dealers in free-made goods."[58] It was "proper" to distinguish between "dealers in these two classes of goods and compel those handling the products of the degraded labor to pay a license fee not charged to other dealers." The cost of producing such goods was lower, and their profitability accordingly higher, so imposing a greater burden of taxation on them was "fair."[59] The "danger" to "welfare of the State latent" in prison-made goods was enough "to warrant singling them out from other classes either for police regulation or for taxation."[60]

In an opinion affirmed *per curiam* by the Court of Appeals later that year, a unanimous five-judge panel of the Appellate Division's First Department rejected O'Malley's argument at every turn. Republican Justice John Proctor Clarke wrote on behalf of Presiding Justice George L. Ingraham and Justice Francis M. Scott, both Democrats, as well as fellow Republican Justices Frank C. Laughlin and Nathan L. Miller. Clarke observed that the "obvious purpose" of the statute, "writ so plain that all may read," was "to prohibit by onerous and exasperating restrictions . . . the buying and selling within this state of convict-made goods." But setting this aside and treating the statute "purely as a revenue or tax law," the court found that its classification was "unreasonable and capricious." "That classification is based upon the origin of the goods dealt in, without regard to the quality or character or nature of the goods themselves." If such classification were valid, the court asked, what was to prevent the legislature from requiring a license to sell goods made in a factory employing union labor, or employing non-union labor? Why not "single out for license dealers in goods made in shops employing members of certain races, religions, or political parties"?[61]

The *Raynes* court did not consider or pass on whether New York's requirement that convict-made goods be labeled was a legitimate exercise of the state's police power. But the decision did focus on the licensing statute's discrimination between goods made by convicts and goods made by free labor, rather than on the evenhandedness of its treatment of convict-made goods produced both within and without the state. This discrimination based on the good's origin or mode of production, the court held, constituted an arbitrary classification, no different constitutionally from discriminations based on race or religion. Even were Congress to enact a Wilson Act for convict-made goods, the opinion suggested, the singling out of prison-made products for adverse treatment would violate the Fourteenth Amendment.

Congressional efforts to pass a divesting statute for prison-made products continued without success for nearly two decades after *Raynes* was decided. In the Seventieth Congress, however, a bill sponsored by Missouri Democrat Harry B. Hawes in the Senate and Ohio Republican John G. Cooper in the House was enacted. The New York legislature transmitted to Congress a communication urging the bill's passage,[62] and at the request of Perry S. Newell, Secretary of the Association of Cotton Textile Merchants of New York, the New York law firm of Breed, Abbott & Morgan prepared a brief presented to the Senate supporting the bill's constitutionality.[63] New York members speaking in favor of the bill on the floors of the House and Senate included Republican Representative Bertrand Snell[64] and Democratic Representative Meyer Jacobstein[65] and Democratic Senator Robert Wagner.[66] And Republican New York Attorney General Albert C. Ottinger filed a statement in support of the bill that largely copied O'Malley's brief in the *Raynes* litigation nearly twenty years earlier. Ottinger acknowledged the Fourteenth Amendment obstacle that *Raynes* presented even were Congress to enact the Hawes-Cooper bill. But he nevertheless urged passage with the observation that "[t]he extension of the principles of the police power, according to the adjudications of our court of appeals during the last 20 years, has been marked," and it was "possible that more weight would be given to [O'Malley's] argument if the case were tried to-day."[67]

Ottinger's characterization of the trajectory of New York jurisprudence is corroborated by William E. Nelson's magisterial study of the subject in *The Legalist Reformation*. "Even in the nineteenth century," he reports, "the courts had construed the police power expansively. But as the center of gravity on the Court of Appeals began to shift" from property-oriented conservatives "toward reformers in the mid-1920s, the judges authored increasingly sweeping statements about its breadth." The police power, wrote Judge Cuthbert W. Pound for a unanimous court in 1930, was "'the least limitable of the powers of government,'" extending "to all the great public needs."[68] During this period, as Nelson relates, the Court of Appeals found less persuasive "constitutional claims about private property and the limited nature of the police power" and became increasingly receptive to legislative measures designed to "prevent exploitation" and "achieve social justice."[69]

This was particularly so with respect to what we might call the constitutional law of competitive injury. Exemplary of this transformation was the 1933 case of *People v. Nebbia*.[70] The case involved the constitutionality of a New York statute setting minimum prices for the sale of milk within the state. The legislative findings and statement of policy accompanying the statute's regulatory measures referred to "unfair, unjust, destructive, demoralizing and uneconomic trade practices . . . carried on in the production, sale and distribution of milk" in the state, which called for an "exercise of the police power" to "protect" the "public welfare." Oversupply led distributors to offer farmers prices below those at which milk could profitably be produced. The farmer was unable to protect himself against these "exactions," and minimum price regulation was necessary "to keep open the stream of milk flowing from the farm to the city and to guard the farmer from substantial loss."[71]

The Court of Appeals upheld the statute by a vote of 5–1.[72] Chief Judge Pound wrote for the majority that "[d]oubtless the statute before us would be condemned by an earlier generation as a temerarious interference with the rights of property and contract," citing the Supreme Court's opinion in *Lochner v. New York*. "But we must not fail to consider," he continued, "that constitutional law is a progressive science; that statutes aiming to establish a standard of social justice, to conform the law to the accepted standards of the community . . . by fixing living standards of prices for the producer, are to be interpreted with that degree of liberality which is essential to the attainment of the end in view." The Due Process Clause did not leave milk producers "unprotected from oppression." The legislature possessed the power to ensure that "a fair return may be obtained by the producer and a vital industry preserved from destruction."[73]

Though the Hawes-Cooper Act was enacted in 1929, its terms provided that it would take effect in January 1934. In the meantime several states, including New York, enacted statutes prohibiting the sale of convict-made goods on the private market within the state after the effective date of the Act. On January 5, 1934, the New York Supreme Court in Albany County ruled in an action to restrain enforcement of the Hawes-Cooper Act and New York's statute.[74] The case was argued before Justice John T. Loughran, who had served on the trial bench for three years and within a matter of months would be elevated by Governor Herbert H. Lehman to the State's Court of Appeals to fill a vacancy created by the resignation of Henry T. Kellogg. Loughran would go on to win election to a full fourteen-year term in November of 1934, and Governor Thomas E. Dewey would appoint him Chief Judge of that Court upon the death of Irving Lehman (Governor Lehman's brother) in 1945. Loughran ran unopposed for that office in 1946 and served as Chief Judge until his death in 1953. In short, he participated in or presided over many of the changes in New York jurisprudence that Nelson describes in *The Legalist Reformation*.

Loughran rejected the contention that the New York convict labor law was "obnoxious to the due process clause." The statute declared it to be the policy of the state "to protect free labor from the unjust competition of convict labor." It was "sound to keep convicts at work," but the products of free labor had to be "marketed at a profit." If there were a "conflict between these objectives, the choice was for the legislature." Loughran pointed out that in *Hawkins* Judge O'Brien had been alone in taking the position that the labeling statute amounted to a denial of due process, and he brushed *Raynes* aside with only a brief mention. The requested relief was therefore denied.[75]

Two years later, Loughran would again support the use of the police power to prevent "unjust competition" in the labor market. Along with Judge Leonard C. Crouch, Loughran would join Judge Irving Lehman's dissent from the majority opinion invalidating New York's minimum wage statute for women in *People ex rel. Tipaldo v. Morehead*. Lehman observed that the legislature had found that "the constant lowering of wages by unscrupulous employers constitutes a serious form of unfair competition against other employers, reduces the purchasing power of the workers and threatens the stability of industry." These "evils of oppressive, unreasonable and unfair wages" were "such as to render imperative the exercise of the police power of the state." Such unscrupulous employers, Lehman argued, forced "more scrupulous employers" to lower their wages. The legislature could "restrain" such "injurious," "unfair," "unjust" practices "in the interest of proper competition." The "vicious result of oppressive wages" paid to "cheap labor" extended "throughout the industry" in question "and in lesser degree even beyond the industry." "Just as experience has shown that, in a community where peonage or slavery exists, free labor cannot flourish, so in an industry, or even community, where oppressive wages are paid to those deficient in bargaining power, it is not unreasonable to believe that such wages affect indirectly but nevertheless very substantially the wages of all others."[76] Here, in a nutshell, was the argument against sale on the open market of convict-made goods, and that argument would be echoed the following year when President Franklin D. Roosevelt called on Congress to enact the Fair Labor Standards Act in order "to protect the fundamental interests of free labor and a free people."[77]

But one did not have to share Roosevelt's and Loughran's views on the constitutionality of the minimum wage to agree with them about the validity of state laws prohibiting open market sale of prison-made products. The day before the New York Court of Appeals decided *Tipaldo*, the U.S. Supreme Court ruled in a case challenging the constitutionality of the Hawes-Cooper Act and an Ohio statute prohibiting open market sale of convict-made goods. The Court unanimously upheld both the federal statute and the Ohio law.[78] The opinion was written by Justice George Sutherland, who is often remembered as one of the conservative Four Horsemen and as a leading proponent of substantive due process. And not without good reason. He had stood foursquare behind the right to liberty of contract when writing the majority opinion invalidating a minimum wage law for women in the 1923 case of *Adkins v. Children's Hospital*,[79] and he would continue to adhere to the views he had expressed there until the end of his career.[80] He had written a series of decisions invalidating price-regulation measures in the 1920s,[81] and he had dissented when the Court affirmed the New York Court of Appeals' decision in *Nebbia*.[82] He would vote to strike down several New Deal initiatives during the Depression decade.[83] But Sutherland was not a dogmatic apostle of *laissez-faire*. Over the course of his tenure on the Court he, like his fellow Horsemen, voted to uphold many more police power regulations than is often recognized.[84] As a member of the Utah legislature and a U.S. senator he had supported several pieces of progressive labor legislation,[85] including the Seamen's Act of 1915, which liberated sailors in the merchant marine from various degrading and unfree conditions of service. The union leader Samuel Gompers later praised the "exceptional" assistance Sutherland rendered in the enactment of that legislation, and Seamen's Union president Andrew Furuseth acclaimed him as "a lover of freedom, a man who understands thoroughly what freedom means, and a man who, in the protection of freedom to all men, regardless of their station in life, may be trusted and relied upon under all possible conditions."[86]

Sutherland's opinion dismissed the contention that the Ohio law deprived dealers in prison-made goods of their property without due process. Ohio's view that "the sale of convict-made goods in competition with the products of free labor is an evil" found "ample support in fact and in the similar legislation of a preponderant number of the other states." Acts of Congress relating to the subject, Sutherland pointed out, also recognized "the evil." The importation of the products of convict labor had been prohibited, and the federal prisons operated on the state-use principle. Such legislation proceeded "upon the view that free labor, properly compensated, cannot compete successfully with the enforced and unpaid or underpaid convict labor of the prison." A state "basing its legislation upon that conception" had "the right and power, so far as the Federal Constitution is concerned, by nondiscriminating legislation, to preserve its policy from impairment or defeat, by any means appropriate to the end and not inconsistent with that instrument." And because the Hawes-Cooper Act divested convict-made goods of their interstate character upon arrival and delivery in the state of destination, the Ohio law was "equally unassailable" on Dormant Commerce Clause grounds.[87]

The final episode in the constitutional battle over the regulation of convict-made goods came the following year. In 1935 Congress had enacted the Ashurst–Sumners Act, which prohibited the interstate shipment or transportation of prison-made products into any state where the goods were intended to be received, possessed, sold, or used in violation of the law of the jurisdiction of destination.[88] The bill was modeled on the Webb–Kenyon Act of 1913, which had imposed a similar scheme of regulation on the interstate shipment of alcohol[89] and which the Court had sustained against constitutional challenge in the 1917 case of *Clark Distilling v. Western Maryland Ry. Co.*[90] The Ashurst–Sumners bill was signed into law by former New York Governor and now President Franklin D. Roosevelt, who had long been a supporter of prison reform at the state and national levels.[91] The Supreme Court would hear a challenge to the statute in *Kentucky Whip & Collar Co. v. Illinois Central Railroad Co.*[92] New York authorities took a keen interest in the case, and the state's Attorney General, John Bennett Jr., filed an *amicus* brief in support of the Act. Bennett's brief placed great emphasis on the power of Congress and the states "to protect free labor from unjust and ruinous competition." It was "a function of government to preserve the freedom of labor," and to prevent "the crushing of free labor in industry." The labor that produced convict-made goods was not free labor, and there was in such labor "no inherent rights of men which are subject to the normal protection of the Constitution." The Due Process Clause did not "preserve for the convict any liberty to contract, or any right of property in his labor or the products of his labor." Accordingly, "other persons" could not "contract with the convict for his labor and thereby acquire rights of property." It was "just as proper for Congress to protect free labor against the interstate transportation of convict-made goods" as it was "to protect free labor against the flooding in from abroad of the products of slave labor." Because convict labor was used "to destroy the property of free men in their labor" and "the property of others in the products of free labor," Congress could "protect interstate commerce in the products of free labor from the demoralizing influence of the competitive products of convict labor."[93]

The Court's unanimous opinion upholding the Act[94] was handed down in early January 1937, less than three months before a sharply divided Court would uphold Washington state's minimum wage statute for women in *West Coast Hotel v. Parrish*.[95] The author of the opinions in both of these cases was Chief Justice Charles Evans Hughes, who had been the progressive Republican governor of New York and a proponent of penal reform in 1910 when *Raynes* was decided.[96] His opinion surveyed the Court's decisions upholding prohibitions on interstate shipment, reiterating the established principle that Congress could prohibit the use of interstate commerce as "'an agency to promote immorality, dishonesty or the spread of any evil or harm to the people of other states from the state of origin.'" Hughes rejected as "inadmissible" the contention that the Act was invalid because the goods in questions were "useful and harmless articles." The liquor cases established that alcoholic beverages were legitimate articles of commerce—indeed, this was why they had enjoyed the protection of the Dormant Commerce Clause. But because of "the effects ascribed to the traffic in intoxicating liquors," the states could exercise their police power to restrict or prohibit internal commerce in them without violating the Due Process Clause, and the same was true of convict-made goods. Though the "subject of the prohibited traffic" and "the effects of the traffic" in the liquor cases were "different," "the underlying principle" was "the same." The "pertinent point" was that Congress could prevent interstate commerce from being used to frustrate the enforcement of valid exercises of the state's police power.[97]

Finally, Hughes found in the Act "nothing arbitrary or capricious" that would bring its provisions "into collision with the requirements of due process of law." The Chief Justice noted that congressional hearings had over many years "thoroughly revealed the evils attending the sale of such goods, in the open market, in competition with goods manufactured and produced by free labor." In exercising the commerce power, Congress was "as free as the states to recognize the fundamental interests of free labor."[98]

As the historian Rebecca McLennan has observed, these decisions "sealed the fate of profit-driven prison industries in the United States."[99] State legislatures were quick to react to the opportunities the decisions presented. By the end of the year only ten states "containing a combined population only slightly in excess of that of the State of New York" permitted "the unrestricted sale of imported convict made goods."[100] "Under these conditions," McLennan reports, "the interstate market in prison-made goods disappeared in a matter of a few years," and "the country's remaining prison industries went into rapid decline."[101]

In the wake of congressional enactment of the Hawes-Cooper Act, an article in *Business Week* had anticipated this result. The author observed that the law would "affect prisons in nearly all states that now permit their products to be sold in the open market because almost all goods of that nature are sold through New York City. And New York State has a 'state use' law, permitting the sale of prison products only for govern-ment use."[102] On this view, the campaign to forbid the open market sale of convict-made goods in New York was tantamount to a movement to prohibit their sale nationwide.

More than a quarter-century ago the historian William Forbath demonstrated that antebellum free-labor ideology left an ambigu-ous legacy, strands of which were capable of nurturing and sustaining visions of the social order offering alternatives to the industrial capital-ism that emerged from the Gilded Age. That ambiguity, Forbath argued, was ultimately resolved in favor of recognition of a right to pursue a lawful calling and enjoy its market-determined rewards, rather than the labor movement's aspiration to a right to be protected from the functionally compulsory sale of one's labor into a system of dependent industrial "wage slavery."[103] The story of convict labor reform in New York reminds us that the Fourteenth Amendment's ambiguous protec-tions of liberty and property also left open how many questions of law and policy would be resolved *within* that system of industrial capital-ism. Throughout this period, free-labor ideology suffused conceptions of both constitutional right and state power in the domain of political economy. For a season, that ideology was a powerful force underwriting constitutional restrictions on government's regulatory competence. But all the while, that multivalent constellation of ideas also supplied a res-ervoir of state authority to order our economic relations. It would take decades of political, legal, and intellectual struggle over the prison labor question, in New York and elsewhere, before the underlying constitu-tional issue would be definitively resolved in favor of the interests of free laborers. And the fact that it was resolved unanimously by Supreme

Court justices otherwise deeply divided on questions of constitutional political economy, and just as the Court was pronouncing the last rites for the doctrine of liberty of contract, serves to highlight the richness and complexity of the ambiguities of free labor that William E. Nelson identified back in 1974.

NOTES

1. William E. Nelson, "The Impact of the Antislavery Movement upon Styles of Judicial Reasoning in Nineteenth Century America," *Harvard Law Review* 87 (1974): 537–38; William E. Nelson, *The Roots of American Bureaucracy, 1830–1900* (Cambridge, Mass.: Harvard University Press, 1982), 52. Other scholars would later build and elaborate upon this insight. Among the most prominent examples are Charles W. McCurdy, "Roots of 'Liberty of Contract' Reconsidered: Major Premises in the Law of Employment, 1867–1937," *Yearbook of the Supreme Court Historical Society* 1984 (1984): 20; William E. Forbath, "The Ambiguities of Free Labor: Labor and Law in the Gilded Age," *Wisconsin Law Review* 1985 (1985): 772–800; Charles W. McCurdy, "The 'Liberty of Contract' Regime in American Law," in *The State and Freedom of Contract*, ed. Harry N. Scheiber (Stanford, Calif.: Stanford University Press, 1998), 167–97.

2. Nelson, "The Impact of the Antislavery Movement," 550–57; Nelson, *The Roots of American Bureaucracy*, 133–38.

3. William E. Nelson, *The Fourteenth Amendment: From Political Principle to Judicial Doctrine* (Cambridge, Mass.: Harvard University Press, 1988).

4. Nelson, "The Impact of the Antislavery Movement," 559–60. See also Nelson, *The Roots of American Bureaucracy*, 67 ("Concepts of human rights . . . are of little help in deciding the great mass of cases in which two or more possible results are equally consistent with the enjoyment of 'natural rights'").

5. Nelson, "The Impact of the Antislavery Movement," 556. See also Nelson, *The Roots of American Bureaucracy*, 138.

6. Rebecca M. McLennan, *The Crisis of Imprisonment: Protest, Politics, and the Making of the American Penal State, 1776–1941* (New York: Cambridge University Press, 2008); Philip Klein, *Prison Methods in New York State* (New York: Columbia University, 1920).

7. Glen A. Gildemeister, *Prison Labor and Convict Competition with Free Workers in Industrializing America, 1840–1890* (New York: Garland Publishers, 1987), 236.

8. Blake McKelvey, *American Prisons: A Study in American Social History Prior to 1915* (Chicago: University of Chicago Press, 1936), 97.

9. Brian Greenberg, *Worker and Community: Response to Industrialization in a Nineteenth-Century American City, Albany, New York, 1850–1884* (Albany: State University of New York Press, 1985), 143.

10. "An Expensive Blunder," *The Nation*, March 5, 1885, 194–95.

11. Gildemeister, *Prison Labor*, 239. *The Nation* would point out that although the proposition attracted the support of a majority of those voting on the issue, a significant portion of those voting in the 1883 election did not vote on the proposition. The editors therefore argued that "[l]ess than a majority of all persons voting favored the change, and it is entirely probable that many thousands of those favoring it had no intelligent idea of what they were doing." "An Expensive Blunder," 194–95.

12. Gildemeister, *Prison Labor*, 222, 239; Laws of New York, 1884, ch. 21; Klein, *Prison Methods*, 259.

13. Gildemeister, *Prison Labor*, 240.

14. McKelvey, *American Prisons*, 98.

15. Klein, *Prison Methods*, 259; Laws of New York, 1886, ch. 432; McKelvey, *American Prisons*, 98.

16. Klein, *Prison Methods*, 260; Laws of New York, 1888, ch. 586; McKelvey, *American Prisons*, 97–99.

17. Klein, *Prison Methods*, 260; Laws of New York, 1889, ch. 382, sections 97, 102, 105; McKelvey, *American Prisons*, 99.

18. N.Y. Const. of 1894, art. III, § 29; McKelvey, *American Prisons*, 99; Klein, *Prison Methods*, 261–62; Gildemeister, *Prison Labor*, 242; E. T. Hiller, "Development of the Systems of Control of Convict Labor in the United States," *Journal of the American Institute of Criminal Law and Criminology* 5 (1915): 262; John Mitchell, "The Wage-Earner and the Prison Worker," *Annals of the American Academy of Political and Social Science* 46 (1913): 12; E. Stagg Whitin, "Trade Unions and Prison Labor," *Case and Comment* 19 (1912): 243 ("labor forced" state-use "from the reluctant New York State Constitutional Convention in 1894"); Collis Lovely, "The Union Man and the Prisoner," in *The Prison and the Prisoner*, ed. Julia Jaffray (1917), 171–72. For a favorable assessment of the Fassett Law and a skeptical appraisal of the 1894 amendment, see W. P. Prentice, "The New Constitution of New York in Relation to Prison Labor," *Albany Law Journal* 52 (1895): 216.

19. 135 U.S. 100 (1890).

20. 26 Stat. 313 (1890).

21. 140 U.S. 545 (1891).

22. *Bowman v. Chicago & Northwestern Railway Co.*, 125 U.S. 465 (1888).

23. H.R. 8716, 50th Cong.,1st Sess. (1888), 19 Cong. Rec. 2262.

24. 19 Cong. Rec. 4528 (1888).

25. Laws of New York, 1896, ch. 931. The preceding year the New York Supreme Court had invalidated under the Dormant Commerce Clause an 1894 labeling statute that applied only to convict-made goods produced in other states. *People v. Hawkins*, 32 N.Y.S. 524 (1895), invalidating Laws of New York, 1894, ch. 698. The first such labeling law was enacted in 1887. Laws of New York, 1887, ch. 323. McLennan, *Crisis of Imprisonment*, 188.

26. *People v. Hawkins*, 51 N.E. 257, 266 (N.Y. 1898).

27. *Id.* at 264.

28. *Id.* at 261.
29. *People v. Hawkins*, 47 N.Y.S. 56, 57 (1897). The sole dissenter was Democratic Presiding Justice Alton B. Parker. The majority opinion was joined by Democratic Justice D. Cady Herrick and Republican Justices Judson S. Landon and Milton H. Merwin.
30. *Id.* at 57.
31. *Id.* at 60.
32. *Id.*
33. *Id.* at 57.
34. *Id.* at 57, 60.
35. *Id.* at 61.
36. *Id.* at 58–60.
37. 51 N.E. at 258.
38. *Id.* at 261–62.
39. *Id.* at 262.
40. In *People v. Hawkins*, 32 N.Y.S. 524, 525 (1895), the Supreme Court reported that "the learned trial judge in the court below" had invalidated the discriminatory 1894 labeling statute in part on the ground that "it operated upon property owned at the time it took effect as well as property thereafter acquired, and thus constituted an unlawful interference with vested rights."
41. 47 N.Y.S. 60.
42. *Mugler v. Kansas*, 123 U.S. 623 (1887).
43. 171 U.S. 1 (1898).
44. *Powell v. Pennsylvania*, 127 U.S. 678 (1888).
45. 51 N.E. 258–60.
46. 51 N.E. 258–59.
47. 51 N.E. 259–60.
48. 51 N.E. 261.
49. *Id.*
50. 120 N.Y.S. 1053 (App. Div. 1910), *aff'd per curiam*, 198 N.Y. 539 (1910).
51. Laws of New York, 1909, ch. 36.
52. 120 N.Y.S. at 1056–57.
53. The brief is reproduced in *Hearing on H.R. 12000, 12001, and 21322, Competition of Penal Labor Before Subcomm. No. 4 of the H. Comm. on Labor*, 61st Cong., 104–15 (1910).
54. *Id.* at 109, 111–13.
55. *Id.* at 106–7.
56 *Id.* at 109–10.
57. *Id.* at 111.
58. *Id.* at 112.
59. *Id.* at 107, 115.
60. *Id.* at 114.
61. 120 N.Y.S. at 1057–58.

62. 69 Cong. Rec. 4373 (1928).

63. 70 Cong. Rec. 668 (1928).

64. 69 Cong. Rec. 8636-38 (1928).

65. 69 Cong. Rec. 4373, 8749 (1928).

66. 70 Cong. Rec. 860 (1928).

67. 70 Cong. Rec. 668–69 (1928).

68. William E. Nelson, *The Legalist Reformation: Law, Politics, and Ideology in New York, 1920–1908* (Chapel Hill: University of North Carolina Press, 2001), 63, quoting *People v. Perretta*, 253 N.Y. 305, 309 (1930).

69. Nelson, *The Legalist Reformation*, 21.

70. 262 N.Y. 259, 186 N.E. 694 (1933).

71. 186 N.E. at 695–98.

72. The majority opinion of now–Chief Judge Pound was joined by Judges Crane, Lehman, Hubbs, and Crouch. Judge Kellogg did not participate. The sole dissenter was Judge John F. O'Brien, son of Judge Denis O'Brien, the author of *Hawkins*.

73. 186 N.E. at 699.

74. Laws of New York, 1930, ch. 136.

75. *Greenthal v. Bennett* (N.Y. Sup. Ct., Albany County, 1934). The text of the opinion is reproduced in Memorandum of New York State, Amicus Curiae, and Motion for Leave to File, Whitfield v. Ohio, 14–15. The court, per Justice Christopher J. Heffernan, issued findings of fact and conclusions of law and entered judgment dismissing the complaint on the merits on August 22, 1934. *Id.* at 7–12.

76. 270 N.Y. 233, 200 N.E. 799, 804-05 (1936).

77. Message from the President of the United States Transmitting a Recommendation that the Congress Enact Legislation "Further to Help Those Who Toil in Factory and on Farm," 75th Cong., 1st Sess., H.R. Doc. No. 255 (1937).

78. *Whitfield v. Ohio*, 297 U.S. 431 (1936). Justices Willis Van Devanter, James C. McReynolds, and Harlan Fiske Stone concurred in the result.

79. 261 U.S. 525 (1923). The majority of the New York Court of Appeals had felt bound by *Adkins* in *Tipaldo*. 270 N.Y. 233, 200 N.E. 799, 800–1 (1936).

80. See *Morehead v. New York ex rel. Tipaldo*, 298 U.S. 587 (1936) (Sutherland joins majority opinion invalidating New York minimum wage law); *West Coast Hotel v. Parrish*, 300 U.S. 379, 400 (1937) (Sutherland dissents from opinion upholding Washington state minimum wage law).

81. *Williams v. Standard Oil Co.*, 278 U.S. 235 (1929); *Ribnik v. McBride*, 277 U.S. 350 (1928); *Tyson & Bro. v. Banton*, 273 U.S. 418 (1927).

82. *Nebbia v. New York*, 291 U.S. 502, 539 (1934).

83. *NLRB v. Jones & Laughlin Steel Corp.*, 301 U.S. 1, 76 (Sutherland joins McReynolds dissent from opinion upholding National Labor Relations Act); *Carter v. Carter Coal Co.*, 298 U.S. 238 (1936) (invaliding Bituminous Coal Conservation Act of 1935); *Railroad Retirement Board v. Alton*, 295 U.S. 330 (1935) (invalidating Railway Pension Act of 1934).

84. See Barry Cushman, "The Secret Lives of the Four Horsemen," *Virginia Law Review* 83 (1997): 566–67, 570–71.

85. These included the eight-hour law for miners that was later upheld by the Supreme Court in *Holden v. Hardy*; the Employer's Liability Act; and the eight-hour day for laborers employed by the United States. Sutherland also chaired the special commission that prepared a federal workmen's compensation bill, for which he was a strong advocate. Joel Paschal, "Mr. Justice Sutherland," in *Mr. Justice*, eds. Allison Dunham and Philip B. Kurland (Chicago: University of Chicago Press, 1964), 222; Joel Paschal, *Mr. Justice Sutherland: A Man Against the State* (Princeton, N.J.: Princeton University Press, 1951), 36, 41, 56, 63, 65–73, 235; Harold M. Stephens, "Mr. Justice Sutherland," *American Bar Association Journal* 31 (1951): 446.

86. Paschal, *Mr. Justice Sutherland*, 72, 97.

87. *Id.*, 439–40.

88. 49 Stat. 494 (1935).

89. 39 Stat. 699 (1913).

90. 242 U.S. 311 (1917).

91. McLennan, *Crisis of Imprisonment*, 420–21, 454, 456–57.

92. 299 U.S. 334 (1937).

93. Brief for the State of New York, 18, 21–22.

94. Justice Stone did not participate. 299 U.S. at 353.

95. 300 U.S. 379 (1937).

96. Merlo J. Pusey, *Charles Evans Hughes* (New York: Macmillan, 1951), 181–258; McLennan, *Crisis of Imprisonment*, 420.

97. 299 U.S. at 346–51.

98. *Id.* at 352.

99. McLennan, *Crisis of Imprisonment*, 465.

100. J. A. C. Grant, "Interstate Traffic in Convict-Made Goods," *Journal of the American Institute of Criminal Law and Criminology* 28 (1938): 857. The states were Alabama, Delaware, Florida, Missouri, Nevada, North Dakota, South Carolina, Vermont, West Virginia, and Wyoming. "State Laws Regulating Sale of Prison-Made Goods," *Monthly Labor Review* 45 (1937): 1424.

101. McLennan, *Crisis of Imprisonment*, 461.

102. *Business Week*, October 12, 1929, 11.

103. Forbath, "The Ambiguities of Free Labor," 767.

6

The Long, Broad, and Deep Civil Rights Movement

The Lessons of a Master Scholar and Teacher

TOMIKO BROWN-NAGIN

How would the legal history of the civil rights movement change if the doctrine of the U.S. Supreme Court and the lawyering of Thurgood Marshall did not dominate analysis? What if the work of local lawyers and activists took center stage? In a recent work, I set out to answer these questions and provide a richer account of the civil rights movement.

This account proposed to add depth and breadth to the "long civil rights movement," a metaphor that rooted the struggle for racial justice in the labor movement's demands for economic justice in the 1930s and stretched it past the landmark civil rights legislation of the 1960s.[1] The portrait of the movement presented in my book *Courage to Dissent: Atlanta and the Long History of the Civil Right Movement* not only lengthens the movement's history in time but also adds new texture to movement history. It does so by merging two methodologies: bottom-up, community-based social history and top-down legal history. This methodological and interpretative synthesis developed out of my convictions that law professors had not fully accounted for the roles of ordinary people at the local level in changing American race relations and that social historians had not fully connected their stories about the grassroots struggle for racial change to the law.

In the process of showing how local people and ordinary Americans shaped and experienced civil rights law, a large cast of characters takes the stage. The work discusses pragmatic and movement lawyers, student radicals and welfare-rights activists, as well as struggles over housing, schools, employment, and war and peace. With these local change agents as centers of attention—rather than elite decision makers at the Court and at the national level, alone—we gain a greater sense of the movement's depth and breadth and thus a different, and perhaps more hopeful, view of the possibilities for social change in a participatory democracy.[2]

This effort to foreground local change agents reflects a scholarly journey that owes much to the sponsorship of William E. Nelson and the Samuel I. Golieb fellowship at New York University School of Law. Nelson taught me the *craft* of legal history. He urged me to take great care to follow my sources—all of them—and to avoid presentism. Nelson's intellectual guidance inspired me to appreciate more fully and to defend my methodological innovations and commitments. His teachings brought great scholarly rewards. The cast of characters whose lives I ultimately recovered in *Courage to Dissent* highlight important political, economic, and cultural dimensions of twentieth-century struggles for racial equality. These strands of movement history often are lost in triumphant, national, NAACP- and court-centered narratives about the civil rights movement. The balance of this essay explores the story of the evolution of my work on these subjects under Nelson's guidance.

The Initial Puzzle: Too Many Sources, Methodologies, and Interpretative Approaches

The coming together of my intellectual journey, Nelson's guidance, and my present book project began in New Haven. I came to New York University and Bill Nelson from Yale Law School, where I had become acquainted with the achievements of the Warren Court and a point of view on the law now associated with "legal liberalism."[3] The Warren Court had put into effect a "program of constitutional reform almost revolutionary in its aspirations, and now and then, in its achievement,"[4] in the words of one eloquent proponent of this school of thought.[5] On this account, the federal courts had been and could ever be protectors of the disadvantaged, as impartial judges set aside politics and pursued the "true" meaning of such constitutional values as equal protection.[6] This attractive and hopeful picture of the federal courts, the Justices, and the Court's role in social change envisioned law as a noble profession.

The liberal vision of the Court fit nicely with the reigning legal history narrative about the country's transition away from Jim Crow. The traditional account of *Brown v. Board of Education* and the civil rights movement placed lawyers and the courts at the center of the narrative of racial change.[7] A heroic narrative hailing Thurgood Marshall as the chief spokesperson of black victims and the NAACP as institutional avenger of black rights firmly anchored the legal history. In this version, the U.S. Supreme Court's unanimous opinion in *Brown* resoundingly validated Marshall's and the NAACP's decisions to attack segregation frontally. Mark Tushnet, the distinguished constitutional scholar and biographer of Justice Marshall, cited the "brilliance of Marshall's strategy" in *Brown*, a decision called "one of the defining moments in Supreme Court history."[8] Many leading works "stressed the role of decisions handed down by the federal courts" as a way of understanding the civil rights movement and set the standard for how to study law and its relationship to society, and to African American communities, during the movement years.[9]

This narrative frame made perfect sense in a world that hailed *Brown v. Board of Education* as a cleansing moment in American constitutional and political history. Why would the history of the struggle for civil rights not revolve around Marshall, the NAACP Legal Defense Fund, *Brown*, and the Justices of the Supreme Court? What else was there?

Nevertheless, I had trouble reconciling the liberal legal understanding of the Court and the heroic narrative of civil rights history with the "bottom-up" and localist methodological approach to the writing of civil rights history.[10] This historical methodology emphasized national developments but at the same time focused on "relatively unknown people in their local contexts."[11] Scholars working in this tradition wrote history in a way that accentuated the agency of the grassroots actors who energized and gave momentum to social movements—such subjects as Fannie Lou Hamer, Ella Baker, and others, often women, whose names were mostly unknown to the general public. The local studies frequently featured the voices of the "inarticulate," on the view that their on-the-ground perspectives could shed light on the functioning of American institutions and democracy.

This approach deviated substantially from scholarly works that analyzed changes in race relations using the members and activities of elite institutions, including the U.S. Supreme Court or Congress, as points of departure. In the view of scholars working in the bottom-up school of thought, studies from that top-down perspective erased "any sense of the complexity of the African-American community and how that complexity shaped responses to oppression." To portray more clearly those historical actors stressed by the bottom-up, community-based perspective, historians adopting that viewpoint even deemphasized the contributions of Rev. Dr. Martin Luther King Jr. and other ministers who had received so much attention in initial historical appraisals of the civil rights movement. These historians invoked and guided their work by an adage associated with the student movement: "Let the people speak. Let the people decide."[12]

The community-study methodology in particular and the concept of bottom-up history more generally held tremendous appeal. Existing narratives about the struggle for civil rights, instructive as they were about the courts and their important roles in processes of historical change, told "partial truths."[13] The court-centered texts elided important social and political contexts in the communities affected by the courts and the civil rights lawyers who deemed themselves representatives of the people. Ironically, this elision occurred not out of spite for African Americans at the local level[14] but because of admiration for the Warren Court and Thurgood Marshall.

*　　*　　*

Nevertheless, the question of how to integrate bottom-up and top-down in proper proportions within the context of civil rights legal history struck me as difficult,[15] for the top-down, court-centric, and bottom-up, localist methodologies—as I hoped to execute them—did not seem that complementary, at least at first.

To be sure, legal historians before me had considered law in context. However, for the scholar interested in how external forces shaped the law, the relevant context tended to be political history, and sometimes economic history.[16] The political actors in question tended to be elites: presidents, or members of Congress and state legislatures who write the laws that become the subject of litigation. In the view of the community-studies scholars with whom I studied, these actors quintessentially represent the "top" of the historical equation. Moreover, even in legal histories that considered context, the law itself dominated analysis, notwithstanding these works' attention to how external factors shaped the law: Statutes, constitutional provisions, cases, doctrine, the Justices who made law, and, occasionally, the lawyers whose cases laid the groundwork for lawmaking took center stage. I thought of William E. Nelson's well-regarded book *The Fourteenth Amendment* as falling within this genre.[17]

By these measures, my civil rights scholarship did not look like classic legal history, and the differences gave me pause. It was not only or primarily concerned with the Constitution itself, or any particular provision of it, or with doctrine, more generally, or even, in a conventional sense, with *Brown v. Board of Education*. The familiar discussion of whether *Brown* was "law" or "politics," whether it was a legitimate exercise of judicial review, and the matter of the counter-majoritarian difficulty did not figure into my work.[18]

Ironically, it seemed to me, the standard inquiries sidelined illuminating consideration of African Americans—the putative beneficiaries of *Brown*—as historical subjects and agents of change. Thurgood Marshall and NAACP LDF ("Inc. Fund") lawyers represented and spoke for black interests. Black opinion at the grassroots level seemed unnecessary to scholarly analysis, or so the existing literature assumed. That framework stood in considerable tension with my project. To the extent that my work did discuss Marshall, it did not make his worldview its critical center. Rather, it took as its central subject the black experience of inequality and the contentious activism that occurred on the ground level as blacks both defined and pursued equality.

But the difference between my work and the leading civil rights histories turned less on absolute methodological conflict—some of those scholars considered aspects of social history, along with their analyses of the law—than on how the sources we chose, and the voices featured in them, influenced interpretation and argument.[19] Given my keen interest in dynamics at the community level, my scholarly gaze turned to different sources and different actors from those who had starring roles in other works. My project, rooted in the study of local African Americans, cast them as members of variegated communities; whites, whether resistors or moderates, played comparatively small roles. The work of the federal courts was less central to my study. Few knew much about the majority of the lawyers discussed in my project; I had to make a case for why they deserved so much attention from a legal historian. In fact, the first part of my book focused on an attorney who did not rely as heavily on civil rights litigation—the avenue through which black lawyers typically obtained notoriety and, ultimately, gained historical notice—as did Marshall and the Inc. Fund. Other lawyers in my book had clashed with Marshall, LDF, and the NAACP at one time or another. This conflict emerged as a major theme of my work. Most important, a large proportion of my work focused on nonlegal actors— on the movement and its agenda, and only secondarily on the law and the lawyers. The work took the movement as distinct from, and yet interactive with, the law.[20]

The activists spoke in distinctive voices. They highlighted the efforts of local people in the struggle for civil rights. Consider the Georgia man who after a sit-in proclaimed, "*I*, myself desegregated a lunch counter . . . not some big man, not some powerful man, but little me."[21] Social activists sometimes rejected court-based change and clashed with civil rights lawyers. Both the leaders of the student movement and the impoverished women activists who populated my work leveled biting criticism at ineffective lawyers, emphasized the degree to which class distinguished blacks from one another, and claimed that the middle-class status of black leaders could undermine good leadership. James Lawson, an architect of the sit-ins, lambasted the national NAACP as a "black bourgeois club." John Lewis, executive secretary of the Student Nonviolent Coordinating Committee (SNCC), a major organization featured in my book, explained, "[W]e were all about" a "mass movement, an irresistible movement of the *masses*. Not a handful of lawyers in a closed courtroom, but hundreds, thousands of everyday people . . . taking their cause and belief to the streets." A speech by Thurgood Marshall, in which he insisted that the students should leave the work of tearing down segregation to the lawyers, led to an epiphany for Lewis. "Thurgood Marshall was a good man, a historic figure," Lewis conceded, "but watching him speak on that April evening in Nashville convinced me more than ever that our revolt was as much against this nation's traditional black leadership structure as it was against racial segregation and discrimination."[22]

The critical perspective on civil rights leaders embraced and displayed by many of these actors contrasted with the viewpoints found in much of legal scholarship, even in the work of legal scholars who otherwise could be acerbic critics of the American legal system and civil rights jurisprudence. Much of critical theory elided any discussion of civil rights lawyers that challenged the heroic, court-centric prevailing narrative. And, unlike many of the subjects whom I had found, these scholars analyzed members of the black middle class with little serious attention to how social status could shape their worldviews or decision making.[23] The critical insights of scholars who *did* seriously consider these matters proved important to my work.[24] If I had questions about how my work would fit with the legal scholarship, I also had concerns about how well it conformed to a bottom-up, social history methodology. As much as a bottom-up, localist orientation framed my work, it also concerned elite lawyers, albeit in relation to grassroots actors. I wondered whether I could analyze the work of civil rights lawyers, their clients, and local communities, all in one text, with adequate attention to locals and non-elites. The social historians who wrote in the bottom-up tradition expected a tremendously detailed analysis of grassroots dynamics, supported by copious amounts of primary and secondary source material. How well could I meet those scholarly expectations, along with those expectations peculiar to the field of legal history?

*   *   *

The task of sorting out these challenges preoccupied me when I met Bill Nelson, after I graduated from law school and found in the Samuel I. Golieb Fellowship year an opportunity to work on the book project. I did not know if my work would find acceptance. In essence, I aimed to link stories about local blacks to the civil rights movement's legal history, as it then stood. In approaching that task, I hoped to follow Steven Lawson's admonition that a "nuanced account of the Black freedom struggle requires an interconnected approach," a mixture of local and national, elite and grassroots, and, for me, legal and social history in equal parts, or as close an approximation as I could achieve. That aspiration was as clear as it was daunting.[25]

Nelson's Validation of Difference

Bill Nelson—an imposing gatekeeper of the field of legal history—established the scholarly standards by which I initially measured my work. Based on what I could learn about Nelson and his preferences to work from written sources, I could not tell what reception my work might receive.

Nelson had written an article commenting on and defining the field of legal history. In an age of scholarly "fragmentation," he offered a capacious definition of scholars and scholarship. Legal historians discovered previously unknown facts, synthesized familiar data into a new interpretation, or provided an analytical structure that deepens understanding of facts, all of these approaches making contributions to scholarship.[26] Nelson also shared an important thought about historical interpretation of texts resulting from the judicial and legislative processes. No historian could be deemed to offer a single, authoritative, objective interpretation of the past, because none existed.[27] By those lights, perhaps, my scholarship was in good standing.

The subjects about which Nelson chose to write demarcated legitimate and important subjects, as well. By this measure, my work might appear to be an outlier. Nelson's book on the legislative debates surrounding the Fourteenth Amendment had impressed me as a classic treatment of the subject.[28] My work differed from that genre of classic legal history in important respects. Nelson's work on U.S. District Judge Edward Weinfeld, then in progress, struck me as falling within another important and familiar genre of legal history: It explored the life and work of an elite figure, a great man who had managed to shape the law from the bench of one of the nation's most important federal district courts.[29] No such figure dominated my work; in fact, my work consciously aimed to explore unknown, non-elite figures. The empirical aspect of Nelson's work on the legalist reformation in twentieth-century New York stood out.[30] After reading thousands of New York court cases, Nelson had drawn conclusions from samples of thousands of trial-court cases. This data supported his conclusions about how New York judges developed a legal ideology and legal doctrines that created opportunity for New Yorkers and, as these ideas and doctrines spread nationwide, for disadvantaged Americans, more generally. Here, again, Nelson's work had placed in the foreground historical actors and concepts that my work, based in the world of grassroots actors and little-known lawyers, relegated to the background. In short, the subjects of Nelson's prior work deepened my sense that my subjects and scholarly approach might appear peculiar or uninteresting to "classic" legal historians.

My anxiety, it turned out, was for naught. Nelson welcomed my particular type of externalist, contextual viewpoint on civil rights history. He showed an interest in the pages of my text recounting the details of daily life and the political struggles waged by grassroots actors who fought for freedom, a concept defined differently by different people. My bird's-eye view of the movement's inception, of who was involved and why, of how it evolved, and of why actors made the choices they did—matters that did not involve the consideration of legal doctrines or questions—gave him little pause.

My interest in local lawyers who might have been dismissed as bit players in the legal world, and in low-status, working-class activists on the margins of the law, all of whom had been overlooked in much of the legal history of the civil rights movement, provoked no resistance from this classic legal historian. Indeed, Bill Nelson embraced the assortment of characters who populated my study.

Nelson's openness cast a different light on his scholarship: Whereas I had once seen differences, now I could see points of similarity. Perhaps it was no long leap for Nelson from his own legal history scholarship on twentieth-century New York or colonial and Revolutionary Massachusetts[31] to my work on the civil rights movement in Atlanta. Although our work was different along many dimensions, at bottom, both of us offered place-based analyses of history. When Nelson published his biography of Judge Edward Weinfeld, I found common ground in it, too. To be sure, any federal judge is rightly understood as "elite." But Nelson's exploration of Weinfeld revealed the humble man beneath the black robes. He described how Weinfeld, the son of Jewish immigrants, rose from an impoverished neighborhood on the Lower East Side of New York to the pinnacle of New York's legal profession.[32] In Nelson's portrait of Weinfeld, readers find the origins of the judge's liberal politics and his fact-driven, "apolitical" jurisprudence. In Nelson's portrait, Weinfeld shared many characteristics of the pioneering lawyers in my work, including Austin Thomas Walden, the son of former slaves and sharecroppers, who rose from abject poverty to the upper reaches of the legal profession and then shaped the meaning of civil rights law. Both Nelson and I told stories about the legal profession, upward mobility, and how racial, ethnic, and religious minorities—outsiders—gained advantage in a hostile world.

Bill Nelson's scholarly voice and mine could coexist. Decades later, I had discovered a truth that Nelson had buried deep in his 1982 article "Standards of Criticism." This illuminating passage followed Nelson's definition of scholarship—written in an age when academics routinely "attacked" the work of those with different views about what constituted legitimate scholarly inquiry. Anticipating criticism of his own scholarly perspective, Nelson wrote:

> Many legal historians continue to judge each other's work by . . . inquiring whether another scholar's writing contributes to the attainment of *their own* understanding of the purposes of legal history research. Criticism of this sort, however, is anachronistic; new standards of criticism and evaluation are needed to accommodate the variety of purposes underlying present scholarship. Legal historians who do not agree about the goals of their discipline must carefully distinguish between critical standards by which all scholarship can be judged and *their own more personal aesthetic and ideological values*, which can give meaning to their own scholarly careers but ought not be forced upon others from those in positions of academic power.[33]

Although some scholars remained closed to difference, Bill Nelson could see that the times had changed and that the profession had to change with the times. Long before I had ever met him, Nelson had accepted the arrival of newcomers and new ideas in the field.

In part because of Nelson's openness to my approach, I became more confident about integrating in my own work the bottom-up, community-based social history methodology with the top-down, legal history methodology. I had come to Nelson as a young scholar, captive to Great Works in two fields, subject to different scholarly expectations, situated in multiple institutions, and experiencing uncertainty about how to practice the historian's craft. Under Nelson's tutelage, I came to embrace the methodological diversity and variegated sources that my project required, instead of viewing them as a problem. More precisely, with Nelson's help, I realized that I had created a good "problem" for myself. I resolved to blend all of these sources, as faithfully as I could, in light of my own commitment to balanced proportions of legal and social history, national and local history, elite and non-elite voices. I would listen to the voices and evidence apparent in my sources, tell the stories that followed, and construct an argument consistent with the multiple stories and competing voices that I found.

The questions that Bill Nelson posed to me and to others who attended NYU's Legal History Colloquium about the relationships among historiography, sources, and interpretation reinforced the idea that a skilled craftsperson could integrate competing methodologies into a coherent narrative. Before long, his admonition that a skilled professional historian (as opposed to a law office historian searching for a usable past) must follow her sources and strive for the unconventional rather than the conventional freed me from any obligation I might have felt to follow any reigning interpretation of civil rights history. I would build on both traditions and, in the process, hope to create something of my own.

Nelson's Lesson about the Perils of Presentism

After I became comfortable with these methodological aspirations, I faced another question: Could I deliver work that met the highest standards of scholarship? I wondered whether one potential impediment might be the reality that any historian's experiences and background will influence what evidence she sees and how she interprets that evidence.

This reality—true of all historians—became obvious to me when I presented a draft chapter of my work at the NYU Legal History Colloquium. The draft chapter focused on Atlanta lawyer A. T. Walden, whom some NAACP Legal Defense Fund lawyers and student activists dismissed as an "accommodationist" of Jim Crow. Walden's reputation had been tarnished because he had deviated from both the mainstream liberal civil rights agenda of the NAACP and the radical agenda of the 1960s student movement. He had pursued a more gradual path toward racial equality than that favored by the NAACP during the late 1940s and 1950s and that embraced by the students during the 1960s. On these bases, Walden found himself labeled an "Uncle Tom," a man unwilling to challenge Jim Crow, even though he had been at the forefront of voting rights activism in Georgia, among other endeavors, for decades.[34]

My draft chapter repeated this perspective on Walden; it uncritically used the term "accommodationist." I had no reason to think twice about the implications of the term or how it might influence my entire interpretative framework. The label, although an insult, jibed entirely with the leading works on Thurgood Marshall's campaign against Jim Crow, which also branded those who did not toe the NAACP's line "accommodationists" of segregation.[35] The existing scholarship took these people to be opponents of civil rights activism and, likely, cowards.[36] More recent scholarship perpetuated the equation of "accommodationism" with opposition to affirmative steps to achieve racial justice and continued to paint those who did not toe the national NAACP's party line as self-interested reactionaries.[37]

Nelson gently but firmly nudged me in a way that led me to reconsider this conventional wisdom. He cautioned that the framework that I had imported to discuss Walden may have crossed the line into presentism. For Nelson, it is a cardinal rule that legal historians should not write histories with an orientation toward contemporary events.[38]

Presentism may have crept into my interpretation of Walden, I came to see, because both the LDF's vision of civil rights and the student activists' perspective had come to define our world today. Few, if any, historians of the civil rights movement publicly argue that the U.S. Supreme Court wrongly decided *Brown v. Board of Education*, LDF's signal achievement. Nor does any historian question the signal achievement for which the students deserve at least partial credit, the Civil Rights Act of 1964. The lawyers of the NAACP Legal Defense Fund and student activists in the SNCC are the heroes and heroines of twentieth-century America. Historians of civil rights tend to embrace these legislative and judicial victories and to celebrate the lawyers and activists who fought for them.[39]

The question whether an allegiance to LDF's worldview might affect a civil rights historian's work loomed especially large during the mid-1990s, when I had begun my research. At the time, the Rehnquist Court continued to push back against liberal-legal civil rights jurisprudence in many ways. School desegregation cases provided a case in point; in a series of decisions, the Rehnquist Court had erected new standards in such cases that made it easier for lower courts to dissolve decades-old desegregation decrees.[40] The decisions had been the topic of much discussion when I was a law student. The Rehnquist Court's school desegregation jurisprudence illustrated, many liberal scholars explained, that legal liberalism—and Justice Marshall's constitutionalism—were under attack.

At that jurisprudential moment, when proponents of integration felt besieged, the idea of recovering the history of a man whose commitment to integration was questionable seemed an untimely and perhaps a dubious endeavor. A. T. Walden's support for desegregation, whether of schools or of residential areas, had been half-hearted. He supported the rhetoric of integration, but in many areas he did not actively pursue that goal. Walden fiercely criticized direct action, the student activists' preferred tool. And he endorsed the Civil Rights Act only after it was enacted. Within this context, many would think without questioning the matter that A. T. Walden had earned the insult that he accommodated segregation.[41]

Hence, when I contemplated Nelson's caution against presentism, I could see a clear connection between narratives about the civil rights past and the contentious racial present. William Faulkner's great comment "The past is never dead. It is not even past" summed up the matter.[42] It seemed right to me to caution historians of the twentieth century's great legal and moral struggle to discern how these monumental events might affect or distort scholarly interpretation.

This concept can be troublesome in application, however. Important and influential scholars privilege the critical lens, "counter-history," and outsider narratives in scholarship.[43] These objectives can conflict with the imperative of scholarly nonpartisanship, the vision of the historian's role in which the caution against presentism is rooted. A scholar's commitment to public intellectualism also can edge out otherwise legitimate concerns about presentism in history.[44] Bearing these caveats in mind, I added my own gloss to Nelson's admonition. Perhaps, I decided, the difficulty occurs when professional historians construct history with the *intention* of advancing a *partisan* view,[45] or when they blithely accept the idea that the past is "usable" in much the same way as any other evidence is used in the adversarial process.[46]

These nuances notwithstanding, I found Nelson's caution against presentism invaluable in the context that I then confronted. As I reflected on my project, it occurred to me that a different and more nuanced interpretative framework could emerge if my work paid even *more* attention to A. T. Walden, a lawyer whose racial "conservatism" appeared antiquated, even embarrassing. The "long civil rights movement" metaphor referenced labor movement activists and others who struggled for economic equality—not "accommodationists." Yet my recalibrated and expanded interpretative framework, inasmuch as it discussed variety and conflict in the movement, would dovetail with the call for a more nuanced understanding of the civil rights era. At the same time, the framework could permit the voices of outsiders to emerge and touch on questions at the intersection of law, society, and inequality.

Resolution, or on Answering "What Else Was There?"

In the book that I ultimately wrote, I am careful to discuss Walden in the context of his time and place. My book pegs him as an elder states-man of the movement whose "pragmatic" approach to civil rights grew out of his experiences as a young man, born and raised in rural Georgia, who had climbed into the professional class on the basis of his "smarts," grit, and strong interpersonal skills. Walden was a member of the NAACP's national legal committee and collaborated with the organiza-tion's Charles Hamilton Houston, chief architect of the NAACP's legal strategy to end Jim Crow. When Thurgood Marshall came to Atlanta, he worked in Walden's office, and Walden served as co-counsel on cases with Marshall and other LDF lawyers. And yet he was not Marshall or Houston, and he did not completely adhere to the NAACP's policy, including questions of school and residential segregation, both of which the national organization hoped to stamp out through litigation.

In the end, relying on the primary sources that I uncovered, I came to interpret Walden's approach as a pragmatic pursuit of civil rights, but an approach no less sincere than that of liberals or radicals, although it certainly was different. Walden fervently believed in black voting rights.

He served as a *Smith v. Allwright* tester by attempting to vote in the wake of the U.S. Supreme Court's decision declaring the white primary unconstitutional.[47] Walden argued that black political power, above all else, held the key to black freedom and economic security. I found his approach prescient, rather than racially retrograde, and, in some respects, more substantive and astute than that of proponents of desegregation. He anticipated the concerns that became dominant during the 1970s, when school desegregation had begun to wane and the passage of the Voting Rights Act had given rise to a new black political class. Walden, a proponent of same-race political representation, bloc voting, and machine politics, believed that blacks could obtain power by means of the model that white ethnic groups had used to achieve standing in America. His viewpoint and approach hardly seem unreasonable.[48]

This interpretation of Walden, not as an (illegitimate) accommodationist but as a civil rights pragmatist, opened my mind to a much broader, deeper, synthetic interpretation of civil rights history. I discovered a fuller spectrum of protest against Jim Crow, including activism taking place inside and outside the courtroom, both well before and well after *Brown v. Board of Education*. Thinking about Walden in context led me to ask the questions: Who else is out there whom I could not see, whom we could not see, because of our present heroes? What other lawyers do not fit inside the "NAACP box," or maybe *did* exist within the NAACP, but only if we understand the organization in terms of its local units, as well as the national organization? The scope and breadth of my work expanded.[49]

As a result of this reorientation of my work, I identified and discussed remarkable figures on the civil rights "left" and "right." The work of Len Holt, an attorney for the Lawyers Guild and the Congress of Racial Equality whom NAACP lawyers had deemed too radical and possibly a Communist, soon became central to mine. Howard Moore Jr., the general counsel of the SNCC and LDF lawyer who represented Angela Davis, all manner of "political prisoners," antiwar activists, and student activists, as well as school desegregation plaintiffs, became the focus of two chapters. I also discovered Margie Pitts Hames, a feminist ACLU lawyer and abortion rights litigator who also handled civil rights cases. She bucked both LDF and the local NAACP chapter on school desegregation.[50]

Together, this fuller complement of lawyers, along with their collaborators in the activist community, led me in much more exciting directions than I would have encountered had I kept my eyes focused on the NAACP "prize." Lawyers Holt and Moore, remarkable for the relationships that they built with local people, seemed far apart ideologically from Walden, the pragmatist. However, I found that all three of these lawyers shared a skepticism of court-centric change and, in particular, of the NAACP's school desegregation remedies. Holt and Moore presented a systemic critique of racism in law, society, and the economic system that anticipated discussions in the legal academy of "illusory" rights.[51] Each of the forms of civil rights leadership, all of which had strengths and weaknesses, raised the question whether any one person can represent a group held together by a social construct with such real ramifications as a "race."[52] Instead, I conclude in my book, we can learn a bit about law and social change, about how all social movements are beset by conflict, from studying the careers of all of these figures together—whether Walden, Marshall, Holt, Moore, Hames, students, or working-class activists. Rather than regarding conflict and failure as problematic, we ought to consider what lessons dissidents have to teach social movements that use law as tool of change.

Ultimately, I conclude that it is unlikely that we can fully understand the arc of history through the grand, top-down narrative of the law. Legal history that considers activists and dynamics on the ground can enhance our understanding of race and democracy and of lawyers' place in the civil rights advances of the past half-century.

To the extent that this point is convincing, and if my work succeeds in showing that the civil rights movement was not only long, but deep and broad, Bill Nelson deserves much of the recognition and credit. His wisdom, open-mindedness, and guidance were both generous and timely in the work's evolution. For these gifts, he has earned my respect and gratitude. Every young legal historian should be so fortunate to cross paths with a master teacher at just the right moment.

ACKNOWLEDGMENTS
Many thanks to Daniel Hulsebosch, R. B. Bernstein, Daniel Nagin, and Lani Guinier for comments on drafts of this essay. This essay meditates on my relationship to Bill Nelson, using as a point of departure the legal history of the civil rights movement, as I understood it when I began a graduate program in history at Duke University

in 1992 and law school at Yale University in 1993. Of course, the field underwent changes over time, as I grappled with the questions I discuss here. I cite below several relevant works and interventions in the historiography; I have further discussion in my book *Courage to Dissent: Atlanta and the Long History of the Civil Rights Movement* (New York: Oxford University Press, 2011).

NOTES

1. Jacquelyn Dowd Hall, "The Long Civil Rights Movement and the Political Uses of the Past." *Journal of American History* 91 (March 2005): 1233–63.

2. Brown-Nagin, *Courage to Dissent: Atlanta and the Long History of the Civil Rights Movement* (New York: Oxford University Press, 2010).

3. Laura Kalman, *The Strange Career of Legal Liberalism* (New Haven, Conn.: Yale University Press, 1986), 3–4, 43, 91–92. Kalman labels Fiss a follower of the "cult of the Court." *Ibid.*, 4.

4. *Ibid.*, 3. The historians Mark V. Tushnet and Morton J. Horwitz also endorsed highly favorable views of the Warren Court and its capacity. *Ibid.* at 43. More recently, Gerald Rosenberg, the political scientist, and Michael Klarman, the constitutional historian, offered revisionist views of law and social change questioning the liberal legal view of the Supreme Court and its capacity. See Gerald Rosenberg, *The Hollow Hope: Can Courts Bring about Social Change* (Chicago: University of Chicago Press, 1991); Michael Klarman, *From Jim Crow to Civil Rights: The Supreme Court and the Struggle for Racial Equality* (New York: Oxford University Press, 2004). My book is in conversation with this revisionist literature.

5. See Fiss, *Law as It Could Be* (New York: New York University Press, 2004), ix–xii, 2–5.

6. *Ibid.*, 10–12, 14.

7. Fiss, for example, wrote that in the school desegregation cases, blacks as a group—the quintessential discrete and insular minority—needed someone to "speak on its behalf." Individual victims, brutalized and vulnerable, could not speak for themselves; an institutional advocate must be "spokesperson for the victim group." *Ibid.*, 17. Here, Fiss, who takes the school desegregation injunction as a paradigm of the structural injunction, referenced prison reform litigation as well. I should note that I am uncertain whether I read the piece quoted here when I was in law school and a student of Fiss's. However, this piece captures essential elements of Fiss's worldview and scholarship of his that I did read at that time.

8. Mark V. Tushnet, *Making Civil Rights Law: Thurgood Marshall and the Supreme Court, 1936–1961* (New York: Oxford University Press, 1994), 216; Mark V. Tushnet, *The NAACP's Legal Strategy against Segregated Education, 1925–1950* (Chapel Hill: University of North Carolina Press, 1987; new edition, 2004), 185; see also Genna Rae McNeil, *Groundwork: Charles Hamilton Houston and the Struggle for Civil Rights* (Philadelphia: University of Pennsylvania Press, 1983). In the words

of Richard Kluger, author of the most celebrated work about the case, *Simple Justice*, *Brown* "represented nothing short of a re-consecration of American ideals." "Black bodies had suddenly been reborn under a new law. Blacks' value as human beings had changed overnight by the declaration of the nation's highest court," Kluger continued. Richard Kluger, *Simple Justice: The History of Brown v. Board of Education and Black America's Struggle for Legal Equality* (New York: Alfred A. Knopf, 1976; revised and expanded edition, New York: Alfred A. Knopf, 2004), 710, 749.

9. See Charles W. Eagles, "Toward New Histories of the Civil Rights Era," *Journal of Southern History* 66:4 (November 2000): 815–48.

10. William Chafe, the author of a landmark community study of the civil rights movement and my graduate school advisor, pioneered this methodology. William H. Chafe, *Civilities and Civil Rights: Greensboro, North Carolina, and the Black Struggle for Freedom* (New York: Oxford University Press, 1981). J. Mills Thornton III also wrote a groundbreaking bottom-up study of the Montgomery bus boycott. J. Mills Thornton, *Dividing Lines: Municipal Politics and the Struggle for Civil Rights in Montgomery, Birmingham, and Selma* (Tuscaloosa: University of Alabama Press, 2002). For a valuable discussion, see Eagles, "Toward New Histories," 827.

11. See Eagles, "Toward New Histories," 827.

12. On the importance of local narratives to understanding the civil rights movement, see, for example, Clayborne Carson, "Civil Rights Reform and the Black Freedom Struggle," in Charles W. Eagles, ed., *The Civil Rights Movement in America* (Jackson: University of Mississippi Press, 1986), 27–28; Steven Lawson, "Debating the Civil Rights Movement: The View from the Nation," in Lawson and Payne, eds., *Debating the Civil Rights Movement* (Lanham, Md.: Rowman & Littlefield, 1998); Charles Payne, "Debating the Civil Rights Movement: The View from the Trenches," in Lawson and Payne, eds., *Debating the Civil Rights Movement*, quote at 110.

13. Jacquelyn Dowd Hall, "Partial Truths," *Signs*, 14:4 (Summer 1989): 902–11 (discussing race and class in women's history).

14. See John Hope Franklin, "The New Negro History," in *Race and History: Selected Essays, 1938–1988* (Baton Rouge: Louisiana State University Press, 1989), 41–43 (noting history of animus-motivated misrepresentation of African Americans in history).

15. I was especially contemplative about striking the proper balance in my telling of civil rights history in light of the fierce battles waged over how much emphasis on violent white resistance to *Brown* was too much. See Michael Klarman, "*Brown v. Board of Education*: Facts and Political Correctness," *Virginia Law Review* 80 (1994): 185; Mark Tushnet, "The Significance of *Brown v. Board of Education*," *Virginia Law Review* 80 (1994): 173; and David Garrow, "Hopelessly Hollow History: Revisionist Devaluing of *Brown v. Board of Education*," *Virginia Law Review* 80 (1994): 151.

16. For a helpful discussion, see Robert W. Gordon, "Critical Legal Histories," *Stanford Law Review* 36 (1984): 57.

17. See, for example, William E. Nelson, *The Fourteenth Amendment: From Political Principle to Judicial Doctrine* (Cambridge, Mass.: Harvard University Press, 1988); cf. Morton J. Horwitz, *The Transformation of American Law, 1870–1960: The Crisis of Legal Orthodoxy* (New York: Oxford University Press, 1992) (discussing economic context of doctrine); Klarman, *From Jim Crow to Civil Rights* (discussing history of Supreme Court's treatment of race and considering how demographic factors, economic change, war, white resistance, and other external forces shaped decisions).

18. For examples of this literature, see Charles L. Black Jr., "The Lawfulness of the Segregation Decisions," *Yale Law Journal* 69 (1960): 421, 421–27 (1960); Herbert Wechsler, "Toward Neutral Principles of Constitutional Law," *Harvard Law Review* 73 (1959): 1.

19. See, for example, Davison M. Douglas, *Reading, Writing, and Race: The Desegregation of the Charlotte Schools* (Chapel Hill: University of North Carolina Press, 1995). In the course of explaining how the NAACP's legal strategy unfolded, Tushnet discusses clients in local communities. See Tushnet, *The NAACP's Legal Strategy*.

20. For a recent discussion of civil rights historiography that provides helpful context and discusses change and stasis in the historiography since I started my project, see Kenneth W. Mack, "Bringing the Law Back into the History of the Civil Rights Movement," *Law and History Review* 27:3 (Fall 2009): 657–69.

21. Quoted in Stokely Carmichael, *Ready for Revolution* (New York: Scribner, 2003), 142.

22. See John Lewis with Michael D'Orso, *Walking with the Wind: A Memoir of the Movement* (New York: Simon and Schuster, 1998), 107–8; *New York Times*, 15 February 1960, p. 1; 21 February 1960, p. E3; 17 April 1960, p. 32; 6 March 1960, p. E3.

23. Consider, for example, that Professor Mari Matsuda, in her incisive, seminal work "Looking to the Bottom," wrote: "There is something about color that doesn't wash off as easily as class. The experience of racism, it seems, causes the normative choices of black capitalists to diverge from the choices of others in their class." Even as I admired Matsuda's work, her widely held assumption, it occurred to me, clashed with a vigorous analysis of civil rights leaders, tactics, and strategies. Mari Matsuda, "Looking to the Bottom: Critical Legal Studies and the Reparations Movement," *Harvard Civil Rights–Civil Liberties Law Review* 22 (1987): 323, 361. I noticed that other works of critical theory similarly glossed over class and intra-racial dynamics. See Mark Tushnet, "An Essay on Rights," *Texas Law Review* 62 (1984): 1363, 1398–403; Patricia J. Williams, *The Alchemy of Race and Rights* (Cambridge, Mass.: Harvard University Press, 1991), 22–28; Neil Gotanda, "A Critique of 'Our Constitution Is Color-Blind,'" *Stanford Law Review* 44 (1991): 1, 36–52; cf. Kimberle Crenshaw, "Mapping the Margins:

Intersectionality, Identity Politics, and Violence Against Women of Color," *Stanford Law Review* 43 (1991): 1241, 1242. On the need for such interpretations, see, for example, Eagles, "Toward New Histories," 840–41. For a recent interpretation that criticizes LDF for abandoning labor cases in favor of school desegregation, see Risa Goluboff, *The Lost Promise of Civil Rights* (Cambridge, Mass.: Harvard University Press, 2007). For different perspectives on the relationship between the civil rights and labor movements, see Paul Frymer, *Black and Blue: African Americans, the Labor Movement, and the Decline of the Democratic Party* (Princeton, N.J.: Princeton University Press, 2008); Nancy MacLean, *Freedom Is Not Enough: The Opening of the American Workplace* (Cambridge, Mass.: Harvard University Press, 2006); Sophia Lee, "Hotspots in a Cold War: The NAACP's Postwar Workplace Constitutionalism, 1948–1964," *Law and History Review* 26 (2008): 327.

24. See Derrick A. Bell Jr., "Serving Two Masters: Integration Ideals and Client Interests in School Desegregation Litigation," *Yale Law Journal* 85 (1976): 470 (questioning who is the true "client" in school desegregation litigation and arguing that educational improvement and "instructional profit" for African American children should be the long-term goals of desegregation campaigns); see also Lani Guinier, "The Triumph of Tokenism: The Voting Rights Act and the Theory of Black Electoral Success," *Michigan Law Review* 89 (March 1991): 1077–154. I reached different conclusions about past events and argue that history teaches different lessons from those that Bell asserted many years ago. See Brown-Nagin, *Courage to Dissent*, chapters 10–12; Tomiko Brown-Nagin, "Race as Identity Caricature: A Local Legal History Lesson in the Salience of Intraracial Conflict," *University of Pennsylvania Law Review* 151 (2003): 1913.

25. Lawson, "Debating the Civil Rights Movement: The View from the Nation," 4.

26. See William E. Nelson, "Standards of Criticism," *Texas Law Review* 60 (1982): 447, 449–50.

27. *Ibid.*, 450–51.

28. Nelson, *The Fourteenth Amendment*.

29. Nelson, *In Pursuit of Right and Justice: Edward Weinfeld as Lawyer and Judge* (New York: New York University Press, 2004).

30. See William E. Nelson, *The Legalist Reformation: Law, Politics, and Ideology in New York, 1920–1980* (Chapel Hill: University of North Carolina Press, 2001).

31. William E. Nelson, *The Americanization of the Common Law: The Impact of Legal Change Upon Massachusetts Society, 1760–1830* (Cambridge, Mass.: Harvard University Press, 1975; new edition, Athens: University of Georgia Press, 1994); see also William E. Nelson, "Authority and the Rule of Law in Early Virginia," *Ohio Northern University Law Review* 29 (2003): 305. This article is one of many he has written as precursors to his multivolume project *The Common Law in Colonial America*. For the first installment, see William E. Nelson, *The Common Law in Colonial America, Volume I: The Chesapeake and New England, 1607–1660* (New York: Oxford University Press, 2008).

32. Nelson, *In Pursuit of Right and Justice*, 3.

33. Nelson, "Standards of Criticism," 451–52.

34. The final version of this chapter is Brown-Nagin, *Courage to Dissent*, chapter 1.

35. See Tushnet, *The NAACP's Legal Strategy*, 107–11, 113–16, 138–41.

36. See Kluger, *Simple Justice*, 3, 7, 11–12, 116–18, 199, 221, 256, 391–94, 460. Kluger repeatedly describes blacks as generally "apathetic" or "complacent" about discrimination and unwilling to protest mistreatment because of fear, intimidation, and self-interest—characterizations that undoubtedly were accurate in many instances but far from the whole story; see also Tushnet, *NAACP's Legal Strategy*, 138–47 (equating opponents of NAACP's desegregation campaign with segregationists).

37. See, for example, Stephen G.N. Tuck's *Beyond Atlanta: The Struggle for Racial Equality in Georgia, 1940–1980* (Athens: University of Georgia Press, 2001), 44–62, which applauds the protest- and integration-oriented struggle for civil rights in Savannah and contrasts it with Atlanta's more cautious movement.

38. See Nelson, "Standards of Criticism," 469.

39. See Eagles, "Toward New Histories," 840–41; but see Rosenberg, *Hollow Hope*; cf. Klarman, *From Jim Crow*, who argues that *Brown* aided the passage of the Civil Rights Act in a perverse way—by provoking a violent white backlash.

40. See *Missouri v. Jenkins*, 515 U.S. 70 (1995); *Board of Oklahoma School District v. Dowell*, 498 U.S. 237 (1991); *Freeman v. Pitts*, 503 U.S. 467 (1992).

41. See Brown-Nagin, *Courage to Dissent*, chapter 8, p. 384.

42. William Faulkner, *Requiem for a Nun* (New York: Random House, 1951), 92.

43. See, for example, Robert Gordon, "Critical Legal Histories," *Stanford Law Review* 36 (1984): 57; Rachel Moran, "Race, Representation, and Remembering," *UCLA Law Review* 49 (2002): 1513 (advocating counter-history and stories that highlight the "authentic" voices of outsiders); Naomi R. Cahn, "Inconsistent Stories," *Georgetown Law Journal* 81 (August 1993): 2475 (noting how legal stories feature conflicting versions of events, making it difficult to distinguish perception from reality and thus to sort out truths).

44. In fact, Jacquelyn Dowd Hall's sense that history should be relevant to present political and legal controversies—in this instance, to continuing battles over race and inequality—inspired her call to historians to reframe the civil rights movement. She believed that historians' tendency to tell morality tales about the movement, in which good prevailed over evil during the period 1954 through 1965, had facilitated the political agendas of those intent on quashing discussion of persistent race- and class-based inequality. See Jacquelyn Dowd Hall, "The Long Civil Rights Movement and the Political Uses of the Past," *Journal of American History* 91 (2005): 1233–63.

45. See John Hope Franklin, "The Historian and Public Policy," in *Race and History: Selected Essays, 1938–1988* (Baton Rouge: Louisiana State University Press, 1989), 309–20 (distinguishing partisan historical scholarship designed to support causes from nonpartisan historical scholarship that, by virtue of its discussion

of socially relevant past events, may be deemed by policymakers to provide rational bases for making public policy decisions, and endorsing the latter).

46. See Martin Flaherty, "History 'Lite' in Modern American Constitutionalism," *Columbia Law Review* 95 (1995): 523; Matthew J. Festa, "Applying a Usable Past: The Use of History in Law," *Seton Hall Law Review* 38 (2008): 479. Discussions of controversies surrounding historians as expert witnesses shed light on the debate over conflicts between the standards of historians and legal advocates and the idea of presentism in legal history. See Thomas Haskell and Sanford Levinson, "Academic Freedom and Expert Witnessing: Historians and the Sears Case," *Texas Law Review* 66 (1998): 1629 (1998); see also Rebecca S. Eisenberg, "The Scholar as Advocate," *Journal of Legal Education* 43 (1993): 391.

47. *Smith v. Allwright*, 321 U.S. 649 (1944). On this case, see Darlene Clark Hine, *Black Victory: The Rise and Fall of the White Primary in Texas* (Millwood, N.Y.: KTO Press, 1979; new edition, Columbia: University of Missouri Press, 2003), and Charles L. Zelden, *The Battle for the Black Ballot: Smith v. Allwright and the Defeat of the Texas All-White Primary* (Lawrence: University Press of Kansas, 2004).

48. Brown-Nagin, *Courage to Dissent*, chapter 2.

49. For important work, with which I am in conversation, that explores the variety of civil rights practice in an earlier era, see Kenneth W. Mack, "Law and Mass Politics in the Making of the Civil Rights Lawyer, 1931–1941." *Journal of American History* 93 (June 2006): 37–62; see also Kenneth W. Mack, "Rethinking Civil Rights Lawyering and Politics in the Era Before *Brown*." *Yale Law Journal* 115 (November 2005): 256–354. For important recent work that expands legal-historical understanding by discussing the legal work of the NAACP, see Lee, "Hotspots." See also Patricia Sullivan, *Lift Every Voice: The NAACP and the Making of the Civil Rights Movement* (New York: New Press, 2009).

50. See Brown-Nagin, *Courage to Dissent*, chs. 7–9.

51. See, for example, Howard Moore, "Racism as Justice." *Black Law Journal* 3 (1973): 54–66. Skepticism among black leaders about using the courts as tools for achieving racial justice was deeply rooted, reaching far back in time. See, for example, Ralph J. Bunche, "A Critical Analysis of the Tactics and Programs of Minority Groups." *Journal of Negro Education* 4 (Jul. 1935): 308–20.

52. On questions of race and representation, see, for example, Guinier, "The Triumph of Tokenism," and Lublin, *The Paradox of Representation*, 4–6, 120–24; cf. Swain, *Black Faces, Black Interests*, 5–19, 34–41, 47–141; J. Phillip Thompson, *Double Trouble*.

7

Counting as a Tool of Legal History

JOHN WERTHEIMER

In the 1960s and 1970s, historical writing in the United States passed through a golden age of quantification. Two developments underlay this trend: advances in computer technology, which enabled scholars to analyze previously unmanageable amounts of data, and the rise of social history, which prompted scholars to seek new ways to study non-elites. Because such groups as workers, slaves, and the poor often left frustratingly scant paper trails, scholars who tried to study these groups using traditional written sources often came up empty. Numerically minded historians realized, however, that even the most marginalized people—even those who, considered individually, left behind few or no words—often, when considered collectively, left behind rich arrays of numbers. Historians who could tease such figures out of archives, who had access to computers, and who were comfortable with statistical analysis could make those numbers talk. "Social science history" was born.

Quantification transformed American historical scholarship. Robert Fogel and Stanley Engerman's head-turning *Time on the Cross* challenged conventional understandings of slavery and turned "cliometrics" into a household word.[1] "New Political Historians" such as Lee Benson, Paul Kleppner, Ronald Formisano, Allan Lichtman, and Samuel P. Hays used sophisticated statistical techniques to rewrite the narrative of American political life.[2] The "New Urban History" used quantitative methods to stretch the study of cities beyond mayors and elites.[3] The

"New Social History" used quantitative analysis to explore social, geo-graphical, and occupational mobility, as well as family history.[4]

By the early 1970s, quantification had permeated the historical disci-pline. Books designed to introduce mathphobic historians to quantita-tive methods proliferated.[5] No fewer than ten sessions at the Organi-zation of American Historians' annual meeting in 1974 dealt with the application of quantitative methods to historical research.[6] That same year saw the birth of the Social Science History Association, which published a journal and held annual meetings designed to encourage historical writing that attempted "generalizations of some breadth" based on quantitative analysis and other forms of systematic research.[7]

American legal history, however, proved comparatively resistant to the quantification craze. As traditionally practiced, legal history empha-sized the evolution of legal doctrine, a quintessentially qualitative, not quantitative, matter. Moreover, many legal historians inhabited law schools, not history departments, making them relatively impervious to the quantifying trends that were sweeping arts and sciences faculties. Thus, although a "new legal history" did develop during these years,[8] it did not share the number-crunching emphasis of the era's "new politi-cal history," "new social history," or "new urban history."

Quantification was in the air, however, and did have a measured impact on the field of legal history. With grant money flowing to schol-ars, including legal scholars, who engaged in number-crunching; with such groups as the Law and Society Association (founded in 1964) promoting social science approaches to the study of law; and with the influential J. Willard Hurst inspiring legal historians, through his schol-arship and mentoring, to look beyond judges and doctrine, quantifica-tion did affect the discipline. Some legal historians embraced quantita-tive methods with at least one arm.

One of the most beneficial consequences of this halting move toward quantification was the identification and exploration of an expanded range of sources. Traditional, doctrinally focused legal historians relied principally on appellate opinions, legal treatises, and other published sources—the sorts of materials that one could conveniently find in law school libraries. Historians of doctrine had little use for, say, musty docket books in remote courthouses. Legal scholars with a quantita-tive mindset, by contrast, realized how valuable such archival materials could be. Old docket-book entries, though essentially meaningless when read singly, could tell important stories when read en masse and summed up smartly. Research trips to musty legal archives increased, inspiring Lawrence M. Friedman's quip that real legal historians should not have allergies.[9]

Two of the most important American legal history books of the 1970s, Morton J. Horwitz's *The Transformation of American Law* (1977) and William E. Nelson's *Americanization of the Common Law* (1975), illustrate both the limits and the benefits of quantification's impact on the field during the golden age of number-crunching.[10] The books' themes are similar; indeed, they could easily have swapped titles. Both explore the interaction between capitalist development and the law in the northern states from the era of the American Revolution to the mid–nineteenth century. The books' research methods, however, differed substantially. For all its substantive revisionism,[11] Horwitz's *Transformation* was methodologically orthodox. Appellate opinions and legal treatises dominate the footnotes; one imagines Horwitz conducting essentially all of his primary source research without leaving Harvard's libraries.

Nelson's *Americanization*, by contrast, carried a bigger carbon footprint. To research it, Nelson gassed up his car—repeatedly—and crisscrossed Massachusetts and Maine, visiting courthouses. Counting helped him make sense of the voluminous material he unearthed. For example, he invoked trial-court numbers to demonstrate the declining power of "puritanical" moral standards in Massachusetts from the mid–eighteenth to the early nineteenth century. In the decade and a half before the outbreak of the American Revolution, he calculated, the colony of Massachusetts initiated some 2,784 criminal prosecutions. Of these, only 13 percent were for "property" offenses (for example, robbery), whereas 38 percent were for "Offenses against God and Religion" (for example, adultery).[12] As Massachusetts commercialized in the decades following the Revolution, those proportions basically inverted; prosecutions for sin decreased and prosecutions for property crimes increased.[13]

Nelson used quantification to great effect. Numerical analysis helped him to sketch the contours of developments in trial courts, legal history's submerged (and often overlooked) bulk. This project beautifully complemented Horwitz's subsequent, provocative, and gripping analysis of the high court rulings that floated above the jurisprudential water line. The Horwitz and Nelson stories differed in many ways but were compatible, in part because they informed each other's creation. The two authors were friends. As they worked on their books, they swapped research notes and numbers. In his *Transformation* acknowledgments, Horwitz reported that Nelson "graciously shared with me the fruits of his own research into the Massachusetts court records."[14]

Even at his most quantitative,[15] however, Nelson was much less obsessed with numbers than were many of his contemporaries in history departments. His math was simple. He did not use "regression analysis" or any other elaborate statistical technique. Rather, he used what might be called commonsense quantification: clear and easy-to-grasp measures of relevant numerical data, such as the ratio of contract cases to total cases in these years as opposed to those.[16] Nelson was not the only legal historian to use commonsense quantification. Lawrence M. Friedman, Michael Hindus, Kermit Hall, and other contemporaries also incorporated the technique.[17] It had a terrifically positive effect on the field.

As time passed, however, quantification fell from favor. Historical scholarship took a cultural turn. Even so, commonsense quantifiers in the legal history guild, never having fully embraced number-crunching during its heyday, did not abandon it when the craze faded. As Nelson reaffirmed decades later in *The Legalist Reformation* (2001), "statistical analysis can help in understanding the impact of doctrine on society."[18]

I agree. Indeed, I believe that simple statistical analysis can help clarify not just the social impact of doctrine but also many other facets of legal history. Although I am not a sophisticated number-cruncher, I frequently rely on commonsense quantification as the best available way to illuminate particular facets of America's legal past. I find it especially useful when seeking to situate historical case studies within broader legal and social contexts. Here are three examples of commonsense quantification, drawn from my research. Each investigates a different aspect of the legal history of race in the United States. The first example explores the legal system's composition, the second examines its actions, and the third considers its impact.

Measuring the Legal System's Composition: Juries

The social backgrounds of judges and jurors can affect their legal decisions. Scholars of judges can assess their social backgrounds both quali-
tatively and quantitatively. The qualitative approach is more common.
Judicial biographers routinely seek to analyze legal rulings in light
of judges' personal histories.[19] For example, scholars have read U.S.
Supreme Court Justice John Marshall Harlan the elder's legal opinions,
including his famous dissent in *Plessy v. Ferguson*,[20] in light of various
facets of his personal history, including his "Old School" Presbyterian-
ism,[21] his Southern Whig nationalism,[22] his troubled relationships with
his siblings,[23] and his slave-owning family's paternalism.[24]

Less commonly, scholars of the judiciary have employed quantitative techniques. During the golden age of number-crunching, Kermit
Hall and other legal historians used statistical analysis to explore the
collective social origins of judges, state and federal, on benches high
and low.[25]

Scholars who wish to learn about the social backgrounds of jurors as
opposed to judges, however, are almost compelled to quantify. Jurors
come and go, leaving behind few words. Qualitative research techniques
can reveal little about them. Counting, however, can shed at least some
light on jury composition, as the case of Arthur Middleton suggests.[26]

In March 1945, South Carolina prosecuted Arthur Middleton for
attempted rape. In that place, at that time, race and sex mattered. It
mattered that Middleton was a black man. It mattered that his alleged
victim was a white woman. And, as Solicitor Robert M. Figg understood, it mattered that the jury was 100 percent white and male. In
his closing statement, Figg urged jurors to look past the prosecution's
evidentiary weaknesses and appreciate the case's broader implications.
"The verdict you bring in," he warned jurors, addressing them as fellow
white men, "may be the safety of *our* womanhood [emphasis added]."[27]
The jury promptly voted to convict. Although a white man had recently
received just eighteen months for raping a white woman,[28] Middleton,
for *attempted* rape, was sentenced to twenty-five years.[29]

Middleton appealed on the ground that African Americans had been
systematically excluded from jury service in his case. Scholars who rely
on the written record might be skeptical of this claim. On its face, South

Carolina law went to elaborate lengths to assure fair jury selection. Stat-utes commanded each county's three jury commissioners to write the names of all qualified electors on separate slips of paper. Each slip was inserted into a separate "opaque capsule, or container, uniform in size, shape, and color." These capsules were then placed in a "strong and sub-stantial" box, which was locked with three "separate and strong" locks, each of which required a unique key. Each key was to be held by a dif-ferent jury commissioner, so that the box could be unlocked only if all three were present.[30] The jury commissioners in Arthur Middleton's case testified that they had scrupulously complied with these rules, that their selections were made "purely by chance,"[31] and that they "never gave [race] any consideration" in picking jurors.[32] On these grounds, the South Carolina Supreme Court denied Middleton's appeal.[33]

Quantitative analysis of the historical record, however, suggests a different story. All evidence indicates that the jury commissioners per-formed their opaque-capsule-and-strong-box routine as ordered, giv-ing the system a patina of legalistic fairness and arguably enabling the commissioners themselves to believe that the rule of law had prevailed. But the system was rife with injustice. The pool of names that formed the starting point of the jury selection process—the list of "quali-fied electors"—was extremely unrepresentative of the population as a whole. Electoral disfranchisement excluded most nonwhites from that initial pool before jury selection even began.[34] Additionally, statutory provisions gave jury commissioners tremendous discretionary power, enabling them to exclude from juries all electors who, in their estima-tion, lacked "good moral character" or "sound judgment."[35] Race and class prejudice affected those decisions. Electoral disfranchisement and jury commissioner discretion combined to filter out the vast majority of nonwhites from possible jury service before the first opaque capsule even entered the triple-locked box.

Quantitative historical analysis substantiates this conclusion.[36] Before describing our results, however, it is worth reflecting on some of the many challenges associated with this sort of research. Imperfections in archival materials often make laboratory-like precision impossible. The key sources in the present study are county-level, Jim Crow–era "voting books" (listing registered voters) and "jury books" (listing prospective jurors) from South Carolina. Some of these books have been preserved;

many others have disappeared. How representative are the books that
remain? Nobody knows. The remaining books are too numerous, and the
research process is too laborious, to be analyzed comprehensively. Time
limitations demand that the researcher seek a representative sample, a
judgment call. Within the chosen books, damaged pages, illegible handwriting, improper spelling, and other such problems make fully authoritative data sets impossible. Unscientific name-skipping is the only option.

Complications continue when scholars seek to determine the races of
the people listed. Some jury commissioners wrote the letter "C" next to
the names of people whom they considered "colored." These written designations appear to have been especially common in the late nineteenth
century. The "C" listings tend to be quite consistent with racial designations contained in U.S. Census reports. But because not all jury books
contain "C's," quantifiers must take the time to cross-reference, name-by-
name, the samples drawn from (imperfect) jury lists against data contained in (imperfect) census reports, in an attempt to determine official
racial designations of all compiled names.[37] This task is easier said than
done. At this writing, name-by-name census reports are available only
through 1930. This research technique, thus, is unworkable for the era of
the Middleton case itself. Even in the available census records, a given
county's census listings might contain, say, three Thomas Smiths, two
black and one white. Which is the Thomas Smith listed in the jury book?
Scratch Thomas Smith. Some spellings are close, but not exact matches.
How many inconsistent letters may the scholar allow and still declare a
match with a clean conscience? Some people are listed by initials, not full
names. Must such entries be ignored? People moved in and out of counties between census years. Is the Joseph Williams listed in a county's 1900
census the same as the Joseph Williams listed in that county's 1905 jury
book? In these and many other scenarios, even the most conscientious
researcher must make difficult judgment calls and, at the end of the day,
accept at least some uncertainty. Results of this sort of research can be
revealing and significant but can never be absolutely precise.

The rewards of quantitative research, however, justify the effort. Data
compiled from South Carolina census reports, voter registration books,
and jury books between 1880 and 1930 indicates that blacks were indeed
severely underrepresented on juries, and that this underrepresenta-
tion resulted from two independent but overlapping factors: the voter

registration process and the jury selection process. The two processes acted as successive filters of increasingly fine weave. Together, they excluded most nonwhite South Carolinians from jury service.

Thus far, our data—which we are still compiling—divides into two chronological periods: from 1880 until the adoption of the disenfranchising constitution of 1895, and from 1896 until 1930. In the pre-disenfranchisement period, the impact of the jury selection process was especially pronounced, for black voting rates were, according to our (still small) data sample, surprisingly (and perhaps inaccurately) high. In the two counties from which we have sampled voter registration figures thus far, African Americans accounted for an average of 65 percent of the populations, and an impressive 55 percent of registered voters. In those same counties, however, African Americans accounted for just 8.5 percent of the names in jury books. Before disenfranchisement, in other words, jury commissioners did much more than voting registrars to exclude blacks.

After the adoption of the 1895 constitution, disenfranchisement became a much more significant factor than it previously had been. Jury commissioners, however, continued to exert an independent and strongly discriminatory effect. In the mix of South Carolina counties for which we were able to find post-1895 voting and jury numbers, African Americans accounted for an average of 46.5 percent of the population, 12.7 percent of registered voters, and just 3 percent of names in jury books.

See the accompanying table for what the numbers look like in tabular form.

Historical Period	Pre-1895[a]	Post-1895[b]
African Americans as a Percentage of the Population in the South Carolina Counties for which We Found Both Voter Registration Lists and Jury Books	64.85%	46.5%
African Americans as a Percentage of Registered Voters in Sampled Counties	55%	12.66%
African Americans as a Percentage of Names Listed in Jury Books in Sampled Counties	8.5%	3%

a. The pre-1895 counties sampled were Newberry County and Charleston County. Voter registration and jury books are held at the State Archives, South Carolina Department of Archives and History, Columbia, South Carolina.

b. Post-1895 counties sampled were Spartanburg, Aiken, Berkeley, Newberry, and Greenville. Voter registration and jury books are held at the State Archives, South Carolina Department of Archives and History, Columbia, South Carolina.

There is nothing transcendently true about these numbers. For one thing, they are based on limited research. Each additional voting book or jury book that we consult will change these numbers—perhaps substantially. But additional research is unlikely to overturn what these preliminary findings indicate: that the jury selection process was significantly discriminatory, well beyond the effects of electoral disenfranchisement.

As the attempted-rape prosecution of Arthur Middleton in Charleston in 1945 shows, the consequences of this discrimination were profound. The all-white jury was a powerful bulwark of white supremacy. This state of affairs was true throughout the Jim Crow era, but it may have been especially true late in that period, during the era surrounding World War II, because by that time lynching had dramatically declined in South Carolina.[38] With lynching no longer a central means of enforcing white supremacy, the World War II–era all-white jury may have been seen as more important than ever as a way of protecting, in the coded words of Solicitor Figg, "our womanhood."[39]

Measuring the Legal System's Actions: How Were Particular Statutes Used?

Historians tend to pay too much attention to the enactment of laws and not enough attention to how those laws were used. For instance, most U.S. history surveys mention the *enactment* of, say, the Pure Food and Drug Act of 1906. Typical accounts present the adoption of this statute as a reflection of muckraking, consumer protection, and administrative governance during the Progressive Era. But few such works say anything about this law's post-enactment history, even though implementation patterns can be just as historically revealing as enactment timing. Counting can reveal implementation patterns.

Note this post–Civil War, Reconstruction-era example. It concerns prosecutions for "fornication and adultery" (that is, out-of-wedlock sex, generally abbreviated in docket books as "F&A") in Mecklenburg County, North Carolina, from the late 1860s to the late 1870s. The legal definition of F&A did not change at all during these years. The enforcement of F&A laws, however, changed dramatically.

Simple counting of the Mecklenburg County criminal docket reveals a sharp increase in F&A prosecutions after 1874, the year when

anti-Reconstruction Democrats wrested control of the local government from pro-Reconstruction Republicans. In 1873, the year before
the Republicans lost power locally, F&A prosecutions accounted for
between 1 and 2 percent of the criminal cases heard in the Mecklenburg
County Superior Court. In the same court's August 1876 term, by contrast, F&A prosecutions accounted for fully 10 percent of the criminal
cases brought before the newly elected Democratic judge (a former Ku
Klux Klan leader) by the newly elected Democratic solicitor.[40]

Simple counting of aggregate numbers, however, is sometimes
too blunt a tool, as this example demonstrates. Based on the figures
described above, we might reasonably conclude that Mecklenburg
County Democrats engaged in a general crackdown on sexual immorality after their electoral victories in 1874. This conclusion, however,
would be wrong, suggesting the dangers of relying on numbers alone.
In this case, qualitative research into the period reveals what underlay
the post-"Redemption" spike in Mecklenburg County F&A prosecutions: a Democratic attempt to stamp out sexual relationships between
black men and white women—relationships that the Republicans had
not endorsed but had tolerated. In the 1874 electoral campaign, Mecklenburg County Democrats were explicit about their aims. "While white
men intend to rule in the county and State Governments, and do not
want any negro office-holders, they . . . intend to accord to the negro
all rights in law and equity," they vowed. "But . . . social equality will
never be tolerated or permitted."[41] In Democratic eyes, few instances of
"social equality" could have been less tolerable than sexual relationships
between black men and white women.

The nature of this Democratic emphasis is evident in the legal
records. Before 1874, under Republican solicitors and judges, F&A prosecutions typically targeted unmarried, same-race cohabiters.[42] Democratic "Redeemers," by contrast, aggressively used F&A prosecutions to
crack down on interracial relationships. As mentioned, fully 10 percent
of all criminal cases heard in the August 1876 term of the Mecklenburg
County Superior Court—12 cases out of 120—were F&A prosecutions.
This was not a general crackdown on out-of-wedlock cohabitation.
Indeed, many of the defendants were married couples. Rather, it was
a targeted crackdown on interracial cohabitation, including interracial marriage. (Interracial marriage was then legal in South Carolina;

several interracial couples had married in South Carolina and moved to North Carolina.) Although the identities of only 6 of the 12 couples tried for F&A in August of 1876 can be determined, all 6 of these couples—and perhaps all 12—were black men paired with white women.[43]

Measuring Law's Impact on Society: Migrations across Legal Borders

Besides measuring the legal system's composition and its actions, counting can help scholars to measure its social effects. One way to achieve this goal is to use census reports to measure the flow of people across state lines, in response to legal differences. Few legal differences among the American states have been as profound as those in antebellum America between slave states and free states. Census records reveal some of this borderland's social contours.

The Ohio River divided slavery from freedom. This fundamental legal difference motivated the movement of people. According to 1860 census records for Hamilton County, Ohio, on the northern banks of the Ohio River migrants dominated the local black community. Only 16 percent of the black heads of family listed in the county's census were native to Ohio; fewer than 10 percent came from other Northern states. All of the remaining black family heads—about 75 percent of the total—had migrated from slave states.[44]

The substantial black migration northward is all the more impressive when contrasted with two other migration statistics. The first is the minimal northward migration of whites. Whereas approximately 75 percent of Hamilton County's black family heads had originated in slave states, just 5 percent of the county's white family heads had come from slave states.[45]

Another way to highlight the impressive magnitude of *northward* black migration is to contrast it with *southward* black migration. The latter scarcely existed. The free black population of Jefferson County, Kentucky, a border county a hundred miles southwest of Hamilton County, Ohio, was substantial. Census records indicate that this county, home to Louisville, included 639 free black heads of household in 1860. None had come from Ohio. (By contrast, 20 percent of the black heads of household in Hamilton County, Ohio, had come from Kentucky.)[46]

Counting demonstrates some of the dramatic demographic effects of the legal distinctions between slave states and free states.

Conclusion

Truth to tell, I use quantification rather little in my legal-historical research. I tend to write detailed case studies, a genre that favors deep, qualitative research over broad, quantitative research. Furthermore, I strive to write engaging narratives, a quality not generally associated with quantitative methods.

And, as noted above, there are problems with quantification. The data sets on which legal historians necessarily rely—courthouse records and the like—are more imperfect than we generally admit, to our readers or even to ourselves. Moreover, our uses of these flawed data, including the categories that we devise to make sense of them, are rarely beyond question.

Such critiques of quantification apply to all fields of historical inquiry but may apply with special force to legal history. One extreme critic in the early 1980s, exasperated by the ubiquity of quantification during the golden age of number-crunching, insisted that particular legal disputes are so inherently fact-specific that all attempts to sort them into countable categories necessarily descend into "speculative numerology."[47] Numerical analysis may shed clarifying light on other fields of history, this critic argued, but statistics "do not appreciably illuminate legal history," for "[a]ny examination of dispute resolution must concentrate on the facts of the disputes."[48]

This critic went too far. Despite these admitted problems, statistical analysis, responsibly employed, can indeed cast clarifying light on the history of law. Quantification helps writers of case studies determine how representative, or how marginal, their chosen cases may be. Archival counting enables scholars to situate easy-to-find appellate cases within the broader and deeper context of courthouse trials. In addition, as suggested in the foregoing examples, quantification can illuminate how a legal system was composed, how it operated, and how it affected society.

In all of these areas, the key to commonsense quantification is not fancy mathematics. Neither computers nor regression analyses are needed. Rather, the key, the part that "law office" historians too often neglect, is the patience to dig through lots of unpublished records, the curiosity to ask good questions of them, and the good judgment to figure out what they reveal.

NOTES

1. Robert William Fogel and Stanley L. Engerman, *Time on the Cross: The Economics of American Negro Slavery* (Boston: Little, Brown, 1974).

2. Quantification enabled new political historians to argue that "ethno-cultural" factors, not social class, best explained the political culture of the nineteenth-century United States, outside of the South. Lee Benson, *The Concept of Jacksonian Democracy: New York as a Test Case* (Princeton, N.J.: Princeton University Press, 1961); Paul Kleppner, *The Cross of Culture: A Social Analysis of Midwestern Politics, 1850–1900* (New York: Free Press, 1970); Richard J. Jensen, *The Winning of the Midwest: Social and Political Conflict, 1888–1896* (Chicago: University of Chicago Press, 1971); Ronald Formisano, *The Birth of Mass Political Parties: Michigan, 1827–1861* (Princeton, N.J.: Princeton University Press, 1971); Allan J. Lichtman, *Prejudice and the Old Politics: The Presidential Election of 1928* (Chapel Hill: University of North Carolina Press, 1979); Allan J. Lichtman and Laura Irwin Langbein, "Ecological Regression Versus Homogeneous Units: A Specification Analysis," *Social Science History* 2:2 (Winter 1978): 172–93; and Samuel P. Hays, *American Political History as Social Analysis: Essays by Samuel P. Hays* (Knoxville: University of Tennessee Press, 1980).

3. See Leo F. Schnore, ed., *The New Urban History: Quantitative Explorations by American Historians* (Princeton, N.J.: Princeton University Press, 1975); Sam Bass Warner Jr., *The Private City: Philadelphia in Three Periods of Its Growth* (Philadelphia: University of Pennsylvania Press, 1968); and Stephan Thernstrom and Richard Sennett, eds., *Nineteenth-Century Cities: Essays in the New Urban History* (New Haven, Conn.: Yale University Press, 1969).

4. See Laurence Veysey, "The 'New' Social History in the Context of American Historical Writing," *Reviews in American History* 7:1 (March 1979): 1–12; Stephan Thernstrom, *Poverty and Progress: Social Mobility in a Nineteenth Century City* (Cambridge, Mass.: Harvard University Press, 1964); Stephan Thernstrom, *The Other Bostonians: Poverty and Progress in the American Metropolis, 1880–1970* (Cambridge, Mass.: Harvard University Press, 1973); Clyde Griffen, "Occupational Mobility in Nineteenth Century America: Problems and Possibilities," *Journal of Social History* 5 (Spring 1972): 310–30; and Michael P. Weber, "Occupational Mobility of Ethnic Minorities in Nineteenth Century Warren, Pennsylvania," in *The Ethnic Experience in Pennsylvania*, John E. Bodnar, ed. (Cranbury, N.J.: Associated University Presses, 1973), 144–74.

5. Charles M. Dollar and Richard J. Jensen, *Historians' Guide to Statistics: Quantitative Analysis and Historical Research* (New York: Holt, Rinehart, and Winston,

1971); Roderick Floud, *An Introduction to Quantitative Methods for Historians* (Princeton, N.J.: Princeton University Press, 1973); William Aydelotte, *Quantification in History* (Reading, Mass.: Addison-Wesley, 1971).

6. Michael P. Weber, "Quantification and the Teaching of American Urban History," *The History Teacher* 8:3 (May 1975): 392.

7. "Editors' Foreword," *Social Science History* 1 (Fall 1976): i–ii.

8. Practitioners of the "new legal history" that developed by the 1970s consciously sought to move beyond doctrinal evolutionism and its Whiggish assumptions. The new legal history was characterized by enhanced attention to civil as opposed to criminal law; enhanced attention to private as opposed to public law; a commitment to seeing legal developments in light of social, political, and economic developments; attention to law-making agencies other than the federal courts; specific focus on the relationship between law and economic development; attention to the consolidation of the legal profession; and attention to legal discourse. See Harry N. Scheiber, "American Constitutional History and the New Legal History: Complementary Themes in Two Modes," *Journal of American History* 68 (September 1981): 337–50; and Alan Hunt, "The New Legal History: Prospects and Perspectives," *Crime, Law, and Social Change* 10 (June 1986): 201–8.

9. The author has heard Friedman deliver this quip orally. A version of it also appears in Lawrence M. Friedman, "American Legal History: Past and Present," in Lawrence M. Friedman and Harry N. Scheiber, eds. *American Law and the Constitutional Order: Historical Perspectives* (Cambridge, Mass.: Harvard University Press, 1988), 470.

10. Morton J. Horwitz, *The Transformation of American Law, 1780–1860* (Cambridge, Mass.: Harvard University Press, 1977); and William E. Nelson, *Americanization of the Common Law: The Impact of Legal Change on Massachusetts Society, 1760–1830* (Cambridge, Mass.: Harvard University Press, 1975).

11. On Horwitz as a "revisionist legal historian," see Victoria Saker Woeste, "Toasting Transformation I," *Law & Social Inquiry* 28 (Autumn 2003): 1122.

12. Nelson, *Americanization*, 37.

13. *Ibid.*, 117.

14. Horwitz, *Transformation*, vii. See also Morton J. Horwitz, "Foreword: Making Legal History," in this volume.

15. See William E. Nelson, *Dispute and Conflict Resolution in Plymouth County, Massachusetts, 1725–1825* (Chapel Hill: University of North Carolina Press, 1981). This *Americanization* spin-off was financed by the sort of grant money that regularly flowed to number-crunching social science projects in those years. A National Science Foundation grant provided the principal financing for this book. Nelson, *Dispute and Conflict Resolution*, x.

16. Tables of this sort abound on the pages of *Dispute and Conflict Resolution in Plymouth County*.

17. Among many other examples, see Lawrence M. Friedman and Robert V. Percival, "Who Sues for Divorce: From Fault through Fiction to Freedom," *Journal*

of Legal Studies 5 (January 1976): 61–82; Robert A. Kagan, Bliss Cartwright, Lawrence M. Friedman, and Stanton Wheeler, "The Business of State Supreme Courts, 1870–1970," *Stanford Law Review* 30 (November 1977): 121–56; Michael S. Hindus, "Contours of Crime and Justice in Massachusetts and South Carolina, 1767–1878," *American Journal of Legal History* 21 (July 1977): 212–37; and Kermit L. Hall, "Social Backgrounds and Judicial Recruitment: A Nineteenth-Century Perspective on the Lower Federal Judiciary," *The Western Political Quarterly* 29 (June 1976): 243–57.

18. William E. Nelson, *The Legalist Reformation: Law, Politics, and Ideology in New York, 1920–1980* (Chapel Hill: University of North Carolina Press, 2001), 2.

19. For a critical discussion of this technique, see Richard A. Posner, "Objectivity and Hagiography in Judicial Biography," *New York University Law Review* 70 (June 1995): 502–24.

20. *Plessy v. Ferguson*, 163 U.S. 537 (1896).

21. James W. Gordon, "Religion and the First Justice Harlan: A Case Study in Late Nineteenth Century Presbyterian Constitutionalism," *Marquette Law Review* 85 (Winter 2001): 317–422.

22. Loren P. Beth, *John Marshall Harlan: The Last Whig Justice* (Lexington: University Press of Kentucky, 1992).

23. Tinsley E. Yarbrough, *Judicial Enigma: The First Justice Harlan* (New York: Oxford University Press, 1995).

24. Linda Przybyszewski, *The Republic According to John Marshall Harlan* (Chapel Hill: University of North Carolina Press, 1999).

25. Kermit L. Hall, "Social Backgrounds and Judicial Recruitment: A Nineteenth-Century Perspective on the Lower Federal Judiciary," *Western Political Quarterly* 29 (June 1976): 243–57; Kermit L. Hall, *The Politics of Justice: Lower Federal Judicial Selection and the Second Party System, 1829–61* (Lincoln: University of Nebraska Press, 1979); John T. Wold, "Political Orientations, Social Backgrounds, and Role Perceptions of State Supreme Court Judges," *Western Political Quarterly* 27 (June 1974): 239–48; and Michael W. Giles and Thomas G. Walker, "Judicial Policy-Making and Southern School Segregation," *Journal of Politics* 37 (November 1975): 917–36.

26. Much of the material in this section originated in a collaborative research seminar taught by John Wertheimer at Davidson College in the fall of 2009. The co-authors of the paper that emerged from that seminar are Peter Bruton, Andrew Jones, Emily May, Kayla McCann, Alexander Merritt, Lee Mimms, Rex Salisbury, Alexander Sineath, and David Warren.

27. "Negro Sentenced to 25 Years in Assault Case," *Charleston* [S.C.] *Evening Post*, March 16, 1945.

28. "Taxi Driver in Rape Case Gets 18-Month Term on Guilty Plea," *The News and Courier* [Charleston, S.C.], September 13, 1944.

29. "James Island Negro Gets 25-Year Term," *The News and Courier* [Charleston, S.C.], March 16, 1945, 1.

30. Statutes at Large of the State of South Carolina, No. 578, Section 3, 1902; Acts of 1933, State of South Carolina, Act 321, Section 3.
31. Testimony of Jury Commissioner W. Lloyd Fleming, *State v. Middleton*, "Case and Exceptions," Court of General Sessions, State of South Carolina, County of Charleston, 1945, p. 15.
32. Testimony of Jury Commissioner W. J. Leonard, *State v. Middleton*, "Case and Exceptions," Court of General Sessions, State of South Carolina, County of Charleston, 1945, p. 16.
33. *State v. Middleton*, 207 S.C. 478 (1946).
34. Voting rolls have been shown to produce unrepresentative juries in terms not just of race but also age, education levels, social class, and sex. See Edward N. Beiser, "Are Juries Representative?" *Judicature* 57 (May 1, 1973): 194–99.
35. Code of Laws of South Carolina, Section 608 (1942).
36. Heidi Rickes, a Davidson College undergraduate, performed the research upon which this section is based. Her work was supported by the Davidson Research Initiative.
37. Names were counted as "black," "white," or "mulatto" only if: (1) the entire name could be corroborated—that is, if the census listed only one such voting-age person during the years in question; (2) there was more than one individual with the same name but all were of the same race; or (3) the first name was merely an initial and there were multiple names with that first initial, but all such individuals belonged to the same race. Otherwise, the race of an individual was deemed to be indeterminate.
38. South Carolina's last known lynching occurred in 1947 and was a national scandal, precisely because lynching, by this point in South Carolina's history, was rare. See Kari Frederickson, "'The Slowest State' and 'Most Backward Community': Racial Violence in South Carolina and Federal Civil Rights Legislation, 1946–1948," *South Carolina Historical Magazine* 98 (April 1997): 177–202.
39. "Negro Sentenced to 25 Years in Assault Case," *Charleston* [S.C.] *Evening Post*, March 16, 1945.
40. Information on the Mecklenburg County Superior Court's criminal docket in 1873 comes from Minute Book, Mecklenburg County Superior Court, 1872–1875, North Carolina State Archives, Raleigh. The following "fornication and adultery" cases were heard in the Mecklenburg County Superior Court on August 28, 1876: *State v. Ben Sharron*, *State v. Isaac Kennedy and Mag Kennedy*, *State v. L. Connor and Mary Sureeh*, *State v. Wyley Davidson and Sallie Lafevers*, *State v. Matt West and* [illegible] *West*. Case of August 29: *State v. Lee Henderson and Nellie Ross*. Case of August 30: *State v. Pink Ross and Sarah Ross*. Cases of August 31: *State v. Joe Jackson and Jane Jackson*, *State v. Isaac Kennedy and Mag Kennedy*, *State v. Jim Jackson and Sarah Jackson*. Case of September 6: *State v. Isaac Kennedy*.
41. "The Election," *Charlotte* [N.C.] *Democrat*, August 10, 1874: 3. For additional evidence of Democratic views on intimate relationships between black men and

white women, see *Charlotte* [N.C.] *Observer*, July 16, 1876: 4; and "Eloping Party Heard From," *Charlotte Observer*, July 16, 1876: 2.

42. In 1872, for instance, the state tried Mary Blythe and William Bryan for F&A. According to the 1870 census, Mary and William lived together, were unmarried, and were both white. *1870 Census Population Schedules, North Carolina, Mecklenburg County*, microcopy M593, reel 1148, p. 73.

43. See Mark Jones and John Wertheimer et al., "Pinkney and Sarah Ross: The Legal Journey of an Ex-Slave and His White Wife on the Carolina Borderlands during Reconstruction," *South Carolina Historical Magazine*, 103 (October 2002): 325–50; and Wertheimer, *Law and Society in the South*, 27–42.

44. Daphne Fruchtman performed research for this section. Her research was funded by a George L. Abernethy grant from Davidson College. Although two-thirds of these black slave-state migrants had come from neighboring Kentucky or Virginia, the remaining third had crossed multiple southern borders to reach free soil. U.S. Census, *1860 Population Schedules Hamilton County, Ohio*; U.S. Census, *1860 Population Schedules Jefferson County, Kentucky*.

45. Just 4.99 percent (3,729 out of 74,582) of white family heads in Hamilton County, Ohio, had migrated from slaves states as of 1860. For secondary-source corroboration of this estimate, see Charles R. Wilson, "Cincinnati a Southern Outpost in 1860–1861?" *Mississippi Valley Historical Review* 24 (March 1938): 474.

46. Although Louisville was a smaller city, with 28,188 households in 1860, as compared with Cincinnati's 76,738 households, the breakdown in composition between white and black households was not too dissimilar: 2.2 percent of Louisville's and 1.5 percent of Cincinnati's total heads of household were listed as black. *1860 Population Schedules Hamilton County, Ohio*; *1860 Population Schedules Jefferson County, Kentucky*.

47. Hiller B. Zobel, review of William E. Nelson, *Dispute and Conflict Resolution in Plymouth County, Massachusetts, 1725–1825*, in *American Historical Review*, 87 (April 1982): 527–28.

48. *Ibid*. Zobel wrote these critical words in response to Bill Nelson´s most quantification-heavy book.

Courts, Judges, and Litigators

8

A Mania for Accumulation

The Plea of Moral Insanity in Gilded Age Will Contests

SUSANNA L. BLUMENTHAL

How uneasy lies the head that wears the name of capitalist.[1]

Rising to address the New York Surrogate's Court on behalf of the disappointed heirs of "Commodore" Cornelius J. Vanderbilt on November
12, 1877, attorney Scott Lord acknowledged the formidable task that lay
before him, mindful that his audience included many luminaries of the
bench and bar as well as members of the press and the general public: "To
say that a man who had the capacity to accumulate $100,000,000, and
who naturally possessed a vigorous will, had not the capacity to dispose
of his estate, or was subject to undue influence, so that the disposition of
his property was controlled by another, presents a proposition which one
unacquainted with the facts would hesitate to believe." Doubts about the
prospects of this contest were all the more warranted in view of the applicable legal rules, Lord further conceded. For under the governing statute,
a competent testator's prerogative to "do what he wills with his own" was
fully protected, regardless of how "repugnant the disposition of his property may be to the just expectations of his kindred and the laws of his
country." However Lord submitted that there was not on record—"in the
history of wills"—a more inequitable and unnatural disposition of a large
estate, the vast bulk being left outright to the testator's eldest son, William, while his siblings were awarded comparatively paltry sums ranging from $200,000 to $500,000. The most galling among these provisions
was that made for the testator's son and namesake, Cornelius, who was
accorded only the annual interest at 5 percent of his $200,000 portion,
which was to leave him "practically disinherited."[2]

More than implying that this document was itself proof of the supposed testator's mental incompetence, Lord assured the assembled crowd that, when all the evidence was in, they would see that the Commodore's commanding exterior was deceiving, as he was, in fact, subject to an overpowering "desire to have his fortune perpetuated in his own name," one that became so controlling as to amount to "a mania." Even as he "held to his railroad projects" by a kind of "force of habit," Vanderbilt's moral and intellectual powers were further undermined by his own vicious indulgences and the ravages of disease in the last year of his life, so that he became an easy mark for the motley assortment of spiritualists, clairvoyants, mesmerists, and gold-digging adventuresses who shamelessly circled around him as he entered his "second childhood." Confined to his sickbed, he was prone to infantile spells of ill temper and was finally and quite literally unmanned by an extremely painful case of cystitis, which caused him to writhe "like a woman suffering from labor pains." Seizing the main chance, the undeserving William staged the most elaborate ruse of all, one diabolically designed to trick the old man into thinking that his younger and needier son— afflicted as he was with epilepsy—was a hopeless degenerate who would certainly squander any share he was given of the Vanderbilt estate. So deceived, the weakened patriarch "put his son who bore his own Christian name under a revolting vassalage." A last testament so obviously extracted under false pretenses, Lord concluded with an air of outraged decency, served only to prove that the proponent had "perpetrated the most infamous offense that a son can commit against his father." It was thus clearly "in the interests of law and good morals" that it be set aside.[3]

While most in the packed courtroom sat forward at riveted attention during the counselor's opening salvo, the alleged usurper of the Railroad King's crown noticeably did not, according to newspaper reports. He instead remained reclined comfortably in his chair, his face almost expressionless in its placidity, save for the occasional sneer or "the slight smile which sometimes flitted across his face," which was "not even expressive of contempt, but rather appeared to indicate that he was just a trifle amused by the fervent remarks of the legal gentleman who was defaming his character."[4] Whether Lord intended to be taken seriously might well be wondered, particularly when his words are placed in the larger context of the proceedings and the wider legal culture of the day. There was, indeed, a unabashed theatricality in Lord's arguments before the surrogate, composed as they were of well-worn lines of attack drawn from a growing repository of capacity contests involving the estates of wealthy men. Lord's showmanship was more than matched by that of the other illustrious lawyers appearing in this case, many of whom were also major players in the epic struggle for control of the Erie Railroad Company and in the contested 1876 presidential election between Samuel J. Tilden and Rutherford B. Hayes. More entertaining still were the colorful array of witnesses called to the stand to provide arresting disclosures of family secrets that often bordered on the ridiculous. Even the Surrogate, Delano C. Calvin, widely reputed to be a tool of the Tammany party machine, was not above playing for laughs on occasion even as he struggled to remain above the fray.[5] A commercial press encouraged this mode of proceeding by according the participants front-page treatment in extensive coverage, with headlines and articles inviting readers to take in the proceedings as theatergoers, reporters speaking in terms of curtains rising and falling, listing the *dramatis personae* set to appear, and critiquing court hearings as acts of a play that were supposed to move the plot along—in other words, presenting the trial as an assemblage of artful maneuvers expected to entertain and intended to achieve a certain result without necessarily revealing the truth of the matter.[6] And perhaps no element of the Vanderbilt case stood out as a more likely bit of chicanery than the insanity claim that the contestants offered to substantiate by means of medical experts. If the mental competence of this titan of industry could be subject to such an undignified legal contest within days of his being eulogized for his indomitable willpower, more than a few commentators reflected, testamentary freedom had become a hollow doctrine indeed.[7]

Considering the way that the trial was conducted by the parties and covered by the press, it is tempting to follow this interpretative line, to view the Great Vanderbilt Will Case as a cynical piece of legal stagecraft that ultimately served its purpose, which was to engineer a financial settlement between the contending children who had survived their father, effectively rewriting what otherwise would have stood as his last will. That liberties were being taken with the truth in this forum was the unmistakable impression conveyed by the newsmen who provided reports of the proceedings for public consumption. Their accounts gave prominent place to the heated exchanges between opposing counselors who routinely accused one another of manufacturing evidence that slandered their respective clients, William at one point becoming so galled by the testimony proffered by his brother as to object on his own motion: "He's making it all up."[8] Writing with the benefit of historical distance, Vanderbilt's most recent biographer, T. J. Stiles, takes a more measured view of the courtroom proceedings, finding both parties guilty of exaggerations and fabrications and ultimately pronouncing the transcript to be "a bizarre, fragmented mosaic of true and false moments in the Commodore's life, lacking context, missing vast stretches of his activities or inner life."[9]

So the record of a will contest might well be viewed from the standpoint of the scholar who seeks to understand a single life. But for the legal historian who aims instead to comprehend the cultural significance of such courtroom struggles, newspaper reports of the Vanderbilt will case constitute the most illuminating of primary sources. Lodged between stories about the end of Reconstruction, persistence of corruption at all levels of government, and intensifying conflicts between capital and labor, the reporters' dispatches from Surrogate Calvin's chambers rapidly spread across the nation, enabling a far-flung reading public to follow the forensic moves of the case. Because no official transcript of the proceedings survives, the press accounts likewise constitute the historian's main means of knowing what was said and done by the participants in this trial.[10] Composed of paraphrases and color commentaries as well as what were represented as direct quotes, the press coverage was far from uniform, though the reporters tended to hit the same high points and low points, thus conveying a common sense of what they and their editors considered newsworthy. Though obviously crafted for instrumental purposes, sometimes without any regard for the truth of the matter, the stories about Commodore Vanderbilt and his will told in the courtroom and repeated in the press are nonetheless revealing in their own way.[11] Here it is instructive to recall what Herman Melville had to say about fiction in his 1856 novel *The Confidence-Man*, intimating that even unabashed practitioners of this literary art are compelled to create narratives that bear some resemblance to the world as their readers know it, ones to which they "feel the tie."[12] Thus we may be warranted in reading the competing characterizations of the Commodore's capacity to make a will as part of a broader cultural ferment about the meaning of freedom in an industrializing age. That his will could be challenged in such a spectacularly crass fashion provides an especially telling indicator of the manipulability and vulnerability of the ideal of autonomy at the heart of the American law of inheritance as it was administered in the last decades of the nineteenth century, an era when the immense fortunes of businessmen like Vanderbilt triggered a crisis of faith in the ethos of personal achievement that drove the process of accumulation in the first place.

To put it bluntly, the great capitalist may have succeeded too well in "the race of life," as daily existence was commonly figured in the Age of Enterprise that he has so often been said to epitomize. At the time of his death on January 4, 1877, at the age of eighty-two, Vanderbilt was widely regarded as one of the richest men in American history, an accomplishment that inspired admiring celebrations of his business acumen as well as more critical appraisals of the ways he made and used his millions over the course of his long and illustrious business career. The size and composition of his estate—principally composed of stocks and bonds— made his declining health a matter of public concern. Hordes of reporters and messengers from the Stock Exchange stood vigil outside the Vanderbilt residence, where they received daily briefings about the bedridden old man for months before he died, a measure deemed warranted because "a slight change in his condition, a little fever, or headache more or less, could affect men's fortunes by thousands of dollars," it being "a favorite system of swindling on the Stock Exchange . . . to start rumors of his death."[13] Being so long anticipated, the actual occurrence of the Commodore's death hardly affected the financial markets, though a fresh news angle was quickly found, journalists now reporting that speculation was rife about the contents of Vanderbilt's will and the likelihood of a legal challenge.[14] No sooner was the document unsealed than headlines announced with an air of inevitability: "Of Course. Vanderbilt's Will to be Contested. Some of the Relatives Not Satisfied, Intend to Make Trouble."[15] This was the peril of dying rich, as the newspapers told the story, for there was "no will which cannot be broken by a discontented heir and a couple of sharp lawyers."[16] These professional men were said to know just how to poke holes in the most carefully crafted document, and they proved equally adept in using the threat of public embarrassment as part of their litigation strategy. Unless and until the quarreling siblings came to terms, reporters assured their audiences, there would be a scandalous will contest, one that effectively placed the testator's character on trial: "his sanity, his kindness, his natural affection, his sense of justice, his morality, his habits."[17]

Owing in no small part to the existence and willing participation of a profit-driven press, this was precisely what happened.[18] For the next two years, two weeks, and four days, the testamentary capacity of the late, great Cornelius Vanderbilt was "litigated over" and "cartooned upon" in the court of public opinion as the parties made their respective cases before Surrogate Calvin.[19] The dueling portraits of the dead millionaire painted for these multiple audiences—the one portraying him as an exemplary entrepreneur, the other as a mental wreck undone by an insatiable avarice—surely stretched the truth. Yet as these trial stories were retold as news stories, they registered a pronounced and widespread ambivalence about "the one-man power" wielded by Vanderbilt during his lifetime and bequeathed by him to his eldest son by way of his alleged will.[20] Though the dynastic ambitions of this "splendid accumulator" may not have constituted sufficient evidence of insanity as a matter of medicine or law, both lay and professional commentators took Vanderbilt's selfish aim of "founding a family on a money basis" to present a serious threat to the health of the republic, its boasted freedom imperiled by the tyrannical rule of a new breed of "moneycrats."[21] In speaking of the testator's acquisitive behavior in terms of monomania, they at once exaggerated and mirrored the moral and mental disorientation occasioned by the sudden appearance (and disappearance) of "New Fortunes" of unprecedented proportions in the "economic chance-world" that was Gilded Age America. Such concentrations of wealth and influence strained conventional notions of property rights and providential order, as they were difficult to justify as the fruits of any one man's labor, let alone that of his heirs. Proceeding with their lawsuit against the violent backdrop of the Great Railroad Strike of 1877, the ridiculously rapacious Vanderbilt children stood as living proof of the debasing impact of a speculative economy that tempted them to try their luck in court.[22] In shining such a bright light on "the trouble of having too much," this sordid trial sparked a spirited national debate about the moral and legal status of inherited wealth, one that ironically left determined dynasts of the Progressive Era more securely positioned to rule from the grave.[23]

Making and Breaking Wills

The "aristocracy of wealth" sustained by the English law of inheritance was an early and symbolically potent target for legal reform after the American Revolution. Leading statesmen took particular aim at the legal devices of primogeniture and entail, seeking thereby to eliminate "the feudal and unnatural distinctions which made one member of every family rich and all the rest poor" and to prevent "the accumulation and perpetuation of wealth" of particular families and individuals, giving them "an unequal and undue influence" in the polity. These egalitarian pronouncements were less thoroughgoing than they sounded, however, as few called for a reversion of property to the state for redistribution upon its owner's death, though his right to dispose of his property at death was generally understood—in line with Blackstone—to be a creature of statute rather than of natural law. The enactments in most newly established states likewise followed English law and colonial precedent regarding testamentary freedom, insofar as they reaffirmed the right of any adult "of sound mind and memory" and "not under any restraint" to dispose of his estate by will. Those deemed legally capable nonetheless found themselves subject to various requirements and prohibitions in most jurisdictions, some expressly intended to safeguard the interests of the testator's spouse and children, others to channel property in conventional directions, and still others limiting the reach of the dead hands of past testators, lest they tie up assets that would otherwise circulate in the marketplace.[24]

The path of inheritance law in the early republic thus proceeded along the general lines that William E. Nelson mapped in his *Americanization of the Common Law*, insofar as the rules governing the intergenerational transfer of property were reconfigured to maintain a delicate balance between founding ideals of liberty and equality and the exigencies of economic development.[25] Although the logic of the statesmen's republican rhetoric might have led them to repudiate the traditional institution of inheritance, theirs was an egalitarianism limited by the

IN THE HOLLOW OF HIS HANDS.
(For further particulars watch the reports of the Vanderbilt will case.)

"In the hollow of his hands." Cartoon in *Puck* magazine calling attention to the reopening of the protracted Vanderbilt will case in September 1878. A grasping William H. Vanderbilt is depicted as the embodiment of money-power, exerting a stranglehold on the courtroom proceedings as well as the operations of the wider political and economic systems of the day. One of his hands holds Surrogate Calvin, who is shown to be abusing his office as an instrument of Tammany Hall, while the other clutches the contestants and court orders excluding their testimony. Signs in the background and foreground suggest that the would-be heir also has a controlling influence on transportation rates and the prices of basic commodities but devotes laughably little of his vast wealth to philanthropic causes.

will of the testator, who remained free to discriminate in favor of his eldest son or deviate more completely from the norms of "natural justice" by disinheriting all of his children. Within the terms of the newly enacted statutes and the cases that construed them in the first decades of the nineteenth century, property holders enjoyed wide discretion to do as they wished with "their own." Conceived as the legislator of his household, the testator was entrusted with the power to determine how his estate was to be distributed upon his death, based on the idea that such a provision not only would spur parents to work to accumulate wealth for the sake of future generations but also would serve as a means to discipline and punish expectant heirs, thereby encouraging the reproduction of virtuous and industrious citizens. Although nothing formally prevented abuses of the liberty of testation, the law of intestate succession had something of a conditioning effect of its own. The norm of equitable division between surviving children expressed in and through its provisions shaped the way that "unequal" wills were read by disfavored heirs as well as by the lawyers, judges, jurors, and members of the general public to whom they appealed. A testator departing from this norm ran the risk of a post-mortem contest, as early republican judges consistently—if somewhat reluctantly—held that an "unreasonable" disposition was at least some evidence that its putative author lacked the mental capacity required to make a valid will.[26]

In making out such a case, contestants could draw upon the expertise of a new band of medical men who specialized in the diagnosis and treatment of mental disease, many of them serving as superintendents of the growing number of insane asylums dotting the American landscape. Convinced that insanity was on the rise in the fluid social conditions that prevailed after the Revolution—this rise showing "the trials of unrestricted freedom" to be too great for some citizens—these doctors were confident that they could cure the disease through humane treatment in carefully regulated institutions. To this end, they engaged in concerted efforts to dispel popular misconceptions about the disease, particularly the notion that insanity entailed a *total* deprivation of reason, which had become embedded in the legal system. They attempted to redress this problem by publishing works on the "medical jurisprudence of insanity," directed first and foremost to lawyers and judges, encouraging them to replace traditional common-law categories and ways of identifying persons *non compos mentis* with scientific alternatives grounded in clinical experience. The most significant of these new diagnostic categories was that of "monomania," referring to a circumscribed derangement, one affecting a single faculty of the mind or concerning a single topic; a person might be afflicted with "moral insanity," leaving the intellect undisturbed, or might exhibit signs of insanity only with respect to a particular subject, usually some religious, political, business, or family matter. It is perhaps no wonder that these disease entities soon found their way into the briefs of lawyers in civil and criminal proceedings, the practice becoming so common by the middle decades of the nineteenth century that it generated complaints from the bench that medical opinions were being "stretched and distorted to save life or defeat a hard will." Even more pointed protests emanated from beyond courtrooms, as doctors and lawyers engaged in a public debate about what the principles of science and justice required when it came to questions of mental soundness and legal responsibility.[27]

Insanity trials involving alleged murders and supposed wills gar-nered the greatest attention during this controversy, and their promi-nence invited comparisons of the standards of capacity applied in civil as distinct from criminal cases. It seemed to many medical commenta-tors that judges displayed far greater receptivity to claims of insanity when made by civil complainants than those made by criminal defen-dants, and they further observed that the threshold of capacity was effectively set at a lower level for purposes of determining whether a crime had been committed, constituting damning evidence that the common law made "more account of property than of life."[28] Crediting these complaints, the historian James C. Mohr has offered an intriguing hypothesis for this judicial tendency, essentially viewing it as a reflec-tion of the social conservatism of the nineteenth-century bench, whose findings of testamentary incapacity would have called into operation the state's intestacy statute, thereby ensuring that the decedent's estate was distributed along conventional lines to his lineal heirs. In other words, the appeal of the doctrine of unsound mind in this civil context largely stemmed from its utility in keeping family property intact dur-ing an era of "rapid democratization," when the country seemed to be careening "toward unfettered market liberalism." Buffeted as they con-tinually were by "tumult and experimentation," Mohr surmises, "Amer-ican courts, consciously or unconsciously, held the line on kin-based inheritance," readily accepting "evidence associated with the radical new theories of insanity" as a scientific basis for declaring eccentric tes-tators to be "both metaphorically and legally" incompetent. Only as the insecurities and disturbances of the early republic receded from view and the country entered a period of material prosperity "beyond any-body's wildest dreams" did judges begin to question seriously the doc-tors' theories, as they "finally felt free, as it were, to indulge the spirit of individualism, even the idiosyncrasies and exaggerated self-importance of their nation's separate sovereign citizens."[29]

This account of the shifting fortunes of the insanity plea in nine-teenth-century will contests certainly captures some of the concerns that animated judicial efforts to delimit the bounds of testamentary freedom in nineteenth-century America. In their concerted efforts to bring the legal category of persons *non compos mentis* in line with the new medical psychology, antebellum judges expanded the grounds for challenging testamentary dispositions and enhanced the power of courts to regulate the intergenerational transfer of wealth.[30] The bringing of capacity challenges was further encouraged by procedural rules allowing both parties to recover costs and counsel fees out of the estate, so long as they proceeded in good faith. These challenges, how-ever, quickly began to look like unseemly scrambles for wealth from the standpoint of those who sat in judgment, not least because of the "one-sided and partisan character" of the testimony elicited from the medical men commonly retained by each side in most will contests.[31] Examination of trial records and appellate decisions in the middle decades of the century reveals members of the bench to have been quite reluctant policemen of testamentary acts, their rulings no doubt shaped more than a little by the disturbing thought that one day they might be subject to like charges of mental incompetence, true or false. Although they were generally permissive in their admission of expert as well as lay testimony on the issue of mental soundness, the judges' instruc-tions to jurors and opinions on appeal were models of equivocation, documenting their own struggles to articulate a scientific and prac-tical basis for distinguishing the insane from the merely eccentric or depraved disposition. Thus it can hardly be said that the late nineteenth century was a time when American courts stopped worrying about the untrammeled exercise of testamentary freedom, as Mohr has suggested. To the contrary, the problem of determining what constituted a valid will grew only more troubling in the Gilded Age as the stakes of these courtroom battles were raised to unprecedented heights by the wealth of a new class of businessmen strangely revered and reviled by their fel-low Americans as "kings" and "princes."[32]

At once awed and galled by these monarchs of money and the vast enterprises they commanded, the reading public more than likely expe-rienced a certain vicarious thrill, and perhaps also a sense of satisfac-tion, as they followed news stories about the challenges to rich men's wills. The shock value would have been especially high in the case of the famously "self-made" and "iron-willed" Cornelius Vanderbilt, reputed as he was to have amassed singlehandedly the largest fortune in his nation's history. Yet as craven and laughable as the heirs' charge of insanity was taken to be in many quarters, the fact remains that this contest was allowed to proceed before Surrogate Calvin for more than two years. Although the courtroom battle of the Vanderbilt children excited concern and prompted calls for reform, the impulse to litigate on the part of disappointed heirs proved difficult to contain. Indeed, the last quarter of the nineteenth century was the heyday of capacity challenges to the wills of dead capitalists, their wealth effectively underwriting the legal proceedings, which regularly featured warring heirs, leading lawyers, disagreeing doctors, long-suffering surrogates, and reporters poised to make the most of all they witnessed. What most obviously brought this cast of characters to the courtroom was encapsulated in a headline aiming to draw a still wider audience to follow the Vanderbilt will case: "There's Millions in it."[33] But these words ought not to be read reductively, if we are to appreciate the cultural significance of this contest as it played out in Gilded Age America. For the amount the Commodore was said to be "worth," the fortune he amassed and sought to perpetuate in his own name, and the last will that caused such strife after his death all stand as telling indicators of how vexed the relationship among money, capacity, and manhood had become by the last decades of the century. Vanderbilt's millions figured as an irresistible lure and a problematic measure of self-sovereignty in the trial as it was covered by the popular press, registering deeper disquiet about the acquisitive spirit of capitalism and its deranging effects upon traditional ways of measuring the value of work and life.

Returning now to the pages of those newspapers, we can see the exaggerated claims and counterclaims about the Commodore's willpower as evidence of a culture internally conflicted about the proper lesson to be drawn from his storied life. Was his "royal way to wealth" a pathway to autonomous selfdom deserving of validation by the law of wills? Or was it a dangerous perversion of the Protestant work ethic that threatened to give rise to a new American aristocracy—to a polity effectively ruled by the "money-mad"? As the lawyer-showmen rose to the occasion of this much-anticipated will contest, so obviously standing to gain from all they said and did on behalf of their clients, they also took part in a sort of morality play, one that remained beyond their creative control, with ramifications far beyond "the House of Vanderbilt."[34]

The Great Vanderbilt Will Case

"I thank God I live in a republican country, which gives all children equal rights, and which does not uphold the will of a man who gives more to one child than the other." So Cornelius Vanderbilt was said to have remarked to one of the contestant's witnesses before falling ill and passing under the controlling influence of his eldest son. The statement was incorrect as a matter of law, and it cannot be presumed to be an accurate expression of the Commodore's testamentary intention, or even what the witness had actually said on the stand, it being the product of a journalist's transcription of the testimony. Although press coverage of the Vanderbilt will case was presented as pure reportage, much of the trial testimony was reproduced in summary form with occasional editorial asides, which could vary in tone and content. Even when reporters selected the same portions for direct quotation, their renditions were not always entirely congruent. In the absence of a surviving official transcript, we can only check the newspaper accounts against one another, making possible the reconstruction of nothing more or less than a composite sketch of the will contest as it unfolded in the New York courtroom. However much was lost in the translation, the surviving news stories allow us to see what nineteenth-century American readers saw as they were lured by headlines into the private reaches of the Vanderbilt residence, where they could view "The Indoor Life of the Wealthiest Man in America." This press coverage was more than simply the means by which the trial became known to the public; it was also an integral part of the proceedings, manifestly shaping the way the case was litigated by the contending parties. From Lord's opening argument forward, the courtroom contest was in significant part a publicity stunt, orchestrated to coerce a settlement or punish the proponent for standing his ground, both of which required the active participation of the popular press. With this end in view, the counselors for the contestants pushed the limits of Victorian propriety, the rules of evidence, and the Surrogate's patience, often seeming more concerned with generating sensational news stories than with obtaining a favorable verdict.[35] If the trial by press is any indication, they succeeded rather well in satisfying the public appetite for scandal but may have underestimated William's resolve in the face of all this mudslinging, and they certainly left many onlookers with reasons for thinking that there was something rotten in an America that permitted the dead capitalist's children to carry on this way in open court.[36]

The tone was unmistakably set by Lord's "remarkable" opening address in November 1877—reportedly "something of a surprise to most of the audience, if not the counsel on the opposite side"—and he continued in this same vein as he called his first witness, the Commodore's estranged son-in-law, Daniel B. Allen. Having established that Allen had been in Vanderbilt's employ from 1834 to 1864, at which time they had a falling-out over an unspecified business matter relating to Allen's son, Lord turned to a far more intimate subject. "Do you remember when the trouble arose which resulted in Mrs. Vanderbilt being sent to the lunatic asylum?" Lord asked his witness, who answered in the affirmative, dating the incident back to 1846. No doubt knowing where his opponent was headed with this line of questioning, the lead counsel for the proponent, Henry L. Clinton, immediately objected on grounds of relevance; he wondered what bearing an episode involving the Commodore's *first* wife, Sophia (who had died in 1868), could have on the validity of a will executed nearly thirty years later, in January of 1875. After a long sidebar, Surrogate Calvin allowed the questioning to continue, expressing a cagey confidence that a counselor of Lord's standing surely would not delve into such delicate family matters unless they shed some light on the matters of testamentary capacity and undue influence that were formally before the court.[37]

If the story that Allen went on to tell was to be believed, the Commodore was a man with far less command over his home life than over his railroad empire, in no small part because of a weakness for women other than his wife. Among the most problematic of such attachments was that to the governess of his Staten Island mansion, which developed around the same time Sophia began to display the signs of mental distress that eventually landed her in the asylum. Allen and his wife were assured by the Commodore that Mrs. Vanderbilt was simply suffering from "the change of life" commonly experienced by women her age. So they agreed to accompany her on a trip to Canada on the theory that a change of scenery would improve her condition. This hoped-for improvement did not come to pass, however, and upon Sophia's return from what Allen now saw as her "forced vacation," the governess left the mansion, doing so against the wishes and much to the consternation of the Commodore. He now began to talk about sending his wife away to an asylum on Long Island, with the hope that the governess could then be persuaded to come back. All of Sophia's children strenuously opposed this move, with the telling exception of William. Desperate to stay in the Commodore's good graces, the strategic son not only took his father's side in this family conflict but procured the services of a new housekeeper for the Vanderbilt residence during the months Sophia was institutionalized, explaining to Allen, "He's bound to fall under the influence of some woman, and I'm bound to control that woman."[38]

This proved to be an eminently quotable line, repeated in the major papers covering the first day of the Vanderbilt will contest, their head-lines promising to reveal "Ugly Secrets" about the "Inhuman Treatment of the First Wife of the Commodore" along with other "Household Skeletons." However, there were two sides to this family feud as it was reported, even in papers that adopted an explicit editorial line concerning the controversy. Those who read the news stories all the way through would have found fairly straightforward accounts of both the direct and cross-examinations of individual witnesses.[39] In Allen's case, the testimony captured in print left plenty of room for doubt whether William was in fact a controlling influence in the Vanderbilt household. Under Clinton's questioning, Allen was pressed to admit that the new "governess" was the cousin of William's wife, a reverend's daughter, and really better characterized as the "companion" of the Commodore's daughter Louisa, summoned to assist her in keeping house until her mother was released from the asylum.[40] Cross-examination also brought out other sorts of nuances, complexities, and ambiguities in the power dynamics between the Commodore and his children. If William was as syco-phantic and spineless as Allen made him out to be, how could he have overwhelmed the will of a man whom this same witness described as growing only more powerful and "determined to have his own way" with every passing year? Arguably the most credible statement made by Allen on the stand concerned a conversation that he recalled having with the Commodore on the subject of wills that was damning to both sides of this suit. "Daniel," the witness recalled the old man's saying when they were still on speaking terms, "when I die there'll be hell to pay." Positioned only slightly above the fray, Surrogate Calvin audibly and acidly quipped, "He seems to have been something of a prophet."[41]

Confirming the acuity of the Commodore's foresight, Lord carried his courtroom campaign into ever deeper reaches of the dead man's private life in the following weeks, calling to the stand a set of physicians who had all taken part in the autopsy of Vanderbilt's body, some having treated him during his lifetime as well. The medical history elicited from these witnesses constituted a form of examination at times too graphic or tedious for public consumption, most papers providing abbreviated coverage under such arresting headlines as "The Commodore Dissected," and "Vanderbilt's Bodily Infirmities Ruthlessly Dragged to Light," the journalists visibly straining to sensationalize the "Painful Diseases that Immense Wealth Could Not Cure" and spice up "His Sick-Bed Talk" to keep their audiences interested. This was no small feat, as it would appear that most of what the doctors were asked to do was read from and elaborate upon a written autopsy report, their testimony essentially providing a guided tour of the patient's internal organs, with a particular emphasis on the maladies that afflicted his urinal and intestinal tracts. The portions that found their way into newsprint went into excruciating detail about what the Commodore's scrotum looked like under a microscope, how "peritonitis" might have affected his bowel movements, and whether this condition was the immediate cause of his death. Within the confines of the courtroom these revelations seemed to bore most of the audience: The proponent's lawyer was observed to be "sound asleep," along with several members of the audience, as the doctors droned on. The sheer tedium of it all was confirmed in a widely reported display of "funereal wit" on Surrogate Calvin's part, inspired by a medical witness's testimony on "the meaning of the term chronic in a medical sense." Upon hearing the doctor state that it connoted a slowly progressing disease, Surrogate Calvin was said to have "yawned and ejaculated, 'In other words, this trial seems to be chronic.'"[42]

Even as laughter again reportedly reverberated throughout the courtroom, the contestants were allowed to continue questioning medical authorities about the Commodore's bodily infirmities. It was only

after most of this evidence had been presented that Clinton raised a formal objection, rather belatedly taking issue with the autopsy's failure
to include any examination of the Commodore's *brain*. "To attempt to
prove a man's insanity . . . by the condition of his bladder and rectum
two years after he made his will" was simply absurd, he now appealed to
the Surrogate, contending that none of the evidence thus far introduced
was even remotely material unless and until there was some actual proof
of the impact of the testator's physical disorders on the operations of his
mind at the time the document at issue was executed. Although agree-
ing with Clinton's assessment of the order of proof, Surrogate Calvin
allowed Lord to finish his examination of the expert witness then on the
stand with the proviso "that this cart-before-the-horse-way of taking
testimony should be reversed after to-day." This direction Lord more or
less followed, though he would have been wise to do so from a strategic
standpoint in any event, as the medical men he put on the stand did
little to advance the case that he was trying to make for the invalidity of
Vanderbilt's will. Indeed, the more they elaborated on the bodily disorders afflicting the testator, the more impressive his mental strength was
made to appear; the proponent's counsel skillfully elicited an admission
to that effect from these experts, who uniformly affirmed that the Commodore remained "quite self-possessed" and "clear-minded" to the end,
even when in the greatest physical agony.[43]

Shifting ground in the face of these damaging assessments, the contestants now emphasized that they never meant to claim "general insanity" but instead aimed to establish that the Commodore was a mono-
maniac—that he labored under a more circumscribed set of manias
with respect to the spirit world and the efficacy of spiritual medicine,
and that he was pathologically avaricious and vain. While there was no
denying that the railroad magnate had "the power to acquire wealth,"
Lord insisted that "he had not the testamentary capacity to transmit it"
because "he labored under a delusion which affected in a great degree
the subjects of his testamentary bounty."[44] Their star witnesses on these
counts were supposed to be the infamously visionary sisters Victoria
Woodhull and Tennessee Claflin, but the two women suddenly and
suspiciously absented themselves from the jurisdiction, amidst rumors
that one of William's agents had bribed them to wait out the trial in
England. As a result, it fell to a "magnetic healer" by the name of Mrs.

Jennie A. Danforth to fill this role. Like the other women, Danforth had stories to tell about the Commodore's belief in clairvoyance and his faith in the healing powers of mesmerism, for she had been called to the Vanderbilt estate by his second wife, Frank, to help ease his suffering through the mechanical technique of "rubbing" in the spring and summer of 1876. At the patient's request, Mrs. Danforth made contact with Vanderbilt's departed first wife, Sophia, and conveyed the dead woman's great distress, which he was convinced had to do with the unequal will that he had written. He expressed regret for following his eldest son's directions in drafting this document and thereupon resolved "to make another tomorrow." This set of disclosures brought Clinton to his feet, objecting that belief in clairvoyant power "had no bearing on the question of insanity or undue influence unless it was supposed to be a delusion," which this counselor denied, adding that the question could not be decided in a courtroom in any event, as "that would open up the whole theory of human belief for discussion."[45]

Recognizing this to be a "grave issue," though only after making light of it in various ways, Surrogate Calvin confessed himself to be uncertain as to the law of the case. Although generally "disposed to leave the door open very wide in this case," he apprehended that if he were "required to test the truth of clairvoyancy the trial might be in court for the next six years." He also wondered more broadly about testators who were known to traffic in controversial ideas, asking Lord what he would say about the validity of "Mr. Darwin's will." This hypothetical disposition, Lord readily responded, was clearly distinguished from the one at bar, for the biologist's evolutionary theory was based upon "logical argument," unlike the spiritualists and their believers, who labored under a patently false belief that mere mortals could do "supernatural things." However, the proponent's counsel were just as quick to invoke precedents establishing that spiritualists were capable of making a will, which the contestants countered with authorities suggesting otherwise, especially in cases also raising claims of mental weakness and undue influence—claims, Clinton acerbically rejoined, that were to be proved by a "crazy witness" by the contestants' own definition. Confounded by these arguments, Surrogate Calvin took the matter under advisement but elected to receive the testimony provisionally while he did, so as not to slow the progress of the trial. This ruling was a victory of sorts for the contestants, at least in view of its publicity effects; newspapers gleefully trumpeted the appearance of this "clairvoyant lady" and her "remarkable revelations," an announcement calculated to awaken audiences within and beyond the New York courtroom.[46]

Though on the following day Surrogate Calvin formally struck from the record the testimony about clairvoyant belief, the contestants' attorneys did not go down without a time-consuming fight, during which they strategically exploited a basic ambiguity at the core of the law of insanity: the distinction between mere eccentricity or depravity and actual mental disease. Though Lord and his co-counsel Jeremiah Black contended that the proffered testimony would corroborate previous testimony showing the Commodore's testamentary incapacity, the Surrogate impatiently interjected, asking "what there was in evidence to show weakness, beyond the unequal distribution of the property." Without pausing to think, Black supplied an almost preposterous response—"Everything he ever said or did"—that became only slightly less absurd as he blustered his way forward; his argument amounted to a mini-dissertation on the doctrine of mental unsoundness as applied to the case at bar. "Sanity," he explained without specific reference to any authorities or evidence in the record, "depends not merely on a man's capability to manage the stock market, or on his riding any hobby, and riding it well, but on the preservation of the balance between his intellectual faculties and his moral sentiments, so that all bore their proper proportions, one to the other." Just as an enlarged liver absorbed the powers of other organs and disrupted their normal operations, so too were mental faculties deranged when one was abnormally developed, as had clearly come to pass within the testator's skull, the counselor bombastically declaring that "Commodore Vanderbilt's bump of acquisitiveness was in a chronic state of inflammation all the time." Black's bit of phrenology prompted a wave of laughter—"in which," a news reporter noted, "the proponent joined heartily," though the press recorded nothing about Black's demeanor as he continued to declaim on the subject of the dead man's supposed brain malformation:

> It grew wonderfully. He cultivated it to the neglect of everything else. Morally and religiously his mind was a howling wilderness. He didn't content himself with worshiping Mammon alone, though he was

certainly a zealous devotee at the shrine of that meanest of all spirits that fell; but he indulged in other follies that are sure to demoralize the mind and weaken it, while they corrupt the understanding. Where such things are carried to such an extent, no man under their influence can be called a sane man.

There could be no question, then, Black concluded, that Vanderbilt's "love of money"—believing as he did that the rolling up of it was "the chief aim of man"—essentially "amounted to a mania," which Black submitted would invalidate "any act which could be shown to result from it." But in the event there was a question, Black insisted that the contestants had a right to present evidence in the alternative "to show the Commodore to be a very weak-minded man, who had made a will which, had he been a stronger man, he would not have made."[47]

In the months to come, the court permitted the contestants to do just that, in their effort to establish what now seemed to be the more plausible claims of undue influence and fraud. Ringing in a new year with no end to the litigation in sight, the witnesses who paraded into the courtroom provided tantalizing hints of a "conspiracy story" to be filled out as soon as the principals could be located and brought to New York City—a search that might be rendered futile, Lord darkly intimated, if the proponent's henchmen got to them first. Trusting that the "eminent" counsel for the contestants was not here attempting "to play the pitiable farce of putting into evidence that which they must know would be of no use," Surrogate Calvin entertained offers of proof by way of the testimony of business associates, employees, household attendants, and physicians of both the magnetic and the more conventional varieties, all intended to show how easily the Commodore would have been taken in by the contrivances of his son and the second (and much younger) wife whom William had procured for his father all too quickly after the death of the first.[48] Over the loud and repeated complaints of the proponent's counselors that this was "to build up a case of defamation of the living and the dead," made all the worse by the use of "crazy witnesses" to demonstrate "impossible facts," these witnesses recounted conversations with the testator both before and after he had made his supposed will, collectively painting a portrait of a man who was duped into believing the younger Cornelius to be an inveterate gambler and whoremonger who always would need a guardian, just as the disfavored son was, in fact, reforming his admittedly dissolute ways and threatening to rival William, who was hell-bent on being the sole successor to the Railroad King's throne. "Young Corneel" himself took the stand to defend his character, only to endure a searing cross-examination by Clinton that left it exceedingly unclear who was conspiring against whom in the months before Vanderbilt's last will was made. On the accounts of this and other witnesses, it was first made to appear that William had hired private detectives to follow a person who was only posing as his younger brother to compile false reports of his carousing ways that were to be turned over to the Commodore. But two of the three hired sleuths who were supposed to testify to this effect abruptly switched sides just before they were to appear in court, testifying that it was young Cornelius who had concocted the whole scheme and secured the services of a whole cast of bogus characters in a desperate attempt to establish a pretext for contesting a will that he knew would not be to his liking.[49]

Winning an adjournment for several months to track down the third of the private detectives, the contestants' counsel reappeared in September 1878 armed with an all-too-familiar line of attack; they now claimed to have witnesses who would reveal how William manipulated his father to make the contested will—a document that was "unjust and against public policy in concentrating such vast wealth upon one child"—with the help of a well-paid "clairvoyant physician" who conveyed messages purportedly from Sophia that actually were ghostwritten by the proponent. Almost exploding with frustration, Clinton protested that his opponent's latest move would simply start the case all over again, but Surrogate Calvin allowed the new testimony, provided mostly by Mrs. Lillian Stoddard, who claimed to be the wife of the now-deceased physician-medium. In a remarkable reversal, however, Clinton exposed Mrs. Stoddard on cross-examination as an "adventuress" with many other aliases before she seduced the doctor and assumed the role of his spouse, to the surprise and outrage of the real Mrs. Stoddard, whose life story became front-page news as Clinton dramatically asked her to stand up and identify herself for all the court to see. Lord attempted to rehabilitate his witness (Hadn't Dr. Stoddard offered her a ring and a certificate of his divorce before they consummated their relationship? he asked), while Clinton endeavored to have charges of perjury drawn up against her (she was surely too ignorant to have invented the testimony all by herself, but it was nevertheless a fraud on the court). In the face of these questionable maneuvers, Surrogate Calvin strongly encouraged the contestants to bring their case to a close. This they finally did, but only after spending two more months of the court's time on testimony by a motley assortment of mediums and medical men; the mediums described many occasions when the Commodore consulted with dead stockbrokers and relatives about a range of financial and personal matters, and the medical witnesses responded to lengthy hypothetical questions, effectively summarizing the contestants' case and then presenting at the attorney's request an expert assessment of the testator's mental condition grounded on the assumption that all they had shown was true.[50] The diagnosis these witnesses consistently gave was that of monomania "on the subjects of the accumulation and acquirement of wealth," with the slight exception of the doctor who cast the Commodore's affliction in terms of "autocracy—a desire to rule and govern everybody!"[51]

Proceeding with comparative dispatch, the attorneys for the proponent dispensed with an opening argument over the contestants' objection and called to the stand a considerably less diverting but more respectable cast of businessmen, ministers, lawyers, and physicians, who testified to the unfailingly rational manner in which the Commodore had governed himself as well as his domestic and business affairs to the end of his life.[52] On their testimony, the testator was, at once, a benevolent and shrewd patriarch, who carefully trained and tested "Billy" before allowing him to "step into his shoes," who protected but did not overindulge his incorrigibly spendthrift younger son Cornelius Jr., and who heeded the entreaties of his anything-but-gold-digging second wife to provide substantial funds for building a church and founding a university that would bear his great name. The cross-examination of the Commodore's business associates predictably brought out less savory aspects of his methods of accumulating capital, for it emerged that "practicing small economies" sometimes did entail "reducing the wages of his railroad employees." And the testimony concerning the couple's charitable giving provided an opening for the contestants' counsel, who delicately but vigorously seized the occasion to engage in another bit of character assassination, this time aimed at the young widow, by intimating that she was someone else's wife when she married the Commodore. In the face of a sharp rebuke from Surrogate Calvin, who instinctively jumped to the lady's defense and preempted any such action on the part of the contestants, Black insisted with what may or may not have been feigned embarrassment that it was his duty to press the point:

> Here is a man eighty years old marrying a woman fifty years his junior, who came here a stranger, after separating from a husband, who is still living. That there should have been bitterness felt toward this woman by the Commodore's daughters, some of whom were already grandmothers, and that this feeling should have turned the heart of the father against them, are natural results. But there was one exception in the family. William H. Vanderbilt encouraged the marriage, and continued to show as much regard for the woman as though she had not done the injury of marrying the Commodore in his dotage. But the aggravation is immense if, in addition to showing the distress and hatred that this marriage caused, we show that it was unlawful, and that, therefore, whatever influence Mrs. Vanderbilt exerted was not only undue, it was unholy. These are the words struggling for utterance here that I am compelled to restrain, and I suppose I have made a bungle of it, but your Honor must understand what I mean. That a stranger should sell herself to this old man for his money, taking advantage of that weakness of his nature, is not a reason why a will made under such circumstances should be allowed to stand.

Understanding perfectly well what Black meant to accomplish by this argument, Surrogate Calvin swiftly and sternly prohibited him from continuing in this vein.[53] But, by playing this particular card in open court, Black seemed to signal that an endgame was in sight, and it was so likely to facilitate an out-of-court compromise that the Surrogate adjourned the trial for two months.[54]

When the trial resumed in early February 1879, the counselors picked up where they had left off, albeit in a decidedly perfunctory manner, fueling speculation that the real work of resolving the family feud was proceeding somewhere outside the courtroom. With an air of indignation, as if his defense of the Vanderbilt will *should* have been entirely unnecessary, Clinton elicited testimony from a number of medical specialists to fill out his side of the case. The key witness among these doctors was the prominent alienist John P. Gray, who voiced the same sort of skepticism about "moral" forms of insanity that he would articulate a few years later when he was called by the prosecution during the celebrated trial of President James A. Garfield's assassin, Charles J. Guiteau.[55] Queried extensively about the details of the autopsy commissioned by the contestants, Gray firmly (if evasively) stated that he could not infer from this post-mortem examination the existence of any mental unsoundness or enfeeblement, and he likewise answered in the negative the carefully framed question "In medical science and classification is there known any such form of insanity as a desire for accumulating wealth followed by large accumulation?" These answers won Gray a measure of ridicule in the press, for they left "the impression that in the opinion of doctors only the men who want to be rich and fail are crazy." Something closer to contempt emanated from Lord as he tried and failed to get Gray to budge from his refusal to diagnose the Commodore; Gray's refusal was reduced in Lord's mind to the scriptural declaration "all things are possible," a literary allusion meant as a swipe at Clinton for his false piety. Giving as good as he got, Clinton shot back that all things were possible, with one conceivable exception: that the contestants were ever going to conclude their case. "What!" Lord erupted, "at $1,000 a day?" to which Clinton rejoined, "You want it prolonged until you have made that much out of it." The rap of Surrogate Calvin's gavel ended this round of verbal sparring, one further punctuated by the Surrogate's stern assessment that "both sides had got more than they had earned."[56]

Moved not so much by this rebuke as by the prospect of even more damaging disclosures about the *finances* of the Vanderbilt family in a parallel lawsuit filed by Cornelius Jr. against his brother that was about to go to trial,[57] Clinton abruptly rested his case on March 4, 1879, though not before calling two final witnesses to the stand, just for the record. The first was the Commodore's trusted personal lawyer and a subscribing witness to his last will, Judge Charles A. Rapallo, who affirmed that his client's testamentary intentions remained steadfast and eminently sound with every redrafting of this document from 1856 to 1875. The

second was the proponent himself; William Vanderbilt calmly and cat-
egorically denied every allegation of undue and fraudulent influence
lodged against him over the course of the trial. After the most cursory of
cross-examinations, Lord rose for the last time to announce that he was
prepared to submit the case without a closing argument as the opposing counsel had done, the contestants' last motion being a request that
the court strike from the record "all offers to prove any conduct reflecting on the character of Mrs. Vanderbilt, the widow of the late Commodore," which had been offered in good faith but were now known to be
untrue. And then, as if on cue, the parties' counselors all shook hands
with one another, Surrogate Calvin gathered his papers, the courtroom
quickly emptied, and newsstands filled with papers reporting that the
sensational trial, with its "strange mingling of farce and more serious
business," had finally "ENDED AFTER MANY DAYS."[58]

The Surrogate's Opinion

On March 19, 1879, amid a veritable "chorus of denials" that the parties
had reached any sort of settlement—as strenuous as they were implausible—Surrogate Calvin issued a hundred-page opinion, affirming the
validity of the Vanderbilt will.[59] Most newspapermen treated this final
act of the courtroom drama as a mere formality, spilling more ink on
the question of how much of his inheritance William had actually given
up to bring all the litigation to an end.[60] Although recognizing the anti-
climactic character of the moment of decision, the Surrogate clearly
aimed to speak to a wider audience than those in attendance as he
spelled out the reasons and authorities supporting his ruling. Though
he had often excoriated the contending lawyers for "playing to the
newspapers" during the trial, the Surrogate now did something of the
same as he laced his opinion with self-justifying and self-congratulating
prose. Posing as the protector of "the memory of the decedent" and the
reputations of countless others (including his own) impugned during
the trial, he promised to give the public a distillation of the facts actually proven by counsel, as distinct from the preposterous "imputations
of social, domestic and business delinquencies" made in arguments
and by means of proffered testimony, which were widely publicized but
never actually admitted into evidence. In drawing these distinctions, the

Surrogate at once sought and claimed a measure of credit for excluding as much "prurient and defamatory matter" as he possibly could, consistent with "the rights of all the parties engaged in this unseemly revelation of family secrets."[61]

Before delving into the specifics of the case, the Surrogate offered a preamble discussing why the trial had generated so much publicity and what was truly at stake, above and beyond the pecuniary interests of the parties before him. That the will of "such a man as the decedent was believed to have been" could be legally challenged was what generated such "extraordinary interest" on the part of the public. Indeed, it was the right of testamentary disposition that was perceived to be "on trial" during the Vanderbilt litigation. "This solicitude," the Surrogate hastened to add, "has not been confined to those of large possessions, but has pervaded the thoughts of those of moderate means, and those who, by years of toil and prudence, have accumulated small savings in the fond hope of providing therewith for the necessities and comforts of infirm and invalid children and parents, as well as of an affectionate and faithful wife." The Surrogate aligned himself with this more sympathetic cast of characters, their family relations contrasting sharply with those of the litigants immediately before him, who were all too eager "to uncover to the public gaze the secrets of a parent's domestic and private life; to belittle his intelligence and his virtues; to distort his providence into meanness; to magnify his eccentricities into dementia; his social foibles into immorality; his business differences into dishonesty and treachery; and to ascribe his disease to obscene practices." Exhibiting perhaps unwarranted optimism about his capacity to discourage this sort of behavior, the Surrogate then clarified the applicable rules of law, strenuously emphasizing it was not his court's province "to *make* a testamentary disposition of other people's property, or to *revise* a decedent's will upon the principles of justice or equity." To the contrary, it was his statutory duty to give effect to the voluntarily drafted wills of all sound-minded testators, however "illiberal and unjust" they might appear to those who survived them. This republican country, that is to say, was not one where all children were guaranteed to inherit equal shares of their father's estate, for it remained the right of the father to make an "undutiful will." In confirming this rule of law, however, the Surrogate never quite confronted the extent to which he was encouraging the growth of a new aristocracy of wealth that threatened to undermine the producer ethos and middle-class way of life that he championed at the outset of his decision.[62]

Training his attention on the authenticity rather than on the fairness of the testamentary disposition before him, Surrogate Calvin sought to determine whether it was the freely expressed will of the Commodore, executed when he was in his right mind. To bring order to the voluminous mass of testimony elicited over the course of the long trial, he organized his analysis under eight headings: (1) evidence from the autopsy of the testator tending to show mental derangement or impairment at the time the will was executed; (2) counter-proof by the proponent's experts; (3) other evidence of mental unsoundness as evidenced by the testator's "alleged weak and irrational conversation, repetitions, declarations and conduct, and so-called monomania for wealth and fame"; (4) testimony that the same man exhibited "uniform rationality, intelligence and coherence in conversations, in business transactions and general conduct"; (5) allegations of fraud perpetrated by the proponent upon his father "respecting the pretended communications from the spirit of his deceased wife, as to the terms of his will," in complicity with assorted mediums; (6) evidence suggesting the "improbability" of this story, in view of the character of the contestants' witnesses and the contradictory testimony offered by the proponent, as well as "the coherent and methodical terms of the will, and of several antecedent wills" executed before the spiritualists entered the picture; (7) allegations of undue influence practiced upon the testator by the proponent; and (8) the testamentary intentions expressed by the decedent over time, "both against and in harmony with the provisions of the will propounded."[63]

The biases inflecting this listing became more pronounced as the Surrogate proceeded with his painstaking review of the trial record. In retrospect, he discerned a large credibility gap between Lord's opening argument and what he was actually able to prove by way of his witnesses, and it had clearly been unwise to reverse the proper order of proof by allowing so much speculative testimony relating to the autopsy before any behavioral evidence had been introduced showing "irrationality or mental alienation" on the testator's part. Some of those who later testified to this effect almost certainly perjured themselves, and the testimony taken as a whole fell far short of the evidentiary showing necessary to make out even a *prima facie* case for setting aside a will.[64] Reasonable people might disagree as to the "propriety" of the Commodore's "ambition to perpetuate the great railroad enterprise to which he had devoted so much of his business, life and energy as a monument to his great business skill and success, and as to the good taste of boasting of it"; however, this aspiration was not unusual, judging from "the common level of commercial incentives and hopes," and it certainly did not make the Commodore insane. One wishing to keep his name alive in this fashion would have been almost crazy not to pick William as his successor, and although "many wise and just men" might hold that his unequal treatment of his other children "betokened a lack of parental affection and justice," these perceived shortcomings were of no moment as a matter of law. In view of how often "*gross injustice and reprehensible cruelty* manifest themselves in men who are in all other respects mentally and morally responsible for their conduct," Surrogate Calvin reasoned, evidence to this effect could not alone support a finding of testamentary incapacity. Moreover, the contestants' charges of undue influence and fraud were even less plausible, the testimony instead establishing that the testator showed "a very vigorous mind and strong nature" even as he lay dying, his chief deficiencies being the want of "education and culture and a delicate respect for the opinions of his fellow-men." Given that these characteristics appeared to be very much in evidence in the contested will, there was all the more reason to find in the proponent's favor.[65]

All that remained, in the Surrogate's judgment, was to draw a few morals from the fabricated stories that the contestants had tried and failed to pass off as the truth. In their spectacularly unsuccessful attempts to smear the reputation of the testator's widow, they had presented an object lesson "to those who are prone to assail the private character and revel in the promiscuous defamation *as a means of intimidating parties and coercing compromises,*" Calvin maintained, censoriously adding that "the tardy apology, after the most diligent and persistent effort to secure witnesses capable of testifying to the charges, while praiseworthy in itself, affords but a sorry and meager amend for the endurance by a delicate, sensitive, cultivated woman, for two years, of a baseless slander of her private character." Calvin could only congratulate himself for maintaining the dignity of the proceedings, admirably

minimizing the number of damaging disclosures during the trial by litigants who were disconcertingly insensible to the moral demands of "fil-
ial and fraternal duty." However, the Surrogate pulled back from such
a dour conclusion as the curtain was about to fall, supplying a happy
ending that in retrospect appears to be wishful thinking:

> When the passions which have been excited by this protracted and acri-
> monious controversy shall have subsided, and a kindlier spirit pervades
> the minds and hearts of those who initiated this proceeding, and they
> reverently turn to the record their father has made upon the business
> annals of his time, and perchance cast their eyes over the record of this
> proceeding, they will rejoice that it is preserved so clean, in spite of all
> their efforts to tarnish it.[66]

The Moral of the Story

"Surely the Vanderbilt money is the root of all evil and brings trouble
to everyone who touches it," the *Chicago Daily Tribune* editorialized in
June 1882, as a new round of litigation began in the Surrogate's Court,
occasioned by the death of "the Commodore's discarded son," Cornelius Jr., by a self-inflicted gunshot to his head. A coroner's jury adjudged
his act to be suicide, committed while the decedent was laboring under
"a temporary mental depression," the witnesses uniformly testifying
that he had lately pronounced himself to be "tired of life" and more particularly "annoyed by the litigations in which he was involved" after the
settlement of his father's estate; that settlement seemed only to spawn
more courtroom disputes of varying kinds, many arising from past
debts that Cornelius Jr. allegedly accrued in anticipation of receiving
some portion of his father's estate. Though he left no note indicating
what finally prompted him to exit the world, he did leave a last will
and testament, awarding the bulk of his $600,000 estate to his long-
time companion and medical advisor, George Terry. This document
provided the basis for "another Chapter in the Courts upon the mental
and physical idiosyncrasies of the Vanderbilt family," as reported in the
Tribune and countless other newspapers; the legal challenge now was
brought by the decedent's sister Mary La Bau Berger, who had fought so

long and hard beside her brother in the attempt to break their father's will. Although the claims of testamentary incapacity and undue influence might have been adjudged more plausible as applied to Cornelius the younger, the court rather handily dismissed them, frustrating the expectations of many newsmen, who nonetheless found ways to fold this disappointingly dull legal episode into a developing story about "the curse of great wealth."[67]

This scourge was visited most immediately and obviously upon rich men and their families, according to the profusion of articles and editorials published on the subject in the last quarter of the nineteenth century. Editorialists described the materialistic behavior of the Commodore and his bickering heirs as lamentably typical of the millionaire class, whose fortunes "were earned in misery, and have left misery behind them." An insatiable appetite for money—"not for the sake of hoarding, nor for the sake of using it for the improvement of the race, but for the joy of holding it, increasing it, and making it grow"—drove men like Vanderbilt to accumulate riches even though the successful pursuit of this end brought "innumerable anxieties," as such men daily were harassed by begging letters and fraudulent schemes ultimately robbing them of their "confidence in humanity." Unable to trust even their own flesh and blood, men burdened with large estates faced death with the added terror of knowing that all their faults and foibles would be exposed and exaggerated by means of a post-mortem legal contest if they dared to make charitable bequests as they saw fit, or otherwise to defy the wills of their children, whose moral sensibilities had been dulled to the point of nonexistence from living amidst such plenty, "which they had no hand in accumulating." So fashionable had such capacity contests become in the Gilded Age that they now appeared to be an unavoidable aspect of "the natural law of mortality," sure to be perpetuated by "speculative lawyers," who could extract huge fees regardless of the merits or outcome of any given case.[68]

In contemplating these courtroom scenes, some sermonizing commentators were prompted to repeat the biblical prayer of Agur, "give me neither poverty nor riches" (Proverbs 30:8), submitting that the miseries and vulgarities suffered and exhibited by the very wealthy "should render professional men content to be poor." Others with otherworldly ambitions found new wisdom in the scriptural passages concerning

Dives and Lazarus as well as "the financially solid man and the dromedary." Yet even though it was consoling to contemplate the difficulty facing any rich man seeking entry into the kingdom of God, there were obvious disadvantages to a scheme barring rich men from taking their accumulated wealth with them on their "last free trip . . . into the afterglow," for this was a great source of conflict among their surviving children, who thought nothing of staining the family name with the imputation of insanity. "Things are getting to that point that we absolutely need a Society for the Suppression of Heirs," or perhaps a "Moribund Millionaire's Club" to check the indefinite multiplication of lawsuits. The sheer threat of a post-mortem capacity contest, another editorialist observed, "virtually compels every dying man to give all his property to his heirs," more than a few commentators regarding this result as tantamount to reinstating the law of entail. Having reverted this far, one journalist wrote with tongue firmly in cheek, legislators might as well declare by statute "that the possession of property worth, say half a million dollars or more, shall be regarded as *prima facie* proof of the testator's insanity, and shall give his next of kin the right to place him in an insane asylum while they seize upon his property," with the further proviso that "the insane man's wishes" with regard to its division "should be as carefully disregarded as possible." Another reasoned that insanity might well be rendered as a perfectly accurate finding in any case where a rich man actually chose to make a will, a patently irrational act given how likely it was to spell his humiliation in a courtroom after his death.[69]

The verdict most commonly drawn from all these Gilded Age will contests, however, was that they served to confirm the truth of an old proverb about family dynasties that had been given new currency at midcentury by the poet and essayist Oliver Wendell Holmes Sr.: "three generations from shirtsleeves to shirtsleeves." Independence, in other words, was apparently not what the capitalist gained in the process of accumulating wealth; his money-getting tendencies proved to be pathologically addictive and positively harmful to his heirs, who themselves were hardly equipped to sustain the sort of democratic republic that architects of the American law of wills had envisioned. This was the Protestant ethic gone horribly wrong, an unintentional parody of the way to wealth promoted by self-help propagandists from Benjamin

Franklin forward, one that begged the question: Should a rich man be free to do as he willed with his own? Lurking between the lines of these mock proposals and comic portrayals of an emergent American "upper class" were serious concerns about the private transfer of wealth—concerns drawing the attention of a widening range of legal professionals, social scientists, ministers, and other reform-minded thinkers as the century drew to a close, some of whom were millionaires themselves.[70]

The most immediate and modest reform efforts were those to deter the "speculative attacks on wills" on the part of disappointed heirs, particularly where these "predatory" practices really reduced to "the looting of dead men's estates." The Vanderbilt will contest became a critical spur to action, the ink on Surrogate Calvin's opinion barely dry when he made his way to Albany to secure the passage of a new law prohibiting the award to unsuccessful contestants of counsel fees out of the disputed estate, a measure he too optimistically predicted would spell "the doom's-day of the will-contesting industry." Albany lawmakers also seriously entertained but never adopted the idea of ante-mortem probate, intended to give the would-be testator the opportunity to establish that he was of sound and disposing mind during his lifetime. Legislation to this effect was enacted in Michigan in 1883, but that state's supreme court soon declared this scheme unconstitutional, finding that the probate process did not constitute a proper judicial proceeding because any judgment rendered remained subject to the testator's own discretion or caprice, because he still was able to "make any subsequent arrangement he may desire." Although law journals and state legislatures bandied about various technical fixes, the dominant opinion among the bench and bar by the end of the nineteenth century was that the proposed cure would prove worse than the disease—that "the proceedings necessary to establish the will during the testator's life" would "cause strife and dissension" considerably worse than that displayed during post-mortem contests, "stirring up bitter hatred" among and between parents and children, probably making passions so intense that they might spark physical violence, all surely "contrary to public policy." As self-serving as this judgment sounded, laymen and lawyers appeared to converge on an alternative solution, one promoted as more Christian and less likely to generate strife and litigation: Wealthy persons should "get rid of their property before the grim messenger knocks imperatively at their doors and calls them hence." Indeed, it was now estimated that "the man who, during his lifetime and under his own supervision[,] organizes and endows public charities is worthy of more praise than he who leaves ten times as much money by his will for similar objects," only relinquishing his "hoarded riches at the brink of the grave because he can't carry cash, stocks, or real estate out of the world with him."[71]

This way of thinking found its most famous advocate and exemplar in the steel magnate Andrew Carnegie, who offered his 1889 *Gospel of Wealth* as a new testament delivered by a millionaire who seemed almost to renounce his self-made status, as he acknowledged that his great fortune—or at least the "surplus wealth" over and above a certain "competence"—belonged to the community, and that he held this property as "a trustee for the poor." The doctrine of Individualism preached by Carnegie required the holder of such a vast estate to administer it during his lifetime for the benefit of mankind rather than disposing of it by will to his children, who should be taught along with their less fortunate fellows to provide for themselves. What was conventionally thought to be an expression of paternal love was in truth a deplorable sort of "family pride," Carnegie insisted, the indulgence of which he adjudged inconsistent with the "responsibilities which attend the possession of wealth." Accordingly, he pronounced what ought to be the public's verdict: "The man who dies thus rich dies disgraced." In so ruling, Carnegie was mainly aiming to speak to the worrying struggles between capital and labor proliferating across the nation rather than to those raging among family members in surrogates' courts. However, in his mind the two were connected: The root cause of the "antagonism between the classes" was to be found in the inheritance practices of the vain and misguided men who injudiciously exercised their testamentary freedom "to found or maintain hereditary families," their charitable bequests appearing as ungracious afterthoughts that would not have been made at all "had they been able to take it with them." So troubled was the reputed Social Darwinist by these misappropriations of money that he hailed "the growing disposition to tax more and more heavily large estates left at death" as a powerful and justifiable means by which the state—proceeding on the community's behalf—could express "its condemnation of the selfish millionaire's unworthy life" and deter others from following the same path. The true disciple of the *Gospel of Wealth* was he who died "poor, very poor, indeed, in money, but rich, very rich, twenty times a millionaire still, in the affection, gratitude, and admiration of his fellow-men, and—sweeter far—soothed and sustained by the still, small voice within, which, whispering, tells him that, because he has lived, perhaps one small part of the great world has been bettered just a little." On the chance that philanthropy's earthly rewards were not incentive enough for his readers, Carnegie concluded with confidence that there was one sure bet: "against such riches as these no bar will be found at the gates of Paradise."[72]

Yet it was with the here and now that Carnegie mainly concerned himself in *The Gospel of Wealth*, taking human nature as he found it with the ultimate aim of making "Home our Heaven." Whereas the spiritualism of his father—a Swedenborgian—might look to an afterlife where "angels derive their happiness, not from laboring for the self, but for each other," the son propagated a Christian capitalism that took for granted the "sacredness" of individual property rights and the fixity of "the Law of Accumulation of Wealth, and the Law of Competition." But if these aspects of the universe made it inevitable that some would be rich and some would be poor, still Carnegie believed that the laws governing the hereditary transmission of property could and should be altered for the common good. Though meant to be magnanimous, his profession of faith was greeted skeptically by many of the less fortunate in his audience, to whom this scheme of things read like the slippery sayings of a confidence man whose only redeeming quality was an uneasy conscience. However, it is precisely for this reason that we can see Carnegie's *Gospel* as an important sign of the times—an indicator of how ambivalent Americans had become about the cultural and legal practices that constituted their system of inheritance. In acknowledging that his financial holdings far exceeded what he could justly claim as his property, this industrialist surely made a significant concession, but the devil was literally in the details: How exactly was this excess to be measured—what was "the test of extravagance"? Appreciating that this conundrum was the nub of the matter, Carnegie stood prepared to allow the community to decide; as was the case with matters of good taste and manners, he declared with assurance, the public's opinion with regard to "the use or abuse of its surplus wealth . . . will not often be wrong." But here he assumed far greater consensus about the rights, wrongs, and responsibilities of the extremely rich than existed at the time, as his contemporaries vividly demonstrated in their words and deeds—not only the editorials, sermons, and works of social science on the subject but also the torched factories and railway cars, the strikers assaulted by federal troops, and the wine-soaked banquets at Delmonico's celebrating the centennial of *The Wealth of Nations* and paying tribute to such new prophets of human progress as Herbert Spencer.[73]

Spencer had returned the compliment and honors paid him on the November evening in 1882 when he was so honored by delivering a fault-finding "homily" (his words) to his American admirers as his after-dinner speech. In this address, he chided his admiring audience for taking life and its struggles too seriously (though he was not one to talk). Maniacally striving well beyond the limits of mental and physical health, those whom the English philosopher had met during his stay in the United States appeared unduly committed to "the gospel of work," so much so that it threatened to unfit them and their heirs for republican government. "Damaged constitutions reappear in children, and entail of them far more of ill than great fortunes yield them of good," he admonished the assemblage of scholars, statesmen, lawyers, clergymen, and industrialists as they digested a twelve-course meal with the help of the best cigars money could buy. "If the ultimate consequence should be a dwindling away of those among you who are the inheritors of free institutions and best adapted to them," the evolutionist prophesied, "there will come a further difficulty in the working out of the great future which lies before the American nation." With a strange admixture of anxiety and philosophic calm, he insisted "there needs a revised ideal of life," forecasting that this "persistent activity has reached an extreme from which there must begin a counterchange—a reaction," essentially amounting to a new dispensation. "Hereafter, when this age of active material progress has yielded mankind its benefits, there will, I think, come a better adjustment of labor and enjoyment," in anticipation of which Spencer exhorted his auditors: "It is time to preach the gospel of relaxation." As with so much of what the Englishman had previously said and wrote, these words were creatively read and misread to differing ends by critics and devotees alike as they struggled to make sense of the widening gap between rich and poor. His notoriety in America is thus perhaps best understood as an index of doubts about the relationship between work and reward—in this world and the next—that accumulated along with the capitalist's wealth. Were millionaires naturally and justly selected to receive high wages and live in luxury, and was this "a good bargain for society," as the sociologist William Graham Sumner so strenuously maintained? Was there always "room at the top" for the industrious, frugal, and sober, as success writers promised, and did the successful actually deserve what they got, as so many ministers tried to convince themselves and their flocks? What did the proverbial movement "from shirtsleeves to shirtsleeves in three generations" ultimately say about the nature of the universe? Was life fair, and if not, would there be some sort of providential allocation of rewards and punishments in a world beyond?[74]

Family Fortunes

In late 1876, as he lay dying and worrying about matters of succession to his throne, concerns about divine justice began to crowd into the head of Cornelius Vanderbilt, or so others said and wrote for purposes of litigation and public consumption. The magnetic physicians in attendance during his last illness conjured up for the contestants' counsel images of a credulous old man prone to erupt with howls of pain accompanied by even louder wonderings "why God should persecute him so." As his condition worsened, he became "greatly worried" that his riches would bar his entry into the kingdom of heaven, and he surely was not consoled by the spirit doctor who reckoned that his talents lay in managing railroads, not playing the harp. To the contrary, the Commodore's disquiet increasingly manifested itself in the form of waking dreams that seemed to presage his death. The vision that recurred most often was of a roadway shaped like a horse-shoe, where he saw himself walking with his friends, some of whom continued all the way to the edge and fell off. Although he had returned safely from these imaginary journeys during earlier stages of his illness, there came a day when the sequence went differently in his head, when he found himself at the end of the road, on the verge of falling off and unable to move back or to see what lay beyond where he stood. The proponents' witnesses recounted similar premonitions, likewise suggesting that Vanderbilt's interest in his spiritual prospects intensified considerably in his last days. In their accounts, however, the Commodore faced his end with greater (and more characteristic) equanimity: He saw many roads as he looked to the future and, although he "couldn't see where they all led to, or whether they became united at the other end," he had resolved none-theless to "put his trust in Providence, 'because Providence was square as a brick.'" As with his education more generally, what he knew of God was mostly self-taught and likely not from the Bible, though it occu-pied a prominent place on the table by his sickbed. For him, the "good book"—and, some intimated, the only one he may have ever read—was John Bunyan's *The Pilgrim's Progress*. Though he did not take up that book for the first time until he was well into his seventies, the Commo-dore commended it ever after as an indispensible guide to living, one that he insisted repaid re-reading by grown men as well as young boys.[75]

"I have used similitudes," read the epigram of Bunyan's archetypal success story of the man Christian, and so it was received by genera-tions of Americans, being second only to the Bible in pious readership from its initial publication in the late seventeenth century through the Civil War. The Pilgrim's harrowing passage from the City of Destruc-tion to the Celestial City resonated with the first colonists, who con-ceived of their own spiritual quest into the American wilderness in similar terms, and it remained a vital narrative well into the second half of the nineteenth century, constituting a "double-edged tradi-tion," as Allen Trachtenberg has aptly observed, one that "bequeathed images of Vanity Fair as well as a city on a hill, a fabric of images of corruption, sin, and destruction, which colored the secular percep-tions of many Americans in the years of the most rapid and thorough and tumultuous urbanization the country had yet experienced." Yet sales of *The Pilgrim's Progress* noticeably plummeted after Appomat-tox, the work suddenly becoming "a fit subject for parody and trav-esty" in this industrializing age, as it was tellingly displaced by a new genre of guidebooks that were quite desperately devoted to the sub-ject of *Getting on in the World*—books that promised to divulge *The Secrets of Success, or Finger Posts on the Highway of Life* and to supply *Portraits and Principles of the World's Great Men and Women* illus-trating the relationship between *Worth and Wealth* explaining *Why Some Succeed While Others Fail*. Against mounting evidence to the contrary, these bestsellers offered assurance to their intended audiences—"discouraged" young men and their "anxious" parents—that the "battle of life" could be won, that "where there's a will there's a way," with Vanderbilt's life story typifying the "Enterprise" required to attain the status of a self-made man, independence being its own and best reward. Although nothing was specifically said about the Commodore's dynastic designs, the Gilded Age success writers tended to treat large fortunes as burdens that weighed upon their possessors like the Christian's knowledge of his own sin, and they were considerably more pessimistic about the fate of children who inherited wealth in such great proportions; expectant heirs were cast as "drones in the hive of human industry" condemned to live lives of "emasculated idleness and laziness" even as their parents were admiringly crowned with such royal titles as "Railroad King." This was the culture that the Protestant ethic had made, the success manuals at once fueling and lamenting a state of overcivilization in which the relatives of rich men came to regard will contests as a sort of sport. In just this sense, the Vanderbilt heirs were exemplary as they opposed one another in Surrogate Calvin's courtroom, the proponents submitting their father's late-blooming interest in *The Pilgrim's Progress* as proof of his spiritual enlightenment, the contestants taking it instead to underscore how credulous and childlike he had become in his old age.[76]

Although not as sybaritic and gaudy as the banquets and costume balls bankrolled by tycoons in *fin de siècle* America, the will contests staged by their covetous heirs were galling in their own way, attracting the attention of an ever-widening array of journalists, scientists, cultural critics, and social reformers, as well as the curiosity seekers who vied for seats in the courtroom day after day after day. In other words, not everyone was laughing, and increasingly those who took such matters lightly appeared to be whistling in the dark. The more it seemed that the sons and grandsons of rich men were not ineluctably cycling back to shirtsleeves again, the louder were the alarms sounded—by middling folks as well as by members of the Brahmin elite—about the coalescence of "a new aristocracy of wealth," a capitalist class of men and women resembling the slaveholders of the antebellum South, who had grotesquely lived on the labor of others.[77] In screeds of self-criticism and protest replete with images of mental distress, strain, and degeneration—of a polity driven "mad" by ambition and convulsed by "panics" and "depressions"—populists and progressives registered fears about the mental and physical health of present and future generations of (white, Anglo-Saxon) Americans. As reformers cast about for solutions, many saw the law of inheritance as an institution especially ripe for renovation. Contending that the accumulated estates of such dead capitalists as Vanderbilt truly belonged to the community rather than to their heirs,[78] who were more harmed than helped by family money in any event, some called for the imposition of a graduated inheritance tax, others for an absolute cap on the amount that any individual could inherit, and still others for the outright abolition of the inheritance system. Of course more than a few prominent men of science balked at this "socialistic" way of thinking and countered it with natural rights–based arguments in support of existing testamentary practices, but their voices were not of sufficient force to block the institution of permanent estate taxes at the federal and state levels in the early decades of the twentieth century. However, the erosion of the rule against perpetuities in this same era and the far-from-coincidental "triumph" of the dynastic trust in the decades that followed more than blunted the impact of this set of reforms. In a certain sense, a man was now freer than ever before to do as he willed with his own.[79]

Although that is a story for another day, I submit in conclusion that the dilemmas posed by the wills of rich men—and women—remain very much with us, as coverage of the Brooke Astor will case and congressional debates about the "death tax" have so vividly exhibited, to say nothing of Warren Buffett's son's memoir, *Life Is What You Make It: Find Your Own Path to Fulfillment*, its very title standing as a powerful reminder of how fraught our relationship to the self-made man continues to be.[80] We are, it seems, as confused and conflicted as ever about the connections linking money-making, self-realization, and social welfare, as once again we find it necessary to dust ourselves off and try, try again, in the wake of another financial disaster, a predicament that history shows to have deeper roots in ambiguities about the morality of the marketplace and the broader universe—ambiguities that a new generation of robber barons have exploited with all too predictable consequences.

NOTES

1. "Battle of the Heirs," *St. Louis Daily Globe-Democrat*, July 4, 1875, p. 11.

2. "Vanderbilt's Home Life," *New York Tribune*, November 13, 1877, p. 2; "The House of Vanderbilt: A Railroad Prince's Fortune," *New York Times*, November 13, 1877. (All articles in the *New York Times* are cited hereafter as *NYT*.)

3. "Vanderbilt's Home Life," *New York Tribune*, November 13, 1877, p. 2; "The House of Vanderbilt," *NYT*, November 13, 1877.

4. "The House of Vanderbilt, November 13, 1877, *NYT*; "The Vanderbilt Will," November 13, 1877, *New York Herald*, New York Public Library file of newspaper clippings relating to the Vanderbilt Will Case, p. 4 [hereafter "NYPL"]; "Scott Lord on Vanderbilt," *The Sun*, November 13, 1877 [NYPL, pp. 13–14]. This file consists of 314 pages of microfilmed newspaper articles (some only in fragmentary form) covering the trial from its first day through April 1878, nearly a year before the trial finally came to a close. Almost all of the articles are from New York papers: the *New York Times*, the *New York Daily Tribune*, the *New York Herald*, the *Sun*, the *World*, the *New York Star*, and the *Sunday Mercury*. Most cover the courtroom proceedings, though there are a number of editorials and items of gossip about members of the Vanderbilt clan and others brought into prominence as a result of the trial. Page references are internal to the file of microfilms, which contains 314 pages. See notes 11, 12, and 38 *infra* for further discussion of these sources and my approach to them.

5. The other members of the contestants' legal team were Jeremiah Sullivan Black, Ethan Allen, David Dudley Field, and Sullivan Tenney. The lead counsel for the proponents was Henry L. Clinton, and he was assisted by George F. Comstock and Theodore E. Leeds. Black appeared in the Surrogate's chambers fresh from Washington, D.C., where he served as one of Tilden's lawyers in the hearings before the Electoral Commission appointed to resolve the disputed election of 1876. See Roy Morris Jr., *Fraud of the Century: Rutherford B. Hayes, Samuel Tilden, and the Stolen Election of 1876* (New York: Simon & Schuster, 2003), 234–35. Field and Tilden represented the Commodore's opponents in the "Erie Wars" fought out in 1868 and 1869 for control of the railroad company, during the course of which injunctions and favors were granted to the highest bidder by Tweed's ring of judges and politicians. Clinton and Tilden were both involved in the anti-corruption initiatives of the newly founded New York City Bar Association, and both took leading roles in the prosecution of Tweed and his confederates, while Field appeared on the side of the defense. By the time of the Vanderbilt will case, Clinton was associated with the administration of Tweed's successor, "Honest" John Kelly, who was rumored to have engineered Calvin's elevation to the bench. For discussions of these interconnected political and legal struggles, see John Steele Gordon, *The Scarlet Woman of Wall Street: Jay Gould, Jim Fisk, Cornelius Vanderbilt, the Erie Railway Wars, and the Birth of Wall Street* (New York: Weidenfeld & Nicolson, 1988), 156–73; Bruce Kimball, *The Inception of Modern Professional Education: C. C. Langdell, 1826–1906* (Chapel

Hill: University of North Carolina Press, 2009), 70–76. For reports linking Calvin to Kelly and to the corrupt practices of the "old Tweed Ring," see, e.g., "Another of Kelly's Candidates: Some Facts in the History of Mr. Calvin—His Employment by the Ring Corporation Counsel—Enthusiastic Letter of Gratitude to Boss Tweed—A Remarkable Document," *NYT*, October 21, 1875, p. 4; "The New Surrogate," *NYT*, April 13, 1876, p. 8. On the jocularity and greed exhibited by the Surrogate and the lawyers see, e.g., "The Vanderbilt Will Case," *Georgia Weekly Telegraph and Georgia Journal & Messenger*, March 11, 1879, Issue 10, col. B (taking note of the Surrogate's "voluminous and heavy jokes," further describing "his humor" as "massive, terrible and perpetual," and predicting that it "will remain an ever enduring monument of judicial pleasantry sharpened by the excitement of extraordinary earnings"—all of which was also said to apply to Lord, Black, and "many others of them").

6. After the Civil War, urban publishers increasingly competed for a national audience and came to depend upon advertisers for revenues while at the same time consolidating their newsgathering efforts and organizing as a profession. For historical treatments of the press and the buying and selling of the news in this era, see Ted Curtis Smythe, *The Gilded Age Press, 1865–1900* (Westport, Conn.: Praeger, 2003); Richard L. Kaplan, *Politics and the American Press: The Rise of Objectivity, 1865–1920* (Cambridge: Cambridge University Press, 2002), 72–139; David Nasaw, *The Chief: The Life of William Randolph Hearst* (Boston: Houghton Mifflin, 2000); Charles Johanningsmeir, *Fiction and the American Literary Marketplace: The Role of Newspaper Syndicates, 1860–1900* (Cambridge: Cambridge University Press, 1997); Andie Tucher, *Froth & Scum: Truth, Beauty, Goodness, and the Ax Murder in America's First Mass Medium* (Chapel Hill: University of North Carolina Press, 1994), 191–209; Mark Walgren Summers, *The Press Gang: Newspapers and Politics, 1865–1878* (Chapel Hill: University of North Carolina Press, 1994); Gerald Baldasty, *The Commercialization of News in the Nineteenth Century* (Madison: University of Wisconsin Press, 1992); John D. Stevens, *Sensationalism and the New York Press* (New York: Columbia University Press, 1991), 57–100; Eugene C. Harter, *Boilerplating America: The Hidden Newspaper* (Lanham, Md.: University Press of America, 1991); Hazel Dicken-Garcia, *Journalistic Standards in Nineteenth-Century America* (Madison: University of Wisconsin Press, 1989), 155–222; Michael McGerr, *The Decline of Popular Politics: The American North, 1865–1928* (New York: Oxford University Press, 1986), 107–37; Dan Schiller, *Objectivity and the News: The Public and the Rise of Commercial Journalism* (Philadelphia: University of Pennsylvania Press, 1981), 180–85; Michael Schudson, *Discovering the News: A Social History of American Newspapers* (New York: Basic Books, 1978), 61–120; W. A. Swanberg, *Citizen Hearst: A Biography of William Randolph Hearst* (New York: Charles Scribner's Sons, 1961).

7. "The Great Will Case," *NYT*, March 6, 1879, p. 4; see also "Ended After Many Days," *NYT*, March 5, 1879, p. 8 (marveling at the idea that this charge could have been leveled at "one of the most sagacious and successful money-kings of

the century"); "Curiosities of the Vanderbilt Will Case," *Baltimore Sun*, March 7, 1879, p. 1; "Vanderbilt Again," *Independent Statesmen*, November 28, 1878, Col. A.

8. "The Great Will Contest," *NYT*, December 19, 1877; "There's Millions in It," *Chicago Daily Tribune*, December 19, 1877, p. 5; "The Vanderbilts," *InterOcean*, December 20, 1877, p. 4, Issue 230, Col. D; "Fighting for Money," *Milwaukee Daily Sentinel*, December 20, 1877, p. 7, Issue 302, Col. A.

9. T. J. Stiles, *The First Tycoon: The Epic Life of Cornelius Vanderbilt* (New York: Alfred A. Knopf, 2009), 563. Alive to the ways that Vanderbilt's life story was distorted by those who participated in the contest over his will, Stiles painstakingly reads the courtroom testimony against other documentary evidence of the episodes recounted by witnesses. However, in his use of this testimony, Stiles is not as attentive to the ways it was mediated by the popular press reports, which constitute the only surviving evidence of what was said by the witnesses and the counselors who questioned them.

10. Though there is at least one fugitive reference to a stenographer charged with the task of transcribing the testimony in the Vanderbilt will case, see "Some Curious Affidavits," *NYT*, October 19, 1878, p. 3, none has survived, raising questions, if it existed, as to why and by whom it might have been destroyed.

11. My treatment of the Vanderbilt trial in this essay draws upon newspaper accounts I have gathered from online databases as well as a set of clippings contained within the Vanderbilt Family Papers at the New York Public Library. In making use of these sources, I do not seek to demonstrate what actually happened in Surrogate Calvin's courtroom. Instead, I use them to illustrate how the contest was represented to a wider reading public—how the trial stories crafted by the counselors and their witnesses were re-told in the form of news stories. That is to say, the news stories are here used to illuminate various strains of thought about the wealth and insanity in late-nineteenth-century American culture; the newsmen's accounts are critical elements of this broader cultural-legal history. For similar approaches that have informed my own, see Richard Wightman Fox, *Trials of Intimacy: Love and Loss in the Beecher-Tilton Scandal* (Chicago: University of Chicago Press, 1999); Laura Hanft Korobkin, *Criminal Conversations: Sentimentality and Nineteenth-Century Legal Stories of Adultery* (New York: Columbia University Press, 1998); Michael Grossberg, *A Judgment for Solomon: The d'Hauteville Case and Legal Experience in Antebellum America* (New York: Cambridge University Press, 1996).

12. Herman Melville, *The Confidence Man: His Masquerade* (London: Longman, Brown, Green, Longmans, and Roberts, 1857), 256.

13. "New York Gossip . . . Com. Vanderbilt's Will," *Chicago Daily Tribune*, June 4, 1876, p. 13; "Commodore Vanderbilt's Will," *Daily Rocky Mountain News*, June 10, 1876, col. C; "Vanderbilt. The Stock-Jobbers again Speculate on the Old Man's Physical Weakness," *Chicago Daily Tribune*, October 17, 1876, p. 7; "The 'Vanderbilt Guard.' Something About the Squad of Benevolent Reporters who

Surround the Sick Commodore's Mansion," *Daily Evening Bulletin*, November 24, 1876, Issue 41, Col. G (reprinted from the *New York Tribune*); "Cornelius Vanderbilt," *Milwaukee Daily Sentinel*, January 6, 1877, Issue 6, Col. C.

14. "Vanderbilt," *Chicago Daily Tribune*, January 5, 1877. Among the sub-headlines of the *Tribune* article was "No Commotion Whatever Among the Gamblers of Wall Street," the article going on to note that "the disposition of his immense railway property was a topic of frequent discussion" and repeating rumors that the bulk of the estate had been willed to William, the eldest son, "who will not 'waste' it." *Id.* For additional examples, see, e.g., "Vanderbilt's Millions: The Relations Said to be Quarreling over the Will—A Contest not Improbable," *St. Louis Globe-Democrat*, January 10, 1877; "Commodore Vanderbilt's Will—Prospect of a Family Contest," *Boston Daily Advertiser*, January 10, 1877, Issue 9, Col. H; "The Vanderbilt Will," *NYT*, February 20, 1877; "The Vanderbilt Will. The Probability of Its Being Contested in Court—The Dissatisfied Heirs," February 26, 1877, *St. Louis Globe-Democrat*, p. 4, Issue 282, Col. D; "Breaking the Vanderbilt Will," February 27, 1877, *Daily Rocky Mountain News*, Col. C.

15. "Of Course. Vanderbilt's Will to be Contested," *Davenport Democrat*, January 11, 1877, p. 2; see also "Commodore Vanderbilt's Will—Prospect of a Family Contest," *Boston Daily Advertiser*, January 10, 1877; Issue 9, Col. H; "Breaking the Vanderbilt Will," *Daily Rocky Mountain News*, February 27, 1877, Col. C.; "The Vanderbilt Will—'Young Corneel,'" *St. Louis Globe-Democrat*, March 2, 1877, p. 2, Issue 286, Col. G.

16. [no title], February 25, 1877, *St. Louis Globe-Democrat*, p. 4, Issue 281, Col. A.

17. "Battle of the Heirs," *St. Louis Globe-Democrat*, July 4, 1875; "The Vanderbilt Will Contest," *Daily Rocky Mountain News*, Saturday, March 3, 1877, Col. C (reprinted from the *New York Tribune*); see also "The Misfortune of Being Too Rich," *Daily Evening Bulletin*, July 13, 1877; "Big Wills," *St. Louis Globe-Democrat*, July 9, 1878.

18. New York dominated the Gilded Age news industry, largely because the member papers of the Associated Press came largely from this city. Among the New York papers, the *Herald* and the *Sun* had the highest circulations in this era; other prominent dailies at the time were the *New York Times*, the *Evening Post*, and the *Tribune*, though they were "all in the doldrums following the deaths of powerful publishers." Stevens, *Sensationalism and the New York Press*, 63–65.

19. "Vanderbiltiana," *Puck*, September 25, 1878, p. 3; Stiles, *First Tycoon*, 563.

20. Perhaps the most telling expression was a cartoon entitled "In the Hollow of his Hands," accompanying the following article: "Vanderbiltiana," *Puck*, September 25, 1878, p. 3; see also "Vanderbilt and His Railroad," *Boston Daily Advertiser*, January 6, 1877, Issue 6, Col. B.; Irenaeus, "Three Rich Men's Wills," *New York Observer and Chronicle*, January 18, 1877; "Highways Not Personal Chattels," *Galveston Daily News*, March 22, 1877, Issue 311, Col. A; "The Vanderbilt Skeleton," *Daily Evening Bulletin*, March 5, 1879. William figured himself as yielding to the "growing public opinion" arrayed "against one-man power" in a November 1879 interview granted after selling his controlling interest in the New York

Central Railroad. "State of Trade," *Daily Inter Ocean*, November 27, 1879, p. 5, Issue 203, Col. C. For a more critical take on William and his claims to public-mindedness, see, e.g., "The Outlook," *Christian Union*, December 3, 1879, p. 463; "The Ambition of Rich Men," *Daily Evening Bulletin*, November 28, 1882.

21. "The Possibilities of Accumulation," *Little's Living Age*, January 16, 1869, p. 190; "Founding a Family," *New York Daily Tribune*, December 6, 1877 [NYPL, pp. 164–66]; "Current Topics," March 28, 1879, *Albany Law Journal*, p. 245. It should be further noted that causal linkages between wealth and insanity were ever more nervously drawn by doctors and laymen during the postbellum era. See, e.g., "Insanity and Death from Intense Devotion to Business," *Merchants' Magazine and Commercial Review*, May 1, 1856, p. 640; "Who of us are Insane?" *Putnam's Magazine*, November 1868; J. S. Jewell, M.D., "Influence of our Present Civilization in the Production of Nervous and Mental Diseases," *Journal of Nervous and Mental Disease*, January 1881, p. 1. It was likewise common in this era to suggest that anxiety and wealth were positively correlated, with the implication that money not only did not buy happiness but brought about the reverse. See, e.g., "The Drawbacks of Riches," *NYT*, November 9, 1878.

22. Steve Fraser, *Everyman a Speculator: A History of Wall Street in American Life* (New York: HarperCollins, 2005), especially ch. 4; Jackson Lears, *Something for Nothing: Luck in America*, esp. chs. 4 and 5 (New York: Penguin Books, 2003); Jonathan Levy, "The Freaks of Fortune: Moral Responsibility for Booms and Busts in Nineteenth-Century America," *Journal of the Gilded Age and Progressive Era* 10:4 (October 2011): 435.

23. "Trouble of Having Too Much," *Frank Leslie's Sunday Magazine*, March 1883, Vol. 13, No. 3.

24. Stanley N. Katz, "Republicanism and the Law of Inheritance in the American Revolutionary Era," *Michigan Law Review* 76 (November 1977): 1; Gregory S. Alexander, *Commodity & Propriety: Competing Visions of Property in American Legal Thought, 1776–1970* (Chicago: University of Chicago Press, 1997); John V. Orth, "After the Revolution: The 'Reform' of the Law of Inheritance," *Law and History Review* 10:1 (Spring 1992): 33; cf. Holly Brewer, "Entailing Aristocracy in Colonial Virginia: 'Ancient Feudal Restraints' and Revolutionary Reform," *William and Mary Quarterly*, 3d series, 54 (April 1997): 307; and C. Ray Keim, "Primogeniture and Entail in Colonial Virginia," *William and Mary Quarterly*, 3d series, 25 (October 1968): 545–86. For an illuminating sociological study considering American institutions and practices from a transatlantic perspective, see Jens Beckert (Thomas Dunlap, translator), *Inherited Wealth* (Princeton, N.J.: Princeton University Press, 2008 [original German edition, Frankfurt/Main, Germany: Campus Verlag, 2004]).

25. William E. Nelson, *Americanization of the Common Law: The Impact of Legal Change on Massachusetts Society, 1760–1830* (Cambridge, Mass.: Harvard University Press, 1975; reprint ed., with new introduction, Athens: University of Georgia Press, 1994).

26. Susanna L. Blumenthal, "The Deviance of the Will: Policing the Bounds of Testamentary Freedom in Nineteenth-Century America," *Harvard Law Review* 119 (February 2006): 959, 969–77.

27. Isaac Ray, "Confinement of the Insane," *American Law Review* 3 (November 1869): 193, 207; David Rothman, *The Discovery of the Asylum: Social Order and Disorder in the New Republic* (Boston: Little, Brown, 1971; revised edition, New York: Aldine de Gruyter, 2002); Susanna L. Blumenthal, "The Default Legal Person," *UCLA Law Review* 54 (June 2007): 1135, 1159; Blumenthal, "The Deviance of the Will," 1007–8.

28. See, for example, Shobal Vail Clevenger, *Medical Jurisprudence of Insanity; or, Forensic Psychiatry* (2 vols.; Rochester, N.Y.: Lawyers Co-operative Publishing Company, 1898), 1:13.

29. James C. Mohr, "The Paradoxical Advance and Embattled Retreat of the 'Unsound Mind': Evidence of Insanity and the Adjudication of Wills in Nineteenth-Century America," *Historical Reflections/Reflexions Historiques* 24 (1998): 415, 425–35.

30. The charge commonly made by doctors that it was easier to establish insanity in civil than criminal cases appears overstated upon close examination of trial records, appellate opinions, and legal treatises; some judges formally applied the same standard in all civil and criminal contexts, and others differentiated on the basis of the doctrinal context and/or the particular circumstances of the case. See generally Blumenthal, "The Default Legal Person," 1166–79.

31. Isaac Redfield, *The Law of Wills: Embracing also, the Jurisprudence of Insanity, the Effect of Extrinsic Evidence, the Creation and Construction of Trusts, so far as Applicable to Wills, with Forms and Instructions for Preparing Wills* (2 vols.; Boston: Little, Brown, 1864–66), 104, 154–56 ("experience has shown, both here and in England, that they differ as widely in their inferences and opinions, as do the other witnesses," it being "so uniform a result with medical experts, of late, that they are beginning to be regarded as much in the light of hired advocates, and their testimony, as nothing more than a studied argument, in favor of the side for which they have been called"; "when we consider the conflicting character of the testimony coming from experts; and often its one-sided and partisan character; and above all, the tendency of the most mature and well-balanced minds to run into the most incomprehensible theorizing and unfounded dogmatism, from the exclusive devotion of study to one subject, and that of a mysterious and occult character, we cannot much wonder that some of the wisest and most prudent men of the age are beginning to feel, that the testimony of experts is too often becoming, in practice, but an ingenious device in the hands of unscrupulous men, to stifle justice, and vindicate the most high-handed crime").

32. Blumenthal, "The Deviance of the Will," 985–1006. For an expression of this dilemma specifically prompted by the Vanderbilt trial, see "Legal Aspects of Insanity," *New York Herald*, Sunday, February 17, 1878 [NYPL, pp. 177–78].

33. "There's Millions in It," *Chicago Daily Tribune*, December 19, 1877, p. 5.

34. "The House of Vanderbilt," *NYT*, November 13, 1877.

35. As will be seen in the pages that follow, Surrogate Calvin was not nearly as exclusionary with respect to the testimony of the contestants' witnesses as he was made out to be in popular renderings of the trial such as that published in *Puck* magazine.

36. "Scott Lord on Vanderbilt. The Indoor Life of the Wealthiest Many in the United States. The Bitter Family Contest over the Millions Left by Commodore Vanderbilt—'Daniel, when I Die there'll be Hell to Pay!'—The Secret History of the Household Recited," *The Sun*, November 13 [NYPL File, p. 13]; "Legal, But Not Wise," *The Sun*, April 14, 1878 [NYPL file, p. 312].

37. "The House of Vanderbilt," *NYT*, November 13, 1877; "Vanderbilt's Home Life," *New York Tribune*, November 13, 1877, p. 2; "Vanderbilt," *Chicago Daily Tribune*, November 13, 1877, p. 1. The audience varied in both size and composition from day to day, according to newspapers, though women were sparse, which was said to be unusual for proceedings of this sort. See, e.g., "Vanderbilt's Money," *New York Herald*, November 15, 1877 [NYPL, p. 39] (observing that "[t]here was not a lady in the room, a fact which was commented upon as rather singular, since at least a few of the gentle sex are to be found at almost every trial which excites any public interest, whatever may be its nature").

38. "Vanderbilt's Home Life," *New York Tribune*, November 13, 1877, p. 2; "The House of Vanderbilt," *NYT*, November 13, 1877; "The Commodore's Money," *NYT*, November 14, 1877; "The Vanderbilt Will," *New York Herald*, November 13, 1877 [NYPL file]; "Scott Lord on Vanderbilt," *The Sun*, November 13, 1877 [NYPL file, pp. 13–14]; "Vanderbilt's Will," *New York Herald*, November 14, 1877 [NYPL file]; "The Great Will Contest," November 14, 1877 [NYPL file]; "The Vanderbilt Will," *The World*, November 14, 1877 [NYPL file]. Although Allen had originally suggested that the woman William procured served in the capacity of a "governess," he was pressed on cross-examination and re-direct examination to acknowledge that she was the cousin of William's wife and served as "an assistant" to the daughter of the Commodore, who had charge of the house during the time her mother was hospitalized. "The Commodore's Money," *NYT*, November 14, 1877.

39. Newspapers covering the Vanderbilt trial tended to present only selected portions of the testimony in question-and-answer format; the remainder appeared in summary form, which consisted of the reporter's glosses, sometimes including direct quotes and other outtakes from the courtroom dialogue, all of which was frequently organized with topical sub-headings, not always indicating what was elicited on direct as opposed to cross-examination.

40. "Vanderbilt's Will," *New York Herald*, November 14, 1877 [NYPL file, p. 19]; scrap, NYPL file, p. 22 (noting that Louisa at the time was eighteen and the cousin twenty-five).

41. "The House of Vanderbilt," *NYT*, November 13, 1877; "The Commodore's Money," *NYT*, November 14, 1877; "The Vanderbilt Will," *New York Herald*,

November 13, 1877 [NYPL file]; "Scott Lord on Vanderbilt," *The Sun*, November 13, 1877 [NYPL file]; "Vanderbilt's Will," *New York Herald*, November 14, 1877 [NYPL file]; "The Great Will Contest," November 14, 1877 [NYPL file]; "The Vanderbilt Will," *The World*, November 14, 1877 [NYPL file].

42. "The House of Vanderbilt," *NYT*, November 13, 1877; "Vanderbilt's Physicians," *New-York Daily Tribune*, November 15, 1877 [NYPL, pp. 49–50]; "The Fight for a Million," *NYT*, November 17, 1877; "The Vanderbilt Fight," *The World*, November 17, 1877 [NYPL, pp. 55–56]; "Vanderbilt's Infirmities," *New York Herald*, November 17, 1877 [NYPL, pp. 64–65]; "The Vanderbilt Will Case," *NYT*, June 26, 1878.

43. "The Commodore's Money," *NYT*, November 14, 1877; "The Vanderbilt Contest," *NYT*, November 15, 1877; "The Fight for a Million," *NYT*, November 17, 1877; "Vanderbilt's Millions," *NYT*, December 5, 1877; "Vanderbilt's Physicians," *New-York Daily Tribune*, November 15, 1877 [NYPL, pp. 49–50]; "The Commodore Dissected. Painful Diseases that Immense Wealth could not Cure," *The Sun*, November 17, 1877 [NYPL, pp. 58–59]; "Vanderbilt's Infirmities," *New York Herald*, November 17, 1877 [NYPL file, pp. 63–65]; "Vanderbilt's Struggle with Disease," *Daily Evening Bulletin*, November 27, 1877, Issue 44, Col. D; "The Sick Commodore," *The World*, December 5, 1877; "The Fight for Millions," *The Sun*, December 5, 1877 [NYPL file, pp. 75–76]; see also "Commodore Vanderbilt's Maladies" [NYPL, p. 48] (summarizing the medical testimony thus: "With at least five maladies from the danger or distress of which he was never free, and with intercurrent troubles that would have carried down many a man physically vigorous, the old Commodore fought on and not only accumulated one of the greatest fortunes ever made in this country, but also achieved successes that were wonderful apart from their financial results. Let no invalid despair with such a history before him.").

44. This was the source of much derisive commentary in the press; see, for example, *The World*, December 9, 1877 [NYPL, p. 98] ("After mature deliberation on the plaintiff's side of the Vanderbilt will case, we have come to the conclusion that they believe that the late Commodore was perfectly rational while accumulating wealth, but hopelessly mad the moment before he came to dispose of it").

45. "Vanderbilt's Millions," *NYT*, December 5, 1877; Vanderbilt's Doctors," *New-York Daily Tribune*, December 5, 1877 [NYPL, pp. 82–83]; "The Fight for Millions," *The Sun*, December 5, 1877 [NYPL file, pp. 75–76]; "The Will of Vanderbilt," *NYT*, December 8, 1877; "The Great Will Contest," *The Sun*, December 8, 1877 [NYPL file, p. 90]; see also "The Commodore's Will," *New York Herald*, December 13, 1877 [NYPL, pp. 101–2] (containing further argument of Comstock: "Half the Christian world believed in the infallibility of the Pope, and on the same ground it might be asserted that this is a delusion. The doctrine of the immaculate conception or the apostolic succession would be subject to the same assertion." From the Surrogate then came the assurance that "the Court is a firm believer in it," to which Comstock replied: "Well, then, counsel on the other side will deny the competency of this court to try this case; they will say the Court is

laboring under a delusion; that the Court is insane."). Similar implications were drawn out in editorials around this time in the popular press; see, for example, "Vanderbilt's Sanity—Who is Sane?," *The Sunday Mercury*, December 9, 1877 [NYPL file, pp. 166] (criticizing the contestants' theory for being over-inclusive on the question of testamentary incapacity: "Every human being has a big or little mania, which makes his mentality oscillate from time to time. There is no such thing as perpetual mental equilibrium. . . . Belief in supernatural agencies is not confined to the few; it is widespread in every nation, and among every race. . . . It is not strange that Vanderbilt should have shared the almost universal belief.").

46. "The Will of Vanderbilt," *NYT*, December 8, 1877; "The Commodore's Sick-Bed," *The World*, December 8, 1877 [NYPL file, pp. 87–88]; "Vanderbilt's Belief," *New-York Daily Tribune*, December 8, 1877 [NYPL file, pp. 96–97].

47. "Suit for $100,000,000," *NYT*, December 13, 1877; "The Commodore's Will," December 13, 1877 [NYPL file, pp. 101–3]; "The Vanderbilt Will Contest," *New-York Daily Tribune*, December 13, 1877 [NYPL, pp. 103–4]

48. Lord was ultimately successful in amending the petition so that the conspiracy count included both the young widow, Mrs. Frank Vanderbilt, and her mother, Mrs. Crawford.

49. "The Great Will Contest," *NYT*, December 19, 1877; "Vanderbilt Will Contest," *New-York Daily Tribune*, December 19, 1877 [NYPL file, pp. 114–15]; "Cornelius J. Vanderbilt," *The World*, December 19, 1877 [NYPL file, pp. 116, 119]; "The Old Commodore's Cash," *The Sun*, December 19, 1877 [NYPL file, pp. 120–21]; "Vanderbilt's Millions," *New York Herald*, December 19, 1877 [NYPL file, pp. 125–26]; "Cornelius J. Vanderbilt," *The World*, December 20, 1877 [NYPL file, pp. 126–27]; "The Great Will Contest," *NYT*, December 20, 1877; "The Vanderbilt Contest," *The Sun*, December 20, 1877 [NYPL file, pp. 128–30]; "Life of a Millionaire's Son," *New-York Daily Tribune*, December 20, 1877 [NYPL file, pp. 132–33]; "The Vanderbilt Will Case," *NYT*, December 22, 1877; "Cornelius J. Vanderbilt," *The World*, December 22, 1877 [NYPL file, pp. 133–34]; "Cornelius J. Vanderbilt Overhauled," *The Sun*, December 22, 1877 [NYPL file, pp. 135–36]; "Vanderbilt's Will," *New York Herald*, December 22, 1877 [NYPL file, pp. 139–41]; "The Vanderbilt Will Suit," *NYT*, December 27, 1877; "The Vanderbilt Will Contest," *New-York Daily Tribune*, December 22, 1877 [NYPL file, pp. 141–42]; "C. J. Vanderbilt's Letters," *The World*, December 27, 1877 [NYPL file, pp. 142–44]; "The Old Commodore's Sons," *The Sun*, December 27, 1877 [NYPL file, pp. 145–47]; "Vanderbilt's Will," *New York Herald*, December 27, 1877 [NYPL file, pp. 151–54]; "The Courts," *New-York Daily Tribune*, December 27, 1877 [NYPL file, pp. 154–55]; "The Vanderbilt Millions," *NYT*, December 29, 1877; "Cornelius J. Vanderbilt," *The World*, December 29, 1877 [NYPL file, pp. 155–56]; "Cornelius J., Spendthrift," *The Sun*, December 29, 1877 [NYPL file, pp. 156–57]; "The Vanderbilt Will," *New York Herald*, December 29, 1877 [NYPL file, pp. 161–62]; "The Vanderbilt Will Case," *New York Herald*, December 29, 1877 [NYPL file, pp.

162–64]; "Discounting his Future," *The Sun*, February 27, 1878 [NYPL file, pp. 179–80]; "The Vanderbilt Will," *New York Herald*, February 27, 1878 [NYPL file, pp. 182–83].

50. By the time the contestants rested, they had reportedly taken more than 1,700 pages' worth of testimony, which was also the approximate number of pages covered by the cross-examination of the witnesses by the proponent. "Some Curious Affidavits," *NYT*, October 19, 1878, p. 3.

51. "The Vanderbilt Will Case," *NYT*, June 26, 1878; "The Vanderbilt Contest," *NYT*, June 27, 1878; "The Vanderbilt Will Contest," *NYT*, June 28, 1878; "The Vanderbilt Will Contest," July 4, 1878; "Fighting for Millions," *NYT*, September 25, 1878; "The Vanderbilt Will Case," *NYT*, September 26, 1878; "Mrs. Stoddard's Story," *NYT*, September 28, 1878; "The Clairvoyant's Widow," *NYT*, September 29, 1878; "Mrs. Stoddard's Career," *NYT*, October 2, 1878; "Spiritualism in Court," *NYT*, October 3, 1878; "Spiritualistic Influence," *NYT*, October 4, 1878; "The Commodore's Money," *NYT*, October 10, 1878; "Vanderbilt and the Mediums," *NYT*, October 17, 1878; "Law Reports," *NYT*, October 23, 1878; "Talking with the Spirits," *NYT*, October 24, 1878; "The Commodore's Pastor," *NYT*, October 26, 1878; "Vanderbilt's Will," *NYT*, October 30, 1878; "Vanderbilt's Will," *NYT*, November 2, 1878; "The Vanderbilt Will Case," *NYT*, November 7, 1878; "The Vanderbilt Will Case," *NYT*, November 9, 1878; "Mrs. La Bau's Case Closed," *NYT*, November 13, 1878.

52. "The Vanderbilt Will Case, *NYT*, November 20, 1878; "The Vanderbilt Will Case," *NYT*, November 21, 1878; "The Vanderbilt Will," *NYT*, November 23, 1878; "The Vanderbilt Will: Did Money Lure the Second Mrs. V. to Marriage?", *St. Louis Globe-Democrat*, November 23, 1878, p. 9, Col. E.; "The Vanderbilt Will," *NYT*, November 27, 1878; "The Vanderbilt Will Case," *NYT*, November 28, 1878; "The Vanderbilt Will Case," *NYT*, February 5, 1879; "The Vanderbilt Will Case," *NYT*, February 6, 1879; "The Vanderbilt Will Case," *NYT*, February 8, 1879; "Some Talks with the Commodore," *NYT*, February 10, 1879; "The Vanderbilt Will Case," *NYT*, February 12, 1879; "The Vanderbilt Will Contest," *NYT*, February 15, 1879; "The Vanderbilt Will Case," *NYT*, February 19, 1879; "The Vanderbilt Will Contest," *NYT*, February 20, 1879; "Vanderbilt's War with Erie," *NYT*, February 22, 1879.

53. "A Dramatic Scene," *Inter Ocean*, November 29, 1878, p. 5, Col. E; see also "The Vanderbilt Will Case: Dramatic Scene in Court," *Galveston Daily News*, November 27, 1878, Col. F; "Vanderbilt's Will: Dramatic Scene on the Cross Examination of Bishop McTyeire," *Georgia Weekly Telegraph and Georgia Journal & Messenger*, November 26, 1878, Col. G; "The Vanderbilt Will: Did Money Lure the Second Mrs. V. to Marriage?", *St. Louis Globe-Democrat*, November 23, 1878, p. 9, Col. E.; "The Vanderbilt Will Case," *NYT*, November 20, 1878.

54. The stated reason for the adjournment, however, was the Surrogate's urgent need to attend to a backlog of cases, which was more than likely an accurate rendering of his docket at the time.

55. For an account of Gray's role in the trial of Guiteau, see Charles E. Rosenberg, *The Trial of the Assassin Guiteau: Psychiatry and the Law in the Gilded Age* (Chicago: University of Chicago Press, 1968), 191–97.

56. "The Vanderbilt Will Case," *NYT*, February 5, 1879; "The Vanderbilt Will Case," *NYT*, February 6, 1879; "The Vanderbilt Will Case," *NYT*, February 8, 1879; "Some Talks with the Commodore," *NYT*, February 10, 1879; "The Vanderbilt Will Case," *NYT*, February 12, 1879; "Vanderbilt's Sanity," *St. Louis Globe-Democrat*, February 13, 1879; "The Vanderbilt Will Contest," *NYT*, February 15, 1879; "The Vanderbilt Will Case," *NYT*, February 19, 1879; "The Vanderbilt Will Contest," *NYT*, February 20, 1879; "Vanderbilt's War with Erie," *NYT*, February 22, 1879; "The Vanderbilt Will Case," February 26, 1879; "An Expert on Insanity," *NYT*, February 27, 1879.

57. One was brought by Cornelius Jr., who contended his brother William breached a promise to give $1,000,000 if he refrained from contesting their father's will. The other was a conspiracy suit, in which William was among the named defendants alleged to have made false statements about him to his father, for which he claimed $7,000,000 in damages. "Vanderbilt Suits Ended," *NYT*, March 26, 1879.

58. "Ended After Many Days," *NYT*, March 5, 1879; "Curiosities of the Vanderbilt Will Case," *Baltimore Sun*, March 7, 1879, p. 1; "The Vanderbilt Will Case," *Daily Evening Bulletin*, March 17, 1879, Issue 145, Col. F.

59. "A Chorus of Denials," *NYT*, March 6, 1879; *La Bau v. Vanderbilt*, New York County Surrogates' Court, December 1877–January 1879, pp. 384–444.

60. The lawsuit Cornelius Jr. had filed against his brother was withdrawn shortly after Calvin issued his decision. "Vanderbilt Suits Ended," *NYT*, March 26, 1879. For examples of press coverage of the aftermath of the trial, see "A Chorus of Denials," *NYT*, March 6, 1879; "Vanderbilt v. Vanderbilt," *The North American*, March 6, 1879; "The Vanderbilt Will Case, and Its Cost to Both Sides," *Washington Post*, March 6, 1879, p. 1; "The Vanderbilt Will to Stand," *NYT*, March 20, 1879; "The Vanderbilt Will Case," *Frank Leslie's Illustrated Newspaper*, March 22, 1879; "The Vanderbilt Will Case," *NYT*, March 25, 1879; "The Vanderbilt Will," *Frank Leslie's Illustrated Newspaper*, April 5, 1879, Issue 1,227, Col. B.

61. *La Bau v. Vanderbilt*, 3 Red. Sur. Ct. 384, 422-44 (N.Y. Sur. Ct. 1879).

62. *Id.* at 423–25.

63. *Id.* at 421–22.

64. *Id.* at 424–44. In reviewing the testimony of a number of the doctors called by the contestants, Calvin suggested the need to raise "a presumption of irrationality in the case of medical experts." *Id.*

65. *Id.* at 430–43.

66. *Id.* at 443–44.

67. *Chicago Daily Tribune*, June 3, 1882, p. 4; "Gossip from Gotham," *Daily Evening Bulletin* (San Francisco, Calif.), June 12, 1882; Issue 56, Col. A. See, generally, Fraser, *Everyman a Speculator*.

68. "Battle of the Heirs," *St. Louis Globe Democrat*, July 4, 1875; "Our New York Letter," *Independent Statesmen*, June 7, 1877; "The Vanderbilt Will," *Chicago Daily Tribune*, December 21, 1877; "The Curse of Dying Rich," *Sunday Times and Messenger*, December 23, 1877 [NYPL]; "Have Fathers Any Rights which Sons are Bound to Respect?", *The Sun*, January 23, 1878; "Legal, But Not Wise," *The Sun*, April 14, 1878; "Dare the Rich Die?", *Daily Arkansas Gazette*, November 12, 1878; cf. "Are we to have Rothschilds in America?", *Milwaukee Daily Sentinel*, November 29, 1875 (answering that "such a family is not among the dangers to which our institutions are exposed"); "American Generosity," *St. Louis Daily Globe-Democrat*, March 31, 1877 (suggesting that most rich men in this country, including "the sordid and grasping Vanderbilt," contributed generously to public purposes as compared with those in other nations). The justice of the criticism of profiteering lawyers is suggested by a striking admission in the *Albany Law Journal*, as the storm that coalesced into the Vanderbilt will contest was brewing: "While it would be well if the last will of a competent testator could be carried out without opposition or interference on the part of the descendants of such testator, we cannot forget that if it were not for sickness physicians would starve, and if it were not for litigation the judicial office would be a sinecure." 15 *Albany Law Journal* 174 (March 10, 1877).

69. "Wealth and Insanity," *St. Louis Daily Globe Democrat*, January 29, 1878, p. 4; "A Mad World, My Masters!," *New York Tribune*, February 1, 1878, p. 4; "The Drawbacks of Riches," *NYT*, November 9, 1878; "Millionaires Miseries," *Puck*, March 5, 1879; "The Great Will Case," *NYT*, March 6, 1879, p. 4; "Current Topics," *Albany Law Journal*, March 28, 1879, p. 245; "Richardson's Millions," *Denver Evening Post*, October 15, 1897, p. 4.

70. Compare "Our 'Upper Class,'" *Munsey's Magazine*, November 1892, Vol. VIII, No. 2; with "American Families," *St. Louis Globe Democrat*, October 29, 1877 (emphasizing the beneficial effects of great fortunes like that of Vanderbilt, which provide stability and generate other social goods: "The man who has more money than he can spend soon finds his fortune overflowing into pursuits which do not pay, and which can only be sustained by immense wealth"); "American Millionaires," *New-York Tribune*, September 6, 1896 (observing the "recent and rapid" formation of American millionaires into "a distinct class" that was here to stay, a development that gave "the lie to the old idea that in the United States 'from shirt sleeve to shirt sleeve is three generations'" and was to be welcomed since this new wealth was not amassed at the expense of other classes); see also "The Power of Capital," *Frank Leslie's Illustrated Newspaper*, September 17, 1887 (occupying a middle ground between these two positions, both in suggesting great fortunes do not inevitably dissipate in three generations' time or prevent concentrations of capital, which are not inherently harmful to society); see, generally, Irvin G. Wyllie, *The Self-Made Man in America: The Myth of Rags to Riches* (New Brunswick, N.J.: Rutgers University Press, 1954); John G. Cawelti, *Apostles of the Self-Made Man* (Chicago: University of Chicago

Press, 1965); Judy Hilkey, *Character Is Capital: Success Manuals and Manhood in Gilded Age America* (Chapel Hill: University of North Carolina Press, 1997); James L. Huston, *Securing the Fruits of Labor: The American Concept of Wealth Distribution 1765–1900* (Baton Rouge: Louisiana State University Press, 1998); Sven Beckert, *The Monied Metropolis: New York City and the Consolidation of the American Bourgeoisie, 1856–1896* (Cambridge and New York: Cambridge University Press, 2001); Jackson Lears, *Rebirth of a Nation: The Making of Modern America, 1877–1920* (New York: HarperCollins, 2009); Oliver Zunz, *Philanthropy in America: A History* (Princeton, N.J.: Princeton University Press, 2011).

71. "The News this Morning," *New York Tribune*, July 23, 1889, p. 4; "The Protection of Testators," *The Nation*, April 12, 1883, pp. 312–13; Editorial, *New-York Tribune*, March 25, 1884, p. 4; "Current Topics," *Albany Law Journal*, May 10, 1884, p. 361; "Current Topics," *Albany Law Journal*, April 16, 1887, p. 301; "Current Topics," *Albany Law Journal*, May 7, 1887, pp. 361–62; "Estates in Probate," *San Francisco Chronicle*, December 1, 1895; "Wills and Will Making," *Independent*, December 27, 1894; Charles C. Moore, "Proposed Ante-Mortem Probate of Wills," *Law Notes*, Vol. 15, April 1911, pp. 6-7; Blumenthal, "Deviance of the Will."

72. Andrew Carnegie, *The Gospel of Wealth and Other Timely Essays* (New York: Century Co., 1900). Carnegie died rich and his will disposed of an estate valued upward of $25,000,000, but whether thus disgraced was the subject of debate. For a strained defense of this testamentary act reported by the *New York Times* right after the will was probated, see "Friend says Carnegie Did Not 'Die Disgraced': Secretary of the Corporation Explains Historic Phrase as to Wealth," *NYT*, August 29, 1919.

73. Carnegie, *Gospel*; David Nasaw, *Andrew Carnegie* (New York: Penguin Press, 2006); Barry D. Karl, "Andrew Carnegie and his Gospel of Philanthropy," in Dwight F. Burlingame, ed., *The Responsibilities of Wealth* (Bloomington: Indiana University Press, 1992), 32–50; Oliver Zunz, *Philanthropy in America: A History* (Princeton, N.J.: Princeton University Press, 2011); Lears, *Rebirth of a Nation*, 51–91; Richard Hofstadter, *Social Darwinism in American Thought* (Philadelphia: University of Pennsylvania Press, 1944; reprint, Boston: Beacon Press, 1992), 31–50; Robert C. Bannister, *Social Darwinism: Science and Myth in Anglo-American Thought* (Philadelphia: Temple University Press, 1979); Wyllie, *Self-Made Man*; T. J. Jackson Lears, *No Place of Grace: Antimodernism and the Transformation of American Culture* (New York: Pantheon, 1981), 20–22; Barry Werth, *Banquet at Delmonico's: Great Minds, the Gilded Age, and the Triumph of Evolution in America* (New York: Random House, 2009).

74. "Farewell Complimentary Dinner at Delmonico's to Mr. Herbert Spencer," *Chicago Daily Tribune*, November 10, 1882; "Philosophy at Dinner: Herbert Spencer's Gentle Reproof to America," *NYT*, November 10, 1882; "Mr. Spencer on Over-Work," *New York Evangelist*, November 16, 1882; "The Herbert Spencer Dinner," *Christian Union*, November 16, 1882; Werth, *Banquet at Delmonico's*;

Hofstadter, *Social Darwinism*; Wyllie, *Self-Made Man*; Hilkey, *Character Is Capital*; Bannister, *Social Darwinism*; Barbara Sicherman, "The Paradox of Prudence: Mental Health in the Gilded Age," *Journal of American History*, 62 (March 1976): 890–912; Richard Wightman Fox, "The Discipline of Amusement," in William R. Taylor, ed., *Inventing Times Square: Commerce and Culture at the Crossroads of the World* (New York: Russell Sage Foundation, 1991), 83–98 (and notes at 382–84).

75. "Vanderbilt's Rich Estate," *NYT*, April 10, 1878; "The Vanderbilt Will," *NYT*, November 23, 1878; "The Vanderbilt Will," *NYT*, November 27, 1878. Further evidence lending credence to the testimony about the Commodore's spiritual anxieties can be found in his second wife Frank's diaries, which noted that "he has queer dreams occasionally," during which he imagined he had fallen "away down to the bottom but was coming up again & that it took all the power of the steamer *Vanderbilt* to pull him out but she did." She also noted that he attempted in the last months of his life to talk with her "about his soul & and salvation" for the first time and actually prayed to Jesus in her presence: "I asked, 'Dear, is it because you love him or is it to be relieved of the pain?' He replied, 'To be candid—both.'" Turning to the attending Dr. Linsly, he further confessed, "it may be selfish, but I would take Frank with me, if I could." Stiles, *First Tycoon*, 560.

76. Alan Trachtenberg, *The Incorporation of America: Culture and Society in the Gilded Age* (New York: Hill & Wang, 1982), 101–2; David E. Smith, *John Bunyan in America* (Bloomington: Indiana University Press, 1966), 15–16; Wyllie, *Self-Made Man*; Hilkey, *Character Is Capital*; Cawelti, *Apostles of the Self-Made Man*; Fraser, *Every Man a Speculator*; Lears, *No Place of Grace*. On Bunyan, see Christopher Hill, *A Tinker and a Poor Man: John Bunyan and His Church, 1628–1688* (New York: Alfred A. Knopf, 1989).

77. See, e.g., Edward Bellamy's *Looking Backward*, which figured late-nineteenth-century society as a "prodigious coach" within which the elite luxuriated while "the masses of humanity" were harnessed to it and tasked with dragging it along under the watchful glare of the driver who was "hunger, and permitted no lagging." Edward Bellamy, *Looking Backward, 2000–1887* (Boston: Ticknor & Company, 1888), 11.

78. See, e.g., Edmund J. James, who made the case for the redistribution of wealth in this fashion: "To test the relative productivity of the state and the individual, compare the fortune accumulated by Cornelius Vanderbilt in America with what he might have accumulated had he been adopted when an infant by a family of Hottentots." E. J. James, "The State as an Economic Factor," *Science*, Vol. 7, No. 172, at 485–91 (quote at 488) (May 28, 1886), quoted in Barbara H. Fried, *The Progressive Assault on Laissez Faire: Robert Hale and the First Law and Economics Movement* (Cambridge, Mass.: Harvard University Press, 1998), 75. For earlier arguments in the popular press to similar effect, see, for example, "Laissez Faire," *Christian Union*, August 28, 1878, p. 162; "Wills," *Independent*, April 14, 1892, p. 15.

79. See, e.g., Charles Joseph Bellamy, *The Way Out: Suggestions for Social Reform* (New York: G. P. Putnam's Sons/The Knickerbocker Press, 1884); George A. Richardson, *King Mammon and the Heir Apparent* (Boston: Arena Publishing Company, 1896); Harlan Eugene Read, *The Abolition of Inheritance* (New York: Macmillan, 1918); see, generally, Fried, *Progressive Assault on Laissez Faire*; Beckert, *Inherited Wealth*; John H. Langbein, "The Twentieth-Century Revolution in Family Wealth Transmission," *Michigan Law Review* 86 (February 1988): 722; Ronald Chester, "Inheritance in American Legal Thought," in Robert K. Miller Jr. and Stephen J. McNamee, eds., *Inheritance and Wealth in America* (New York: Plenum Press, 1998), 23–44; Lawrence M. Friedman, *Dead Hands: A Social History of Wills, Trusts, and Inheritance Law* (Stanford, Calif.: Stanford University Press, 2009); Ray Madoff, *Immortality and the Law: The Rising Power of the American Dead* (New Haven, Conn.: Yale University Press, 2010); Huston, *Securing the Fruits of Labor*; James T. Kloppenberg, *Uncertain Victory: Social Democracy and Progressivism in European and American Thought, 1870–1920* (New York: Oxford University Press, 1986); Daniel T. Rodgers, *Atlantic Crossings: Social Politics in a Progressive Age* (Cambridge, Mass.: Belknap Press of Harvard University Press, 1998).

80. Meryl Gordon, *Mrs. Astor Regrets: The Hidden Betrayals of a Family Beyond Reproach* (New York: Houghton Mifflin Harcourt, 2009); Frances Kiernan, *The Last Mrs. Astor: A New York Story* (New York: W. W. Norton, 2007); Steve Fishman, "Mrs. Astor's Baby: The Fight for a Mother's Love, and Money," *New York*, November 12, 2007, http://nymag.com/news/features/40662/?ftr-promo (accessed 26 February 2013); Peter Buffett, *Life Is What You Make It: Finding Your Own Path to Fulfillment* (New York: Harmony Books, 2010).

9

The Political Economy of Pain

JOHN FABIAN WITT

One of the great successes of William E. Nelson's massive *The Legalist Reformation: Law, Politics, and Ideology in New York, 1920–1980* is its expert doctrinal unpacking of the dense case law in the New York law of personal injury.[1] As Nelson notes, he starts with a couple of assumptions. The first is that New York was the leading jurisdiction in the recreation of the common law. The second is "the common lawyer's faith that analysis of judicial opinions is key to understanding law." Considering that he perused 620 volumes of the *New York Supplement*, 400 volumes of the *Federal Reporter*, 500 volumes of the *Federal Supplement*, and a sample of some 50,000 unreported trial-court cases, we can hardly doubt the depth of Nelson's faith in cases as historical evidence and in New York as the geographic center of the reformation of American law. Nelson's faith sometimes seems virtually catechistic.[2]

Nelson's common-law faith in the religion of the case raises an important question for the history of modern tort law. What exactly do cases and doctrine tell us about the twentieth-century history of torts? Nelson is absolutely right to describe tort law—and in particular the law of personal injury and accidents—as central to what he calls the "reformation" of the common law in the twentieth century. (To be fair, I should add that my agreement with Nelson is likely no coincidence: I came to many of my views about the history of tort law under his wise supervision when I was a Samuel I. Golieb Fellow.) And though Nelson's stupendous work ethic and the sheer volume of cases with which he works separate him from the pack, he is hardly alone in his focus on decided cases. In the law of torts—and indeed across the common-law curriculum—judicial opinions are the core materials from which legal scholars (including legal historians) draw conclusions about the structure of tort law and its change over time.[3]

Nelson's focus on cases, however, confronts us with a conundrum in the history of tort law, one that is clearest in the twentieth- and twenty-first-century development of the field. The literature on twentieth-century tort doctrine makes it increasingly plain that there were fewer doctrinal transformations in the law of torts than scholars once imagined. As Robert Rabin and the late Gary Schwartz have pointed out, supposed revolutions in twentieth-century common-law doctrine never really came to pass. Instead, the negligence idea has remained the core concept in tort doctrine for about a century and a half. The most marked trend in the evolution of tort law since the 1850s has been the slow and partial working out of the negligence principle and the removal of the limited-duty and no-duty rules that got in its way in cases involving landowners and occupiers, emotional distress, sovereign immunity, familial torts, product-related injuries, and more. Even here, the trend to abolish what used to be known as the "old fashioned" limited-duty and no-duty rules has not swept the field. Indeed, in some jurisdictions, the old rules seem likely to become the new rules![4]

And yet, doctrinal continuity notwithstanding, the changes in the torts system have been dramatic. No one doubts that tort law as a system experienced exponential growth over the twentieth century, especially in the subfield of accident law. In the decade from 1950 to 1960, the total cost of the American tort system grew by nearly $3.5 billion, nearly doubling the tort system's share of the nation's gross domestic product (from 0.6 percent to 1 percent). Today the cost of the tort system is estimated at somewhere around $200 billion, or 2 percent of GDP, roughly the cost of Social Security old-age pensions. No one really knows for certain how much money runs through the tort system. All the estimates are controversial. But everyone agrees that, despite continuity in the doctrine, the tort system of today is dramatically different from the tort system of the first half of the twentieth century.[5]

Here, then, is tort law's conundrum: How can the experience of tort law have changed so dramatically while the rules articulated in judicial opinions have retained such fidelity to the basic outlines of the law as it was handed down from the nineteenth century?

In this essay I take up the pattern of continuity and change in the law of damages for pain and suffering. Nowhere is the pattern more pronounced. In the course of the twentieth century, pain and suffering damages went from being a backwater of American law to one of its raging currents. At the beginning of the century, pain and suffering damages were a relatively insignificant part of American tort practice, meriting little if any notice or comment. By the end of the century, observers believed, pain and suffering damages accounted for roughly half of all tort damages, aggregating to about $50 billion a year, nearly twice the size of the damages produced by the entire tort systems of Germany and Japan in the same period. The historical puzzle of the law of pain and suffering damages is to explain this startling development. How—for better or for worse—did pain and suffering damages become so crucial to the operation of our tort system?[6]

The inquiry into pain and suffering damages that follows is quintessentially Nelsonian. It requires that we take him seriously when he calls on us to "rediscover forgotten data rather than rehash what is already familiar." And, as we shall see, the real story of pain and suffering damages in the history of American law produces precisely the kind of "new knowledge" that Nelson delights in. It even corrects an erroneous interpretation of the history of pain and suffering that has recently appeared in the decisions of the U.S. Supreme Court.[7]

Pursuing the history of pain and suffering damages vindicates the Nelsonian study of legal history in several important respects. It requires that we follow Nelson's understanding that "law is deeply embedded in the culture and political economy of its time." It will send us into the archives, where he has sent generations of students. And when we emerge on the other side, dust-covered and pallid from lack of sun, I think we will see that Nelson's master narrative of "reformation" explains the history of tort law more effectively than does Morton Horwitz's rival "transformation" narrative. Reformation better explains the history of tort law in general and of pain and suffering damages in particular.[8]

Yet the history of pain and suffering damages in torts also offers a pair of qualifications to Nelson's story of twentieth-century legalist reformation. The first is that the story of pain and suffering—like much of the history of tort law over the past century—is a story about the limits of the case law in which Nelson has so much faith. One of the most striking features of the modern law of accidents is the limits on judges' capacity to shape the vast, decentralized tort system. Judges often play little more than a guest-star cameo role. Instead, the stars in the story of pain and suffering damages are the members of the plaintiffs' bar: The trial lawyers whose sudden rise to prominence in the years immediately following World War II probably did more to reform American tort law than did any judicial decision in torts.

The second qualification to Nelson's story is geographical. Reorganizing the master narrative of reformation in twentieth-century tort law to include the trial bar requires that we reorient our field of vision to the west. New York has long been notorious among tort lawyers for its resistance to the doctrinal trends that in the 1960s and 1970s seemed likely to sweep away many of the old-fashioned pro-defendant rules of limited- and no-duty. California, by contrast, touched off those trends. It is in California that we find the roots of the plaintiffs' bar as we know it today. And if the twentieth-century common-law process of reformation was central to the creation of the modern policy-oriented legal system that we know today, California has a prominent place alongside New York in that story.

I

Damages for pain and suffering seem to have been available in legal systems since antiquity. The Roman doctrine of *iniuria* authorized the award of damages for "pain or distress of mind or body." Such damages were available only in cases of intentional injury to free persons.[9]

Medieval English law also seems to have recognized something approximating damages for pain and suffering. The scheduled damages of the medieval English "bot" were designed first and foremost to allow an offender to purchase peace from a vengeful victim. But these damages payments almost certainly reflected in part the pain and suffering caused by the offending injury. Later in the medieval period, according to Pollock's and Maitland's magisterial history of the English common law, plaintiffs in the English local courts regularly sought damages for the shame and loss of honor that arose out of an injury.[10]

By the end of the eighteenth century, English pleading manuals instructed lawyers to allege pain and suffering in actions of trespass on the case (the plaintiff "suffered and underwent great and excruciating pains and tortures both of body and mind," recounted one such model pleading). A popular pleading manual by Joseph Chitty included model pleadings alleging pain and suffering for cases such as dog bites ("thereby suffered and underwent great pain") and carriage accidents ("during all which time . . . [plaintiff] suffered great pain"). Chitty's influential manual was published in multiple English and American editions in the early nineteenth century, with further additions of model pain and suffering pleadings. And in 1822, apparently for the first time, the English Court of Exchequer upheld a damages award that expressly included money for the pain and suffering of a victim of medical malpractice.[11]

The difficulty of reconstructing the law of pain and suffering for personal injury in the early periods of Anglo-American law is that essentially there was no organized common-law category known as "torts" before the rise of the negligence action in the middle of the nineteenth century. But almost as soon as the Industrial Revolution gave life to tort law, tort law began allowing damages for pain and suffering to the smashed victims of industrial progress. Pain and suffering damages were present at the creation.[12]

Thanks to Chief Justice Lemuel Shaw and his colleagues, Massachusetts was to the antebellum common law what Nelson's New York is to the common law of the twentieth century. Shaw wrote many of the founding opinions in the American law of torts while sitting on the Massachusetts Supreme Judicial Court. And lo and behold—in 1835, the Supreme Judicial Court recognized pain and suffering damages when it upheld an award of damages that included payment for "great bodily and mental suffering" of a plaintiff who had fallen through a hole in a railing on the Canal Bridge over the Charles River. The doctrine quickly spread. Seven years later, a wagon accident on a road in Connecticut produced a damages award that included compensation for the plaintiff's "bodily pain" and "mental anguish." In neither case did the defendant challenge the legitimacy of awards for pain and suffering damages.[13]

By the time that some defendants finally did challenge the availability of such awards, courts in states across the country made clear that it was too late in the day to call them into question. "Pain," ruled the Maine Supreme Judicial Court in 1850, was "a part of bodily injury" and indeed was "inherent in it" for purposes of the law of torts. In 1851, a justice writing for a three-judge appellate panel of the New York Supreme Court presented the state of the law forthrightly: "bodily pain and suffering is part and parcel of the actual injury, for which the injured party is as much entitled to compensation in damages as for loss of time or the outlay of money." It was true, Justice Thomas A. Johnson conceded, that "the footing for a precise and accurate estimate of damages may not be quite as sure and fixed . . . as where a loss has been sustained in time or money." But the "actual damage is no less substantial and real." Johnson concluded, "I am confident" that the availability of pain and suffering damages "has been generally understood, and uniformly administered by our courts . . . in all cases of this kind, where one person has received personal injury and mutilation, by the careless or negligent act of another."[14]

Of course, the need for courts to address the issue at all—along with the existence of an occasional dissenting voice—suggests that the practice of pain and suffering damages generated some controversy in the middle of the nineteenth century. But virtually every common-law authority on the subject treated such damages as longstanding parts of the common law. If there were relatively few such authorities until the middle of the nineteenth century, that was simply because the matter was settled and uncontroversial. As Judge Hiram Denio of the New York Court of Appeals explained, "no doubt was ever supposed to exist" on the question. "It has always been assumed," Denio concluded, "that personal suffering was to be compensated in damages, in an action by the person injured."[15]

The first generation of treatise writers all concurred with Judge Denio's assessment. We see uncontroversial endorsements of pain and suffering damages by Francis Hilliard in his *The Law of Remedies for Torts*, by Thomas Shearman and Amasa Redfield in their influential *Treatise on the Law of Negligence*, and by Thomas Cooley in his *Treatise on the Law of Torts*. By the 1890s, treatise writer Arthur Sedgwick could confidently say that as to "physical pain . . . resulting from personal injury, there has never been any question." And at the turn of the twentieth century, when the editors of the West Publishing Company sorted and organized the accumulated cases of the common-law tradition for their seminal *Century Digest* project, they included as a matter of course a category in the law of damages for "Physical Suffering and Inconvenience."[16]

Another way of getting at the deep roots of pain and suffering damages in common-law doctrine is to look at the practicing lawyer's categories in litigation over damages. Still today, lawyers and insurance company claims adjusters regularly refer to pain and suffering damages as "general" damages, as distinct from a plaintiff's economic losses (costs of medical care, lost wages, and the like). The categories are practitioner's categories rather than academic categories. One rarely encounters them in the academic literature. But in practice they have long been invaluable tools. Among other things, the distinction between "general damages" and so-called "specials" underlies the formulae that claims adjusters and plaintiffs' lawyers often use to settle personal injury claims out of court. Total damages equal to "three times specials" is one such formula. It uses a plaintiff's economic losses as a basis for total settlement value, effectively allocating damages equally among the plaintiff's economic losses, her pain and suffering, and her contingent-fee lawyer's bill.[17]

For our purposes, what is striking about the distinction between special and general damages is that its history reveals just how deeply pain and suffering damages are rooted in the soil of the common law. We can see the distinction—apparently for the first time—in the earliest nineteenth-century tort decisions recognizing pain and suffering damages. General damages, the courts explained, were those that necessarily resulted from the wrong in question. Special damages, by contrast, were not the "necessary consequences of the act complained of" but rather consequences that arose contingently out of the defendant's act in the particular case. What damages were general, then, and which were special? The Connecticut Supreme Court explained the categories this way:

> If [the damages] necessarily result, such as the loss of the value of an article of property which is carried away or destroyed, or of a sum of money which is not paid to the plaintiff according to the contract, *or . . . the endurance of pain consequent upon having one's limb fractured*, they are called general damages.

Pain and suffering naturally and necessarily flowed from an injury and in this way became *general* damages rather than *special* damages.[18]

The significance of the distinction was that general damages such as pain and suffering did not have to be set out expressly in the plaintiff's complaint. They were covered by a generalized *ad damnum* clause, or general allegation of damage in the complaint. Special damages such as wage loss and costs of medical care were different. Because they did not follow inevitably from the defendant's actions, special damages needed to be specially alleged in the plaintiff's pleadings. Specific allegation was required to give the defendant sufficient notice that the plaintiff would be seeking recovery for economic losses.

From an early-twentieth-century perspective, this is an especially arresting way to distinguish between non-economic and economic damages. Today it is the practice of non-economic damages that raises notice and due process concerns that such damages are too unmanageable. But a century and a half ago, courts saw the same problem in reverse. Economic damages—not pain and suffering damages—raised the notice and due process concerns. Pain and suffering was just the ordinary, everyday stuff of tort litigation.[19]

II

So far the history of pain and suffering damages has been one that sits very nicely in Nelson's case-centered approach to legal history. It has also been a history that significantly revises the current understanding of the story. For not everyone agrees with this narrative. Indeed, some of its most important detractors have sat on the U.S. Supreme Court, which in recent years has described a very different history for pain and suffering damages in the United States.

In a 1991 dissent in *Pacific Mutual Life Insurance v. Haslip*, Justice Sandra Day O'Connor wrote that historically the common law had declined to compensate injuries such as "pain, humiliation, and other forms of intangible injury." Punitive damages, in her view, served the function of compensating such injuries.[20]

A decade later, the Supreme Court as a whole embraced this historical claim in *Cooper Industries v. Leatherman Tool Group*. Writing for the Court, Justice John Paul Stevens explained that "until well into the 19th century" compensation for intangible injuries often was not "available under the narrow conception of compensatory damages prevalent at the time." Punitive damages, Stevens asserted, frequently operated as compensation for otherwise unrecognizable intangible injuries. Even more recently, the same idea has appeared in the pages of the *New York Times*.[21]

There is some truth to the notion that punitive damages once may have performed some of the work done today by pain and suffering or emotional distress damages. But with respect to personal injury cases this historical story is badly misleading. For as we have seen already, in personal injury cases the separation of pain from punishment occurred virtually simultaneously with the birth of tort law, the negligence action, and personal injury accident law in the middle of the nineteenth century.[22]

We can see this best in Justice Johnson's New York decision from 1851, which we have already had occasion to discuss for its clear statement about the availability of damages for pain and suffering in the common law. In *Morse v. The Auburn and Syracuse Railroad Company*, the plaintiff had been badly burned when a locomotive smashed into the passenger train in which he was traveling, scalding him with steam from the locomotive's steam engine. After establishing that plaintiffs could seek pain and suffering damages, Justice Johnson rejected the argument of the railroad lawyer that pain and suffering damages were a form of exemplary or punitive damages. The trial judge in the case had mixed the two together in his jury instruction. But Johnson sharply distinguished the two forms of damages. Pain and suffering damages, the court explained, were "strictly compensatory for the actual pain, of which the bodily pain and suffering were an essential part." Such damages, Johnson's opinion continued, "are not exemplary, or punitory in their character."[23]

By the end of the decade of the 1850s, a number of additional cases (along with Francis Hilliard's early torts treatise) had strengthened the distinction between pain and suffering damages, on the one hand, and punitive damages, on the other. The former, Hilliard explained, were "strictly compensatory for the actual injury, of which bodily pain and suffering were an essential part."[24]

Hilliard's distinction was more than just conceptual. Separating pain and suffering damages from punitive damages played a critical role in

the development of common-law tort doctrine. As the New York case
reporter Oliver L. Barbour observed in his headnote to the *Morse* case,
Morse stood for the proposition that "physical pain and suffering ought
to be taken into the account in estimating the damages in every action
to recover for a personal injury occasioned by negligence." In actions
for personal injury, it seemed—in *"every action,"* Barbour emphasized—damages would necessarily involve pain and suffering awards.
A plaintiff wanting to recover punitive damages had to make a showing
of intent or recklessness by the defendant. But there would be no intent
or motive requirement for plaintiffs seeking pain and suffering awards.
Any plain-vanilla negligence verdict would support awards of pain and
suffering.[25]

Barbour's gloss on the *Morse* case aptly summarizes the status of
pain and suffering damages in nineteenth-century common law. At the
creation of modern tort law, pain and suffering damages were unexceptional and unproblematic. They were a routine and not even a very
interesting dimension of the new field called torts.

III

With Barbour, the twentieth-century conundrum begins to come
into view. For if Barbour was right that awards for pain and suffering
were routinely available in the middle of the nineteenth century, what
explains the dramatically increased significance of pain and suffering
damages in American tort law a full century later? Why had pain and
suffering damages only recently become so important if they had been
available for so long?

In other areas of tort law, after all, courts had made intangible recov-
eries very hard to get. The most important limit on intangible damages was the longstanding common-law physical impact rule, requiring some physical impact and bodily injury to sustain a common-law
tort recovery. "The general rule," as one federal court explained in the
1880s, was that "'pain of mind' is only the subject of damages *when connected with bodily injury.*" Injuries "to the feelings, independently and
alone," were thus not recoverable in tort actions when they occurred
"apart from corporal personal injury." Mental distress alone, the courts
ruled, was "something too vague to enter into the domain of pecuniary

damages,—too elusive to be left . . . to the discretion of a jury." But as soon as there was a bodily or physical injury—even "though that injury may have been very small"—then the "mental suffering to the plaintiff" was "a part of the injury for which he was entitled to have damages."[26]

The reasoning here is familiar—only in the past half-century since the *Falzone* case in New Jersey and the *Dillon* case in California have common-law courts thought otherwise. Even now the central problems in negligent infliction of emotional distress cases are to manage the domain of recoverable mental distress damages and to draw lines between recoverable and unrecoverable damages. In the nineteenth century, courts drew such lines all the time, and indeed they did so more aggressively than do most late-twentieth-century and early-twenty-first-century courts. Only in limited and sharply contained categories of cases such as interference with corpses, the desecration of burial grounds, and *per se* defamation did nineteenth-century courts allow mental distress damages without physical impact and physical injury.[27]

Nineteenth-century courts sought to prohibit recovery for such intangible injuries as pain and suffering and mental distress in cases in which the question for the courts was whether there had been a legally cognizable injury—*any* legally cognizable injury—such that liability could be established. But in the ordinary run-of-the-mill personal injury case, in which the plaintiff had sustained a cognizable physical injury, courts created few if any restraints on compensatory damages for pain and suffering. To put it another way, nineteenth-century common-law courts aggressively policed the valuation of intangible injuries at the *liability margin* but were receptive to their valuation at the *damages margin*.

Why did the courts adopt this seemingly inconsistent posture? Why did the law seek to guard against an imagined avalanche of new cases that might follow the recognition of a cause of action for pure negligent infliction of emotional distress even as they made it relatively easy for tort plaintiffs with bodily injuries to add intangible pain and suffering components to their lists of injuries?

The best answer seems to be that the value of such intangible awards was almost always relatively minor. In all but a handful of the decided nineteenth-century pain and suffering cases that I have encountered, the pain and suffering awards were small. Typical cases include $600 in 1835 (a little more than $13,000 in 2012 dollars) for the "great bodily and mental suffering" of a man who fell through a hole in an unlighted canal bridge into the icy waters below. An Arkansas court in 1893 upheld a jury award of $2,500 in pain and suffering damages ($63,000 in 2012 dollars) in a death case involving a railroad brakeman who spent twenty-four hours in gruesome pain before his death from a railroad accident. In such cases, the economic loss component of damages awards seems to have been substantially larger than the pain and suffering component. In the Arkansas brakeman's case, for example, the award of $2,500 in pain and suffering damages was accompanied by $4,000 for economic losses.[28]

Interestingly, the exceptional cases—those with higher damages awards—tended to be those involving injuries to middle-class and upper-class women for whom there were few other bases for personal injury damages under nineteenth-century law. In the nineteenth century, middle-class women typically did not work for pay outside the home and thus could rarely claim significant economic losses in the form of lost wages. Costs of medical care were relatively low during the period as well. As a result, gruesome injuries to women sometimes were compensated with large undifferentiated awards that presumably included substantial pain and suffering components. In the largest such award that I have been able to locate, the Massachusetts Supreme Judicial Court in 1857 upheld a massive damages judgment of $22,250 (a half million dollars in 2012 funds) awarded to a woman named Sarah Shaw. Miss Shaw had been horribly injured in a railroad accident that had resulted in the amputation of one arm and the permanent disabling of the other. According to the court, Shaw could not feed or dress herself, her head was badly cut, an eye badly injured, several teeth broken, and "her body much bruised." Her health and memory had been impaired, and "she suffered constant pain."[29]

Today, cases such as Shaw's might produce large damages awards, but such awards would include substantial economic loss components for medical care, nursing assistance, and lost future earnings. In Shaw's case, few such bases for compensation seem to have existed, and the Supreme Judicial Court's reasoning about the damages in the case focused on the pain that Shaw had undoubtedly suffered.

If all nineteenth-century pain and suffering awards had been worth what such plaintiffs as Shaw received, nineteenth-century law might not have been nearly so comfortable leaving pain and suffering awards to the unfettered discretion of juries. Perhaps we would have seen some approximation of the difficult line-drawing exercise that the courts adopted to limit the legal recognition of intangible injuries in the no-impact and no–physical injury cases.

A century after the *Shaw* decision, American tort law began to treat all plaintiffs as it once had treated some female plaintiffs. Pain and suffering awards rose across the board. By that time, however, a new cast of players had come on the scene. The group was the trial lawyers. What the trial lawyers realized was that the common law was very well suited to the charismatic creativity of attorneys such as themselves. In the decades after World War II, the trial lawyers turned pain and suffering damages into the comparatively booming field we know today.[30]

IV

Among literary critics it has become fashionable to say that pain resists language. The inarticulate scream, not the word, is the common tongue of the body in pain. Lawyers—especially in the mandarin institutions of the legal academy—have sometimes agreed. Converting pain into currency, Harvard law professor Louis L. Jaffe wrote in 1953, is like "evaluating the imponderable." Jaffe was one of the twentieth century's leading scholars and teachers of administrative law. To him, as to so many others in the academy, pain and suffering damages seemed to be a quagmire of irrationality, something like what Max Weber famously called the "Khadi justice" of the Anglo-American jury system.[31]

In the years following World War II, however, a very different class of American lawyers crafted a new vocabulary for translating pain and suffering into the language of the law and, more important, into the language of dollars and cents. The San Francisco trial lawyer Melvin Belli led the way for an entire generation of lawyers when he wrote in the 1950s, "Relief from pain is the physician's purpose, compensation from pain is the lawyer's duty."[32]

For the first one-and-a-half centuries of U.S. history, the plaintiff's lawyer barely existed as a category. The first generation of accident lawsuits in the 1830s and 1840s featured lawyers who shifted back and forth between representing defendants and plaintiffs. Charles G. Loring in Massachusetts was one such lawyer, a man from an influential New England family who represented both work accident plaintiffs and the railroads they sued. After the turn of the twentieth century, the bar swelled with new members from the ranks of southern and eastern European immigrants. These lawyers were much more likely to be repeat-play plaintiffs' representatives, and some of them developed substantial portfolios of cases.[33]

Through the first half of the twentieth century, plaintiffs' lawyers remained relatively diffuse and disorganized. The American common-law system—with its dozens of state court systems, its jury decision makers, and the like—was about as decentralized and disorganized as the plaintiffs' lawyers themselves were. However, as twentieth-century reformers sought to bring greater organization to the torts system, tort lawyers organized as well.[34]

Workmen's compensation statutes, first enacted in the United States beginning in the 1910s, moved the center of energy for one of the most important fields of accident law out of the decentralized courts, away from the lay juries, and into administrative agencies controlled by state legislatures. The statutes thus placed a premium on precisely what plaintiffs' lawyers had never before needed—namely, collective organization and lobbying before centralized state agencies and legislatures. Only on the floors of state legislatures and in the halls of state agencies could compensation rates be raised and legal fee provisions made more generous. And only at the legislature and in the agencies could the lobbying power of defendants' interest groups be met.[35]

Indeed, defense interests seem to have beat their plaintiffs' lawyer counterparts to the punch. Even as workmen's compensation statutes were enacted around the country, such repeat-play defendants as railroads and insurance companies already had begun to organize themselves to minimize their liability in personal injury litigation. At the federal level, railroad lawyers' associations lobbied and cajoled Congress to minimize liability under the Federal Employers' Liability Act, or FELA, which governed interstate railroad injuries. At the state level, such employers' associations as the National Association of Manufacturers and state chambers of commerce lobbied for pro-employer workmen's compensation benefit rate increases.[36]

For more than three decades, defense-side interests had the field virtually to themselves. But in 1946, a small band of claimant's lawyers led by a Massachusetts union-side workmen's compensation lawyer named Samuel Horovitz met in a back room at a convention of insurers and defense-side workers' compensation attorneys to forge their own organization, the National Association of Claimants' Compensation Attorneys (NACCA). On the defense side, lawyer organizations had found that collective action brought with it ancillary benefits. Coordination of litigation strategies and sharing of information helped defendants to achieve better litigation outcomes in the courts as well as better legislative outcomes in the statehouses and better rulemaking outcomes in the agencies. The NACCA lawyers who banded together to push for more generous benefit rates in the state legislatures soon realized that collective action in the courts had even more upside potential for them than it did for their adversaries. Such repeat-play tort defendants as railroads and liability insurers had built-in economies of scale and information-collection mechanisms. But isolated plaintiffs' representatives had no such advantages. Collective organization, however, could begin to deliver some of these economies of scale and information-sharing advantages that the defense bar had long enjoyed.[37]

Collective action around common-law courts proved so effective for plaintiffs' lawyers that the NACCA soon abandoned its workers' compensation efforts to focus on transforming the tort system. Within a few short years, the NACCA had become an organization dedicated not to the improvement of the workmen's compensation system but to its rollback. By the early 1950s, NACCA advocated the abolition of workmen's compensation. At the very least, NACCA representatives argued, it was important to end the spread of the rationalizing workmen's compensation principle into other areas such as the automobile accident field. In the middle of the 1960s, the organization that had begun as an effort to improve the administrative law of workmen's compensation renamed itself the Association of Trial Lawyers of America (ATLA), an organization that eventually would become one of the most powerful lobbying organizations in the nation.[38]

V

The shift from the NACCA to ATLA plays out in miniature the reformist story that Nelson describes in the twentieth-century common law
more generally. Workmen's compensation was one of the great examples of the administrative agencies of the Progressive Era and the New
Deal. It held the potential to introduce new, transformative principles
into American law, principles that might have licensed the far-reaching
use of statistics and actuarial techniques in the law, or a sharp increase
in the significance of administrative agencies, or perhaps even substantial new redistributive regulation. In the first half of the twentieth century, many leading observers of American public policy anticipated that
the problems of mass industrial society inevitably would shift the center
of gravity from courts and the market to administration and active government intervention. The NACCA seemed at first to be a concession
by the plaintiff's lawyers that their field would be swallowed up by the
industrial bureaucracies of the mid–twentieth century. But the shifts
that took place were never more than partial, and courts effectively
reasserted themselves in the administrative state. To use Nelson's term,
a legalist reformation took place, one that adapted the common law for
the new era of industrial life and mass urban society. The trial lawyers
of the NACCA and later of ATLA rededicated their efforts to defending
the common law and the courts.[39]

The significance of the plaintiffs' bar is easily missed if one focuses
too closely on the work of judges alone. The trial lawyers make virtually no appearance in Nelson's account of New York. That's a shame,
because some of the leading members of the early trial bar were based
there. Stuart Speiser was an early aviation litigation lawyer in New
York who pioneered the mass treatment of airplane disasters in the
years after World War II. Jacob D. Fuchsberg was the president of the
New York State Trial Lawyers Association and then of ATLA itself in
the late 1960s and early 1970s before becoming a judge on the New
York Court of Appeals. Nelson describes Fuchsberg's checkered career
in the New York judiciary relatively sympathetically. But in the long
run, Fuchsberg's work in the trial bar may have been more significant
than his work on the bench. In the trial lawyers' organizations, Fuchsberg helped to develop (among other things) a centralized database of

information through which member lawyers could share information with one another. Insurers and repeat-play defendants had a built-in ability to share information about prior lawsuits. Fuchsberg managed to deliver some of the same advantages of scale to the decentralized trial lawyers as well.[40]

Introducing the trial lawyers to the story helps make sense of a dimension of Nelson's history that otherwise goes unexplained. According to Nelson, cultural changes outside the courts changed tort litigation inside the courts. What this argument omits is that the trial bar formed an increasingly well-organized interest group powerfully motivated to encourage a new culture of risk and injury and to deliver that culture to the courthouse steps. It was the trial lawyers who breathed new life into a doctrine that had lain dormant in American tort law for a century.[41]

VI

Melvin Belli led the way. The Belli whom many remember today was a flamboyant, decadent, embarrassing, self-promoting, and ethically challenged showman lawyer. The "King of Torts," as *Life* magazine dubbed him in 1954, was a man of scarlet silk–lined suits, of multicolored Rolls-Royces, of courtroom theatrics and Hollywood hijinks. He was the oafish lawyer for Jack Ruby in Ruby's trial for the murder of Lee Harvey Oswald, and he was the crass ambulance chaser who landed in Bhopal, India, to sign up plaintiffs while people were still dying of exposure to the poisonous cloud at the Union Carbide plant. As early as the middle of the 1960s, such behavior by Belli caused the trial lawyers' organization to distance itself from him. But the early Belli, the Belli of the 1940s and 1950s, had been a dynamo, a man who almost singlehandedly galvanized the trial lawyers and reoriented them away from the administrative bureaucracy of workmen's compensation and back toward the courts, where the cases were more lucrative and more congenial to Belli's brand of showmanship.[42]

Belli's contributions to modern plaintiffs' practice were legion. He litigated the *Escola v. Coca-Cola Bottling Company* case that produced Justice Roger Traynor's first great announcement of the logic of strict liability in products cases. Along with Horovitz, the Massachusetts workmen's compensation lawyer who founded the NACCA, Belli brought the aging Roscoe Pound into the plaintiffs' lawyers' organization, where he added a much-needed reputational boost to the low-status plaintiffs' bar. Belli also helped propel the litigation campaign launched by the NACCA against the nineteenth-century doctrines that had limited the recovery of damages for such intangible injuries as pain and suffering. The old physical impact rule, which had limited the recovery of damages for mental distress and suffering, came under sustained attack from NACCA and its affiliated lawyers, and when the California Supreme Court finally overturned the common-law rule in 1968 in *Dillon v. Legg*, ATLA lawyers once again were litigating the case. Few doctrinal developments in tort in the twentieth century garnered more attention from the law professoriate.[43]

Perhaps more significant than the establishment of liability for intangible injuries with no physical impact or bodily injury was the work that Belli did to expand the size of pain and suffering damages in otherwise unexceptional personal injury cases. Belli's campaign began in 1951, when he published a long article in the law review of his alma mater, the law school at the University of California, Berkeley. The article, titled "The Adequate Award," aimed to raise the value of personal injury cases. Professional baseball players earned $100,000 for a season's work. Racehorses fetched $300,000 on the market. Works of art and fine violins sold for hundreds of thousands of dollars. And yet, Belli contended, the value of personal injury awards lagged behind the increasing cost of everything from haircuts to housing.[44]

Front and center in Belli's efforts were pain and suffering damages. It was true, he conceded, that "pain is not a readily measurable commodity." But the speculative character of pain and suffering awards did not mean that they should be prohibited. "Too many decided cases awarding specific damages for the intangibles of pain and suffering have surmounted the problem of measurability." And understood properly, pain and suffering damages were both the core of tort law and an opportunity for the common-law plaintiffs' lawyer.[45]

What was tort law about? According to Belli, tort law in its essence was about "man's right to live out his life free from pain and suffering, with his mind and body intact." Pain and suffering damages, in turn, allowed the creative plaintiffs' lawyer the opportunity to vindicate that right. Damages for such intangible injuries as pain and suffering, Belli observed, "depend upon counsel's imagination." Their value turned on the "vividness" of the trial lawyer's portrayal of the pain of his client. By using the courtroom for the theatrical reconstruction of the victim's pain and suffering, the trial lawyer could push the value of pain ever upward. Indeed, there was no logical upward boundary to the value of intangible injuries. In a contingency-fee world in which the lawyer took a third of the winnings, that was precisely their appeal.[46]

Illustrating pain and suffering played to the strong suit of such charismatic midcentury trial lawyers as Belli. They liked to farm out the doctrinal niceties to specialist brief-writers. Courtroom theatrics, by contrast, were their specialty, and this is where Belli excelled. In packed lecture halls and in bestselling books he taught overflow audiences and tens of thousands of readers how to describe and (better yet) reconstruct pain for a jury. The per-diem method was among his best-known contributions to the art of presenting pain. How much money would it take, Belli liked to ask his juries, to make you whole for even a day of the pain of the plaintiff? Take that number and multiply it by the plaintiff's life expectancy, and the pain and suffering damages seemed sure to be higher than the defense would like.[47]

Belli's multi-volume book *Modern Trials*, published at the height of his powers in the late 1950s and early 1960s, was the midcentury equivalent to the trial-in-a-box preparations issued by trial lawyers' organizations a half-century later. Here Belli showed trial lawyers the myriad ways to dwell on and describe pain in the courtroom. Pictures, he wrote, were worth a thousand words. And photographs that sought to capture his clients' pain were one of Belli's calling cards. The more gruesome the imagery, the better the photo. Badly burned hands, mangled bodies, and more—all featured in Belli's photographic shop of horrors.[48]

What Belli called "demonstrative evidence" was sometimes even better. One of Belli's best-known courtroom tricks was the prosthetic limb hidden in thickly wrapped butcher paper in a case involving an amputated leg. In another case, he used a crane to lift a 600-pound bedridden client through the window of a second-floor courtroom. One way or another, Belli explained, the trial lawyer needed to get the jury to try to "picture" the plaintiff's pain. The more lurid the picture, the better. But in a pinch, even the accumulated prescription slips for pain medication would do.[49]

Words were good, too, of course. Belli talked about pain as the apocryphal Eskimo talks about snow.[50] There were at least forty different kinds of pain, he asserted, and he instructed his audiences in an elaborate taxonomy of the kinds and types of pain that their clients might be suffering. He distinguished "physical pain and suffering" from "mental pain and suffering," which in turn he distinguished from "embarrassment, ridicule, and humiliation," each of which he insisted could be an independent basis for intangible damages without an impermissible double counting. Belli became an ersatz expert in the budding science of pain measurement, and he encouraged his peers at the bar to do the same. He painstakingly described "the pathways of pain," which he likened to an elaborate telephone system managed by a central operator's station in the thalamus.[51]

In the decade after Belli and the ATLA transformed the practice of personal injury law, the size of damages awards for pain and suffering injuries increased dramatically. Belli himself reported the new trends in his companion to *Modern Trials*, the massive, multi-volume treatise *Modern Damages*, published with pocket-part updates to keep plaintiffs' lawyers around the country informed on the latest damage verdicts and settlements.[52]

VII

For better or worse, Belli's successes are the kind of legalist reformation that Nelson seems to want to describe. They are not transformations of the law of torts. Nelson's reformation has Horwitz's transformation beaten here. Had the rationalist reformers in the twentieth century prevailed, the story might well be one of the law's transformation—from common law to bureaucratic rulemaking, from juries and judges to administrators, from trials to hearings. But the triumph of the trial lawyers was a triumph of reformation. Pain and suffering damages were one of law's oldest doctrines. They were almost as old as the common law itself. They were firmly rooted in the nineteenth-century origins of torts as a field of law. Indeed, the substantive law had barely changed in a century. Yet in Belli's hands, the law-in-action dramatically altered the law that had been on the books all those years.

The irony of American tort law in the twentieth century is that Belli's successes in breathing new life into the once-moribund doctrine of pain and suffering damages were an unanticipated consequence of the kinds of rationalist reforms promoted in the twentieth century. Workers' compensation programs had adopted a basic bureaucratic administrative logic: They sought to eliminate the lay participation, the unpredictability, and the gamesmanship of the common law, and to substitute the certainty and bureaucratic rationality of the twentieth-century administrative state. They even sought to eliminate pain and suffering damages from the law of accidents, replacing them with rationalized compensation for lost wages and medical care. But workmen's compensation was only an incomplete regulation of a highly decentralized common-law field. In the domains of tort law left untouched by workmen's compensation, the common law had its revenge.

The history of accident law in the twentieth and twenty-first centuries is the story of dynamic interaction between systemic reformers, on the one hand, and interest groups, on the other. Beginning a century ago, we see a series of attempts to bring order and bureaucratic rationality to the tangled skein of the common law. Workmen's compensation was the first such systematic effort at reform. It was also far and away the most important effort, though it was followed by further reform proposals for automobile accidents as well as niche programs for childhood vaccines, black lung, and nuclear disasters.[53]

Across the middle two-thirds of the twentieth century, however, interest groups from at least two sides eroded the value of these rationalizing reforms. On one side, employers' lobbies systematically destroyed the value of workmen's compensation benefits. Only in the 1970s would legislative readjustment of benefit rates and the indexing of benefit rates for inflation solve what by then had become an acute crisis.[54]

From the other side—and often at precisely the same time—trial lawyers worked to rehabilitate the common law and the courts in the modern state and to increase tort liability by leaps and bounds. Consider the rise of third-party product liability cases in workplace accidents. The law pressed its thumb down on lawsuits against employers, only to see those suits reappear in the guise of actions against manufacturers. By the 1980s, between one-half and two-thirds of product liability cases were workplace cases in which plaintiffs' lawyers defeated the compensation statutes by bringing tort actions against the third-party products manufacturer. The manufacturer often impleaded the employer, and in such cases workmen's compensation's administrative replacement of tort law collapsed. Employers and employees were back in court litigating common-law negligence questions against one another—only now the contests were even more complex than they had been before. Even where the law barred the manufacturer from impleading the employer, the costs of these product liability suits were nonetheless built into the prices of the products. Employers paid the costs either way. Product cases thus proved to be the partial common-law undoing of workmen's compensation bargain.[55]

A second effect of partial rationalization was cross-fertilization—or cross-contamination, depending on your view—between the decentralized common law and the rational compensation systems. In workers' compensation, lawyers quickly smashed the streamlined administrative aspirations of reformers by importing common-law adversarial tactics into administrative hearings. In the common law, the no-fault reforms of workmen's compensation influenced the liability standards of common-law jurists, establishing the intellectual underpinnings of strict liability doctrine in the common law. All of the basic elements in the strict liability cases of the 1950s and 1960s, all of the ideas of a judge such as Traynor in California, are to be found in the logic of workmen's compensation, which sought to substitute a rational enterprise-based liability for the expensive fault litigation of the common law. Of course, even when it adopted the workmen's compensation liability standard of strict liability, the common law preserved its far more generous damages provisions and its expensive jury system.[56]

The basic pattern here ought to be familiar from other areas of the law. In criminal justice, the Warren Court's liberal criminal-procedure decisions were, in William Stuntz's brilliant account, incomplete regulatory moves that left the regulated entities (state legislatures and Congress) free to respond by increasing sentences dramatically. In election law, Samuel Issacharoff and Pamela S. Karlan have identified the hydraulic effect of campaign-finance regulations, in which regulation drives partisan competition underground and into more pernicious forms.[57]

Pain and suffering damages in American tort law present much the same kind of incomplete regulation or hydraulic story. The rationalizing impulse of the twentieth-century law reformers, from the Progressive Era workmen's compensation advocate to the 1960s automobile no-fault supporter, called forth a defensive collective action on the part of

THE POLITICAL ECONOMY OF PAIN >> 257

American trial lawyers, which in turn helped to produce even more of the common-law litigation that the reformers had sought to prevent in the first place. The efforts to subvert or replace the common law produced a legalist reformation that allowed the common law to carry on with many of its old tools in innovative new ways.

VIII

Twenty years ago, Robert Gordon identified one of the chief virtues of Morton Horwitz's seminal second *Transformation of American Law* volume. The book's rich material, Gordon wrote, cascaded over the powerful but sometimes narrow arguments into which Horwitz sought to confine it.[58] Much the same can be said for *The Legalist Reformation*. Even where his argument focuses on the work of the judiciary, Nelson understands the conundrum of tort law in the twentieth century. He grasps precisely the juxtaposition of continuity in the doctrine with change in the practice exemplified by the story of pain and suffering damages. The reformation of tort law, Nelson argues, retained "superficial continuity" in doctrine even as it was put to "new and more expansive uses." The change, Nelson writes, took place at a "deeper level."

What I have tried to offer here is a theory of what was going on underneath the superficial continuity of tort doctrine that Nelson describes. The reformation of the common law in the torts field was indeed being accomplished at a deeper level. But that does not mean that it was happening outside the law. It means only that we will need to follow Nelson's injunction to follow the history of the law into new and unknown territory in hopes of finding the delight of discovery that he has so movingly described as the soul of legal-historical research. Maybe if we're lucky—just maybe—we'll be able to offer our readers the same delight in discovery that Bill Nelson has given his readers.

NOTES

1. Many thanks to Kellen Funk at Yale Law School and Kristin Yemm at Columbia Law School for superb research assistance.
2. William E. Nelson, *The Legalist Reformation: Law, Politics, and Ideology in New York, 1920–1980* (Chapel Hill: University of North Carolina Press, 2001), 2.
3. John Fabian Witt, *The Accidental Republic: Crippled Workingmen, Destitute Widows, and the Remaking of American Law* (Cambridge, Mass.: Harvard

University Press, 2004), 297 (Nelson's supervision in the Golieb Fellowship). On the centrality of judicial opinions, see, e.g., Jules Coleman, *The Practice of Principle* (New York: Oxford University Press, 2001) (purporting to identify the moral core of tort law from the opinions of judges); G. Edward White, *Tort Law in America: An Intellectual History* (New York: Oxford University Press, 2nd ed., 2003) (describing the history of tort law as the story of leading cases decided by judges).

4. For the idea of doctrinal transformations in tort law, see Morton J. Horwitz, *The Transformation of American Law, 1780–1860* (Cambridge, Mass.: Harvard University Press, 1977) and George L. Priest, "The Invention of Enterprise Liability: A Critical History of the Intellectual Foundations of Modern Tort Law," *Journal of Legal Studies* 14 (1985): 461. For examples of courts' retaining the old rules on negligent infliction of emotional distress, see *Tobin v. Grossman*, 24 N.Y.2d 609 (N.Y. 1969) and *Guilmette v. Alexander*, 259 A.2d 12 (Vt. 1969). For retention of landowners duties, see *Mallet v. Pickens*, 522 S.E.2d 436 (W. Va. 1999) (noting that only twenty-five states have followed California's lead in abolishing or modifying landlords' duties). Robert L. Rabin, "Some Thoughts on the Ideology of Enterprise Liability," *Maryland Law Review* 55 (1996): 1190; Gary Schwartz, "The Beginning and the Possible End of the Rise of Modern American Tort Law," *Georgia Law Review* 26 (1992): 601.

5. For the tort system's share of the GDP, see Tillinghast Towers-Perrin, *2008 Update on U.S. Tort Cost Trends*, p. 3, available at http://www.towersperrin. com/tp/getwebcachedoc?webc=USA/2008/200811/2008_tort_costs_trends.pdf (accessed 7 March 2010).

6. On the size of pain and suffering damages, see Tillinghast Towers-Perrin, *U.S. Tort Costs: 2003 Update—Trends and Filings on the U.S. Tort System*, p. 15, available at http://www.towersperrin.com/tillinghast/publications/reports/2003_ Tort_Costs_Update/Tort_Costs_Trends_2003_Update.pdf (accessed 7 March 2010); see also Neil Vidmar et al., "Jury Awards for Medical Malpractice and Post-Verdict Adjustments of Those Awards," *DePaul Law Review* 48 (1998): 265, 296; W. Kip Viscusi, "Pain and Suffering in Product Liability Cases: Systematic Compensation or Capricious Awards?" *International Review of Law and Economics* 8 (1988): 203. For the size of the German and Japanese tort systems, see Tillinghast-Towers Perrin, *U.S. Tort Costs and Cross-Border Perspectives: 2005 Update*, p. 4, available at www.towersperrin.com/tillinghast/publications/ reports/2005_Tort_Cost/2005_Tort.pdf (accessed 7 March 2010).

7. Nelson, *Legalist Reformation*, 1 ("forgotten data").

8. *Ibid.*, 3 ("political economy").

9. M. de Villiers, *The Roman and Roman-Dutch Law of Injuries* (Cape Town: J. C. Juta and Co., 1899), 182.

10. James Q. Whitman, "At the Origins of Law and the State: Supervision of Violence, Mutilation of Bodies, or Setting of Prices?" *Chicago-Kent Law Review* 71 (1995): 41 (purchase peace); Sir Frederick Pollock and Frederic William

Maitland, *The History of English Law Before the Time of Edward I* (Cambridge: Cambridge University Press, 1899), 2: 537–38.

11. Joseph Chitty, *A Treatise on Pleading* (London: W. Clarke and Sons, 1809), 2: 243 ("suffered"). For an example of a model pleading, see Joseph Chitty, *Supplement to A Treatise on Pleading* (Philadelphia: Isaac Riley, 1818), 408.

12. See Witt, *The Accidental Republic*; Thomas C. Grey, "Accidental Torts," *Vanderbilt Law Review* 54 (2001): 1225. To be sure, the word "torts" was used from time to time to describe legal wrongs; witness the clause on causes of action by aliens "for a tort only" in the Judiciary Act of 1789, 1 Stat. 79-93 (1789), now codified in the Alien Tort Statute, 28 U.S.C.A. § 1350 (St. Paul, Minn.: West Publishing Co., 2011). Similarly, cases that today we would categorize as torts cases pop up throughout the history of the common law, running back deep into the Middle Ages. Such cases presented the early common law with an ad hoc assortment of actions for wrongful injury. Most of these cases were for intentional injury, but until the mid–nineteenth century, no English or American lawyer conceived of them as falling together into a common category called torts. As another giant of Nelsonian proportions in the field of legal history has put it, the "modern law of torts" was an invention of the Industrial Revolution; see Lawrence M. Friedman, *A History of American Law*, 3rd ed. (New York: Simon & Schuster, 2005), 350.

13. *Worster v. Proprietors of the Canal Bridge*, 33 Mass. 541, 547 (Mass. 1835); *Linsley v. Bushnell*, 15 Conn. 225, 1842 WL 510 at *8 (Conn. 1842).

14. *Verrill v. Minot*, 31 Me. 299, 299 (Me. 1850); *Morse v. Auburn & Syracuse R.R.*, 10 Barb. 621, 621 (N.Y. Sup. 1851).

15. For a dissenting voice see, for example, Pollock in *Theobald v. Railway Passengers' Assurance Co.*, 26 Eng. L. & Ex. R. 438 (1862), contending that it was "an unmanly thing" to make claims for pain and suffering damages and reporting that as a barrister he had never made such claims; *Ransom v. New York & E.R. Co.*, 15 N.Y 415, 419 (N.Y. 1857) ("no doubt").

16. Francis Hilliard, *The Law of Remedies for Torts* (Boston: Little, Brown, 1867); Thomas G. Shearman and Amasa A. Redfield, *A Treatise on the Law of Negligence* (New York: Baker, Voorhis, 1869); Thomas Cooley, *A Treatise on the Law of Torts: Or the Wrongs Which Arise Independent of Contract* (Chicago: Callaghan, 1879); Arthur G. Sedgwick, *Elements of Damages: A Handbook* (Boston: Little, Brown, 1896), 97; *Century Edition of The American Digest: A Complete Digest of All Reported American Cases from the Earliest Times to 1896*, 50 vols. (St. Paul, Minn.: West Publishing Co., 1897–1904).

17. When scholars do take notice of the general damages category, it is most often to advocate for its abolition; see Joseph Sanders, "Reforming General Damages: A Good Tort Reform," *Roger Williams University Law Review* 13 (2008): 115, and Richard Abel, "General Damages are Incoherent, Incalculable, Incommensurable, and Inegalitarian (But Otherwise a Great Idea)," *DePaul Law Review* 55 (2006): 253. On adjusters' formulae, see Samuel Issacharoff and John Fabian

Witt, "The Inevitability of Aggregate Settlement: An Institutional Account of American Tort Law," *Vanderbilt Law Review* 57 (2004): 1571; see also H. Laurence Ross, *Settled Out of Court: The Social Process of Insurance Claims Adjustments* (Chicago: Aldine Publishing Co., 1970) (distinction in usage); Corydon T. Johns, *An Introduction to Liability Claims Adjusting* (Cincinnati: National Underwriter Co., 1965), 367–68 ("three times specials").

18. See *Olmstead v. Burke*, 25 Ill. 86, 1860 WL 6505 at *1 (Ill. 1860) (general damages necessary); *Roberts v. Graham*, 73 U.S. 578, 579 (1867) ("necessary consequences"); *Bristol Mfg. Co. v. Gridley*, 28 Conn. 201, 1859 WL 1265 at *7 (Conn. 1859) (emphasis added).

19. Jeffrey O'Connell and Theodore M. Bailey, "Appendix V: The History of Payment for Pain and Suffering," *University of Illinois Law Forum* (1972): 83. However, some still see problems with economic damages; see Catherine M. Sharkey, "Unintended Consequences of Medical Malpractice Damages Caps," *New York University Law Review* 80 (2005): 391 (arguing that economic damages may be almost as malleable as non-economic damages); see also Jonathan Klick and Catherine M. Sharkey, "The Fungibility of Damage Awards: Punitive Damage Caps and Substitution" (FSU College of Law, Law and Economics Paper No. 912256, 2007), http://ssrn.com/abstract=912256 (accessed 7 March 2010).

20. *Pacific Mutual Life Ins. Co. v. Haslip*, 499 U.S. 1, 61 (1991) (O'Connor, J., dissenting).

21. *Cooper Industries v. Leatherman Tool Group*, 532 U.S. 424, n.11 (2001); Adam Liptak, "Foreign Courts Wary of U.S. Punitive Damages," *New York Times*, March 26, 2008, p. A1.

22. The standard citations on punitive damages' doing the work of non-economic damages are Linda L. Schlueter, *Punitive Damages* (Newark, N.J.: LexisNexis, 5th ed., 2005), 8–9, and Note, "Exemplary Damages in the Law of Torts," *Harvard Law Review* 70 (1957): 517, 519–20. For updates, see Thomas B. Colby, "Beyond the Multiple Punishment Problem," *Minnesota Law Review* 87 (2003): 583, 613–37, and especially Anthony J. Sebok, "What Did Punitive Damages Do?" *Chicago-Kent Law Review* 78 (2003): 163, 180–204, which offers the most insightful review of the nineteenth-century punitive damages cases and treatises I have encountered.

23. *Morse v. Auburn & Syracuse R.R.*, 10 Barb. 621, 621 (N.Y. Sup. 1851).

24. See, e.g., *Shaw v. Boston & Worcester R.R.*, 74 Mass. (8 Gray) 45, 82 (1857); *Merrill v. City of St. Louis*, 12 Mo. App. 466 (Mo. 1882); *Lake Shore & M.S. Ry. Co. v. Prentice*, 147 U.S. 101, 107 (1893); Hilliard, *Remedies for Torts*, 252. In the treatise literature, Hilliard was adopting what would become the orthodox view as against the view of Simon Greenleaf, who insisted that punitive damages ought not be available in private tort suits but who held a view of compensatory damages that swept in much of what the coming orthodoxy would label as punitive. For a review of the nineteenth-century controversy, see Sebok, "What Did Punitive Damages Do?", 182–87.

25. *Morse v. Auburn & Syracuse R.R.*, 10 Barb. at 621.

26. *Morse v. Duncan*, 14 Fed. 396, 398 (S.D. Miss. 1882) ("pain of mind"; emphasis added); *Curtin v. Western Union Tel. Co.*, 42 N.Y.S. 1109, 1111 (N.Y.A.D. 1897) ("to the feelings . . . of a jury"); *Canning v. Inhabitants of Williamstown*, 55 Mass. 451, 452 (Mass. 1848) ("part of the injury").

27. *Falzone v. Bush*, 45 N.J. 559 (N.J. 1965); *Dillon v. Legg*, 68 Cal. 2d 728 (Cal. 1968); on the line-drawing problem see, e.g., *Metro-North Commuter Railroad v. Buckley*, 521 U.S. 424 (1997) and *Norfolk & Western Ry. v. Ayers*, 538 U.S. 135 (2003); *Larson v. Chase*, 47 Minn. 307 (Minn. 1891) (interference with corpses); *Bessemer Land & Improvement Co. v. Jenkins*, 111 Ala. 135 (Ala. 1895) and *Meagher v. Driscoll*, 99 Mass. 281 (Mass. 1868) (desecration of burial grounds); Hilliard, *Remedies for Torts*, 301 (per se defamation).

28. *Worster v. Proprietors of the Canal Bridge*, 33 Mass. 541 ($600); *St. Louis, I.M. & S. Ry. Co. v. Robbins*, 21 S.W. 886 (Ark. 1893) ($2,500). Conversions to 2012 dollars calculated using http://www.westegg.com/inflation.

29. Women play an increasingly important role in the history of nineteenth-century tort litigation; see Barbara Young Welke, *Recasting American Liberty: Gender, Race, Law and the Railroad Revolution, 1865–1920* (New York: Cambridge University Press, 2001); Martha Chamallas and Linda Kerber, "Women, Mothers, and the Law of Fright: A History," *Michigan Law Review* 88 (1990): 814; Margo Schlanger, "Injured Women Before Common Law Courts, 1860–1930," *Harvard Women's Law Journal* 21 (1998): 79; and John Fabian Witt, "From Loss of Services to Loss of Support," *Law and Social Inquiry* 25 (2000): 717, 722 (economic losses rare); see generally Viviana Zelizer, *Pricing the Priceless Child: The Changing Social Value of Children* (Princeton, N.J.: Princeton University Press, 1994) (undifferentiated awards); *Shaw v. Boston & Worcester R.R.*, 74 Mass. 45, 81 (Mass. 1857).

30. Historian Barbara Welke argues that the phenomenon of taking standards generated in the nineteenth century for women plaintiffs and making them the general standards is characteristic of twentieth-century tort law more generally. See Welke, *Recasting American Liberty*.

31. Elaine Scarry, *The Body in Pain: The Making and Unmaking of the World* (New York: Oxford University Press, 1985) (common tongue); Louis L. Jaffe, "Damages for Personal Injury: The Impact of Insurance," *Law and Contemporary Problems* 18 (1953): 219, 233 ("the imponderable"). For more on the problems of calculating pain and suffering damages in a contemporary context, see Randall R. Bovbjerg, Frank A. Sloan, and James F. Blumstein, "Valuing Life and Limb in Tort: Scheduling 'Pain and Suffering,'" *Northwestern University Law Review* 83 (1989): 908; see also Ronen Avraham, "Putting a Price on Pain and Suffering Damages: A Critique of the Current Approaches and a Preliminary Proposal for Change," *Northwestern University Law Review* 100 (2006): 87; Mark Geistfeld, "Placing a Price on Pain and Suffering: A Method for Helping Juries Determine Tort Damages for Nonmonetary Injuries," *California Law Review* 83 (1995): 773;

David W. Leebron, "Final Moments: Damages for Pain and Suffering Prior to Death," *New York University Law Review* 64 (1989): 256; Stephan D. Sugarman, "A Comparative Law Look at Pain and Suffering Awards," *DePaul Law Review* 55 (2005–2006): 399. More details on Jaffe's career can be found in his obituary, "Louis L. Jaffe, 90, Noted Legal Scholar," *New York Times*, December 15, 1996, p. 168; Max Weber (G. Roth & C. Wittig, eds.), *Economy & Society* (Berkeley: University of California Press, 1978) 2: 767–68, 814 ("khadi justice").

32. Melvin M. Belli, *Modern Trials: Abridged Edition* (Indianapolis: Bobbs-Merrill, 1963), 636.

33. See Witt, *The Accidental Republic*, 196 (absence of plaintiff lawyer category until twentieth century); Randolph Bergstrom, *Courting Danger: Injury and Law in New York City, 1870–1910* (Ithaca, N.Y.: Cornell University Press, 1992) (same); Louis Anthes, *Lawyers and Immigrants, 1870–1940: A Cultural History* (El Paso, Tex.: LFB Scholarly Publishing, 2003) (same). Two examples of Loring's representing plaintiffs and railroad defendants are *Farwell vs. The Boston and Worcester Rail Road Corporation*, 45 Mass. (4 Metcalf) 49 (1842) and *Shaw v. Boston & Worcester R.R.*, 74 Mass. 45; see also Christopher Tomlins, *Law, Labor, and Ideology in the Early American Republic* (New York: Cambridge University Press, 1993), 348; Witt, *The Accidental Republic*, 61 (immigrants at the bar); Issacharoff and Witt, "The Inevitability of Aggregate Settlement" (repeat players); John Fabian Witt, "Bureaucratic Legalism, American Style," *DePaul Law Review* 56 (2007): 261–91 (same).

34. John Fabian Witt, "The King and the Dean: Melvin Belli, Roscoe Pound, and the Common-Law Nation," in John Fabian Witt, *Patriots and Cosmopolitans: Hidden Histories of American Law* (Cambridge, Mass.: Harvard University Press, 2007), 211–78.

35. Witt, "The King and the Dean," 213, 239.

36. William G. Thomas, *Lawyering for the Railroad: Business, Law, and Power in the South* (Baton Rouge: Louisiana State University Press, 1999) (federal level); Philippe Nonet, *Administrative Justice: Advocacy and Change in a Government Agency* (New York: Russell Sage Foundation, 1969) (state level).

37. Witt, "The King and the Dean," 241–42.

38. For the name changes of the organization, see John Fabian Witt, "First, Rename All the Lawyers," *New York Times*, October 24, 2006, p. A29.

39. Daniel Rodgers, *Atlantic Crossings: Social Politics in a Progressive Age* (Cambridge, Mass.: Harvard University Press, 2000) (workmen's compensation as progressive administration); Witt, "The King and the Dean," 252 (turn to defending common law).

40. Nelson, *Legalist Reformation*, 349–52.

41. *Ibid.*, 186–87 (cultural changes).

42. See the sensationalistic new biography of Belli: Mark Shaw, *Melvin Belli: King of the Courtroom* (Superior, Colo.: Six Dog Books, 2011).

43. *Escola v. Coca Cola Bottling Co. of Fresno*, 24 Cal. 2d 453 (1944) (Traynor, J., concurring) (logic of strict liability); Witt, "The King and the Dean," 246–52

(reputational boost from Pound); *Dillon v. Legg*, 68 Cal.2d 728; Richard S. Jacobsen and Jeffrey R. White, *David v. Goliath: ATLA and the Fight for Everyday Justice* 126–28 (Washington, D.C.: ATLA Press, 2004) (ATLA lawyers involved in *Dillon v. Legg*).
44. Melvin M. Belli, "The Adequate Award," *California Law Review* 39 (1951): 1.
45. *Ibid.*, 1.
46. *Ibid.*, 37, 1 ("mind and body intact"; "counsel's imagination" and "vividness").
47. *Ibid.*, "The Adequate Award," 1.
48. Melvin Belli, *Modern Trials* (Indianapolis: Bobbs-Merrill, 1954). For the latest edition of Belli's photo gallery, see Belli, *Modern Trials: Abridged Edition*, 501–63.
49. Witt, "The King and the Dean," 236–37 (prosthetic leg in butcher paper); Belli, *Modern Trials: Abridged Edition*, 638, 639 ("picture"; prescriptions).
50. On this popular anthropological-linguistic myth, see John Steckley, *White Lies About the Inuit* (Toronto: University of Toronto Press, 2007), chapter three, "Fifty-Two Words for Snow," at 51–76.
51. Melvin Belli, *Modern Trials: Abridged Edition*, 642–45.
52. Melvin Belli, *Modern Damages* (Indianapolis: Bobbs-Merrill, 1959–63).
53. See, e.g., Jeffrey O'Connell and John Linehan, "Neo No-Fault Early Offers: A Workable Compromise Between First and Third-Party Insurance," *Gonzaga Law Review* 41 (2005–2006): 103.
54. Walter F. Dodd, *Administration of Workmen's Compensation* (New York: The Commonwealth Fund, 1936); see also *Report of the National Commission on State Workmen's Compensation* (Washington, D.C.: Government Printing Office, 1972).
55. Kenneth Abraham and Lance Liebman, "Insurance, Social Insurance, and Tort Reform: Toward a New Vision of Compensation for Illness and Injury," *Columbia Law Review* 93 (1993): 75.
56. Nonet, *Administrative Justice*; see also Jerry L. Mashaw and Michael J. Graetz, *True Security: Rethinking American Social Insurance* (New Haven, Conn.: Yale University Press, 1999) (infusion of common law into administration of workmen's compensation); and see John Fabian Witt, "Speedy Fred Taylor and the Ironies of Enterprise Liability," *Columbia Law Review* 103 (2003): 1 (strict liability).
57. William J. Stuntz, "The Political Constitution of Criminal Justice" *Harvard Law Review* 119 (2006): 780; Samuel Issacharoff and Pamela S. Karlan, "The Hydraulics of Campaign Finance Reform," *Texas Law Review* 77 (1999): 1705; see also *FEC v. Wisconsin Right to Life*, 127 S.Ct. 2652 (2007); *McConnell v. FEC*, 540 U.S. 93 (2003) ("Money, like water, will always find an outlet").
58. Robert W. Gordon, "The Elusive Transformation," *Yale Journal of Law and the Humanities* 6 (1994): 137, 139 ("The problem is that Horwitz is too conscientious a historian for his Idea to work. The intricate details of his story keep messing up its architectonic simplicity. In the end, Horwitz's orderly structuralist garden (to switch metaphors) is overrun by its sprawling poststructuralist undergrowth: a luxuriant, unruly proliferation of divergent interpretations"); Nelson, *Legalist Reformation*, 199.

10

An Unexpected Antagonist

Courts, Deregulation, and Conservative Judicial Ideology, 1980–94

REUEL SCHILLER

Generalizing about the work of a historian as prolific as William E. Nelson is a daunting and perhaps futile task. However, Nelson's works have certain methodological and substantive characteristics in common. Methodologically, Nelson's scholarship demonstrates a deep commitment to the importance of detail. In examining the relationship among law, ideology, and society, Nelson's work repeatedly emphasizes the importance of looking not just at constitutions, "blockbuster" cases, and "red-letter" statutes (though, to be sure, he has written compellingly about each). Instead, he has demonstrated how much we can learn by studying the entire fabric of a legal system—the warp and weft of individual, obscure cases that, taken as a whole, tell us more about the relationship between law and society than do the signature cases of a given jurisdiction.

Substantively, Nelson has returned repeatedly to the theme of chaos and conflict within and between legal regimes: for example, the conflicting goals of colonial American law and its conflict with imperial law;[1] the tensions between local autonomy and the nationalizing impulses of the administrative state;[2] the contradictory goals of egalitarianism and libertarianism in postwar liberalism.[3] Though Nelson would, I'm sure, reject such a facile generalization, it's hard not to read his work and come to believe that such conflict is endemic to legal systems. Certainly it is part of the small story that this paper tells: that of the battle between the Reagan administration and the federal judiciary over deregulation during the 1980s.

To the extent that Nelson's work teases the subtle textures of a legal regime from a detailed study of the routine functioning of a legal system, it is difficult to replicate his methodology in a brief essay. Nonetheless, I have tried to do so by taking a narrow legal issue—the judicial response to deregulation—and examining it exhaustively. I have tried to identify and read all the cases between 1981 and 1992 in which federal courts adjudicated issues related to the Reagan and George H. W. Bush administrations' policies of deregulation. A particular narrative emerges from these cases—namely, that federal judges, regardless of their political beliefs, were hostile to each administration's actions.

In the early 1980s, the Reagan administration discovered that it could not pursue much of its deregulatory agenda through legislation because of opposition in Congress. Accordingly, it instituted a policy of "executive deregulation." This policy sought to implement deregulation through the administrative state, using the discretion that the administration claimed it had under a multitude of existing statutes. This strategy was unsuccessful. In case after case, the federal courts rejected the Reagan administration's attempts to do this, even during Reagan's second term when his appointees had come to dominate the federal judiciary.

Having used Nelson's methodology, I was pleased to find that a study of courts and deregulation revealed a story that is consistent with some of his substantive themes. In particular, examining the deregulation cases revealed a host of contradictory impulses within the case law. Judicial objections to executive deregulation stemmed from a number of factors. Some judges found deregulation ideologically objectionable. More interesting, however, were the judges who did not object to deregulation as a matter of ideology but nonetheless struck down the administration's deregulatory actions. For these judges, two other impulses were at work.

First, because executive deregulation required courts to adopt a highly deferential posture toward executive action, courts allowing it would have been forced to endorse administrative law doctrines that transferred a great deal of power from courts to the executive. Conservative judges were unwilling to take this step, particularly in the face of the ham-handed power grab that was obvious in many instances of executive deregulation by the Reagan administration. Their institutional interests trumped their political loyalties.

Second, judicial rejection of executive deregulation illustrates some of the contradictions in late-twentieth-century conservative politics. There is no doubt that Reagan-era conservatives were committed to anti-statist beliefs, from which deregulation naturally flowed. However, modern conservatism also was committed to a variety of mechanisms for controlling what conservatives called "judicial activism." These mechanisms included textualist approaches to statutory interpretation and a commitment to originalism in both constitutional and statutory interpretation. These approaches undermined executive deregulation. The Reagan administration's claims of deregulatory powers under regulatory statutes, while not necessarily implausible, required very generous, expansive readings of those statutes. These readings were available only under theories of statutory interpretation known to initiates as "intentionalism" or "purposivism" that conservative legal thinkers and the people within the Reagan administration who selected candidates for judicial appointment had explicitly rejected. Thus, conflicting impulses within late-twentieth-century conservativism limited the ability of conservatives to put their reform agenda into effect.

*   *   *

The story of deregulation has been told many times.[4] In the 1970s, a broad consensus emerged that certain types of regulation harmed the economy (and consumers in particular) by sheltering important industries from competition. According to these critics, the regulation of transportation, power, and telecommunications, for example, by independent federal commissions simply protected these businesses from the rigors of the marketplace. Consequently, market mechanisms that would have kept prices down and forced companies to innovate had no effect on these industries. By the late 1970s, the political will existed to begin to remove these regulatory barriers to market discipline. The relevant agencies began the deregulatory process, their actions confirmed and encouraged by legislation.

When the Reagan administration took office in 1981, it shifted the emphasis of deregulatory activity from widely disfavored regulatory regimes that inhibited competition (as in the transportation and communications sectors) to regimes that, although they imposed costs on businesses, were widely viewed as having obvious benefits to the public (such as environmental or consumer products safety regulation).[5] This change of emphasis from what economists call "economic" regulation to "social" regulation resulted in a change in the political dynamic surrounding deregulation. The consensus for deregulation evaporated. Consequently, social deregulation would have to be carried out entirely within the executive branch, under existing legislation, without the cooperation of Congress.

The new administration moved rapidly to put executive deregulation into effect.[6] Two days after taking office, President Reagan created the Task Force on Regulatory Relief, chaired by Vice President George H. W. Bush, and ordered it to launch a review of existing and proposed regulations to generate a list of those to be eliminated or scaled back. The following week, Reagan suspended all regulations that had been promulgated by the Carter administration but that had not yet gone into effect. Finally, and most important, in mid-February, Reagan issued Executive Order 12291, which established the institutional mechanisms that would carry out executive deregulation.

E.O. 12291 centralized the regulatory process within the White House.[7] It required executive agencies to submit proposed regulations to a newly established Office of Information and Regulatory Affairs (OIRA) within the Office of Management and Budget (OMB), itself controlled by the White House. These submissions had to be accompanied by a cost/benefit analysis demonstrating how a given regulation maximized social benefits while minimizing the cost to society. OIRA was empowered to delay and ultimately to prevent the issuing of regulations of which it did not approve, subject to an appeal by the agency to the Task Force or to the president directly.

E.O. 12291's emphasis on cost/benefit analysis and centralized control of the administrative processes, as well as its creation of additional roadblocks to the promulgation of regulations, demonstrated the administration's desire to tame the regulatory process and to encourage deregulation. Indeed, one stated purpose of the order was to provide institutional support for the deregulators whom Reagan appointed to key positions at executive agencies.[8] Reagan feared that these appointees would meet resistance to their deregulatory goals from the professional staff at the agencies. OIRA, newly empowered by E.O. 12291, would provide a counterbalance to a bureaucracy that the administration considered predisposed to oppose deregulatory activities. Not only would OIRA prevent Reagan's appointees from being captured by their pro-regulatory staff; it could act as a weapon that those appointees could use to bring the recalcitrant bureaucracy around to the administration's regulatory philosophy.

Having created the institutional mechanisms to promote deregulation, the Reagan administration developed legal arguments to achieve the same ends. The administration's decision to pursue deregulation through executive action—a decision driven by the controversial nature of the regulatory regimes that it wished to limit—gave federal courts a substantial role in the deregulatory process. Barring a constitutional problem, federal courts give Congress essentially unfettered discretion when it legislates. A court will not strike down legislation that is illogical, based on faulty facts, or downright arbitrary. The same cannot be said of executive action. The Administrative Procedure Act (APA) empowers federal courts to review executive actions and measure them against more exacting standards than those required of Congress.[9] As with legislative action, executive action that violates the Constitution will be overturned. However, judicial review of executive action does not stop there. The APA requires courts to ensure that executive action is permitted by the statute pursuant to which the executive proposes to act. Regulating widget production may be a good idea, but if Congress has not given the president the power to regulate widgets, he may not. Additionally, the APA requires courts to review executive action to ensure that it is not arbitrary. Legislatures can act in an illogical, unreasonable fashion and courts will not stop them. Executive agencies that act the same way may have their actions overturned by the judiciary.

The Reagan administration was aware that much of its deregulatory agenda would have to be approved by the courts. Consequently, it formulated a legal strategy that went along with the policy of deregulation. In particular, the Justice Department argued that deregulatory administrative action should be subject to less stringent judicial review than actions that increased the amount of regulation.[10] The theoretical basis for this assertion was simple, if somewhat outdated: Regulation, the administration's lawyers argued, infringed individual liberty, while deregulation increased individual liberty. Consequently, given that the job of courts in the administrative process was to protect individuals from state action, structuring judicial review to make regulation difficult but deregulation easy was consistent with that principle.

Thus, by the middle of 1981, with the Task Force, OIRA, and E.O. 12291 in place, Reagan appointees ensconced at the agencies, and legal arguments in favor of deregulation developed, the process of deregulation began. The number of new rules being issued dropped dramatically during the administration's first year, and the agencies began to take action on the regulations targeted by the Task Force. Only one obstacle to deregulation remained: the federal judiciary. As it turned out, this obstacle was a substantial one. Throughout the Reagan administration's first term, the federal courts, carrying out their responsibilities under the APA, reviewed dozens of instances of executive deregulation.[11] In doing so, the courts handed the deregulators defeat after defeat.

*   *   *

In Reagan's first four years in office, only a few instances of social deregulation survived the scrutiny of the federal courts. Indeed, the most politically visible of the administration's attempts to deregulate—its attacks on the National Highway Transit Safety Administration (NHTSA) and the Occupational Safety and Health Administration (OSHA)—were overturned by the U.S. Court of Appeals for the Circuit of the District of Columbia, the circuit court that, by virtue of its location, heard the lion's share of appeals concerning the actions of federal agencies.[12] Attempts to rein in the similarly disfavored Environmental Protection Administration (EPA) also met judicial resistance,[13] as did miscellaneous deregulatory rulemakings with respect to wage and hour laws,[14] alcoholic beverage labeling,[15] and smoking prohibitions.[16] More surprising, even the Reagan administration's attempts to further economic deregulation met judicial resistance. Even though this resistance was not as all-encompassing as with respect to social deregulation, throughout the early 1980s, federal circuit courts rejected certain elements of transportation, power, and telecommunications deregulation.[17]

Part of the problem the deregulators encountered was ideological. In the early 1980s, the D.C. Circuit was dominated by judges such as J. Skelly Wright, Spottswood Robinson, Ruth Bader Ginsburg, Abner

Mikva, and Patricia Wald, all Democratic appointees whose politics may have predisposed them to view deregulation with hostility. Additionally, the Reagan administration's initial attempts at deregulation were ham-handed, at best—deregulation by "legal politicians" rather than "legal craftsmen," to take Peter Irons's language from his study of New Deal lawyers.[18] Indeed, the foot soldiers of the "Reagan Revolution" had much in common with the "boys with their hair ablaze" who populated the agencies during the early days of the Franklin D. Roosevelt administration. Both groups possessed a messianic conviction that their boss had been put into office with such a resounding mandate for change that legal formalities could be dispensed with in carrying out such change. Managerial talent, technical expertise, or legal ability were not the skills that Reagan sought in the deregulators he appointed to the agencies. Indeed, when it came to qualifications, Reagan advisor Lyn Nofziger stated the administration's basis for its appointments with admirable bluntness: "As far as I'm concerned, anyone who supported Reagan is competent."[19] As a result of this approach, the agencies were populated with ideological true believers with little or no ability or desire to thread their way through the complicated legal constraints on administrative action.

Indeed, in many of the cases from Reagan's first term, courts overturned agency actions because the agency gave no explanation for its decisions to deregulate other than a "general desire for a bare minimum of regulation."[20] This lack of a substantive explanation for deregulatory activity occurred frequently in the early years of the Reagan administration. For example, when the Bureau of Alcohol, Tobacco, and Firearms (now the Bureau of Alcohol, Tobacco, Firearms and Explosives) revoked a Carter administration regulation requiring ingredient labeling on alcoholic beverages, it did so without stating why its previous reasons for issuing the regulation were invalid. It did not refute the scientific data upon which the original regulation was based, nor did it respond specifically to comments it received that supported the old regulation. Instead, invoking E.O. 12291, it simply stated that the cost of the regulation outweighed any health benefits that the labeling could provide.[21]

Similarly, in 1981, the Civil Aeronautics Board revoked regulations limiting smoking on domestic flights without any explanation and without responding to a number of alternatives suggested to the agency during the rulemaking process.[22] Indeed, failure to address reasonable alternatives to deregulation seemed to be standard operating procedure in the Reagan administration. When Secretary of Labor Raymond J. Donovan deregulated the "homework" segment of the textile industry, he did so without considering a number of ways to enforce the Fair Labor Standards Act while at the same time achieving his goal of increasing employment opportunities in the industry.[23] Similarly, when NHTSA revoked the Carter administration's passive-restraint requirements for motor vehicles, it spent nine pages in the *Federal Register* explaining why detachable seatbelts would not increase passenger safety, while rejecting requirements for airbags and nondetachable seatbelts with cursory comments in a single paragraph.[24]

The federal courts made mincemeat of these administrative actions and others similar to them, because the errors that the agencies made were so elementary. When Congress required regulation regardless of cost, an executive order that imposed cost/benefit analysis was "an insufficient basis for [an agency] to disregard [its] statutory duties. . . ."[25] The political preferences of the administration could not relieve agencies of their duty to disclose the factual bases for their conclusions and to engage in "reasoned consideration of competing objective and alternatives."[26] If the agencies had offered some explanation why they were deregulating or if they had responded to the reasonable alternatives suggested by various interest groups, then these might have been more difficult cases. But Reagan's crusading deregulators refused to be distracted by the niceties of administrative law. The courts did not punish Reagan's deregulators for poor reasoning. They punished them for not reasoning at all.

Consider the NHTSA's elimination of the passive-restraint requirement.[27] While running for president, Reagan had repeatedly asserted that one way to help the American automobile industry out of its desperate financial straits was to ease its regulatory burdens.[28] Consequently, one of his first acts on taking office was to revoke the Carter administration's regulations requiring passive restraints in automobiles. These regulations would have required automakers to install one of three types of passive restraints: airbags, spooling seatbelts, or detachable automatic seatbelts. As previously noted, the NHTSA revoked the standard by focusing on the failings of detachable automatic seatbelts without addressing the possibility of requiring airbags or spooling seat-belts instead. The Supreme Court unanimously rejected the agency's action under such circumstances:

> Given the effectiveness ascribed to airbag technology by the agency, the mandate of the act to achieve traffic safety would suggest that the logi-cal response to the faults of detachable seatbelts would be to require the installation of airbags. . . . [T]he agency not only did not require compli-ance through airbags, it also did not even consider the possibility in its 1981 rulemaking. Not one sentence of its rulemaking statement discusses the airbags-only option.[29]

Indeed, it appeared to the Court that the only reason the agency addressed the issue of detachable belts was that they were the device that auto manufacturers chose to install. "[T]hat the regulated industry has eschewed [airbags] . . . hardly constitutes cause to revoke [the air-bag requirement]."[30]

The passive-restraints case—known as *Motor Vehicle Manufacturers Association v. State Farm Mutual Automobile Insurance Co.*—was the Reagan administration's deregulatory Waterloo. Its loss on the substan-tive issue was decisive—an increasingly conservative Supreme Court had rejected a deregulatory action that was, symbolically, at least, at the center of the Reagan administration's drive for deregulation. Even more devastating for the administration was the case's procedural hold-ing that courts should review decisions to deregulate with at least the same vigor they applied to reviewing decisions to regulate. The case was the one in which the administration had asked the Supreme Court to endorse its theory that deregulatory activities should be more leniently reviewed than agency decisions to regulate. The Supreme Court would have none of this. The Court acknowledged that agencies were allowed to change or even to eliminate their regulations, but it rejected the idea that the direction of the change should determine the intensity of judi-cial review:

> [T]he forces of change do not always or necessarily point in the direction of deregulation. In the abstract, there is no more reason to presume that

changing circumstances require the rescission of prior action, instead of a revision in or even the extension of current regulation. If Congress established a presumption from which judicial review should start, that presumption—contrary to petitioners' views—is not against safety regulation, but against changes in current policy that are not justified by the rulemaking record.[31]

Such language was the final nail in the deregulatory campaign's coffin. Reagan's administrators had carried out much of their deregulatory business with such disregard for the forms of administrative law that deregulation could survive judicial scrutiny only under a substantially reduced standard of review. What the *Motor Vehicle Manufacturers* case represented was the opposite: "hard look review," as administrative-law cognoscenti called it. Courts would be particularly vigorous in reviewing agency actions in circumstances where the agency was reversing itself.

Thus, by June 1983, when the Supreme Court decided *Motor Vehicle Manufacturers*, deregulation's best days had passed. Political and legal defeats had resulted in little or no actual deregulation. Additionally, the administration had discovered that political support for elimination of social regulations was less widespread than it had expected. Indeed, after scandals touched two of Reagan's most ideologically potent deregulators—Anne Gorsuch Burford, administrator of the EPA, and Secretary James Watt of the Department of the Interior—the political operatives within the White House began to view deregulatory initiatives as a political liability.[32] Consequently, the Task Force of Regulatory Relief disbanded and deregulation ceased to be a priority for the Reagan administration.

* * *

That deregulation was no longer a priority in Reagan's second term does not mean that no deregulation cases arose after 1984.[33] Several cases from the first term dragged into the late 1980s and the administration was not averse to putting deregulatory policies into effect when it had a chance, albeit in a more piecemeal fashion than during the halcyon days of 1981 and 1982. Indeed, in 1984 and 1985, the Reagan administration won two legal victories in the Supreme Court, each of which suggested that the federal judiciary might be embracing a more positive view of deregulation.

The first of these was *Chevron v. National Resources Defense Counsel*,[34] decided in June 1984. Destined to become one of a handful of canonical administrative law cases, *Chevron* stemmed from a mildly deregulatory EPA rulemaking. At issue was whether the Clean Air Act required each source of air pollution within a factory to meet the Act's standards or whether only the total emissions for the factory had to meet the standards, thereby allowing newer, cleaner sources to compensate for older, unmodified, dirtier sources. The EPA had issued a rule imposing the latter standard, but the D.C. Circuit had set aside the regulation, holding that it was an impermissible interpretation of the Clean Air Act.[35] A unanimous Supreme Court reversed the Court of Appeals.

What made *Chevron* so significant for executive deregulation was not the small victory for market-based environmental protection that resulted from the Court's substantive holding. Instead, its significance was the Court's stated basis for that decision. The Court's unanimous decision held that if a statute was unclear with respect to a particular legal issue (in *Chevron*, whether the definition of a "stationary source" of air pollution had to include each smokestack rather than the entire factory), then courts should defer to any reasonable executive interpretation of that legal issue. When congressional intent was vague, courts owed executive interpretations of a statute considerable deference. This holding appeared to be a dramatic windfall for would-be deregulators in the executive branch. After all, regulatory statutes were frequently vague, delegating broad authority to the executive. After *Chevron*, the judiciary's diminished role might prevent them from checking executive interpretations of statutes that would allow the introduction into regulatory regimes of cost/benefit analysis or other deregulatory mechanisms.

The Reagan administration's second victory was in an unusual case called *Heckler v. Cheney*,[36] decided in early 1985, nine months after *Chevron*. Cheney, an inmate on death row, had requested that the Food and Drug Administration enforce the provisions of the Food, Drug, and Cosmetic Act that prohibited "unapproved use of an approved drug."

He argued that because the drugs used for lethal injections had never specifically been approved for such uses by the FDA, the agency should commence enforcement actions to prevent states from using them for executions. The FDA refused to do so, saying that its limited resources did not permit it to pursue every unapproved use. Instead, it initiated such proceedings only when the unapproved use constituted "a serious danger to public health or a blatant scheme to defraud." The D.C. Circuit ordered the FDA to begin an enforcement action and, as in *Chevron*, the Supreme Court reversed. .

Once again, the significance of this case was not its specific outcome—which was agreed to by all nine members of the Court—but in the logic of Justice William H. Rehnquist's majority opinion. Decisions not to commence enforcement actions, the Court held, are presumptively unreviewable. Courts must defer to an agency's decision not to begin an adjudication. For the deregulators within the Reagan administration, *Heckler v. Cheney* was another victory. After all, even if an agency could not undo a regulation through a rulemaking, it could simply decline to enforce a regulation that remained on the books. Additionally, the seven members of the Court who joined Justice Rehnquist's opinion accepted, at least in this context, the one-way ratchet that the justices had rejected in *Motor Vehicle Manufacturers*: Judicial review of agency inaction could be reduced or eliminated because the deregulatory posture was the least threatening to individual liberty. "[W]e note," Rehnquist wrote, "that when an agency refuses to act it generally does not exercise its *coercive* power over an individual's liberty or property rights, and thus does not infringe upon areas that courts often are called upon to protect."[37]

Thus, by early 1985, it appeared that the federal courts might be easing up on judicial review of deregulation. Indeed, that is how contemporary observers interpreted *Chevron* and *Heckler*.[38] Furthermore, by the end of 1985, the D.C. Circuit had been ideologically transformed by Ronald Reagan. Many of Reagan's appointees to the D.C. Circuit have since become household names, paragons of a conservative legal worldview: Robert Bork, Kenneth Starr, Antonin Scalia. His other appointees (as of 1986: Laurence Silberman, James Buckley, Stephen Williams, and Douglas Ginsburg) may be less well known, but each was a reliable soldier in the Reagan revolution.[39] Surely with increasingly friendly doctrines and ideologically sympathetic judges populating the bench of the Circuit Court that heard the bulk of appeals of administrative action, the Reagan administration's attempts at executive deregulation might be considerably more successful. Such turned out not to be the case.

Reagan-appointed judges struck down attempts to deregulate natural gas markets,[40] shipping markets,[41] advertising on children's television,[42] animal protective regulations,[43] and pesticide limitations on imported produce,[44] as well as the use of cost/benefit analysis in licensing nuclear power plants and in setting clean air standards.[45] The new deference to agency action suggested by *Chevron* did not seem to make its way into judicial review of the Reagan administration's deregulatory actions.[46] Indeed, the deregulatory cases citing *Chevron* predominantly involved economic deregulation under legislation that explicitly authorized deregulation.[47] All in all, between 1985 and 1992, the D.C. Circuit struck down twenty out of twenty-nine deregulatory administrative actions.[48]

Just as *Chevron*'s potential as a deregulatory tool went unfulfilled, so too did *Heckler v. Cheney*'s potential.[49] Federal judges read *Heckler* narrowly, repeatedly crafting exceptions to the presumption in favor of unreviewability that *Heckler* created. Additionally, courts refused to extend that presumption to rulemaking. Unlike the decision to commence an enforcement action, a decision by an agency not to issue regulations was presumptively reviewable. Indeed, the D.C. Circuit made something of a habit of compelling reluctant administrators to issue regulations on a diverse range of topics including shipping fees,[50] agricultural sanitation,[51] animal protection,[52] and formaldehyde exposure standards.[53] Thus, in the end, *Heckler* was of little solace to those within the administration who sought to promote deregulation through inaction. Just as the courts were reluctant to allow the Reagan administration to undo social regulations directly, they were also disinclined to allow it to do so through neglect.

This is not to say that, as in the early 1980s, the D.C. Circuit never upheld an instance of social deregulation. The alcohol-labeling regulation made its way back to the D.C. Circuit by 1986 and it was upheld,[54] as were some aspects of power and transportation deregulation.[55] Similarly, the court upheld deregulatory rulemakings in the areas of used car sales,[56] vinyl chloride emissions,[57] automobile bumper performance standards,[58] and radio station licensing requirements.[59] Yet, the D.C Circuit's reaction to most of the administration's deregulatory action during the second half of the 1980s was decidedly tepid. During Reagan's first term, judicial hostility could be explained by a collision between profoundly ideological administrators, disinclined to follow the formal requirements of administrative law, and a D.C. Circuit dominated by Democrat-appointed judges. The deregulation cases of the second term cannot be explained that way. Reagan appointees dominated the D.C. Circuit, and many of the administration's most ideological administrators had been replaced by less controversial people with a greater degree of managerial and technical competence.[60] Why then the continued resistance?

*   *   *

Obviously, political ideology was not the cause of this resistance. By 1985 Reagan's appointees dominated the D.C. Circuit, and several of them had explicitly stated a policy preference for deregulation.[61] Additionally, it is possible to identify only a few deregulation cases in which political ideology seems to have made a difference. Of the twenty-nine deregulation cases that the D.C. Circuit heard between 1985 and 1992, seven generated dissents, five of them breaking along ideological lines.[62] Of these cases, two were only partial dissents, with a third on a fairly small issue.[63] Thus, in the vast majority of cases, the Democratic and the Republican appointees on the D.C. Circuit agreed in their judgments about the Reagan administration's deregulatory actions. Accordingly, the reasons for judicial hostility toward deregulation must lie outside the realm of simple partisan ideology.

One explanation for the D.C. Circuit's hostility toward executive deregulation is that it was driven by institutional interests that transcended the more obvious ideological ones. Federal judges, regardless of their political ideology, have shown a consistent interest in defending their own power against the encroachments of the administrative state.[64] Such institutional self-interest suggests that decisions limiting judicial authority, such as *Chevron* and *Heckler*, should be read narrowly. After all, interpreted expansively, each decision would have transferred a great deal of power from courts to agencies.

278 << REUEL SCHILLER

Indeed, Judges Starr and Scalia both downplayed the significance of *Chevron*, suggesting that standard techniques of statutory construction (engaged in by judges, of course) would render the meaning of most statutes clear, thereby relieving courts of the obligation to defer to agencies.[65] More significantly, despite the Supreme Court's clear instructions, the D.C. Circuit was singularly unresponsive to *Chevron's* call for increased deference. The year after *Chevron*, the D.C. Circuit actually affirmed a lower percentage of agency actions than the year before the case was decided (52.6 percent as compared to 58.6 percent). This trend continued through the rest of the 1980s.[66] By way of contrast, the average affirmance rate for all federal courts of appeal increased more than 10 percent in 1985 and remained higher in seven of the nine circuit courts based outside the District of Columbia.[67] The D.C. Circuit, claiming a special competence in administrative law and a special role in the administrative process, refused to give up that role even while other courts, with no particular institutional commitment to administrative law, acquiesced to the Supreme Court's instructions without complaint.[68]

This denigration of *Chevron* (and the concomitant embrace of "hard look" review) caused trouble for executive deregulation, because deregulation under existing statutes often required strained readings of those statutes. Indeed, the consensus among the members of the D.C. Circuit on the deregulation cases was remarkable. By the mid-1980s, the Circuit had gained a reputation for being particularly polarized politically.[69] However, this polarization was simply not apparent with respect to deregulation cases.

Another factor driving this judicial consensus against deregulation was that, even in the late 1980s, many of the Reagan administration's attempts at deregulation were not particularly skillful. For example, in *Independent U.S. Tanker Owner's Committee v. Dole*, Judge Bork took the Department of Transportation to task for trying to deregulate entrance into the United States' domestic shipping market (one effect of which would be to reduce dramatically the size of the United States' international shipping capacity) in the face of a statute designed to "foster the development and encourage the maintenance of an American merchant marine. . . ."[70] When confronted with the clash between the agency's policy and the goals of the statute, the agency stated, with admirable candor, that "'it would not be appropriate to let the . . . objectives reflected in the Act stand in the way of achieving the Act's broader policy mandates, including promoting a more competitive and efficient merchant fleet.'"[71] Unfortunately for the agency, as far as Judge Bork and his colleagues were concerned, "promoting a more competitive and efficient merchant fleet" was "not among the objective specified in the Act."[72] The agency was simply "not free to substitute new goals in place of statutory objectives. . . ."[73] Reagan appointees also wrote decisions overturning attempts to deregulate pesticides[74] and vinyl chloride[75] for the same reason—rejecting agencies' attempts to substitute deregulatory policy preferences for the explicitly stated intent of the statute.

Trying to wring deregulatory interpretations out of statutes that were clearly regulatory in purpose was only one problem to which Reagan's appointees to the D.C. Circuit objected. There were also cases in which agencies failed to provide any reason for deregulation at all, even if the relevant statute might allow it. "Far be it from us to demand long-winded tiresome explanations. But the Commission's barebones incantation of two abbreviated rationales cannot do service as the requisite 'reasoned basis' for altering its long established policy," wrote Judge Starr in a case overturning the Federal Communications Commission's attempt to remove advertising restrictions for children's television shows.[76] In six separate cases, Reagan appointees to the D.C. Circuit vacated elements of the administration's attempts at natural gas deregulation because of the Federal Energy Regulatory Commission's disinclination to explain its reasoning.[77] As Judge Scalia wrote:

> It would be an exaggeration to say that this petition for review has required us to evaluate whether the Commission had, if not the better side, at least the reasonable side, of the argument. . . . On a number of obviously significant points . . . there is simply no argument to evaluate: the Commission proceeded on its course with no comment, or with comment that was patently unresponsive.[78]

Similar unresponsiveness plagued Reagan administration attempts to lessen regulatory burdens on the nuclear power industry,[79] to adopt lower standards for both formaldehyde and ethylene oxide exposure,[80] and to refuse to issue regulations on agricultural workplace safety and animal cruelty.[81] Indeed, even in cases where the agency provided a more detailed explanation for their deregulatory action, the D.C. Circuit's commitment to "hard look" review made judicial acceptance of agency action less likely.[82]

The final reason for the federal judiciary's hostility toward executive deregulation stems from conservative judicial ideology itself. The judiciary's animosity toward deregulation continued even as Republican appointees came to dominate the D.C. Circuit because conservative judicial ideology dictated approaches to statutory interpretation that were particularly unsympathetic to attempts at executive deregulation. Within the Reagan administration, conservative legal ideology was most frequently articulated in the context of constitutional interpretation. Reagan pledged to replace "activist" judges who, he claimed, used the Constitution to further their own policy preferences with judges who would interpret the meaning of the Constitution according to its "original intent."[83] Additionally, conservative legal thinkers, both within the administration and outside it, developed a theory of statutory interpretation that similarly sought to limit judicial discretion in nonconstitutional cases.

In particular, these thinkers, who included Reagan appointees to the D.C. Circuit Scalia, Starr, and Buckley, as well as Ninth Circuit Judge Alex Kozinski and Seventh Circuit Judge Frank Easterbrook, advocated using formal, textualist approaches to statutory interpretation.[84] Judges, they argued, had fallen into the habit of determining legislative intent by looking at too broad a range of materials. By the time a judge had looked at statutory language, as well as at all the possible sources of legislative history (committee reports, statements by the legislation's drafters, colloquies among legislators or between legislators and witnesses at hearings), that judge could find whatever meaning he or she wanted to find. As Starr wrote: "[O]ne generally finds in the legislative history only that for which one is looking."[85] Scalia, as usual, was more piquant: "[U]nder the guise or even self-delusion of pursuing unexpressed legislative interests, common-law judges will in fact pursue their own objectives and desires. . . ."[86]

The solution to this problem, according to conservative legal thinkers, was for judges to forsake dependence on legislative history and focus exclusively on the "plain meaning" or "actual meaning" of the statute. This focus, they believed, would prevent judges from replacing the will of the democratically elected legislature with their own policy preferences. Indeed, for its most committed acolytes, textual, plain-meaning interpretation of statutes was required by the Constitution. When judges rummaged through a statute's legislative history to determine its "purpose" or "intent," they were upsetting the constitutionally ordained distribution of powers among the three branches of government by inferring statutory meaning from a sentiment that had not been approved by both houses of Congress and the president.[87] By the end of Reagan's second term, this approach to statutory construction had become the official policy of the administration.[88] Yet as the administration engaged in executive deregulation, its commitment to plain-meaning interpretation would prove a severe obstacle to that goal. The conservative judges' rejection of legislative history and their preference for a textualist mode of statutory interpretation caused problems for executive deregulators in any case in which they wished to deregulate under the authority of an obviously regulatory statute.

Consider, for example, administrative deregulation of certain aspects of municipal waste disposal. Throughout the 1980s, environmental groups fought a running battle with the EPA over the proper disposal of municipal waste. At issue was whether the ash produced by municipal incinerators should be disposed of as toxic waste—and therefore be highly regulated by the Resource Conservation and Recovery Act (RCRA)—or as nontoxic waste, subject to considerably less regulation. The dispute focused on household waste. Could a municipality assume that the ash from incinerated household waste was nontoxic even though such waste might contain toxic trash such as batteries and cleaning fluid?

The EPA's instincts were deregulatory.[89] If the agency declared that the ash produced by municipal incinerators was toxic, the cost of its disposal would increase dramatically. Either this cost would be passed along to businesses and consumers, or cities would simply stop incinerating household waste and instead dispose of it in already overused landfills. Furthermore, to the extent that incineration generated energy, the agency believed it should be encouraged as a form of recycling. By limiting the extent to which the disposal of household waste was regulated, the agency would achieve these policy goals. Environmental groups begged to differ. If the ash that emerged from municipal incinerators was toxic, the RCRA required stringent regulation, regardless of the source of the waste.

In the 1980s, the circuit courts split on this issue. The Second Circuit held that though the text of the RCRA itself was unclear on this issue, its legislative history revealed congressional intent to exclude from the Act's requirements the ash derived from incinerating municipal waste.[90] The Seventh Circuit addressed the same issue seven months later and reached the opposite result. The court, after reviewing the legislative history, dismissed it; quoting Justice Scalia and his fellow textualist Judge Easterbrook, the court noted that legislative history was "unreliable evidence" of the meaning of a statute.[91] Instead, the court turned to the literal language of the statute, which it believed explicitly extended the RCRA's coverage to the ash.

Thus, when in 1994 the Supreme Court resolved the split between the two circuit courts, it had to choose not only between outcomes (more or less regulation) but also between methods of statutory interpretation. Should the Court focus on the RCRA's broad purposes: encouraging resource recovery and preventing environmental contamination? Or, should it focus on the specific language of the statute, which the Seventh Circuit thought unambiguous? For Justice Scalia, whose majority opinion struck down the EPA's deregulatory rule, this was an easy case. The "plain meaning" of the statute did not exclude the ash that a municipal facility produced.[92] Whereas the facility would not be deemed to be "treating, storing, or disposing of" hazardous waste, the statute said nothing about the waste that it "generated."[93] Accordingly, if the incinerator generated ash, that ash would be subject to regulation as a hazardous material.

Justice John Paul Stevens dissented. The statutory language, he asserted, was much more ambiguous than Scalia allowed. On the other hand, the legislative history of the Act, as embodied in the Senate committee's report on the legislation, explicitly stated Congress's desire to exclude municipal ash from regulation.[94] Furthermore, Justice Stevens noted, excluding the ash from regulation would serve at least two of the broad purposes of the RCRA: to conserve landfill space and to encourage the recovery of energy and resources from waste.

The contrast between Scalia's and Stevens's methods of interpretation was obvious. Scalia derived congressional intent from the absence of a single word in the statute. If Congress had meant to exclude materials generated by the incinerator, it would have used the word "generate" in the statute. Stevens, by contrast, was willing to look at the Act's legislative history and its broader statutory purposes. Congress had said what it was planning to do when it passed the statute. Additionally, the agency's interpretation of the Act furthered the RCRA's statutory goals. Accordingly, Stevens stated that the deregulation should be allowed, even if doing so stretched the actual language of the statute. Stevens's use of legislative history and his focus on the Act's overall purpose were anathema to Scalia. The Senate committee report might have stated an intent to exclude "generated" waste from regulation, but the language of the statute did not: "[I]t is the statute and not the Committee Report, which is the authoritative expression of the law. . . . 'Why should we, then, rely upon a single word in a committee report that did not result in legislation? Simply put, we shouldn't.'"[95]

The dispute over municipal waste was not the only instance in which textualist approaches to statutory interpretation interfered with deregulatory impulses. When the FCC attempted to eliminate tariff-filing requirements for telecommunications companies, conservative jurists (Silberman on the D.C. Circuit and Scalia on the Supreme Court) forbade it. In Scalia's words, both judges had "considerable sympathy" for the agency's deregulatory goals.[96] However, the text of the Communications Act stated that telephone companies "shall" file their rates. This was "the language of command."[97] Although the Act allowed the Commission to "modify" the tariff-filing requirements, the word "modify" necessarily connoted small, incremental changes, not wholesale detariffing.[98] The dissenters argued that detariffing would serve the broader purpose of the Act—assuring reasonably priced phone service—by promoting competition. According to the majority, that fact was irrelevant. It was concerned with fidelity to the text, not with some broader, easily manipulated understanding of what Congress intended. Indeed, even before this telecommunications case, the Supreme Court had rejected similar detariffing initiatives at the Interstate Commerce Commission using the same textualist logic.[99] A dissent, based on the statute's purpose, was summarily rejected by Justice Scalia: "[The Court's decision is] based not on 'the regulatory scheme as a whole,' . . . by which [the dissent] appears to mean the regulatory climate within which the statute then operated . . . but rather on the text of the statute."[100]

* * *

Irony can be a satisfying theme to draw from a historical narrative. Indeed, Nelson's substantive theme of contradiction within legal systems can frequently lead to ironic outcomes: Liberalism runs aground on its own libertarian foundations, or the emergence of illiberal formalism in the nineteenth century as a response to the profoundly illiberal *Dred Scott* decision.[101] The story of courts and deregulation has its own obvious irony: conservative judges using a technique of statutory interpretation espoused by conservatives to strike down the actions of a conservative administration. Beyond this irony, two things make the story of courts and deregulation particularly worth telling. First of all, rarely can you find such an explicit connection between the rise of a specific intellectual movement—the "new textualism"—and specific doctrinal changes. One need not speculate about whether changing "patterns of legal thought"[102] cause doctrinal changes when the actual purveyors of the thought are placed on the courts. Second, the story nicely illustrates how courts impose their own autonomous interests on the administrative state in a manner that warps and, in this case, inhibits the policy goals of political and administrative actors. Conservative judges held fast to their own interests: preserving the power of the federal courts over the administrative state, and promoting a particular method of statutory interpretation. These autonomous interests were strong enough to undermine deregulatory goals that coincided with their political preferences. Thus, they became surprising antagonists to deregulation because they preferred other values that were also part of the late-twentieth-century conservative movement.

ACKNOWLEDGMENTS
My thanks to Ash Bhagwat, Barry Cushman, and Norman Williams, each of whom read a draft of this article and provided me with thoughtful comments. Kate Feng's research assistance was fantastic. Thanks also to Daniel Hulsebosch and R. B. Bernstein for both inviting me to participate in this conference and for their work putting together this volume. Finally, my thanks to Bill Nelson for all his help, both intellectual and professional, throughout my career.

NOTES

1. William E. Nelson, *Americanization of the Common Law: The Impact of Legal Change on Massachusetts Society, 1760–1830* (Cambridge, Mass.: Harvard University Press, 1975).

2. William E. Nelson, *The Roots of American Bureaucracy, 1830–1900* (Cambridge, Mass.: Harvard University Press, 1982).

3. William E. Nelson, *The Legalist Reformation: Law, Politics, and Ideology in New York, 1920–1980* (Chapel Hill: University of North Carolina Press, 2001).

4. Barry D. Friedman, *Regulation in the Reagan-Bush Era: The Eruption of Presidential Influence* (Pittsburgh: University of Pittsburgh Press, 1995), 7–105; George C. Eads and Michael Fix, *The Reagan Regulatory Strategy: An Assessment* (Washington, D.C.: Urban Institute Press, 1984); Charles Noble, *Liberalism at Work: The Rise and Fall of OSHA* (Philadelphia: Temple University Press, 1986), 99–175; Chester A. Newland, "Executive Office Policy Apparatus: Enforcing the Reagan Policy Agenda," in Lester M. Salamon and Michael S. Lund, eds. *The Reagan Presidency and the Governing of America* (Washington, D.C.: Urban Institute Press, 1984); Lawrence E. Lynn Jr., "The Reagan Administration and the Renitent Bureaucracy," in Salamon and Lund, eds., *The Reagan Presidency*; Martha Derthick and Paul J. Quirk, *The Politics of Deregulation* (Washington, D.C.: Brookings Institution Press, 1985); Lou Cannon, *President Reagan: The Role of a Lifetime* (New York: Simon and Schuster, 1991), 819–28; Thomas K. McCraw, *Prophets of Regulation* (Cambridge, Mass.: Harvard University Press, 1984), 222–99; Joseph D. Kearney and Thomas W. Merrill, "The Great Transformation of Regulated Industries Law," *Columbia Law Review* 98 (1998): 1323–409.

5. Isabel V. Sawhill, "Reaganomics in Retrospect," in John L. Palmer, ed., *Perspectives on the Reagan Years* (Washington, D.C.: Urban Institute Press, 1986), 104.

6. Eads and Fix, *The Reagan Regulatory Strategy*, 2–3, 108–12; Noble, *Liberalism at Work*, 154–61; Friedman, *Regulation in the Reagan-Bush Era*, 31–58; Newland, "Executive Office Policy Apparatus," 162–63.

7. Elena Kagan, "Presidential Administration," *Harvard Law Review* 114 (2001): 2245, 2277–80; Friedman, *Regulation in the Reagan-Bush Era*, 31–39, 43–49.

8. Friedman, *Regulation in the Reagan-Bush Era*, 49–52; Eads and Fix, *The Reagan Regulatory Strategy*, 139–45. For a contemporary description of the relationship between OIRA and Reagan's appointees to the agencies, see Timothy B. Clark, "OMB to Keep Its Regulatory Powers in Reserve in Case Agencies Lag," *National Journal* (March 14, 1981), 424–29.

9. 5 U.S.C. sections 551 et seq. Judicial review of administration actions is authorized by sections 701–6.

10. Merrick B. Garland, "Deregulation and Judicial Review," *Harvard Law Review* 98 (1985): 505, 513–20, 542.

11. Garland lists all the deregulation cases from Reagan's first term in "Deregulation and Judicial Review," at 540nn. 185, 186, 541n. 188.

12. *State Farm Mutual Auto Insurance Co. v. Dep't of Transportation*, 680 F.2d 206 (D.C.Cir. 1982); *Public Citzien v. Steed*, 733 F.2d 93 (D.C.Cir. 1984); *Public Citizen Health Research Group v. Auchter*, 702 F.2d 1151 (D.C.Cir. 1983).

13. *National Resources Defense Council v. EPA*, 683 F.2d 752 (3d Cir. 1982); *Environmental Defense Fund v. Gorsuch*, 713 F.2d 803 (D.C.Cir. 1983).

14. *ILGWU v. Donovan*, 722 F.2d 795 (D.C.Cir. 1983).

15. *Center for Science in the Public Interest v. Department of the Treasury*, 573 F.Supp. 1151 (D.D.C. 1983).

16. *Action on Smoking and Health v. Civil Aeronautics Board*, 699 F.2d 1209 (D.C.Cir. 1983).

17. *Wheaton Van Lines v. ICC*, 671 F.2d 520, 527 (D.C.Cir. 1982); *National Ass'n of Broadcasters v. FCC*, 740 F.2d 1190, 1199–1206 (D.C.Cir. 1984); *Coal Exporters Ass'n v. United States*, 745 F.2d 76, 95–99 (D.C.Cir. 1984); *Global Van Lines v. ICC*, 714 F.2d 1290, 1291 (5th Cir. 1983).

18. Peter H. Irons, *The New Deal Lawyers* (Princeton, N.J.: Princeton University Press, 1982), 5–6.

19. Quoted in Friedman, *Regulation in the Reagan-Bush Era*, 50.

20. *Action on Smoking and Health*, 699 F.2d at 1217.

21. *Center for Science in the Public Interest*, 573 F.Supp at 1174–78; 46 Fed Reg. 55,094 (1981).

22. *Action on Smoking and Health*, 699 F.2d 1216–17; 46 Fed Reg. 45,936 (1981).

23. *ILGWU v. Donovan*, 722 F.2d 795 (D.C.Cir. 1983).

24. 46 Fed. Reg. 53, 419–27 (1981).

25. *Center for Science in the Public Interest*, 573 F.Supp. at 1175.

26. *Action on Smoking and Health*, 699 F.2d at 1216.

27. *Motor Vehicle Manufacturers Association v. State Farm*, 463 U.S. 29 (1983).

28. Jerry L. Mashaw and David L. Harfst, *The Struggle for Auto Safety* (Cambridge, Mass.: Harvard University Press, 1990), 207–8.

29. *Motor Vehicles Manufacturers Association*, 463 U.S. at 48 (1983).

30. *Id.* at 49.

31. *Id.* at 42.

32. Eads and Fix, *The Reagan Regulatory Strategy*, 3–6, 177–79; Charles Fried, *Order and Law: Arguing the Reagan Revolution: A Firsthand Account* (New York: Simon and Schuster, 1991), 136; Cannon, *President Reagan*, 823.

33. Not only did the Reagan administration lose interest in deregulation after the first term; legal academics did as well. Consequently, there is no definitive list of deregulation cases for the second term as there is for the first. I have identified twenty-nine deregulation cases decided between 1985 and 1992. *Center for Auto Safety v. Peck*, 751 F.2d 1336 (D.C.Cir. 1985); *Maryland People's Counsel v. Federal Energy Regulatory Commission*, 761 F.2d 768 (D.C.Cir. 1985); *Maryland People's Counsel v. Federal Energy Regulatory Commission* 761 F.2d 780 (D.C.Cir. 1985); *MCI v. Federal Communications Commission*, 765 F.2d 1186 (D.C.Cir. 1985); *Office of Communications of the United Church of Christ v. Federal Communications*

Commission, 779 F.2d 702 (D.C.Cir. 1985); *Coalition for the Environment, St. Louis Region v. Nuclear Regulatory Commission,* 795 F.2d 168 (D.C.Cir. 1986); *Public Citizen Health Research Group v. Tyson,* 796 F.2d 1479 (D.C.Cir. 1986); *Center for Science in the Public Interest v. Department of the Treasury,* 797 F.2d 995 (D.C.Cir. 1986); *Consumers Union of U.S., Inc. v. Federal Trade Commission,* 801 F.2d 417 (D.C.Cir. 1986); *Natural Resources Defense Council, Inc. v. Environmental Protection Agency,* 804 F.2d 710 (D.C.Cir. 1986); *Independent U.S. Tanker Owners Committee v. Dole,* 809 F.2d 847 (D.C.Cir. 1987); *National Coalition Against the Misuse of Pesticides v. Thomas,* 809 F.2d 875 (D.C.Cir. 1987); *Farmworker Justice Fund v. Brock,* 811 F.2d 613 (D.C.Cir. 1987); *American Horse Protection Association, Inc. v. Lyng* 812 F.2d 1 (D.C.Cir. 1987); *Associated Gas Distributors v. Federal Energy Regulatory Commission,* 824 F.2d 981 (D.C.Cir. 1987); *Action for Children's Television v. Federal Communications Commission,* 821 F.2d 741 (D.C.Cir. 1987); *Consolidated Edison Company of New York, Inc. v. Federal Energy Regulatory Commission,* 823 F.2d 630 (D.C.Cir. 1987); *Natural Resources Defense Council, Inc. v. Environmental Protection Agency,* 824 F.2d 1146 (D.C.Cir. 1987); *Union of Concerned Scientists v. Nuclear Regulatory Commission,* 824 F.2d 108 (D.C.Cir. 1987); *Center for Auto Safety v. Dole,* 828 F.2d 799 (D.C.Cir. 1987); *Public Citizen v. National Highway Traffic Safety Administration,* 848 F.2d 256 (D.C.Cir. 1988); *Syracuse Peace Council v. Federal Communications Commission,* 867 F.2d 654 (D.C.Cir. 1989); *United Mine Workers of America v. Dole,* 870 F.2d 662 (D.C.Cir. 1989); *International Union, United Automobile, Aerospace and Agricultural Implement Workers of America v. Pendergrass,* 878 F.2d 389 (D.C.Cir. 1989); *National Customs Brokers & Forwarders Association of America, Inc. v. Federal Maritime Commission,* 883 F.2d 93 (D.C.Cir. 1989); *American Gas Association v. Federal Energy Regulatory Commission,* 888 F.2d 136 (D.C.Cir. 1989); *Associated Gas Distributors v. Federal Energy Regulatory Commission,* 893 F.2d 349 (D.C.Cir. 1989); *Williams Natural Gas Company v. Federal Energy Regulatory Commission,* 943 F.2d 1320 (D.C.Cir. 1991); *The Society of Plastics Industry, Inc. v. Interstate Commerce Commission,* 955 F.2d 722 (D.C.Cir. 1992); *AT&T v. Federal Communications Commission,* 978 F.2d 727 (D.C.Cir. 1992).

I have excluded from these cases one obvious instance of deregulatory rulemaking—the Reagan administration's attempt to lower automobile fuel efficiency standards. This rulemaking was the subject of three cases before the D.C. Circuit—*Center for Auto Safety v. National Highway Traffic Safety Administration,* 793 F.2d 1322 (D.C.Cir. 1986); *Center for Auto Safety v. Thomas,* 847 F.2d 843 (D.C.Cir. 1988); *Public Citizen v. National Highway Traffic Safety Administration,* 848 F.2d 256 (D.C.Cir. 1988)—in which the court upheld the administration's deregulatory action. These cases caused a great deal of conflict on the court. Each case generated dissents, and one case resulted in an evenly divided *en banc* decision by the court. However, the issue that so divided the court in these cases was not the merits of the administration's deregulatory policy. The dispute was over whether the parties challenging the order had standing to bring the case at all. While some scholars have read the Republican appointees' hostility toward standing to be evidence of their support of deregulation, I don't think there is evidence for this conclusion. See Christopher P. Banks, *Judicial Politics in the D.C. Circuit* (Baltimore: Johns Hopkins University Press, 1999), pp. 56–64. When a court narrows standing, it prevents parties from challenging regulatory actions regardless of whether they are regulatory or deregulatory. Indeed, the use of standing doctrine to exclude people from challenging regulatory actions was pioneered by judges who wished to prevent such challenges to Progressive-era and New Deal regulatory initiatives. Daniel E. Ho and Erica L. Ross, "Did Liberal Justices Invent the Standing Doctrine? An Empirical Study of the Evolution of Standing, 1921–2006," *Stanford Law Review* 62 (2010): 591, 634–45; Cass R. Sunstein, "Standing and the Privatization of Public Law," *Columbia Law Review* 88 (1988): 1432, 1436–38; Steven L. Winter, "The Metaphor of Standing and the Problem of Self-Governance," *Stanford Law Review* 40 (1988): 1371–516.

34. *Chevron v. NRDC*, 467 U.S. 837 (1984).
35. *NRDC v. Gorsuch*, 685 F.2d 718 (D.C. Cir. 1982).
36. *Heckler v. Cheney*, 470 U.S. 821 (1985).
37. 470 U.S. at 832.
38. Kenneth Starr et al., "Judicial Review of Administrative Action in a Conservative Era," *Administrative Law Review* 39 (1987): 355.
39. Silberman served in the Nixon administration as a Deputy Attorney General and the Solicitor of the Department of Labor. Immediately prior to his appointment he was a policy fellow at the conservative American Enterprise Institute. Reagan had made Buckley an Undersecretary at the State Department and then the Director of Radio Free Europe. Before that, he was a Republican U.S. senator from New York. Buckley was the older brother of conservative intellectual William F. Buckley Jr. Before Reagan placed Ginsburg on the D.C. Circuit, he was the head of both OIRA and the Justice Department's Antitrust Division. Williams had no previous connection to the Reagan administration. For biographical information on these judges see the Federal Judicial Center's *Biographical Directory of Federal Judges*, http://www.fjc.gov/history/home.nsf/page/judges.html (accessed 15 July 2011).
40. *Maryland People's Counsel v. Federal Energy Regulatory Commission*, 761 F.2d 768 (D.C.Cir. 1985); *Maryland People's Counsel v. Federal Energy Regulatory Commission* 761 F.2d 780 (D.C.Cir. 1985); *Associated Gas Distributors v. Federal Energy Regulatory Commission*, 824 F.2d 981 (D.C.Cir. 1987); *Consolidated Edison Company of New York, Inc. v. Federal Energy Regulatory Commission*, 823 F.2d 630 (D.C.Cir. 1987); *American Gas Association v. Federal Energy Regulatory Commission*, 888 F.2d 136 (D.C.Cir. 1989); *Associated Gas Distributors v. Federal Energy Regulatory Commission*, 893 F.2d 349 (D.C.Cir. 1989).
41. *Independent Tankers Committee v. Dole,*809 F.2d 847 (D.C.Cir. 1987).
42. *ACT v. FCC*, 821 F.2d 741.
43. *American Horse Protective Association v. Lyng*, 812 F.2d 1 (D.C.Cir. 1987)

44. *National Coalition Against Pesticides v. Thomas*, 809 F.2d 875

45. *Union of Concerned Scientists v. NRC*, 824 F.2d 108 (Williams concurring); *NRDC v. EPA*, 824 F.2d 1146, 1164.

46. See Peter H. Schuck and E. Donald Elliot, "To the *Chevron* Station," *Duke Law Journal* 1990 (1990): 1041–42; Thomas Merrill, "Textualism and the *Chevron* Doctrine," *Washington University Law Quarterly* 72 (1994): 351.

47. See, for example, *Society of Plastics v. ICC*, 955 F.2d 722; *Williams v. FERC*, 943 F2d 1320; 757 F.2d 301.

48. The nine cases in which deregulatory actions were upheld are listed in notes 53 through 58, below. In every other case listed in note 33, the court struck down the deregulatory action.

49. The material in the paragraph is drawn from Ashutosh Bhagwat, "Three-Branch Monte," *Notre Dame Law Review* 72 (1996): 157–92.

50. *National Customs Brokers and Forwarders v. United States*, 883 F.2d at 93–94.

51. *Farmworker Justice Fund v. Brock*, 811 F.2d at 613.

52. *American Horse Protective Association v. Lyng*, 812 F.2d at 1.

53. *UAW v. Pendergrass*, 878 F.2d at 389–90.

54. *Center for Science in the Public Interest*, 797 F.2d. at 995.

55. *Williams Natural Gas Co. v. FERC*, 943 F2d at 1320; *The Society of Plastics Industry, Inc. v. Interstate Commerce Commission*, 955 F.2d at 722–23; *National Customs Brokers & Forwarders Association of America, Inc. v. Federal Maritime Commission*, 883 F.2d at 93–94; *Coalition for the Environment, St. Louis Region v. Nuclear Regulatory Commission*, 795 F.2d at 168–69.

56. *Consumers Union v. FTC*, 801 F.2d at 417–18.

57. *NRDC v. EPA*, 804 F.2d at 710.

58. *Center for Auto Safety v. Peck*, 751 F.2d at 1336.

59. *Syracuse Peace Council v. FCC*, 867 F.2d at 654.

60. The most obvious example was the appointment of William Ruckelshaus to replace Anne Gorsuch at the EPA. See also Lynn, "The Reagan Administration and the Renitent Bureaucracy," 339–70.

61. For Scalia and Silberman, see below at note 95. Ginsburg had run OIRA before his appointment. See *supra*, note 39.

62. In *NRDC v. EPA*, 804 F.2d 710 (D.C.Cir. 1986) and *Center for Auto Safety v. Peck*, 751 F.2d 1336 (D.C.Cir. 1985), Judge Wright dissented in cases in which the majority consisted of one judge appointed by a Democratic administration and one judge appointed by a Republican administration.

63. *Associated Gas Districbuters v. FERC*, 824 F.2d at 1044 (Mikva, J., concurring in part and dissenting in part); *Syracuse Peace Council v. FCC*, 867 F.2d at 669 (Wald, J., concurring in part and dissenting in part).

64. Reuel Schiller, "Rulemaking's Promise: Administrative Law and Legal Culture in the 1960s and 1970s," 53 *Administrative Law Review* 53 (2001): 1139, 1181–81; Nicholas S. Zeppos, "The Legal Profession and the Development of Administrative Law," *Chicago-Kent Law Review* 72 (1997): 1119, 1139–52; Ronen Shamir,

Managing Legal Uncertainty: Elite Lawyers in the New Deal (Durham, N.C.: Duke University Press, 1995), 100–13, 131–32.

65. Starr, "Judicial Review of Administrative Action in a Conservative Era," at 363; Kenneth Starr, "Observations about the Use of Legislative History, *Duke Law Journal* 1987 (1987): 371, 373; Antonin Scalia, "Judicial Deference to Administrative Interpretations of Law," *Duke Law Journal* 1989 (1989): 511, 521.

66. Banks, *Judicial Politics in the D.C. Circuit*, 82–85; Schuck and Elliot, "To the *Chevron* Station," at 1042.

67. *Id.*

68. Indeed, judging by its attempts to narrow *Chevron* in recent years, it appears that even the Supreme Court seems to have had regrets about the amount of institutional power the decision gave away. See *FDA v. Brown and Williamson*, 529 U.S. 120 (2000); *United States v. Mead*, 533 U.S. 218 (2001).

69. See Banks, *Judicial Politics in the D.C. Circuit*, 56–64, 87–116; Richard L. Revesz, "Environmental Regulation, Ideology, and the D.C. Circuit," *Virginia Law Review* 83 (1997): 1717–72 (1997).

70. *Independent Tankers*, 809 F.2d at 852.

71. *Id.* at 853 (internal citation omitted).

72. *Id.* (internal citation and quotation omitted).

73. *Id.*, 854.

74. *National Coalition Against the Abuse of Pesticides v. Thomas*, 809 F.2d 875, 882 ("The defect in these proceedings, however, is that the EPA has failed entirely to take into account factors that section 346a(b) clearly requires the agency to consider. . . .").

75. *NRDC v. EPA*, 824 F.2d 1146 (D.C.Cir. 1987).

76. *Action for Children's Television v. FCC*, 821 F.2d at 746.

77. *Maryland People's Counsel v. FERC*, 761 F.2d 768 (D.C.Cir. 1985); *Maryland People's Counsel v. FERC*, 761 F.2d 780 (D.C.Cir. 1985); *Consolidated Edison v. FERC*, 823 F.2d 630 (D.C.Cir. 1987); *Associate Gas Distributors v. FERC*, 824 F.2d 981 (D.C.Cir. 1987); *American Gas Association v. FERC*, 888 F.2d 136 (D.C.Cir. 1989); Associated Gas Distributors, 893 F.2d 349 (D.C.Cir 1989).

78. *Maryland People's Counsel v. FERC*, 761 F.2d 768, 779.

79. *Union of Concerned Scientists v. NRC*, 824 F.2d 108, 121–2 (Williams, J., concurring).

80. *United Automobile, Aerospace and Agricultural Implement Workers of America v. Pendergrass*, 878 F.2d 389 (D.C.Cir. 1989); *Public Citizen Health Research Group v. Tyson*, 796 F.2d 1479 (D.C.Cir. 1986).

81. *American Horse Protective Association v. Lyng*, 812 F.2d 1 (D.C.Cir. 1987); *Farm Worker Justice Fund v. Brock*, 811 F.2d 613 (D.C.Cir 1986).

82. For examples of the D.C. Circuit's engaging in hard-look review, see *State Farm v. Department of Transportation*, 680 F.2d 206 (D.C.Cir. 1982); *Public Citizen Health Research Group v. Tyson*, 796 F.2d 1479 (D.C.Cir. 1986); *Syracuse Peace Council v. Federal Communications Commission*, 867 F.2d 654 (D.C.Cir. 1989);

United Mine Workers of America v. Dole, 870 F.2d 662 (D.C.Cir. 1989); *International Union, United Automobile, Aerospace and Agricultural Implement Workers of America v. Pendergrass*, 878 F.2d 389 (D.C.Cir. 1989).

83. See Laura Kalman, *The Strange Career of Legal Liberalism* (New Haven, Conn.: Yale University Press, 1996), pp. 132–34. Reagan's two attorneys general, William French Smith and Edwin Meese III, were particularly vocal in their opposition to "judicial activism," and this opposition became a central part of Reagan's strategy for selecting federal judges. See William French Smith, *Law and Justice in the Reagan Administration: The Memoirs of an Attorney General* (Stanford, Calif.: Hoover Institution Press, 1991), pp. 57–73; Edwin Meese III, *With Reagan: The Inside Story* (Washington, D.C.: Regnery Gateway, 1992), pp. 315–16; United States, Department of Justice, *Major Policy Statements of the Attorney General: Edwin Meese, III, 1985–1988* (Washington, D.C.: United States Department of Justice, 1989), pp. 1–68; Cannon, *President Reagan*, 803–11. For a fascinating discussion of the institutional origins of conservative legal ideology, see Steven M. Teles, *The Rise of the Conservative Legal Movement* (Princeton, N.J.: Princeton University Press, 2008).

84. For accounts of the rise of textualism, see Jonathan T. Molot, "The Rise and Fall of Textualism," *Columbia Law Review* 106 (2006): 1, 23–29; William Eskridge, "The New Textualism," *UCLA Law Review* 37 (1990): 621, 646–66. In addition to those identified in Molot's and Eskridge's articles, Jane S. Schacter identifies textualist judges in "The Confounding Common Law Originalism in Recent Supreme Court Statutory Interpretation: Implications for the Legislative History Debate and Beyond," *Stanford Law Review* 51 (1998): 1, 3 n. 3.

85. Quoted in Eskridge, "The New Textualism," at 648 n. 104.

86. Antonin Scalia, *A Matter of Interpretation: Federal Courts and the Law* (Princeton, N.J.: Princeton University Press, 1997), pp. 17–18.

87. United States Department of Justice, *Using and Misusing Legislative History: A Re-Evaluation of the Status of Legislative History in Statutory Interpretation* (Washington, D.C.: United States Department of Justice, 1989), pp. 26–33; Molot, "The Rise and Fall of Textualism," at 26–28.

88. The Justice Department published *Using and Misusing Legislative History* in January 1989.

89. 45 Fed. Reg. 33,084 (1980). For the specific discussion of household waste, see *id.* at 33,098–99. For a discussion of the overall goal of avoiding use of landfills and encouraging refuse-derived fuel, see *id.* at 33,091. The facts for these cases can be found in *Environmental Defense Fund v. Wheelabrator Technologies*, 725 F.Supp. 758 (S.D.N.Y. 1989), and *Environmental Defense Fund v. City of Chicago*, 948 F.2d 345 (7th Cir. 1991).

90. *Environmental Defense Fund v. Wheelabrator Technologies*, 725 F.Supp. 758 (S.D.N.Y. 1989).

91. 948 F.2d at 351.

92. *City of Chicago v. Environmental Defense Fund*, 511 U.S. 328, 334 (1994).

93. *Id.* at 336.

94. *Id.* at 344–45.

95. *Id.* at 337, quoting the lower court.

96. *MCI v. AT&T*, 512 U.S. 218, 233 (1994), *AT&T v. FCC*, 978 F.2d 727, 736 (D.C.Cir. 1994).

97. *MCI v. AT&T*, 765 F.2d 1186, 1191-92 (D.C.Cir. 1985).

98. 512 U.S. at 227–29; 765 F.2d at 1192.

99. *Maslin Industries v. Primary Steel*, 497 U.S. 116, 117–18 (1990).

100. *Id.* at 136 (internal citation omitted).

101. Nelson, *The Legalist Reformation*; William E. Nelson, "The Impact of the Anti-slavery Movement upon Styles of Judicial Reasoning in Nineteenth Century America," *Harvard Law Review* 87 (1974): 513–66.

102. The phrase is Ted White's. See G. Edward White, *Patterns of American Legal Thought* (Indianapolis: Michie-Bobbs-Merrill, 1978).

BIBLIOGRAPHY OF THE SCHOLARSHIP
OF WILLIAM E. NELSON, 1963–2012

BOOKS

The Common Law in Colonial America: Volume II: The Middle Colonies and the Caroli-nas, 1660–1730 (New York: Oxford University Press, 2012).

The Common Law in Colonial America: Volume I: The Chesapeake and New England, 1607–1660 (New York : Oxford University Press, 2008).

Fighting for the City: A History of the New York City Corporation Counsel (New York: New York Law Journal in association with the Law Department and the Mayor's Fund to Advance New York City, 2008).

In Pursuit of Right and Justice: Edward Weinfeld as Lawyer and Judge (New York: New York University Press, 2004).

The Legalist Reformation: Law, Politics, and Ideology in New York, 1920–1980 (Chapel Hill: University of North Carolina Press, 2001).

Law as Culture and Culture as Law: Essays in Honor of John Phillip Reid. William E. Nelson and Hendrik Hartog, editors (Madison, Wis.: Madison House Publishers, 2000).

Marbury v. Madison: The Origins and Legacy of Judicial Review (Lawrence: University Press of Kansas, 2000) (*Landmark Law Cases and American Society* series).

Liberty and Community: Constitution and Rights in the Early American Republic (Dobbs Ferry, N.Y.: Oceana Publications, 1988) (with Robert C. Palmer) (*New York University School of Law Linden Studies in Legal History*).

The Fourteenth Amendment: From Political Principle to Judicial Doctrine (Cambridge, Mass.: Harvard University Press, 1988).

The Literature of American Legal History (Dobbs Ferry, N.Y.: Oceana Publications, 1985) (*New York University School of Law Linden Studies in Legal History*) (co-author, with John Phillip Reid).

The Roots of American Bureaucracy, 1830–1900 (Cambridge, Mass.: Harvard University Press, 1982).

Dispute and Conflict Resolution in Plymouth County, Massachusetts, 1725–1825 (Chapel Hill: University of North Carolina Press, 1981) (*Studies in Legal History* series).

Americanization of the Common Law: The Impact of Legal Change on Massachusetts Society, 1760–1830 (Cambridge, Mass.: Harvard University Press, 1975) (*Studies in Legal History* series).

BOOK CHAPTERS

"The Historical Foundations of the American Judiciary," in *The Judicial Branch*. Kermit Hall and Kevin McGuire, editors (New York: Oxford University Press, 2005).

"Government Power as a Tool for Redistributing Wealth in Twentieth-Century New York," in *Law as Culture and Culture as Law: Essays in Honor of John Phillip Reid*. William E. Nelson and Hendrik Hartog, editors (Madison, Wis.: Madison House Publishers, 2000).

"Transformation of State Laws," in *The Spirit of American Law*. George S. Grossman, editor (Boulder, Colo.: Westview Press, 2000).

"Property," in *Fundamentals of American Law*. Alan B. Morrison, editor (New York: Oxford University Press, 1996).

"The American Revolution and the Emergence of Modern Doctrines of Federalism and Conflict of Laws," in Daniel R. Coquillette, ed., *Law in Colonial Massachusetts, 1630–1800*, 62 *Publications of the Colonial Society of Massachusetts* 419 (Charlottesville: University Press of Virginia, for the Colonial Society of Massachusetts, 1984).

"Court Records as Sources of Historical Writings," in Daniel R. Coquillette, ed., *Law in Colonial Massachusetts, 1630–1800*, 62 *Publications of the Colonial Society of Massachusetts* 419 (Charlottesville: University Press of Virginia, for the Colonial Society of Massachusetts, 1984).

"Introductory Essay: The Larger Context of Litigation in Plymouth County, 1724–1825," in 1 *Plymouth Court Records*, 1686–1859. David T. Konig, editor. Wilmington, Del.: M. Glazier, 1978) (funded by NSF grant).

"Emerging Notions of Modern Criminal Law in the Revolutionary Era," in *Crime, Law, and Society*. Joseph Goldstein and Abraham S. Goldstein, editors (New York: Simon and Schuster, 1971).

ARTICLES

"The Lawfinding Power of Colonial American Juries," *Ohio State Law Journal* 71 (2010): 1003–30.

"Politicizing the Courts and Undermining the Law: A Legal History of Colonial North Carolina, 1660–1775," *North Carolina Law Review* 88 (2010): 2133–97.

"Legal Turmoil in a Factious Colony: New York, 1664–1776," *Hofstra Law Review* 38 (2009): 69–162.

"The Height of Sophistication: Law and Professionalism in the City-State of Charleston, South Carolina, 1670–1775," *South Carolina Law Review* 61 (2009): 1–62.

"The Liberal Tradition of the Supreme Court Clerkship: Its Rise, Fall, and Reincarnation," 62 *Vanderbilt Law Review* 62 (2009): 1749–814. With Harvey Rishikof, I. Scott Messinger, and Michael Jo.

"The Supreme Court Clerkship and the Polarization of the Court: Can the Polarization Be Fixed?", *Green Bag (New Series)* 13 (2009): 59–70. With Harvey Rishikof, I. Scott Messinger, and Michael Jo.

"Summary Judgment and the Progressive Constitution," *Iowa Law Review* 93 (2008): 1653–66.

"Government by Judiciary: The Growth of Judicial Power in Colonial Pennsylvania," *SMU Law Review* 59 (2006): 3–54.

"Utopian Legal Order of the Massachusetts Bay Colony, 1630–1686," *American Journal of Legal History* 47 (2005): 183–230.

"*Marbury v. Madison*, Democracy, and the Rule of Law," *Tennessee Law Review* 71 (2004): 217–40.

"*Brown v. Board of Education* and the Jurisprudence of Legal Realism," *Saint Louis University Law Journal* 48 (2004): 795–838.

"The Province of the Judiciary," *John Marshall Law Review* 37 (2004): 325–56.

"Justice Byron R. White: His Legacy for the Twenty-First Century," *University of Colorado Law Review* 74 (2003): 1291–304.

"Authority and the Rule of Law in Early Virginia," *Ohio Northern University Law Review* 29 (2003): 305–62.

"Marbury, Madison, Marshall and Massachusetts," *Massachusetts Legal History* 9 (2003): 49–66.

"*Marbury v. Madison* and the Establishment of Judicial Autonomy," *Journal of Supreme Court History* 27 (2002): 240–56.

"The Law of Fiduciary Duty in New York, 1920–1980," *SMU Law Review* 53 (2000): 286–314.

"Moral Perversity of the Hand Calculus," *Saint Louis University Law Journal* 45 (2001): 759–68.

"Suburbanization and Market Failure: An Analysis of Government Policies Promoting Suburban Growth and Ethnic Assimilation," *Fordham Urban Law Journal* 27 (1999): 197–236.

"From Morality to Equality: Judicial Regulation of Business Ethics in New York, 1920–1980," *New York Law School Law Review* 43 (1999): 223–300.

"From Fairness to Efficiency: The Transformation of Tort Law in New York, 1920–1980," *Buffalo Law Review* 47 (1999): 117–226.

"Two Models of Welfare: Private Charity versus Public Duty," *Southern California Interdisciplinary Law Journal* 7 (1999): 295–316.

"Integrity of the Judiciary in Twentieth-Century New York," *Rutgers Law Review* 51 (1998): 1–44.

"A Man's Word and Making Money: Contract Law in New York, 1920–1960," *Mississippi College Law Review* 19 (1998): 1–52.

"Civil Procedure in Twentieth-Century New York," *Saint Louis University Law Journal* 41 (1997): 1157–242.

"Growth of Distrust: The Emergence of Hostility toward Government Regulation of the Economy," *Hofstra Law Review* 25 (1996): 1–82.

"Patriarchy or Equality: Family Values or Individuality," *St. John's Law Review* 70 (1996): 435–538.

"Changing Meaning of Equality in Twentieth-Century Constitutional Law," *Washington and Lee Law Review* 52 (1995): 3–104.

"Justice Byron R. White: A Modern Federalist and a New Deal Liberal," *Brigham Young University Law Review* 1994 (1994): 313–48.

"Criminality and Sexual Morality in New York, 1920–1980," *Yale Journal of Law & the Humanities* 5 (1993): 265–342.

"Role of History in Interpreting the Fourteenth Amendment," *Loyola of Los Angeles Law Review* 25 (1992): 1177–86.

"Contract Litigation and the Elite Bar in New York City, 1960–1980," *Emory Law Journal* 39 (1990): 413–62.

"Moral Ethics, Adversary Justice, and Political Theory: Three Foundations for the Law of Professional Responsibility," *Notre Dame Law Review* 64 (1989): 911–31.

"An Exchange on Critical Legal Studies Between Robert W. Gordon and William Nelson," *Law and History Review* 6 (1988): 139–86.

"Deference and the Limits to Deference in the Constitutional Jurisprudence of Justice Byron R. White," *University of Colorado Law Review* 58 (1987): 347–64.

"Reason and Compromise in the Establishment of the Federal Constitution, 1787–1801," *The William and Mary Quarterly* 3d.ser., 44 (1987): 458–84.

"History and Neutrality in Constitutional Adjudication," *Virginia Law Review* 72 (1986): 1237–96.

"Ideology and Racial Progress," *Rutgers Law Journal* 17 (1986): 607–14.

"Legal and Constitutional History," *Annual Survey of American Law* 1984 (1984): 227–64.

"Standards of Criticism," *Texas Law Review* 60 (1982): 447–94.

"Legal History: A Review of Recent Literature," *Annual Survey of American Law* 1980 Supp. (1981): 1–25.

"Legal and Constitutional History," *Annual Survey of American Law* 1978 (1978): 395–410.

"The Eighteenth-Century Background of John Marshall's Constitutional Jurisprudence," *Michigan Law Review* 76 (1978): 893–960.

"Legal and Constitutional History," *Annual Survey of American Law* 1976 (1976): 427–500.

"Officeholding and Powerwielding: An Analysis of the Relationship between Structure and Style in American Administrative History," *Law & Society Review* 10 (1976): 187–234.

"Judge Weinfeld and the Adjudicatory Process: A Law Finder in an Age of Judicial Lawmakers," *New York University Law Review* 50 (1975): 980–1007.

"Legal Restraint of Power in Pre-Revolutionary America: Massachusetts as a Case Study, 1760–1775," *American Journal of Legal History* 18 (1974): 1–32.

"Legal History," *Annual Survey of American Law* 1974 (1974): 625–40.

"Impact of the Antislavery Movement upon Styles of Judicial Reasoning in Nineteenth Century America," *Harvard Law Review* 87 (1974): 513–66.

"Reform of Common Law Pleading in Massachusetts 1760–1830: Adjudication as a
Prelude to Legislation," *University of Pennsylvania Law Review* 122 (1973): 97–136.
"Changing Conceptions of Judicial Review: The Evolution of Constitutional Theory
in the States, 1790–1860," *University of Pennsylvania Law Review* 120 (1972):
1166–85.
"Legal History," *Annual Survey of American Law* 1971 (1971–1972): 627–44.
"Legal History," *Annual Survey of American Law* 1969 (1969–1970): 657–767.
"Continuity and Change in Constitutional Adjudication," *Yale Law Journal* 78 (1969):
500–15.
"Legal and Constitutional History," *Annual Survey of American Law* 1968 (1968):
359–64.
"Legal and Constitutional History," *Annual Survey of American Law* 1967 (1967):
547–54.
"Emerging Notions of Modern Criminal Law in the Revolutionary Era: An Historical
Perspective," *New York University Law Review* 42 (1967): 450–83.
"Constitutional History," *Annual Survey of American Law* 1966 (1966): 687–98.
Note, "Section 1983: A Civil Remedy for the Protection of Federal Rights," *New York
University Law Review* 39 (1964): 839–57.
Note, "Drug Amendments of 1962," *New York University Law Review* 38 (1963):
1082–132.

COMMENTS
"Categorizing Zipporah's Petition," *Hofstra Law Review* 38 (2009): 279–84.
"Defending the Historian's Art: A Response to Paul A. Crotty's Attack on *Fighting for
the City*," *New York Law School Law Review* 53 (2008–2009): 533–40.
"Tribute to John Sexton," *New York University Annual Survey of American Law* 60
(2004): 19–22.
"Byron R. White: The Justice Who Never Thought about Himself," *Harvard Law
Review* 116 (2002): 9–18.
"Multiple Voices as a Means to Legal Reform (A Response to Martha Fineman)," *Yale
Journal of Law & the Humanities* 5 (1993): 351–54.

BOOK REVIEWS
"Emulating the Marshall Court: The Applicability of the Rule of Law to Contemporary
Constitutional Adjudication," reviewing George Lee Haskins and Herbert A. John-
son, *Foundations of Power: John Marshall* (1981), *University of Pennsylvania Law
Review* 131 (1982): 489–515.
Reviewing John Phillip Reid, *A Better Kind of Hatchett: Law, Trade, and Diplomacy in
the Cherokee Nation During the Early Years of European Contact* (1976), *University
of Chicago Law Review* 44 (1977): 911–21.
Reviewing Lawrence M. Friedman, *A History of American Law* (1973), *American Journal of Legal History* 18 (1974): 182–85.

ACKNOWLEDGMENTS

The editors acknowledge the support of Dean Ricky Revesz of New York University School of Law, who embraced from its inception the idea of a conference and volume for Bill Nelson. We also thank our editors at New York University Press: Deborah Gershenowitz, who helped us organize the volume and edit the essays; and Clara Platter, who jumped in toward the end and made sure the book got finished. The anonymous reviewers for the Press offered invaluable suggestions on the essays, as did the tireless Alfred L. Brophy. Alexia Traganas provided helpful production editing on the manuscript. Warm thanks are also due to Judge Morris Arnold, Sir John Baker, Chris Beauchamp, Lauren Benton, Jerry Cohen, Willy Forbath, Dirk Hartog, Morton Horwitz, Larry D. Kramer, David Konig, Harvey Rishikof, Jed Shugerman, Steven Wilf, and President John Sexton for memorable remarks and tributes at the conference in May 2010. They all helped make it a special weekend. Many people at the Law School helped plan the conference. To name only a few: Trish McNicholas, David Mora, and Sterling Waters in the Special Events office helped organize the conference events and made sure they went off without a hitch. Vice Deans Barry Friedman, Randy Hertz, and Liam Murphy provided gracious support. John Phillip Reid offered wise advice at several key junctures along the way, while Dan Evans and Shirley Gray played essential roles behind the scenes. Ron Brown and Gretchen Feltes undertook the heroic task of compiling the bibliography. Peter Freedberger provided cheerful assistance as we turned the presentations into essays. Before the conference, Leila Nelson supplied us with a veritable archive of information and photographs, and during the conference Greg Nelson contributed his boundless good cheer. It's possible that the conference might never have happened without a timely intervention by Elaine Nelson, for which we are extremely grateful. Our largest debt of gratitude is to Bill Nelson.

R. B. BERNSTEIN is Distinguished Adjunct Professor of Law at New York Law School and Adjunct Professor of Political Science and History in the Skadden, Arps Honors Program in Legal Studies at City College of New York. His books on American constitutional and legal history include *Thomas Jefferson*; *The Founding Fathers Reconsidered*; and *The Education of John Adams* (forthcoming).

SUSANNA L. BLUMENTHAL is Associate Professor of Law and History at the University of Minnesota. She is the author of *Law and the Modern Mind: Consciousness and Responsibility in American Legal Culture* (forthcoming).

TOMIKO BROWN-NAGIN is Professor of Law and Professor of History at Harvard University. She is author of *Courage to Dissent: Atlanta and the Long History of the Civil Rights Movement*, winner of the 2012 Bancroft Prize.

BARRY CUSHMAN is John P. Murphy Foundation Professor of Law and Concurrent Professor of History and Political Science at the University of Notre Dame. His book *Rethinking the New Deal Court: The Structure of a Constitutional Revolution* was awarded the American Historical Association's Littleton-Griswold Prize in American Law and Society.

CORNELIA H. DAYTON, Associate Professor of History at the University of Connecticut, and SHARON V. SALINGER, Professor of History and Dean, Division of Undergraduate Education, at the University of California, Irvine, are authors of *Warning Out: Robert Love Searches for Strangers in Pre-Revolutionary Boston*.

SARAH BARRINGER GORDON is Arlin M. Adams Professor of Constitutional Law and Professor of History at the University of Pennsylvania. She is the author of two works on the legal history of religion: *The Mormon Question: Polygamy and Constitutional Conflict in Nineteenth-Century America* and *The Spirit of the Law: Religious Voices and the Constitution in Modern America.*

DANIEL W. HAMILTON is Dean of the William S. Boyd School of Law at the University of Nevada–Las Vegas. He is the author of *The Limits of Sovereignty: Property Confiscation in the Union and Confederacy During the Civil War.*

DANIEL J. HULSEBOSCH is the Affiliated Charles Seligson Professor of Law and Professor of History at New York University. He is the author of *Constituting Empire: New York and the Transformation of Constitutionalism in the Atlantic World, 1664–1830.*

THOMAS C. MACKEY is Professor of History, University of Louisville, and Adjunct Professor of Law, Brandeis School of Law, University of Louisville. His most recent project is an edited three-volume work, *A Documentary History of the American Civil War Era* (2012–).

REUEL SCHILLER is Professor of Law at the University of California, Hastings College of the Law. His new book is *Forging Rivals: Labor Law, Racial Discrimination, and the Decline of Postwar Liberalism* (forthcoming).

JOHN WERTHEIMER is Professor of History at Davidson College in North Carolina. His works on U.S. and Latin American legal history include *Law and Society in the South: A History of North Carolina Court Cases.*

JOHN FABIAN WITT is the Allen H. Duffy Class of 1960 Professor of Law at Yale Law School. His most recent book is *Lincoln's Code: The Laws of War in American History*, winner of the 2013 Bancroft Prize.